Third Edition

Beyond POLICY ANALYSIS

Public Issue Management in Turbulent Times

Third Edition

Beyond POLICY ANALYSIS

*Public Issue Management
in Turbulent Times*

Leslie A. Pal
Carleton University

THOMSON
NELSON

stralia   Canada   Mexico   Singapore   Spain   United Kingdom   United States

THOMSON

NELSON

Beyond Policy Analysis:
Public Issue Management in Turbulent Times

Third Edition

by Leslie A. Pal

Editorial Director and Publisher:
Evelyn Veitch

Publisher for Social Sciences and Humanities:
Chris Carson

Executive Marketing Manager:
Don Thompson

Senior Developmental Editor:
Rebecca Rea

Permissions Coordinator:
Kristiina Bowering

Senior Production Editor:
Natalia Denesiuk

Copy Editor and Proofreader:
Karen Rolfe

Indexer:
Christopher Blackburn

Senior Production Coordinator:
Helen Locsin

Creative Director:
Angela Cluer

Interior Design:
Katherine Strain

Cover Design:
Peter Papayanakis

Cover Images:
Gears and clouds: Scott Morgan/Taxi/Getty Images
People: Roz Woodward/Photodisc Red/Getty Images

Compositor:
Interactive Composition Corporation

Printer:
Transcontinental

Library and Archives Canada Cataloguing in Publication Data

Pal, Leslie A. (Leslie Alexander), 1954–
    Beyond policy analysis: public issue management in turbulent times / Leslie A. Pal. — 3rd ed.

Includes bibliographical references and index.
ISBN 0-17-641678-1

    1. Policy sciences.
    2. Political planning— Canada. I. Title.

H97.P343 2005   320.6
C2004-906692-7

Table of Contents

Preface

I titled the first edition of this book *Beyond Policy Analysis* because, as I said then, I was convinced that the world of policymaking had changed so dramatically that it was time to go beyond conventional categories and concepts. I pointed to three broad factors affecting both the theory and practice of policy analysis. The first was the changing nature of governance under the pressures of globalization, information technology, new demands for leaner government, and more deeply diverse societies and cultures. The second was an emerging demand for better and more effective government in the face of these challenges and forces. One could see that these pressures were not making the state—and good public policies—irrelevant, but were in fact sustaining demands for effective state action in a host of new areas, from global human security to dealing with genetically modified organisms. The third factor was fresh debate within the discipline of policy analysis about its intellectual foundations and practical accomplishments. Combined, it seemed to me in 1997 that these factors forced a reconsideration of what it is that we do when we engage in policy analysis.

The forces that I identified in the first and second editions have, if anything, intensified, though they have morphed in some interesting ways as well. It is virtually impossible today to engage in any serious discussion of public policy challenges without addressing globalization, information technology, changing public values and cultural assumptions, citizen distrust, new public management techniques, policy networks, consultation, or decentralization and subsidiarity. In Canada and abroad, it is widely accepted that Western governments have gone through wrenching changes in the way they manage public issues and organize their policy work. In varying degrees, the shape and nature of the public sector has changed everywhere. More remarkably, many of these changes have been similar in nature and direction. This is due in part to the emergence of a global conversation about public sector reform and renovation, a conversation to which Canadians have made some significant contributions, and in part to the fact that many states are facing similar challenges and so are keen to exchange experiences. The Organization for Economic Co-operation and Development, for example, has been a particularly important clearinghouse and catalyst for public sector management trends. As well, the collapse of communism and the emergence of new post-communist states in Central and Eastern Europe set the stage for massive governmental and nongovernmental efforts to modernize governance in that region—successful efforts in that ten new states joined the European Union in 2004. Public sector reform projects have been sponsored by government agencies such as the Canadian International Development Agency and by non-government foundations such as the Open Society Institute. Part of the modernization and reform effort includes sharing expertise in policy analysis as a foundation for good governance.

Of course, some things have changed since the second edition of this book was published in 2001. Most interestingly from a Canadian perspective, after almost 25 years of deficits, the federal government and most provincial governments now boast fiscal surpluses. Some of the trends that marked the mid-1990s—such as program review, downsizing, cuts to social programs, increased taxes, municipal restructuring, reorganization of core services in health and education, and deregulation—seem in part to have been driven by limited financial resources and the need to reduce if not eradicate the deficit. In retrospect, this may have been a unique historical moment when governments were briefly willing to embrace fiscal discipline and managed to ride a booming American economy into budget surpluses. After the 2004 federal election, it seems likely that program spending, particularly on health, will come back into vogue. Democratic governments have to get elected, and to do that they have to provide services to citizens. New programs and new services, perhaps even deficits, should not be surprising. The real challenge will be to merge this new, tentative magnanimity with the new public management ethos that emerged in the 1990s. This book will show, nonetheless, that many of the key changes in the last decade in how we think about and implement public policy have been fundamental and irreversible, largely because they are not so much reflections of ideology and available resources as they are responses to the major forces I outlined at the outset of this preface.

This third edition has been thoroughly revised and updated, though I have kept the basic structure of the last. All weblinks have been updated, and new cases and illustrations have been incorporated. As with the last edition, I have tried to include international examples and citations, though the focus remains on Canadian policy issues. A completely new Chapter 8 deals with something that policymakers increasingly have to grapple with: policymaking under pressure. It looks at risk analysis, emergencies, and crises. As with the second edition, I have divided each of the chapters roughly in two: the first half reviews the current literature in the field on the chapter's subject, and the second half goes beyond and looks at contemporary changes and challenges. Chapter 9 concludes the book with a discussion of what distinguishes good policy and good governance. Each chapter concludes with a list of key concepts, which are printed in bold in the text, along with suggestions for further readings and Internet resources.

This edition, as the other two, was graced by the advice and support from several colleagues: James Lightbody, University of Alberta; Byron Sheldrick, University of Winnipeg; and Stephen Brooks, University of Windsor.

Students in my undergraduate course at Carleton's Kroeger College were especially helpful in shaping some of the new ideas and arguments that form this text. The project would have been impossible without the superb organizational and research support of Tatyana Teplova, who mobilized a mass of materials and updates in a remarkably short space of time.

The team at Thomson was, as usual, thoroughly professional: my thanks to Rebecca Rea, Murray Moman, Natalia Denesiuk, and freelance editor Karen Rolfe.

My unlikely muse was my ten-year-old daughter, Meredith. Some chapters were written as she practised multiplication tables next to me, or as I called out words for an impending spelling test. She drew pictures and cartoons, made jokes, walked the dog, sang endlessly, and sometimes worried that I worked too hard. *Buongiorno, principessa!*

Chapter 1

Policy Analysis: Concepts and Practice

Public policies are an essential element in modern democracies in that they provide both guidance for government officials and accountability links to citizens. Governments may do things for a wide variety of reasons—patronage, political competition, reflex, tradition—but when their actions are grounded in policy, they presumably are taking a course of action that has been thought through in terms of the nature of the problem they are addressing and the circumstances they face. Insofar as these policies are visible and measurable to the public, they become key tests of the government's record at election time. Thus, organizing policy work in government and developing a public conversation about policy is central to healthy democratic politics. Despite general misgivings about the specific analytical techniques used by policymakers to achieve their objectives, the importance of policy to democratic governance has enjoyed a resurgence in recent years. Indeed, there has been growing international interest in developing policy capacity. This chapter introduces the key concepts of public policy and policy analysis and explores some of their characteristics. It then reviews some prominent Canadian and international examples of the global policy "movement" that have developed recently in the face of new governance challenges. These challenges are taken up in detail in Chapter 2.

WHAT IS PUBLIC POLICY?

Citizens expect many things from their governments, but at the very least they expect intelligent decisionmaking. Perhaps even more importantly, however, they expect those decisions to flow from some general position or vision. Unfortunately, governments can be very decisive without being terribly intelligent. Intelligent decisions come from operating within some consistent framework, however general. We will return to this issue of consistency below, but for the moment it should be clear that the very nature of intelligent and accountable **governance** in a democracy demands more than mere decisions—it demands decisionmaking guided by a framework. In short, we demand that our governments have policies.

For the purpose of this book, **public policy** will be defined as a course of action or inaction chosen by public authorities to address a given problem or interrelated set of problems. Several aspects of this definition bear emphasis. First, note that it refers to a course of action. This picks up on the idea of frameworks or patterns—policies are guides to a range of related actions in a given field. A "policymaker" is someone who develops these guides, a "policy-taker" is someone who operates within that **policy framework,** applying it to new situations. Immigration policy, for example, is a broad framework that structures the actions of a host of different organizations, from our foreign embassies to refugee boards at home. When political parties differ over their immigration policies, we know that they differ over first principles (e.g., open versus closed immigration, admission based on family considerations or economic contributions). When a policy is changed, the actions that take place within its framework are reconfigured to yield different results.

Another aspect of the definition is that it refers to action as well as inaction, as long as it has been chosen by public authorities. As Howlett and Ramesh put it, "Public policy is, at its simplest, a choice made by government to undertake some course of action" (2003, p. 5). Consider the issue of recognizing same-sex marriages. Until a few years ago, it never would have entered the minds of most policymakers that this was a policy issue to be addressed, and so the absence of action on this front cannot be seen as a policy decision. On the other hand, once the Supreme Court decided in May 1999 in *M. v. H.* that existing federal and provincial legislation discriminated against gay and lesbian couples, and once litigation around the issue occurred in British Columbia, Ontario, and Quebec, government inaction could properly be defined as a policy choice. In the United States, President George W. Bush was moved in the run-up to the 2004 elections to state that he would support a constitutional amendment protecting marriage as a union of a man and a woman. Something that had been an unspoken assumption became crystallized as policy through this deliberate choice. Not everything that governments do is policy driven, of course. Indeed, in a "crisis situation" governments have little option but to react. As deLeon (1988) points out, a crisis is a surprise, it is "unpredictable and unavoidable" (p. 116). Rochefort and Cobb (1994) note that decisionmaking in crisis situations is synonymous with an emergency mentality that enables "quick responses but also tended to produce temporary

Band-Aid solutions" to major public problems (p. 21). As well, some actions taken by government agencies are so far down the chain of implementation that they are properly seen as reflections of organizational routine rather than policy *per se*. The municipal bus driver's route is a function of policy; changes in routes due to road construction or seasonal weather are just administrative decisions.

Finally, note that the definition refers to problems and interrelated sets of problems. Public policy, whatever its symbolic dimensions, is seen by policymakers and citizens as a means of dealing with problems or sometimes with opportunities. In this sense, policies are largely "instrumental"—that is, they are not ends in themselves, or even good in themselves, but are instruments or tools to tackle issues of concern to the political community. But the instrumental character of public policy does not remove it from the realm of values. For one thing, problems and opportunities are defined as such only in relation to goals or things we value. For another, means and ends are not so easily separated—in public policymaking, to use the "right tool" means both using the tool best suited (in an instrumental sense) to the task as well as the tool that is consistent with a morally acceptable range of government behaviour. The appropriate balance of technical or instrumental analysis and values in policy work is a perennial debate in the field. The rationalist roots of policy analysis in the 1960s held out the hope that with enough data and analysis, policy problems could be solved largely in technical terms, without too much contamination by values. A more recent trend in the literature has argued that almost everything in policy analysis is affected by values and that consequently the challenge is to develop techniques and processes of tackling public problems that encourage exchanges and ultimately consensus-building among citizens, politicians, and experts (Stone, 2001; Fischer and Forester, 1993; Fischer, 1993). As we will note below, the contemporary practice among policy analysts seems to have settled on working conscientiously within policy "visions" articulated by democratically elected governments but being sensitive to the way in which both analysts' and citizens' values will affect each phase of the analytical process as well as **policy development**, implementation, and evaluation.

This mix of values and technical analysis can be illustrated with reference to a policy field that at first blush seems almost completely technical—taxation. At its most basic level, tax policy is about generating revenue for government. Taxes can also be used, however, as instruments that encourage or discourage certain kinds of behaviour; lower business taxes, for example, might encourage investment, while higher "sin" taxes on alcohol and cigarettes might discourage drinking and smoking. Both of these dimensions entail technical considerations: what is the ideal or best level and incidence of taxation to both produce revenues and have the desired policy outcomes? Overly high levels of taxation will encourage tax evasion, thus lowering yields. Then there are questions of the progressivity of tax rates, the number of income brackets and so on. But the actual policy debate around taxes in Canada and in other countries is also strongly affected by values. During the 2004 federal election, for example, the New Democratic Party (NDP) proposed tax increases on wealthier Canadians, not simply for technical revenue considerations, but because the party believes that higher income groups should carry a larger share of tax burden so that poorer Canadians can get some relief. The same is true of the debate over flat taxes (Alberta has had a flat income tax for years). While there are important technical issues over the efficacy of flat versus progressive taxes, a good part of the debate is between alternative visions of social justice.

Policies rarely tackle single problems; rather, they deal with clusters of entangled problems that may have contradictory solutions. Many policy problems are complex "because of their size and breadth; they comprise *sets* of other, perhaps smaller problems whose very interconnectedness makes them difficult to comprehend, and whose boundaries are difficult to define across issues and over time" (Desveaux, Lindquist, and Toner, 1994, p. 497). Policy design therefore becomes a process of balancing different solutions that address different aspects of a cluster of problems. In 2002, for example, the House of Commons ratified the Kyoto Protocol, and since then has found itself working "to resolve the inherent contradiction between two of its stated policy goals: first, the extraction and sale of fossil fuel in order to contribute to economic development, and second, reductions in fossil fuel consumption" (Vannijnatten and MacDonald, 2003, p. 72). Canada has committed itself to reducing annual emissions of carbon dioxide and other greenhouse gases by 2012 to below 1990 levels. One approach to achieve that objective is to move the Canadian economy to a lower-carbon profile; others involve encouraging technological changes that will reduce dependency on carbon-producing energy sources. Apart from the sheer scale of policy interventions required to achieve the goal, climate change is clearly a bundle of issues, and not a unidimensional issue. Most obviously, there is the trade-off between economic growth and jobs associated with the energy sector, and lower greenhouse gas emissions. Lowering those emissions does not necessarily mean slower economic growth, but the risk is there. Compounding the policy problem about climate change is the regional character of the Canadian economy—Western provinces, in particular Alberta, are most exposed if the federal government moves seriously to curtail energy consumption. But the effects could be quite different in the Ontario industrial heartland. Finally, Kyoto is an international agreement (which the United States has refused to sign), and so brings a host of complicated foreign policy considerations. Unsurprisingly, given the technical, regional, and international dimensions of this policy issue, Ottawa has grappled for consistency and coherence without much luck.

The general character of a public policy therefore is that it is a guide to action, a plan, a framework, a course of action or inaction designed to deal with problems. This fits with the classic definitions of public policy in the field. Thomas Dye simply defined policy as "whatever governments choose to do or not to do" (1984, p. 1), and Harold Lasswell, arguably the originator of the modern policy sciences, defined it as "the most important choices" (1951, p. 5). Colebatch uses the term "coherence" to describe the same thing: "the assumption that all the bits of the action fit together, that they form part of an organized whole, a single system, and policy has to do with how this system is (or should be) steered" (Colebatch, 1998, p. 3). All of these definitions are grounded in a **rational model** of what it means to make decisions and respond to problems: "policy or strategy is formulated consciously, preferably analytically, and made explicit and then implemented formally" (Mintzberg and Jørgensen, 1987, p. 216). The intentional aspect, as we noted above, is important in this classic approach to defining policy. Another approach is to de-emphasize intention in favour of action: organizations can engage in consistent patterns of behaviour that emerge or form rather than being planned. Mintzberg and Jørgensen refer to this as **emergent strategies** that bubble up from all corners of an organization. In this perspective, policy is what governments actually do, not what they say or intend (Burt, 1995). As they point out, however, this concept is at most a corrective, since no organization could survive through the "hothouse" generation of uncoordinated strategies.

The definitional exercise does not end there, however. Of what does this guide or framework consist? If someone asked you to search out the government's policy on X and summarize it, what would you look for and where? Let's begin with the "where" since it takes us to yet another aspect of the definition that seems so natural that it is easily overlooked. Policies emanate from public authorities, but that is not to say that every public servant has the power to articulate policy. Since policy is a guide, it has a normative or coercive dimension: if the policy says you must do X, then you must (should) do X. Of course, not everyone is empowered to make these sorts of statements. Policies get made in organizations all the time, and typically they are made by "management." When we speak of public policy, we are referring to policies that deal with public problems, not organizational routines or structure.

Policy, to put it simply, comes from those who have the legitimate authority to impose normative guidelines for action. In a democracy, policy is made by elected officials in concert with advisors from the higher levels of the administration. In strongly hierarchical systems of government like Canada's, public servants often ruefully joke that policy is whatever the minister says it is. The hard truth behind the humour is that since the minister is the elected official at the apex of the government department, only he or she has the right to enunciate policy. If the written documents say one thing, and the minister says something else, then that "something else" (at least temporarily) is the policy. Of course, once a policy has been authoritatively announced, nonelected officials can—and usually are required to—re-articulate and fine-tune policy. They also have an obligation to implement policy through programs. As well, the judiciary can get into the policy game by rendering judgments as to whether legislation is constitutional; progress toward the legalization of same-sex marriages in Canada and in the United States has come about completely as a result of courts striking down existing marriage laws as contravening human rights.

Not everyone, therefore, is empowered to articulate policy. But for those who are, what is it that they are saying in a **policy statement**? Every policy has three key elements. The first is the definition of the problem, the second is the goals that are to be achieved, and the third is the instruments or means whereby the problem is to be addressed and the goals achieved.

Problem definition will be considered the central element of a policy statement. If there is no perceived problem, or a problem seems insoluble, one would hardly expect a public policy to solve it. In Chapter 3 we will consider the nature of problem definition more closely, but several points should be noted here. First, problems have to be recognized and defined. Recognition might be nothing more than a sense that "something is wrong" or that some new situation is looming. This often happens as a result of changes in some fairly systematic indicator that suggest a problem: "Such indicators abound in the political world because both governmental and non-governmental agencies routinely monitor various activities and events: highway deaths, disease rates, immunization rates, consumer prices, commuter and inter-city ridership, costs of entitlement programs, infant mortality rates, and many others" (Kingdon, 1995, p. 90). Second, the process of problem definition can either be exhaustive or casual. The Royal Commission on Aboriginal Peoples, for example, spent five years and over $50 million dealing with a two-page mandate calling for it to "investigate the evolution of the relationship among aboriginal peoples (Indian, Inuit and Métis), the Canadian government, and Canadian society as a whole"

(P. C., 1995; 1997). On the other hand, the editorial pages overflow with instant experts on every conceivable public problem, and the policy positions of many groups are quite predictable since they base those positions less on analysis than on ideology. Third, as noted above, problems usually come in clusters, and so problem definitions typically operate across a range of dimensions; the Kyoto Protocol and climate change is as much about economic policy and innovation strategies as it is about the environment. Fourth, problems can sometimes appear in the guise of a substantially changed context or situation, more like new realities or opportunities to which we have to adapt. The most arresting example of this aspect comes from our foreign policy. The impact of 9/11 and the destruction of the World Trade Center on Canada's security posture, our relations with the United States, our immigration and refugee policies, and our defence policy have been profound. Fifth, all problem definitions have a causal character: they indicate what the problem or issue is, and bundle that with some indication of the factors that led to it in the first place. Without this causal connection, it would be difficult to determine what to do about the problem.

The irony of problem definition is that while it is central to understanding public policy, it is rarely articulated in great detail in a policy statement itself. Interest groups and the media spend a great deal of time debating problem definitions and causal factors, and governments cannot avoid rooting their policy reactions in the often exhaustive analyses undertaken by their departments or other agencies. However, the policy statement in itself will rarely reflect this level of detail. As the definitions of public policy cited earlier suggest, policy is about action or deliberate inaction. It is the framework or guide, and while problem definition is crucial to understanding the rationale for policy, it is not in itself crucial to the statement of what that guide is to be. From a purely practical point of view as well, the rationale for an action is often considerably more complex than the action (or statement of what that action will be). The importance of this is simply that doing policy analysis—trying to make sense of a policy statement—involves a fair amount of detective work in tracking down both the policy statement and the supporting rationale in terms of problem definition.

Problem definitions are inextricably bound to **policy goals.** A key distinction, however, is between **general goals** and **policy-specific goals.** Health care policy, for example, has as its most general goal the maintenance and improvement of health among the Canadian population. At this level, almost no one disagrees about goals—the same is true of general goals in foreign policy, education policy, social policy, and so on. As policies get more specific, however, so do their goals. Those goals are still related to the broader ones, but they are contributory rather than final. A provincial health care policy to improve services for at-risk youth will have goals that are directly tied or related to those youth (e.g., safer pregnancies, reduced substance abuse). If achieved, those goals will contribute to the larger goals in the health care field.

As with problem definitions, intermediate policy goals sometimes have to be inferred since they are not always clearly stated. Occasionally, policymakers do articulate clear objectives and measureable intermediate goals. One of the most famous of these was the federal Liberal promise in its 1993 election platform to reduce the national annual deficit to 3 percent of GDP. In the 2004 federal election campaign, the prime minister may have won the election by making a similarly clear promise on health care. In announcing an additional $4 billion in transfers to the provinces for health, the prime minister promised a new National Waiting Times Reduction Strategy, and a new "Five in Five" plan to reducing waiting times for five specific types of care: cancer, heart, diagnostic imaging, joint replacements, and sight restoration. However, most policy goals are fuzzy: in these cases, the mere fact that the problem is not getting worse is sometimes used as a claim that the policy goals are being met. Another problem, of course, is that the real goals of the policy might be quite different from the stated goals. Politicians may decide that they want to "send a message" rather than solve a specific problem; the promise by the federal Conservative party to scrap the national gun registry might be a case in point. The gun registry was introduced in 1995, but took until 2003 to fully implement. Originally estimated to cost roughly $80 million, it was tagged by the auditor general of Canada as approaching $1 billion. The registry has become a lightning rod for public anger over waste, and so is a fine symbol to attack. But it is unclear whether the Conservatives would seriously considering scrapping the entire program. Enormous efforts have gone into improving the registry, and public opinion polls (even among long-gun owners) indicate that there is growing if still sometimes grudging public support.

The third key component of a public policy statement is some indication of the nature of the **policy instruments** or means whereby the problem is to be addressed and the goals achieved. Defining a policy problem and determining a solution are frequently overshadowed in the policymaking process by the question of "how." The choice of instruments is also entangled with a choice of the means of implementing those instruments. A government might choose, for example, to dissuade substance abuse through advertising. But who will do the advertising, and how? The first is an instrument choice issue, the second is an implementation issue. In principle governments have a wide range of instruments from which to choose to tackle a policy problem and achieve their goals. They can rely on information (the advertising example), they can spend or tax, they can regulate, or in some instances they can set up agencies that combine these instruments under public auspices and address the problem directly. Linder and Peters (1989, p. 56) list as many as twenty-three types of instruments (see Chapter 4).

The theoretically wide range of choices over instruments is actually quite constrained in the real world. For one thing, even as policies change from time to time, governments take for granted the instruments to achieve their goals. Canadian broadcasting policy, for example, has evolved substantially since the 1960s, but the key instruments of achieving its policy goals—the Canadian Radio-Television and Telecommunications Commission and the Canadian Broadcasting Corporation—have remained. Health policy has changed marginally from time to time, and yet the key delivery mechanisms of hospitals, health care professions, and public expenditures have been quite stable since the 1960s. Recent restructuring in most provinces, however, with the closure of hospitals and the possible greater reliance on private clinics, does represent a fundamental shift. Sometimes, of course, policy changes so radically in terms of problem definition and goals that instruments get reconfigured quite dramatically as well. The federal government, for example, decided some years ago that innovation and research were keys to a productive, high-tech economy, and that universities in turn were the keys to fostering research and innovation. Over the last five years, Ottawa has become a major funder of university research through a host of new policy instruments such as Canada Research Chairs and the Millennium Foundation.

Instrument choice can also be significantly constrained by perceptions of legitimacy. In only rare cases, for example, are Canadians prepared to accept government coercion over matters of sexual behaviour. Therefore, government action to deal with problems like sexually transmitted diseases has had to rely primarily on informational instruments. Legitimacy is elastic, and will change with circumstances (e.g., an epidemic of sexually transmitted diseases could lead to acceptance of stronger government action, just as the SARS crisis in 2003 gave public health and border officials legitimacy to impose stringent controls), and it is also culturally contingent. The Vancouver Health Authority, for example, has for several years been operating a safe injection site for heroin addicts, where they can come and get clean needles and shoot up under some degree of supervision. As a "harm reduction" strategy, this may make sense in the local context, but the practice has been widely criticized both in Canada and by the United States.

Finally, instrument choice can be limited by legal restrictions—a constitutional division of powers or international agreements that prohibit the use of some policy tools—or by practical constraints. Both are important. In the Canadian case, federalism divides sovereignty among two levels of government, so that the provinces, for example, have control over health and education whereas Ottawa has exclusive powers over employment insurance and banking. Governments can still use some instruments to effect policy changes in fields outside their jurisdiction— the classic Canadian case is Ottawa's use of its spending power in the health care and postsecondary education fields. The North American Free Trade Agreement is a good example of an international agreement that limits the trade policy instruments governments can use. Canada, the United States, and Mexico, for example, cannot give preferential treatment to their own national firms in contrast to those from the other two countries. Consequently, a host of traditional economic policy tools to pump up one's own companies against their competitors are simply not available by agreement—though this should not be taken to mean that governments will give up trying to find a way around the rules. Human rights conventions do much the same thing in fields as diverse as language and the treatment of children. These legal constraints can be joined by more practical ones. Examples include limits on spending programs due to high deficit levels or limits to taxation and regulatory policies in a global environment where investors and capital are increasingly mobile and can go anywhere they please. Also, instrument choice is often constrained by organizational routines and preferences: regulatory departments reach first for regulatory instruments; finance departments reach first for fiscal instruments, and so on.

Figure 1.1 summarizes the preceding discussion of policy content. If one were asked to find out the government's policy on X, one would (1) seek an authoritative source for the policy statement, and (2) search relevant documents for clues on problem definition, goals, and instruments. All of these concepts and some of their nuances will be explored in greater detail in subsequent chapters. Note that Figure 1.1 connects these elements in a loop. While problem definition is central to an understanding of policy in a logical sense, in reality the three elements are inextricably entwined. Policymakers' goals orient them toward certain problems they think need solving; expertise with a set of policy tools encourages one to seek out problems and goals that are consistent with what is achievable with the tools. Moreover, it is virtually impossible to understand any one of these elements without considering the others. In this sense, policy analysis is usually iterative: it moves through the loop several times, refining an understanding of any one element in light of the others.

The loop also suggests that there will be consistency between the different elements. A definition of a problem should "fit" somehow

Figure 1.1   Elements of Policy Content

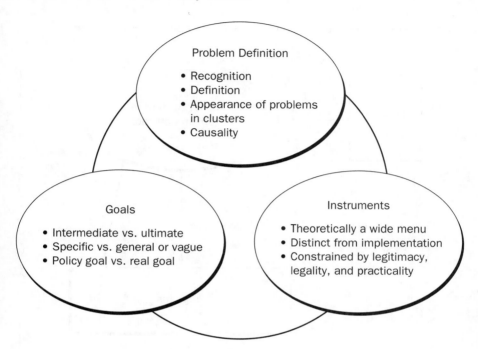

with the instruments and goals. **Policy consistency** is an important concept to appreciate, since it underpins both what we do as policy analysts and how we perceive public policies as citizens. Policies are expected to be consistent in several interrelated ways (see Figure 1.2 on page 12). First, as noted above, we expect policies to have an **internal consistency** among the three elements of problem definition, goals, and instruments. Second, we expect a policy to be **vertically consistent** in the sense that the programs and activities that are undertaken in its name are logically related to it. This is in part the nub of implementation. Policy statements are normally fairly abstract and general. They must be actualized through an implementation process that elaborates programs and activities to give the policy effect. A municipal policy to maintain the livability of the downtown core assumes programs and initiatives that support business and residential developments in that area. If the municipality simultaneously had programs to disproportionately encourage suburban development, these would on their face appear inconsistent with the larger policy framework.

Figure 1.2   Policy Consistency

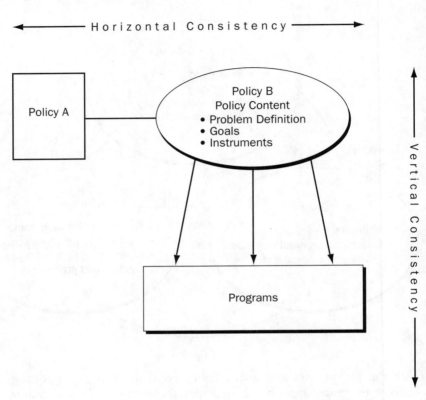

A third type of consistency is **horizontal consistency,** or consistency across policy fields, not just within them. This is an expectation that what governments do in one field will not contradict what they do in another. A fiscal policy of restraint coupled with high spending in a wide variety of areas makes no sense. An open trade policy would be inconsistent with an industrial policy to encourage domestic producers and limit competition. This type of consistency is important in democratic politics, since it implies that there is an underlying philosophy of government that cuts across all policy fields. From a policy perspective, when people vote, they often vote less for specific policies than for the "whole package." It is a way of ensuring a degree of accountability, since every part of the government is expected to follow a broadly consistent line of policy. Horizontal consistency varies considerably in the real world, both because of the sheer sprawl of government and the existence of multiple jurisdictions. There are so many actors with some influence over the policy process, and so many agencies with relatively autonomous control of their policy fields, that it is not unusual to have quite widely disparate policy frameworks operating at the same time. In systems like Canada's, where the executive has greater control over the policy agenda and is internally more coherent due to the role of the prime minister and the governing party, there is a higher degree of policy consistency. Even here however, where strong ministers can control their own departments, horizontal consistency is never perfect. Nonetheless, the concept (if not the term) seems to be gaining favour. There have been examples at both the federal and provincial level of governments/parties putting coherent and detailed proposals before the electorate (though this varies by election and by party), and there has been growing emphasis in administrative circles on "horizontality." It is tempting to speculate that budgets recently have become and may continue to be the great engines of horizontal policy consistency for many governments. In the old days, when fiscal constraints did not matter or were ignored, the budget was little more than a compendium of spending initiatives undertaken by departments. Now that money is tight (or our attitudes have changed toward deficits), everything gets measured against the bottom line, which in turn becomes a compelling reference point for all departments (more on this in later chapters).

In reflecting on the nature of public policy, we also have to realize what it is not. It is not the implemented program, the behaviours of public servants who put it into effect, or indeed the reactions of citizens affected by it. If we take the definition developed above, we are forced to realize that public policy—as a course of action—is not the action itself, in the same way that a map is different from travelling. Policies are mental constructs, strings of phrases, and ideas. The text of a policy statement and the programs and actions that follow it are simply evidence for the mental construct. Analyzing policy is akin to trying to figure out which maps people used by studying the paths they took on their journey. The fact that there was a journey and a destination is not proof that maps were in fact used, as anyone who's taken a pleasant ramble in the woods can attest. But we presume that our governments are doing more than rambling, that they have a plan, that their journeys and their destinations are guided by policy. This presumption will often be proven wrong—government actions may be the result of accident, instinct, or habit, rather than of policy. Once we understand this, we understand the challenge of doing policy analysis—it is nothing less than an attempt to grasp an underlying structure of ideas that supposedly guide action.

WHAT IS PUBLIC POLICY ANALYSIS?

In this book, **policy analysis** will be defined as the disciplined application of intellect to public problems. This is similar to Dunn's definition: "policy analysis is a process of multidisciplinary inquiry designed to create, critically assess, and communicate information that is useful in understanding and improving policies" (Dunn, 2004, pp. 1–2). Apropos of the last point in the previous section, policy analysis is a cognitive activity—a thinking game, if you will—a large part of which focuses on public policy outputs in terms of their problem definition, goals, and instruments. As Wildavsky (1979) pointed out, it is not exclusively a matter of "cogitation" but of "interaction" as well—of letting problems get solved through experimentation, bargaining, and exchange, rather than exclusively through planning—but the reflective, cognitive aspect is central (p. 11). Ours is a broad definition and is complemented by a thicket of other conceptual terms such as "policy studies," "policy science," and "policy evaluation." The central distinction to keep in mind is between a style of policy analysis that is more explanatory and descriptive and a style that is more applied or prescriptive or between what Harold Lasswell (1970) called "knowledge *of* the policy process" and "knowledge *in* the policy process" (p. 3). Hogwood and Gunn (1984) point out that the broad term **policy studies** is often used to indicate "an essentially descriptive or explanatory set of concerns" while "policy analysis" is usually reserved "for prescriptive activities" (p. 29). The distinctions among these terms are less important than what they have in common:

> Obviously, the conceptual distinction between these terms is rather indistinct. It would appear that, when the word policy appears as a prefix to the words science, studies, and analysis, we are talking about activity that investigates some form of government problem or output. This includes studies that examine the policy-making process to determine how it affects the output of that process. (McCool, 1995, p. 10)

Or, as George Graham (1988) argues: "The policy orientation provides a means for dealing with human purposes in the best scientific framework possible to aid those who will make social choices. The instrumental end is better intelligence" (p. 152; quoted in McCool, 1995, p. 10).

All these definitions stress the degree to which this reflection is more than just casual observation—the idea that analysis is disciplined implies that it is both grounded in some method and that it is systematic and multidisciplinary. Dunn (2004, p. 3) stresses the multidisciplinary nature of policy analysis in that it draws on a range of social and behavioural sciences, ethics and other branches of social and political philosophy, normative economics, and decision analysis. Indeed, the formal dictionary definition of "analysis" is that it is the process of breaking something complex down to its various simple elements—in our sense, into problem definition, goals, and instruments, but possibly even further with respect to each one of those three key dimensions. The methodological basis can vary from a generic (and usually multidisciplinary) approach to one that is solidly grounded in either natural or social sciences. Policy analysis of environmental issues, for example, will be informed by several natural sciences, but this is not to say that only natural scientists can analyze environmental policy. Economics offers an intellectual apparatus that is broadly applicable to a wide range of policy issues, but once again the central concerns of the policy analyst have less to do with the disciplines that seem to be "naturally" aligned to the policy issue than with the larger issues discussed in the previous section: how well is the problem defined, what are its characteristics, what goals are being pursued, and are the instruments adequate and likely to produce results? In fact, as we will see in a moment, there is a host of supplementary issues that also are well within the scope of policy analysis *per se,* rather than separate disciplines. The other aspect of policy analysis is that it is systematic—it proceeds logically through a series of clearly defined stages to come to its conclusions. It should be possible, in other words, to see how someone arrived at his or her conclusions.

All this may seem self-evident, but it holds three implications of great importance to the way that we view contemporary policy analysis. The first is that, at least insofar as policy analysis seems to be allied with scientific disciplines, not just anyone can do it properly. Ordinary citizens have opinions about public policy, but their views may be determined by prejudice or what happened to be on that morning's front page. Sometimes people have extraordinarily strong views about policy that they cannot explain. Once again, this would seem to fall short of policy analysis. The issue this raises of course is the division between citizens and experts. Can policy analysis be performed only by those trained to do it? Put another way, do citizens, when they contemplate public policy issues, engage in "real" policy analysis or merely in fuzzy thinking, and can experts put aside their own personal opinions?

The second implication, given that policy analysis should be disciplined and systematic, is that there will be both good and bad analysis. More disciplined and systematic analysis will be superior to the less disciplined and systematic. This implies some intersubjective standard of judgment that will act as a benchmark for all participants in the analytical process. Once again this implies some training, especially in

the use of more technically oriented forms of analysis and data generation (e.g., opinion surveys, cost-benefit analysis). Nonetheless, it has to
be acknowledged that policy analysis contains an irreducible element of
interpretation and perspective. There is no exact science, for example,
of structuring policy problems. As we noted earlier, policy problems are
almost always complex and multifaceted, and so defining or structuring
the problem depends very much on which elements the analyst emphasizes and how those elements are imaginatively combined. This does
not mean that all analysis is consequently purely subjective. As was
mentioned, a substantial part of policy analysis does rely on specific
methodological techniques of data-gathering, research, and assessment.
Moreover, in a democratic policy process, policy problems should be
debated and exposed to discussion and criticism, and this is a means
of correcting mistakes as well as generating intersubjective consensus.
But policy analysis has as well to be self-aware and self-critical in an
effort to remove as much unintentional bias as possible. One major
example of this type of effort is the treatment of gender in policy analysis. Critics of traditional public policy analysis argue that it neglects
the interests of women because of the "early adoption of rational, self-
interested man as the reference point for both policy development
and policy studies" (Burt, 1995, p. 357). A partial solution has been
the development in the last decade of specific techniques of **gender-
based analysis (GBA),** which seek to assess the differential impact of
public policies, programs, and legislation on women and men. GBA
is designed not to simply be an add-on in the analytical process, but
a perspective that is woven through each step and phase (Status of
Women Canada, 1996). A complementary concept is **gender mainstreaming,** which is an organizational strategy to ensure that a gender
perspective is reflected in all types of organizational activities. The United
Nations has made a strong commitment to gender mainstreaming,
"ensuring that gender perspectives and attention to the goal of gender
equality are central to all activities—policy development, research,
advocacy/dialogue, legislation, resource allocation, and planning, implementation and monitoring of programmes and projects" (United
Nations, 2004).

Policy analysis is also complicated by possible cultural biases. An
extreme example of policy work that had to grapple with different
cultural perspectives is the Royal Commission on Aboriginal Peoples.
Hundreds of researchers from across Canada were invited to participate,
but the Commission was well aware of the problem that Aboriginal
peoples had been "studied" for generations and felt very much like the
objects of policy rather than its agents. Moreover, the research directors
were sensitive to the issue that Aboriginal peoples themselves might see

their problems through a different cultural lens:

> The Research Directorate, both in its staffing and commission-
> ing, strives to achieve a balance between Aboriginal and
> non-Aboriginal researchers, and among Indian, Inuit and
> Métis. Much of our work will take place outside universities in
> Aboriginal cultural institutes and communities. We hope that
> this innovative approach will allow our research to speak in two
> voices—and be heard by both Aboriginal and non-Aboriginal
> people in Canada. (Hawkes and Castellano, 1993, p. 7)

The Commission's ethical guidelines for research were even more clear about this juggling act. All Commission research would have to display respect for "the cultures, languages, knowledge and values of Aboriginal peoples, and to the standards used by Aboriginal peoples to legitimate knowledge" (Royal Commission on Aboriginal Peoples, n.d., p. 1). Most public policy issues will not be as strongly marked by cultural differences between participants but, as we noted earlier, values are at the heart of all policy debates, no matter how apparently techni-cal. And values can be strongly linked to "ways of life" or community sensibilities. Consider for a moment the response governments face when they might decide, for rational reasons, to reallocate educational resources by closing schools. Or what municipalities might have to deal with when suggesting name changes to streets.

The third implication is that policy analysis, however much it may draw on other scientific disciplines, is itself a specific form of inquiry. Policy analysis, for example, has a unique focus when compared to other disciplines: public policies themselves and the several elements that com-prise them, along with the processes that produce them and the impacts they ultimately have. It has its own traditions of debate, its journals, its schools, and its characteristic intellectual paradigms and issues.

It is important not to paint too rigid a picture of policy analysis. Taking the two elements of the definition—(1) the disciplined applica-tion of intellect and (2) public problems—it is easy to see that if we break each one down into its possible elements that there is a wide va-riety of possibilities and permutations that might come under the broad rubric of policy analysis. The first category is really about styles of rea-soning, as long as these styles are disciplined and systematic in some recognizable sense. The second is about the various aspects of process, content, and outcome that are relevant to policy. As Figure 1.3 (page 18) shows, one can reason about (or analyze) policy in several equally legit-imate ways: normative, legal, logical, and empirical.

Normative analysis measures some aspect of policy against an ethical standard: secular morality, the Bible, the Koran, the Canadian Charter

Figure 1.3   Policy Analysis: Types of Reasoning

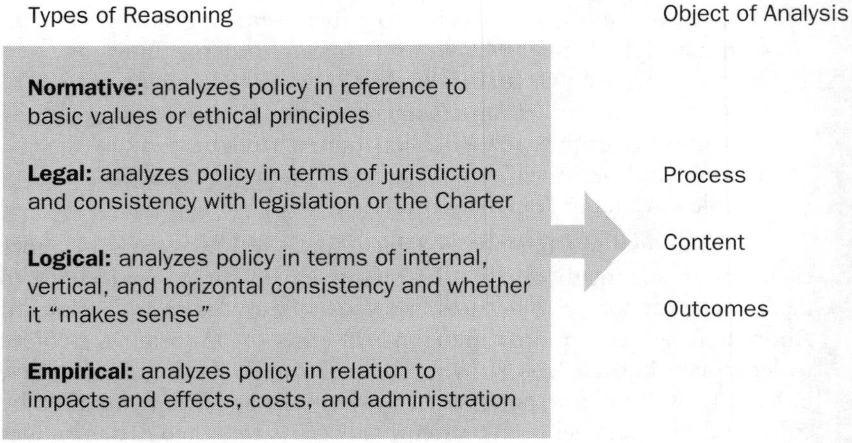

Types of Reasoning   Object of Analysis

Normative: analyzes policy in reference to
basic values or ethical principles

Legal: analyzes policy in terms of jurisdiction   Process
and consistency with legislation or the Charter

Logical: analyzes policy in terms of internal,   Content
vertical, and horizontal consistency and whether
it "makes sense"   Outcomes

Empirical: analyzes policy in relation to
impacts and effects, costs, and administration

of Rights and Freedoms, the UN Universal Declaration of Human Rights. This type of analysis is remarkably important in today's world but is rarely acknowledged in the literature on policy analysis (though see Dunn, 2004, Chap. 7). But as Peters (1999) points out, "both the policy maker and the citizen must be concerned also with the criteria of justice and trust in society. It may be that ultimately justice and trust make the best policies—and even the best politics" (p. 454). It is included here both for its importance and because it fits the definition of disciplined and systematic; while one may not agree with the conclusions, at least one can see how they were arrived at.

Legal analysis looks at public policy through the prism of law: constitutionality, consistency with statute, the practices of legal convention. This overlaps slightly with the previous category in that a prime measure of contemporary morality is human rights, and hence constitutional provisions on human rights. But this category also contains questions about jurisdiction and legality in the more technical sense.

Logical analysis deals with questions of consistency and coherence such as were raised earlier in this chapter: is the policy internally consistent, is it vertically consistent, and is it horizontally consistent? This kind of analysis can be done without extensive empirical research and so is a favourite of media pundits. The fact that these pundits shape the opinion of millions of people should underscore how important a form of analysis it is.

Empirical analysis takes logical analysis one step further by actually posing the same questions in the light of empirical evidence; not what might be the *likely* effect of policy X, but what was its actual effect? Impact questions can be about the direct intended impact, unintended consequences on other targets, or surveys of client satisfaction.

Figure 1.3 also highlights some of the dimensions of policy that can be analyzed: process (the various determinants of a policy, the actors and institutions that shaped it), content (problem definition, goals, instruments), and outcomes (legislation, regulations, actual impact or effect).

Defining policy analysis in this way—as the disciplined application of intellect to public problems—deliberately excludes some "other ways of knowing." It does so because it is itself based on a certain epistemology or system of knowledge. That system is **rationalism,** the characteristic form of knowing in the West that is rooted in the Greek and European civilizations. This is hardly the place to discuss the intellectual history of Western civilization, but it is important to understand what this form of reason implies about how we come to decisions, and what counts as knowledge and what does not. The rational decisionmaking paradigm, a feature of virtually every introductory textbook on policy analysis, is outlined in Box 1.1 (page 20). Note that the procedure is a generic one: it should apply as well to deciding public policy as it does to choosing a mate or choosing one's wardrobe.

Few of us are this systematic when we make everyday decisions, but the more important a decision, the more likely that we will think about it carefully and perhaps approximate this model. Will this make for a better decision? Maybe. But making decisions rationally is not the same as making reasonable decisions. A reasonable or good decision is defined less by the process that produced it than by its appropriateness as a solution to the initial problem. While the rational model could in principle be used to choose a mate, most people would argue that it is more reasonable to make this type of decision with the heart or one's emotions. By the same token, non-Western cultures are often more comfortable with decisionmaking processes that rely less on systematic analysis than on wisdom, intuition, or even "signs" (Suzuki and Knudtson, 1992).

It is worth taking a moment to consider the implications of the rational model for policy analysis and decisionmaking, if only because "rational" seems synonymous with "reasonable" and the opposition of "rationality" and "intuition" seems to give preference to the former. For one thing, the rational model has embedded in it a strong concern with efficiency, which Herbert Simon (the most important decision theorist) defined as choosing alternatives that provide the greatest results for the least cost (Simon, Smithburg, and Thompson, 1958, p. 60).

Box 1.1   THE RATIONAL
DECISIONMAKING MODEL

Choose objectives: The first step in making a decision is knowing what one wishes to do or accomplish. This necessarily involves a *statement* of the problem as well as of goals.

Consider alternatives: Once the problem and goals are identified, the second step is to identify the means by which the objectives may be attained.

Outline impacts: Each alternative will consist of a bundle of costs and benefits, positive and negative impacts on the problem. Measure them.

Determine criteria: A fourth step is to rank all of the alternatives in order of desirability, but this requires some explicit criterion, such as least cost, for a given objective.

Apply models/scenarios: The final step before actual implementation is the construction of a model or a scenario to help predict and map out the potential empirical consequences of the chosen alternative.

Implement preferred option: Put the preferred option into effect.

Evaluate consequences: What happened, and how well do the real impacts fit with predicted outcomes?

Simon was convinced throughout his long and distinguished career (he was born in 1916, won the Nobel Prize for Economics in 1978, and died in 2001) that social betterment would come from the application of rational techniques to complex decisions. He acknowledged that pure rationality in decisionmaking was an impossibility, and that instead human beings made decisions under various constraints, in a model he described as **bounded rationality** in search of **satisficing** solutions. In 1957 he was excited about the use of the "digital computer and the tools of mathematics and the behavioral sciences on the very core of managerial activity—on the exercise of judgment and intuition; on the process of making complex decisions" (Simon and Newell, 1957, p. 382). Mintzberg (1994) has noted how, for Simon, "the fundamental assumption is that continuous knowledge can be broken down into discrete elements, that is, decomposed for the purposes of analysis. . . . [I]ntuition gets reduced to analysis" (pp. 310–11). The pure rational model presumes certain patterns of thought: it is linear, systematic, self-conscious, purposive, and efficient.

Another way of putting this is that policy analysis, and the rationalism in which it is rooted, is part and parcel of the way "the state sees." James C. Scott (1998) points out the difficulties states had in pre-modern times in fulfilling classic state functions such as raising taxes, conscripting armies, or preventing rebellions. Societies were not "legible" or visible because pre-modern states, confronting patterns of social life that were suited to local conditions, knew very little about the identities, location, holdings, wealth, or personal conditions of their subjects. Scott's book traces the way in which the state developed this knowledge through focusing on and analyzing specific bits of information to the exclusion of others. With simplification "an overall, aggregate, synoptic view of a selective reality is achieved, making possible a high degree of schematic knowledge, control, and manipulation" (Scott, 1998, p. 11). Things we take for granted today, such as standard weights and measures, freehold land tenure and cadastral maps (showing plots of individually owned land), grid systems for the layout of cities, official languages, and even permanent patronyms (inherited last names date only from the twentieth century in Europe) all had to be invented, and they were invented largely to benefit state administration. As Scott (1998) argues, "the modern state, through its officials, attempts with varying degrees of success to create a terrain and a population with precisely those standardized characteristics that will be easiest to monitor, count, assess, and manage" (pp. 81–82). The statecraft that can be exercised on a "legible" society can be either sinister or benign, organized for oppression or public welfare. The point is that rationalism, as a key part of the modernist project, has deep roots in an impulse to centralize, categorize, and control. It should come as no surprise that the first burst of interest in policy analysis occurred just at the time that the United States was preparing to launch massive new social intervention programs in the 1960s and 1970s; new forms of information and "ways of seeing" had to be organized. That these were driven by a desire to improve public welfare is undeniable, but it is also important to realize that in practice rationalism and its offspring, policy analysis, may be closed to more complex social realities grounded in local practice and informal and complex social and economic patterns of behaviour.

This should remind us of the limits of policy analysis and rational technique. It may be that better policy will flow from disciplined analysis (methodologically rigorous, systematic, organized, and geared to the breaking down of complex phenomena into their simple components), but it is no guarantee. As we will note in a moment, there is also the possibility that rational technique might blind us to other, equally legitimate, ways of knowing. But at the very least, we should remember that all of the technique and discipline in the world will still run up against uncertainty. We cannot know everything, and hence our policy interventions may go wrong, fall short, or have unintended consequences. Henry Aaron (2000) has underscored the degree to which the policy sciences tend to ignore the challenges of uncertainty:

> The reason is straightforward. The task is laughably beyond our current analytical capacities. We simply cannot simultaneously handle the direct consequences of a policy change (presuming that our data and models are exactly right); *and* the direct consequences under alternative properly-weighted uncertain contingencies; *and* the direct consequences under plausible models different from the one that we have used; *and* the impacts on future legislation of the different legislative *and* political environment brought about by current actions; *and* whether it would be better to act now or defer action until the future; *and* if we act now, whether it would be better to implement policy changes promptly or at some time in the future. (pp. 201–02)

The standard definition of policy analysis therefore clearly carries with it some cultural and historical baggage. Even if we substantially relax the definition to include a wider variety of ways of knowing and thinking, it is hard to escape the core assumptions that analysis will demand, at minimum, (1) expertise, (2) reliance of Western science, (3) deductive logic, (4) measurement, and (5) clear and replicable steps or stages. For the last fifty years, this model of rationality has been at the heart of what people do when conducting policy analyses. For almost as long, that model has been challenged and criticized for what it leaves out. So what's wrong with being rational? It may seem a bit mechanical and plodding but is hardly sinful or dangerous. In summary, the main challenges and criticisms have been:

The real world is "incremental," not rational. In a famous 1959 article, Charles Lindblom argued that the unforgiving strictures of rational decisionmaking were so unrealistic in terms of the cognitive and political situation faced by most decisionmakers that in fact they made choices by "muddling through." In later work, Lindblom (1979) refined the model, both as a normative and a descriptive framework. In other words, incrementalism better described what really went on and, moreover, it had certain advantages over its apparently superior rival. In the real world of politics and administration, of course, there are multiple decisionmakers with conflicting perspectives and priorities, information is in short supply or contradictory, and everything has to be done immediately. In this situation, Lindblom and others argued, decisions get made on the basis of "successive limited comparisons." In this method, goals and values are not neatly separated from each other or from the process of choice. In making decisions, we often clarify what we want and what we believe only through the process of concrete choices in specific situations. As well, we usually make choices against a backdrop of what has been done before—we move in usually small increments from one situation to the next. Incrementalism seems a sorry standard in many respects, slow, halting, without clear vision or conviction, but it probably captures routine, day-to-day public policy-making in most organizations (Weiss and Woodhouse, 1992).

"Facts" lie at the heart of the rational model, but "facts" are constructed through values and theories. The rational model presumes that there are such things as "facts," but critics point out that facts are always constructed through values and perceptions, or more accurately, through deep theories that structure our cognition of reality. These theories are sometimes chosen rationally in the sense of deliberation among a range of alternatives according to multiple criteria, but "however exhaustive the arguments advanced in support of one position, considered judgments concerning the best theory will remain contentious and tentative . . ." (Hawkesworth, 1988, p. 87). Frank Fischer and John Forester (1993) have termed this emphasis the "argumentative turn" in policy analysis and planning. For them, policymaking is a "struggle over the criteria of social classification, the boundaries of problem categories, the intersubjective interpretation of common experiences, the conceptual framing of problems, and the definitions of ideas that guide the ways people create the shared meanings which motivate them to act" (Fischer and Forester, 1993, p. 2). The argumentative turn entails, among other things, the critical study of the structure of argument in policy analysis (Fischer, 1980); the role of values (Fischer and Forester, 1987); and the deep impact of positivism through its associated logic of technocratic mastery (Fischer, 1990). This has been complemented by work such as Dryzek's (1990), exploring the epistemological foundations of policy analysis. This is not merely a methodological debate: for deLeon (1997) as for his colleagues in the "post-positivist" school, the issue is developing a "policy sciences of democracy" (esp. Chap. 4).

Policy analysis actually has relatively little influence on policymaking. The high point in the fortunes of policy analysis and scientific decisionmaking was in the 1960s, when the United States decided to adopt the Planning-Programming-Budgeting System (PPBS), later adopted in Canada as well, and then made program evaluation mandatory, thus setting off a boom in the industry in the 1970s. A natural question was whether all this activity was having any effect on the policy process. Carol Weiss and her colleagues began a series of studies through the

1970s to answer this question. Their conclusion was that the "implications of explanatory studies and the recommendations from policy-oriented studies seemed to have little effect on either the day-to-day operations of program management or the long-term directions of public policy" (Weiss, 1983, p. 217). If it was clear that policy analysis did not influence the policy process directly, then what contributions did it make? One early argument was that policy analysis and the rest of the social sciences have a broad "enlightenment" function, providing broad ideas, concepts, insights, and theoretical perspectives (Janowitz, 1972). Another version of this image is the "limestone" metaphor, to capture how science enters politics: "It relies on indirect or cumulative interest and requires no action other than the research itself and the presentation of the findings in a readable way. If circumstances permit (and the research has no control over many of them) the work may, in combination with other work with a similar theme and message, seep into the public consciousness" (Thomas, 1987, p. 57).

There is much to these criticisms, and they have had powerful impacts on the way in which policy analysis is theorized and practised. However, in recent years there has been a resurgence of interest in policy and in developing strong **policy capacity**, a resurgence that has been evident both in Canada and abroad. There are several broad explanations for this. In many countries, after a long focus on management of existing resources through the 1990s to deal with deficits and financial constraint, the realization dawned that just "minding the store" was not enough. Countries faced major challenges and rapidly shifting environments, and without guides, strategy, or vision—in short, public policy—they would be rudderless. Other countries, such as those in Central and Eastern Europe, lacked a policy tradition—orders had come down from the Communist Party in Moscow—and so they found themselves grappling with similar imperatives, but from a position that forced them to reinvent and reconsider the assumptions both of their state systems and of policy analysis (as understood in the Western state tradition) itself.

Policy is popular again. The next section provides some examples of the international policy movement that is emerging and some of its characteristics. The deeper forces that underlie the rise of this movement will be explored in the next chapter.

THE POLICY MOVEMENT

To understand the recent resurgence in policy analysis one has to understand its rise and temporary decline. The social sciences, particularly economics, political science, public administration, and planning, developed in the late nineteenth and early twentieth centuries. Whereas in continental Europe sociology tended to be the umbrella discipline for all of these, in the Anglo-Saxon tradition of England and North America they developed as separate disciplines. Just as important, political science was distinct from law, another difference from the continental tradition. The idea that these disciplines could be integrated into something distinct—the policy sciences—can be conveniently dated from some key publications by American social scientist Harold Lasswell. As early as 1951, he and colleagues were arguing for a distinct approach they termed the "policy sciences of democracy" and a distinct role for policy analysts (Lasswell, 1951). In Lasswell's view, the policy sciences would integrate the other social sciences in a multidisciplinary enterprise devoted to dealing with public problems and the policy processes of democracy. It was an ambitious vision but clearly gathered momentum through the 1960s. By 1972, for example, leading American social scientists were seriously debating the possibility that policy analysis might become the integrating medium for the social sciences (Charlesworth, 1972).

The terms "public policy" and "policy analysis" began to be used more frequently in the 1960s as the American government began to try to solve "problems" in a host of areas from racial conflict, urban renewal, transportation, and education (Parsons, 1995, pp. 20–21). Hofferbert (1990) notes that between 1960 and 1975 "national research priorities drew many American social scientists out of the ivory tower and into the political arena, not as politicians or bureaucrats but as experts in the evaluation of public programs" (p. 4). The same was true of Canada. Sutherland (1993) reports that by the mid-1970s "after several years of expansionary budgets and in a climate of general high faith in rationalism, many policy departments and some central agencies had built up good-sized cadres of professional researchers and analysts" (p. 95). Both Hofferbert and Sutherland claim that after this heyday came decline. This was due in part to overweening optimism and the ultimate failure to deliver much except bad news. In the Canadian case as well, the newly elected Conservative government cut 15 000 person-years between 1984 and 1992, hitting staff advisory functions quite hard. As well, the federal Tories were less interested in building internal research capacity than buying the necessary services from think-tanks or universities.

By the late 1990s the pendulum was swinging back, and "policy capacity" and "policy analysis" were once more key terms in debates over governance and appropriate public management. Why? The reasons will be developed in greater detail in the next chapter, but generally had to do with several broad but common factors. First, the collapse of the Soviet Union in 1990–91 ended the Cold War and led to the creation of a host of new states in Central and Eastern Europe (including the

Russian Federation). These events required a shift in foreign policy in the West, but also gradually created a demand for training in public administration and policy in these countries. Examples will be given below, but the problem for newly independent countries like the Baltic states and Ukraine was that they had had no tradition of distinct public administration or indeed of policy development. As these states struggled to modernize, it became abundantly clear that good public policy was a key ingredient in the success of post-communist societies. Second, many Western states in the 1990s experienced an unusual degree of political polarization. The Canadian variant was the rise of the Reform (then Canadian Alliance, and finally Conservative) party in the early 1990s and the prominence of the Ontario and Alberta Tory parties as they pursued major program reforms. In the United States, President Bill Clinton had to deal suddenly with a Republican-dominated Congress through the mid-1990s. The rhythms varied, but many European countries saw sharper competition between right and left. The upshot was that, by the end of the decade, debates over policy—and often diametrically opposed policy approaches—were suddenly important. Third, there was a growing sense that the solutions and frameworks of the 1980s would no longer suffice for the modern world (Giddens, 1999; Pal, 1999), and this too led to more concentrated discussion and debate about public policy issues. Fourth, and partly in response to the previous factor, the early 1990s were a decade of public sector reform in the light of new management theories, but eventually the question arose "reform for what?" Changing administrative structures and processes could not be completely divorced from substance. And finally, after a decade of criticism of the traditional state, it was clear that an effective public sector was an important ingredient in social harmony and economic progress. Health and educational services, transportation, communications, security, and biotechnology are all affected by, if not dependent on, state action.

If anything, the emphasis on policy capacity has continued, though for complicated and not always mutually consistent reasons. As mentioned above, a key factor has been the realization of the importance of the state and state policy for a host of social and economic activities. The sterile debate of the 1980s and 1990s over a "minimalist state" has been eclipsed by several realities. The post-9/11 international and domestic security situation demands both policy and operational responsiveness by government. Modern economies depend increasingly on new technologies, innovation, and research, and governments find themselves having to design new, more supple, forms of regulation, intervention, and support. A factor peculiar to Europe is the recent accession of ten new states to the European Union (EU) (Latvia, Estonia, Lithuania, Poland, Czech Republic, Slovakia, Slovenia, Hungary, Cyprus, and Malta). In order to be admitted to the EU, applicant countries must make their laws and most policy frameworks consistent with the *"acquis communautaire,"* or the body of laws, treaties, declarations, and resolutions that make up the EU. This requires a tremendous amount of policy-oriented work. For other countries that are eyeing EU membership, there is an equivalent pressure to enhance their policy capacity in order to engage with Brussels.

More detail on these factors will be developed in the next chapter, but the following provides some examples from Canada and the rest of the world on the flavour of this policy movement.

CANADA

The first alarm about Canada's policy capacity was sounded by the clerk of Privy Council, Jocelyne Bourgon, in 1995 in her Third Annual Report to the Prime Minister on the public service:

> All of the governments in Canada are making significant changes to their roles and functions. While certain determinants of change are unique to Canada, others are affecting all western nations. One of the most striking features of western democratic nations in recent years has been that they have all been engaged in rethinking the role of government and the organization of their public sectors. In many nations the essence of governance is being redefined. (Privy Council Office, 1995)

Bourgon sketched out the government of Canada's responses, but she highlighted the importance of developing policy capacity: "The strategic policy capacity of the federal public service must be strengthened. This is essential, given the complexity of issues that governments must address, and the increasingly horizontal and cross-sectoral nature of these issues." She identified the development of policy capacity as a key priority for the public service over the coming years (Bakvis, 2000).

Bourgon's concern about policy capacity helped propel two important initiatives under her tenure. The first was *La Relève.* As outlined in her Fourth Annual Report, it was directed at what she called a "quiet crisis" in the federal public service. After years of downsizing that had seen almost 55 000 public servants leave the federal public service, after years of criticism of their efficiency and competence, after pay freezes and cuts, the public servants who were left felt demoralized. Those who left the federal public service were either retiring in record numbers or being recruited, ironically, by the private sector. *La Relève* was dedicated to nothing less than the renewal of the federal public sector. For our purposes, what was most interesting about the initiative was the assumption of the importance of a well-functioning public sector. As

Bourgon put it: "In today's global environment, the quality of the public sector will continue to make a significant difference to the performance of nations. A high quality public sector contributes to competitiveness, provides countries with a comparative advantage in their competition for trade and investment, and contributes to the quality of life and the standard of living of citizens" (Privy Council Office, 1997). The second initiative was the creation of the **Policy Research Initiative** (PRI), which was directed specifically at enhancing policy capacity. A Policy Research Committee had been established in 1996, involving over thirty departments and agencies. By November 1997, some 300 public service policy analysts met at a conference to discuss strategic policy issues, and in November 1998 the first National Policy Research Conference was held with both government and nongovernment participants, followed by a second one in November 1999 with over 750 Canadian and international participants. In 2001, the PRI (in the form of the Policy Research Secretariat that was formed in 1997) was organizationally affiliated with the Privy Council Office. As of 2004, it was focusing on five research areas: population aging and life-course flexibility, poverty and exclusion, social capital, North America linkages, and sustainable development.

It must be said that the federal government's emphasis on policy capacity declined in the dying days of the Chrétien regime. With the exception of health care and a vague innovation agenda, the national government slipped into a tired semi-paralysis as it waited for the transition to Paul Martin. That occurred on December 12, 2003, and was accompanied with a flurry of announcements on restructuring the machinery of government, new initiatives on health care and cities, and a federal budget in February 2004. The new policy energy was quickly dissipated, however, as the government became mired in the sponsorship scandal (it was alleged that the Liberal party for years had been loosely managing $100 million worth of advertising contracts in Quebec), and finally decided to call an election for June 28, 2004.

INTERNATIONAL EXAMPLES

The Organisation for Economic Co-operation and Development (OECD) is an international body of thirty member states "sharing a commitment to democratic government and the market economy" (OECD, 2004). Its original membership has expanded beyond North America and Western Europe to include Japan, Australia, New Zealand, Finland, Mexico, the Czech Republic, Slovakia, Hungary, Poland, and Korea. The OECD also has interactions with states in the former Soviet bloc and in Latin America. Much of the focus of its work is on key policy issues, such as aging, agriculture, biotechnology, education, energy, health, security, sustainable development, trade and transport, and, more recently, corporate governance.

The OECD also has an interest in governance issues and public sector management, principally through its Directorate for Public Governance and Territorial Development (of which the Public Management Committee (PUMA) is a part). Its rationale is as follows:

> Good governance is critical to long-term economic, social and environmental development. The Public Governance and Territorial Development Directorate (GOV) identifies changing societal and market needs, and helps countries adapt their governmental systems and territorial polices. This involves improving government efficiency while protecting and promoting society's longer-term governance values. . . . GOV supports improved public sector governance through comparative data and analysis, the setting and promotion of standards, and the facilitation of transparency and peer review. This involves promoting understanding of the dynamics of public management and territorial development policies in different societal and market conditions, with a view to the long-term interests of all citizens. (OECD, 2004)

PUMA has published several key international reports on governance. For example, a 1995 report entitled *Governance in Transition: Public Management Reform in OECD Countries* argued that "OECD countries are undergoing profound structural change. An increasingly open international economy puts a premium on national competitiveness and highlights the mutual dependence of the public and private sectors. Citizen demand is more diversified and sophisticated, and, at the same time, the ability of governments to deal with stubborn societal problems is being questioned. . . . Traditional governance structures and managerial response are increasingly ineffectual in this context. Radical change is required in order to protect the very capacity to govern and deliver services. (OECD [PUMA], 1995).

In 2003 the Directorate published a policy brief on public sector modernization that surveyed twenty years of OECD member country attempts at reform. The report had a somewhat sober tone, noting that two decades of reform had yielded some clear improvements but had also created unanticipated problems. The pursuit of efficiency, which characterized most of this period, had been myopic and sometimes counterproductive. But the document still emphasized the need for better policy capacity—indeed the very problems created by the reforms demanded improved governance systems:

> To complicate matters, governments are now under pressure for more profound changes to meet the requirements of contemporary society. A concern for efficiency is being supplanted by problems of governance, strategy, risk management, ability to adapt to change, collaborative action and the need to understand the impact of policies on society. To respond to this challenge, member countries, and the OECD, need better analytical and empirical tools and more sophisticated strategies for change than they have generally had to date. (OECD, 2003)

The OECD's focus on policy development as a key aspect of public sector reform is not restricted to its members alone but has formed part of the organization's efforts at international aid focused on formerly communist regimes. Its SIGMA program (Support for Improvement in Governance and Management in Central and Eastern European Countries), which is a joint effort by the OECD and the European Union (under its Phare program, which since 1989 has been channelling EU financial and technical support for transition and reform efforts, and more recently, to prepare countries in Central and Eastern Europe to successfully join the EU), provides support to Albania, Bosnia-Herzegovina, Bulgaria, Croatia, the Czech Republic, Estonia, the Former Yugoslav Republic of Macedonia, Hungary, Latvia, Lithuania, Poland, Romania, Russia, Serbia and Montenegro, Slovakia, Slovenia, and Turkey (SIGMA, 2004). Priority reform areas include anti-corruption and integrity, policymaking and regulatory capacities, and public expenditure management. The importance of policy capacity is clear:

> Sigma activities to support policy-making and co-ordination focus on four sub-areas: policy and strategic capacities; co-ordination structures; regulatory reform, including impact assessment; and management of EU integration.

> Sigma assists partner countries in strengthening policy-making capacities and in setting up co-ordination mechanisms at the centre of government, usually in the Office of the Government and/or the Prime Minister's Office, to ensure coherence among sectoral policies of ministries and consistency of government policy-making and implementation. Support is also given to developing methodologies for assessing the impact of legislation on the budget and the economy as a whole—including such aspects as labour market, social and political impact—and on the management, organisational structures and process of adopting the acquis communautaire. (SIGMA, 2004)

The World Bank is another influential international organization that has turned its attention to governance and policy capacity in recent years. Founded in 1944, the bank currently channels some US$18 billion to more than 100 countries for development assistance loans. In its 1997 annual report, entitled *The State in a Changing World,* the bank highlighted the importance of good governance to sustainable economic development:

> For human welfare to be advanced, the state's capability— *defined as the ability to undertake and promote collective actions efficiently*—must be increased. This basic message translates into a two-part strategy to make every state a more credible, effective partner in its country's development:
>
> *Matching the state's role to its capability* is the first element in this strategy. Where state capability is weak, how the state intervenes—and where—should be carefully assessed. Many states try to do too much with few resources and little capability, and often do more harm than good. A sharper focus on the fundamentals would improve effectiveness. But here it is a matter not just of choosing what to do and what not to do— but of how to do it as well.
>
> But capability is not destiny. Therefore the second element of the strategy is to *raise state capability by reinvigorating public institutions.* This means designing effective rules and restraints, to check arbitrary state actions and combat entrenched corruption. (World Bank, 1997) [emphasis in original]

This was followed in 2000 by a World Bank strategic document entitled *Reforming Public Institutions and Strengthening Governance* (World Bank, 2000). In its most recent reports, the Bank has emphasized empowerment and participation of the poor in the development process, and this has led it to highlight well-functioning public institutions as a key crucible of that participation.

Not only governments participate in this worldwide movement to develop policy capacity and good governance. There are numerous foundations supporting a host of initiatives to develop democracy and policy capacity. An interesting example of private, nongovernment action is the Open Society Institute (OSI), with headquarters in New York. It serves as the hub for a network of autonomous foundations and networks active in over fifty countries, principally in Central and Eastern Europe, Central Eurasia, the Caribbean and South America, and Africa. The organization is funded by billionaire philanthropist George Soros. According to OSI, "open societies are characterized by the rule of law; respect for human rights, minorities, and minority opinions; democratically elected governments; market economies in which business and government are separate; and thriving civil societies" (OSI, 2002). A representative program of the OSI efforts is the International Policy Fellowships (IPF), administered in cooperation with the Centre for Policy Studies at the Central European University in Budapest, Hungary. Launched in 1998, the program seeks to identify the "next generation of open society leaders" and equip them with policy analysis and advocacy skills so that they may put forward innovative policy solutions in their respective countries. The IPF "identifies and nurtures the next generation of open society leaders in the countries of the former Soviet Union, Central and Eastern Europe, and Mongolia. IPF joined forces with the Center for Policy Studies when it was established in late 1999 and began offering training to policy fellows to develop their capacity to write professional policy documents, identify appropriate policy instruments, and effectively advocate polices—skills that remain underdeveloped in countries where the Soros foundations work" (IPF, 2004).

These Canadian and international examples demonstrate the enormous energy that has gone into public sector reform in the last decade, and the prime importance of developing policy capacity as part of the reform agenda. The pace has varied in different countries, as have the circumstances (particularly in Central and Eastern Europe), and even the concepts—sometimes policy is used, sometimes strategy, sometimes horizontal co-ordination. Hood (1998) properly cautions us to be skeptical about the degree of international convergence around "modern" public administration:

> Convergence is a powerful rhetorical theme, because by providing apparently convincing backing for the claim that the same thing is happening everywhere, it suggests (typically by suppressed premiss again) that running with the herd must be the best—or at least the only—thing to do. It is thus hardly surprising that both domestic reformers and international agencies like OECD and the World Bank tend to lay heavy stress on 'convergence' . . . [I]nternational organizations are almost by their *raison d'être* committed to a view of international convergence on some single 'best-practice' model which it is their role to 'benchmark' and foster, helping the 'laggards' to catch up with the best-practice techniques of the vanguard. (p. 202)

At the heart of all this international activity, however, is the simple insight that a society's quality of life depends in large measure on the quality of its government, and that the quality of governmental responses to problems depends in large measure on its capacity to think through those problems and develop appropriate and effective solutions. Public policymaking is no more, and no less, than that.

CONCLUSION

This chapter defined public policy and policy analysis, along with some key associated concepts, and showed how the discipline and practice of policy analysis in its modern guise goes back to the immediate post–World War II era. At the same time, in the second section of the chapter, we showed how after a period of decline, policy and the development of policy capacity have been enjoying a resurgence, not only in Canada but also throughout the world. We provided some reasons for this shift earlier, but it is important to recall that the interest in policy has been part of a larger effort at **public sector reform.** If reform has been the name of the game, can we expect that the type of policy analysis and the type of policy capacity that is being demanded will be the same as that of the 1960s and 1970s? Will old tools be adequate when the edifice is being drastically renovated?

This book's answer is no. Many of the tools remain useful, as do the concepts, but they are being revised and changed to come to terms with a situation where the role and nature of government is very different from what it was a generation ago. Policymaking and policy analysis have to adapt to at least three fundamental shifts that have occurred in the last decade. First, the nature of some old policy problems has changed, and they have been joined by some entirely new issues. Poverty, for example, which a generation ago was most acute among families with a male breadwinner, is now in many countries a phenomenon concentrated among single mothers. The new problems countries face are often an artifact of new technologies, for example, how to create regulatory frameworks for e-commerce or for the bio-engineering of genetically modified organisms?

Second, many key policy processes have changed. It is almost universally acknowledged that citizens today want a more direct say in both policy development and program implementation. The Internet gives people, nongovernmental organizations, and the private sector unprecedented and instant access to materials and information that previously would have been primarily in government hands. Government departments themselves are different from what they were before—they are generally smaller, more knowledge-based, and focused more on evaluation of results and outcomes. Government responsibilities have been shuffled as well: in most provinces, notably Ontario and Quebec, major provincial responsibilities have been shifted to municipalities and *vice versa*. Today, policy analysis for a major urban centre in Canada is likely to include issues that previously would have been provincial or even federal responsibilities.

Third, there has been a subtle but important change in the way governments view their relationship with the private sector and civil society. Whereas a generation ago it might have seemed normal for the state to dominate both these sectors, today there is a sense that government actions should in most instances complement markets and support civil society. As broad a change as this is, it does have important implications for how governments go about implementing public policy.

At its best, policy analysis provides guidance to governments as they try to address public problems. In practice, of course, governments are political creatures interested in re-election and in power, and so they may eschew "guidance" in favour of more politically motivated behaviour. But from a citizen's perspective, governments are democratically elected to address public problems and provide core public services in the public interest, not in their own interest. The definition of the public interest will be contested of course, but it is this formula that provides the foundation for policy analysis and civic dialogue around policy issues. Policy analysis can then pose its core questions: what is the nature of the problem, what are we trying to achieve, how shall we go about addressing it, and how will we know if we have been successful or not? These are the key questions, but this book argues that the context in which they are asked—both in Canada and around the world—has changed dramatically in recent years. It is to these changes that we now turn.

KEY TERMS

bounded rationality—a term invented by Herbert Simon to capture the idea that most human decisionmaking takes place under various constraints rather than ideal conditions of complete information and unlimited processing capacities

emergent strategies—consistent patterns of behaviour that emerge or form rather than being planned

empirical analysis—takes logical analysis one step further: not what might be the *likely* effect of policy X, but what was its actual effect?

gender-based analysis (GBA)—a process that assesses the differential impact of public policies, programs, and legislation (proposed or existing) on women and men in terms of their social and economic circumstances, as well as their relationships in key social institutions such as the family

gender mainstreaming—an organizational strategy to ensure that a gender perspective is reflected in all types of organizational activities; championed by the United Nations as a means for achieving gender equality internationally

general goals—policy goals that enjoy a majority consensus or that express the broadest objectives of the policy initiative as a whole

governance—the process of governing or steering complex systems in cooperation with a variety of other actors

horizontal consistency—consistency across policy fields, not just within them

internal consistency—consistency among the three elements of problem definition, goals, and instruments

La Relève—the initiative started by the clerk of Privy Council, Jocelyne Bourgon, during the mid-1990s to address the "quiet crisis" in the federal public service and rebuild motivation and pride

legal analysis—looks at public policy through the prism of law: constitutionality, consistency with statute, the practices of legal convention

logical analysis—deals with questions of consistency and coherence: is the policy internally consistent, is it vertically consistent, is it horizontally consistent?

normative analysis—measures some aspect of policy against an ethical standard: secular morality, the Bible, the Koran, the Canadian Charter of Rights and Freedoms, or the UN Universal Declaration of Human Rights

policy analysis—the disciplined application of intellect to public problems

policy capacity—the institutional ability to conduct policy analysis and implement its results effectively and efficiently

policy consistency—agreement between the different elements of public policy, embracing horizontal, vertical, and internal consistency

policy development—the process of shaping policy initiatives, from problem recognition to implementation and evaluation

policy framework—a guide to a range of related actions and decisions in a given field

policy goals—the objectives to be achieved by a given public policy

policy instruments—means chosen on how to address the problem and achieve the policy goals

Policy Research Initiative—an initiative directed at developing a sustained demand for policy among a community of collaborating federal departments and the wider research community focused on long-term, research-based, and reflective issues

policy-specific goals—goals related to the broader ones but more directly connected to the programs that give the policy effect

policy statement—defines the problem, sets the goals that are to be achieved, and indicates the instruments or means whereby the problem is to be addressed and the goals achieved

policy studies—the broad range of research literature that is relevant to the study of and reflection upon public policy

problem definition—indicates what the problem or issue is and some of the causal factors behind it

public policy—a course of action or inaction chosen by public authorities to address a given problem or interrelated set of problems

public sector reform—attempts to change management practices and institutional design in the public sector to enhance efficiency and effectiveness

rational model—a systematic approach to problem-solving that lays out the problem, reviews options, and makes recommendations based on the intersection between goals and factual circumstances

rationalism—the characteristic form of knowing in the West that emphasizes empirical knowledge, science, objectivity, and systematic analysis

satisficing—the objective in most human decisionmaking to find a workable rather than perfect solution to problems

vertical consistency—consistency between the broad policy framework and the specific programs that implement that framework

Weblinks

Canadian Policy Research Networks
http://www.cprn.com/en/

Institute for Research on Public Policy
http://www.irpp.org/indexe.htm

OECD
http://www.oecd.org

Open Society Institute
http://www.soros.org

Policy Research Initiative
http://policyresearch.gc.ca/

Privy Council Office (Canada)
http://www.pco-bcp.gc.ca

World Bank Group
http://www.worldbank.org

Further Readings

Bardach, E. (2000). *A practical guide for policy analysis: The eightfold path to more effective problem solving.* New York: Chatham House Publishers.

Clemons, R. S. and McBeth, M. K. (2001). *Public policy praxis: Theory and pragmatism: A case approach.* Upper Saddle River, NJ: Prentice-Hall.

Dunn, W. N. (2004). *Public policy analysis: An introduction,* 3rd ed. Englewood Cliffs, NJ: Prentice-Hall.

Howlett, M. and Ramesh, M. (2003). *Studying public policy: Policy Cycles and Policy Subsystems,* 2nd ed. Don Mills, ON: Oxford University Press.

Parsons, W. (1995). *Public policy: An introduction to the theory and practice of policy analysis.* Aldershot, UK: Edward Elgar.

REFERENCES

Aaron, H. J. (2000). Presidential address: Seeing through the fog: Policy-making with uncertain forecasts. *Journal of Policy Analysis and Management,* 19(2), 193–206.

Bakvis, H. (2000, January). Country report: Rebuilding policy capacity in the era of the fiscal dividend: A report from Canada. *Governance,* 13, 71–103.

Burt, S. (1995). The several worlds of policy analysis: Traditional approaches and feminist critiques. In S. Burt and L. Code (Eds.), *Changing methods: Feminists transforming practice* (pp. 357–78). Peterborough, ON: Broadview Press.

Charlesworth, J. C. (Ed.). (1972). *Integration of the social sciences through policy analysis*. Philadelphia: The American Academy of Political and Social Science.

Colebatch, H. K. (1998). *Policy*. Minneapolis: University of Minnesota Press.

deLeon, P. (1988). *Advice and consent: The development of the policy sciences*. New York: Russell Sage.

deLeon, P. (1997). *Democracy and the policy sciences*. Albany: State University of New York.

Desveaux, J. A., Lindquist, E. A., and Toner, G. (1994). Organizing for policy innovation in public bureaucracy: AIDS, energy and environmental policy in Canada. *Canadian Journal of Political Science, 27,* 493–528.

Dryzek, J. S. (1990). *Discursive democracy: Politics, policy and political science*. Cambridge, MA: Cambridge University Press.

Dye, T. R. (1984). *Understanding public policy,* 5th ed. Englewood Cliffs, NJ: Prentice-Hall.

Dunn, W. N. (2004). *Public policy analysis: An introduction,* 3rd ed. Englewood Cliffs, NJ: Prentice-Hall.

Fischer, F., and Forester, J. (Eds.). (1987). *Confronting values in policy analysis: The politics of criteria*. Newbury Park: Sage.

Fischer, F., and Forester, J. (Eds.). (1993). *The argumentative turn in policy analysis and planning*. Durham, NC: Duke University Press.

Fischer, F. (1980). *Politics, values, and public policy: The problem of methodology*. Boulder, CO: Westview Press.

Fischer, F. (1990). *Technocracy and the politics of expertise*. Newbury Park, CA: Sage.

Fischer, F. (1993). Citizen participation and the democratization of policy expertise: From theoretical inquiry to practical cases. *Policy Sciences, 26,* 165–87.

Giddens, A. (1999). *The third way: The renewal of social democracy*. Malden, MA: Polity Press.

Graham, G. (1988). "The policy orientation" and the theoretical development of political science. In E. Portis and M. Levy (Eds.), *Handbook of political theory and policy science* (pp. 150–61). New York: Greenwood Press.

Hawkes, D. C., and Castellano, M. B. (1993, January). Research: A challenging agenda. *The Circle* (Royal Commission on Aboriginal Peoples) 2, 1, 7.

Hawkesworth, M. E. (1988). *Theoretical issues in policy analysis.* New York: State University of New York.

Hofferbert, R. I. (1990). *The reach and grasp of policy analysis: Comparative views of the craft.* Tuscaloosa: The University of Alabama Press.

Hogwood, B. W., and Gunn, L. A. (1984). *Policy analysis for the real world.* Oxford: Oxford University Press.

Howlett, M. and Ramesh, M. (2003). *Studying public policy: Policy cycles and policy subsystems,* 2nd ed. Don Mills, ON: Oxford University Press.

Hood, C. (1998). *The art of the state: Culture, rhetoric, and public management.* Oxford: Clarendon Press.

IPF (International Policy Fellowships). (2004). *About the Initiative.* Retrieved September 5, 2004, from http://www.soros/org/initiatives/IPF/about

Janowitz, M. (1972, July). Professionalization of sociology. *American Journal of Sociology,* 78, 105–35.

Kingdon, J. W. (1995). *Agendas, alternatives, and public policies,* 2nd ed. New York: HarperCollins.

Lasswell, H. (1951). The policy orientation. In D. Lerner and H. Lasswell (Eds.), *The policy sciences* (pp. 3–15). Stanford, CA: Stanford University Press.

Lasswell, H. (1970). The emerging conception of the policy sciences. *Policy Sciences,* 1, 3–13.

Lindblom, C. E. (1959). The science of muddling through. *Public Administration Review,* 19, 79–88.

Lindblom, C. (1979, November–December). Still muddling, not yet through. *Public Administration Review,* 39, 517–26.

Linder, S., and Peters, B. G. (1989). Instruments of government: Perceptions and contexts. *Journal of Public Policy,* 9, 35–58.

McCool, D. C. (Ed.). (1995). *Public policy theories, models, and concepts: An anthology.* Englewood Cliffs, NJ: Prentice-Hall.

Mintzberg, H. (1994). *The rise and fall of strategic planning: Reconceiving roles for planning, plans, planners.* New York: The Free Press.

Mintzberg, H., and Jørgensen, J. (1987, Summer). Emergent strategy for public policy. *Canadian Public Administration,* 30, 214–29.

OECD. (2003). *Public sector modernisation.* Paris: OECD. Retrieved August 5, 2004, from http://www.oecd.org/dataoecd/31/56/29888169.pdf

OECD. (2004a). *About OECD*. Paris: OECD. Retrieved August 5, 2004, from http://www.oecd.org/about/
0,2337,en_2649_201185_1_1_1_1_1,00.html

OECD [PUMA]. (1995). *Governance in transition: Public management reform in OECD countries*. Paris: OECD. Retrieved August 5, 2004, from http://www.oecd.org/puma/gvrnance/general/pubs/git95/
gitexsum.pdf

OSI (Open Society Institute). (2002). *Soros Foundations Network, 2002 Report*. Retrieved August 5, 2004, from http://www.soros
.org/resources/articles_publications/publications/
sorosannual2002_20030801/a_complete_report.pdf

Pal, L. A. (Ed.). (1999). *How Ottawa spends: 1999–2000: Shape shifting: Canadian governance toward the 21st century*. Toronto: Oxford University Press.

Parsons, W. (1995). *Public policy: An introduction to the theory and practice of policy analysis*. Aldershot, UK: Edward Elgar.

Peters, B. G. (1999). *American Public Policy*, 5th ed. New York: Chatham House.

Privy Council Office (Canada). (1995). *Third annual report to the Prime Minister on the public service of Canada*. Retrieved September 5, 2004, from http://www.pco-bcp.gc.ca/default
.asp?Language=E&Page=clerk&Sub=AnnualReports

Privy Council Office (Canada). (1997). *Fourth annual report to the Prime Minister on the public service of Canada*. Retrieved September 5, 2004, from http://www.pco-bcp.gc.ca/default
.asp?Language=E&Page=clerk&Sub=AnnualReports

Rochefort, D. A., and Cobb, R. W. (1994). Problem definition: An emerging perspective. In D. A. Rochefort and R. W. Cobb (Eds.), *The politics of problem definition: Shaping the policy agenda* (pp. 1–31). Lawrence: University of Kansas Press.

Royal Commission on Aboriginal Peoples. (1991). *The Mandate: Royal Commission on Aboriginal peoples: Background documents* (Ottawa: Royal Commission on Aboriginal Peoples).

Royal Commission on Aboriginal Peoples, (Canada) (n.d.). *Ethical guidelines for research* (Ottawa: Royal Commission on Aboriginal Peoples).

Scott, J. C. (1998). *Seeing like a state: How certain schemes to improve the human condition have failed*. New Haven: Yale University Press.

SIGMA. (2004). Policy-making and Co-ordination. Paris. Retrieved September 5, 2004, from http://www.sigmaweb.org/reforms/pmc.htm

Simon, H., and Newell, A. (1957). Heuristic problem solving: The next advance in operations research. Reprinted in H. A. Simon. (1982). *Models of bounded rationality: Volume 1: Economic analysis and public policy.* Cambridge, MA: MIT Press, 380–89.

Simon, H., Smithburg, D. W., and Thompson, V. A. (1958). *Public administration.* New York: Alfred A. Knopf.

Status of Women Canada. (1996). *Gender-based analysis: A guide for policy-making.* Ottawa: Status of Women Canada.

Stone, D. (2001). *Policy paradox: The art of political decision making.* Rev. ed. New York: W. W. Norton and Co.

Sutherland, S. L. (1993). The public service and policy development. In M. M. Atkinson (Ed.), *Governing Canada: Institutions and public policy* (pp. 81–113). Toronto: Harcourt Brace Jovanovich.

Suzuki, D. T., and Knudtson, P. (1992). *Wisdom of the elders: Sacred native stories of nature.* New York: Bantam.

Thomas, P. (1987). The use of social research: Myths and models. In M. Bulmer (Ed.), *Social science research and government: Comparative essays on Britain and the United States,* (pp. 51–60). Cambridge, UK: Cambridge University Press.

United Nations, Office of the Special Advisor on Gender Issues and Advancement of Women. (2004). *Gender mainstreaming.* Retrieved August 5, 2004, from http://www.un.org/womenwatch/osagi/gendermainstreaming.htm

Vannijnatten, D. L. and MacDonald, D. (2003). Reconciling energy and climate change policies: How Ottawa blends. In G. B. Doern (Ed.), *How Ottawa spends 2003–2004: Regime change and policy shift,* (pp. 72–88). Don Mills, ON: Oxford University Press.

Weiss, A., and Woodhouse, E. (1992). Reframing incrementalism: A constructive response to critics. *Policy Sciences, 25,* 255–73.

Weiss, C. H. (1983). Ideology, interest, and information: The basis of policy positions. In D. Callahan and B. Jennings (Eds.), *Ethics, the social sciences, and policy analysis* (pp. 213–45). New York: Plenum Press.

Wildavsky, A. (1979). *Speaking truth to power: The art and craft of policy analysis.* Boston: Little, Brown & Co.

World Bank. (1997). *World development report 1997: The state in a changing world (summary).* Washington, D.C.: The International

Bank for Reconstruction and Development/The World Bank. Retrieved August 5, 2004, from http://www.worldbank.org/html/extpb/wdr97/english/wdr97su1.htm

World Bank. (2000). *Reforming public institutions and strengthening governance*. Washington, DC: The International Bank for Reconstruction and Development/The World Bank. Retrieved August 5, 2004, from http://www1.worldbank.org/publicsector/Reforming.pdf

Chapter 2

Modern Governance: The Challenges for Policy Analysis

Policy analysis, in the service of the public interest, makes its contributions by asking certain questions and using certain tools. It cannot make those contributions in a vacuum, however, and the nature of policy work depends on context. As the last chapter suggested, that context has been changing in the last decade. This chapter reviews the key forces underpinning this change: globalization, political culture, and governance. They are closely entangled, and sometimes conflicting, but with broad consequences that make a substantial difference to the nature of policymaking and analysis. Globalization involves deeper and more intense economic and political interdependencies and challenges fundamental assumptions about sovereignty and the role of the nation-state. In Canada as well as other industrialized countries, political culture is less deferential and more individualist and participatory. Changing notions of governance reflect these forces but also have their own dynamic that stresses smaller government and new forms of public management. Subsequent chapters take up the detailed implications of these forces for problem definition, policy design, implementation, agenda-setting, evaluation, and policymaking under conditions of turbulence and crisis.

In Chapter 1, public policy was defined as a course of action or inaction undertaken by public authorities to address a problem or interrelated set of problems. Policy analysis was defined as the disciplined application of intellect to public problems. If the nature of public problems changes, if the broad context within which problems arise and are addressed is altered, then both public policy and policy analysis should change as well. This is precisely what has been happening in the past decade in industrialized countries—Canada included—and a revitalized policy analysis has to come to terms with what is different about modern **governance**. It is a cliché, of course, that our times (like all times!) are marked by change. But it is in the nature of clichés to expose obvious truths, and no truth is more obvious than that we are surrounded and affected by changes of unparalleled magnitude and scope. On a global level, recent years have seen the collapse of the Soviet empire and of apartheid in South Africa, the rise of new security threats and global terrorism, the emergence of the United States as the world's "hyperpower," European Union enlargement, Internet viruses that spread around the world in minutes, the rising threat of pandemics such as SARS, and devastating crises in our food supply such as Mad Cow disease and avian flu. In 1995, few people had heard of the Internet; by 2005 wireless access through cell phones and PDAs was routine. Canada experienced the impact of each of these forces, and had its own developments to contend with: the end of the decade-long Chrétien era in late 2003, the creation of the Canadian Conservative party out of the ashes of the Canadian Alliance and Progressive Conservative parties, and a national election that created a minority government for the first time in a generation, facing a strong separatist opposition.

These changes are more than merely numerous—they have altered key social and political systems in both the industrialized and developing world. "Indeed, in Canada, as elsewhere, the impact of the new economic order, the information revolution and the growing populist demand for greater public participation as a means of solving problems is being felt in virtually every sector and in every area of government activity" (Courchene and Savoie, 2003, p. 4). Clarkson (2002) is so concerned about the triple effects of globalization, continentalism, and neo-conservatism that he worries about the continued existence of the country. In examining both modes of governance and substantive changes in public policy, Clarkson echoes a broad consensus that the country has changed fundamentally in the last ten years.

These changes are massive and unrelenting, but the trick is to try to make some sense of the broad pattern and to tease out the implications for policy analysis and governance. This chapter argues that there are three powerful undercurrents beneath the waves of political turmoil and **policy reversal** evident in Canada and throughout the industrialized world. They are globalization, shifts in **political culture**, and new ideas about governance and **public management**. Each of these is multi-faceted, of course, and connected intimately to the others. Nonetheless, it is possible to outline at least a few of their most important features. They have been building for over twenty-five years, and in some respects are so natural a part of our political, economic, and social environment that we take them for granted. A policy analysis that fails to come to grips with these forces and their implications for policy and governance is doomed to irrelevance.

GLOBALIZATION

ECONOMIC GLOBALIZATION

The modern phenomenon of globalization has to be carefully distinguished from the mere fact of international connectedness. The British Empire was global in scope, and other imperial systems like the Romans' covered enormous tracts of territory. The Moors extended their empire as far as Spain, and the Portuguese in turn established outposts as far away as Goa, India. Marco Polo travelled from the Mediterranean to China in the late 1200s. The city states of medieval Europe had extensive trade connections of their own to the Orient, and vast, complex, and virtually global systems of trade developed by the 1700s around sugar, spices, and slaves. In short, human history in the last 1000 years has been clearly marked by internationalism that sometimes came close to embracing the entire planet. What is different about the present situation?

American journalist Thomas L. Friedman (1999) captures the differences as well as anyone else. His point of comparison is not the ancient world but the Cold War and what he calls the "**globalization system**" that has replaced it. For Friedman, globalization "is not a phenomenon. It is not just some passing trend. Today it is the overarching international system shaping domestic politics and foreign relations of virtually every country" (p. 7). Globalization has several important features. It is not a static system but a dynamic process that "involves inexorable integration of markets, nation-states and technologies" to an unprecedented degree (ibid.). Its driving idea is **free market capitalism**—the more countries integrate with the world economy and allow global economic forces to penetrate domestic economies, the more they will prosper. It has its own dominant culture—largely American—and so tends to be homogenizing. It has its own defining technologies organized around computerization, digitization, satellites, the Internet, and mobile communications. It has its own international balance of power—between nation-states (the traditional geo-political balance, but wherein the United States is now the only global superpower), between nation-states and markets (global investment markets driven by the "Electronic Herd"), and between individuals and nation-states (the ability of individuals to act directly on the world stage). While an enthusiast of globalization, Friedman is savvy enough to know that in the real world people live in communities, traditions, customs, and languages that are deeply rooted—what he calls the "olive tree"—and that will bend only so far in the face of global economic, technological, and cultural forces. The policy trick for most states is to come to terms with globalization but also balance it against identity and community.

In understanding globalization, it is important also to understand what it is not. Scholte (2003) identifies what he calls four cul-de-sacs in conceptualizing globalization: globalization-as-internationalization ("the growth of transactions and interdependence between countries"); globalization-as-liberalization ("a process of removing officially imposed restrictions on movements of resources between countries in order to form an 'open' and 'borderless' world economy"); globalization-as-universalization ("a process of dispersing various objects and experiences to people at all inhabited parts of the earth"); and globalization-as-westernization ("social structures of modernity [capitalism, industrialism, rationalism, urbanism, etc.] are spread the world over, destroying pre-existent cultures and local self-determination in the process"). Scholte sensibly argues that understanding globalization in these terms is redundant—the phenomena of internationalization, liberalization, universalization, and westernization have existed much longer than contemporary globalization, and simply redefining these phenomena as globalization does not add anything to our understanding. He then goes on to argue that contemporary globalization should be identified as the spread of transplanetary and supraterritorial connections between people. "People become more able—physically, legally, culturally, and psychologically—to engage with each other in 'one world'" (Scholte, 2003, p. 7). Contemporary globalization is characterized by "**globality**," or the sense that the entire planet is a single social space, that people carry on conversations in that space irrespective of territoriality, that they pay collective attention to "global events"—that there is a quality of simultaneity. While globality depends on modern means of transportation (i.e., the spread of SARS as a global event would simply not be possible without modern air travel), it is clear that information and communications technologies and the Internet are a crucial foundation—indeed the very concept of "cyberspace" expresses the notion of a supraterritorial space within which there can be social interactions distinct from those that occur in real space and time (Rheingold, 2003). In this sense, contemporary globalization is defined by globality, which in turn is defined (in large part) by information and communications technologies and the Internet. Examples of simultaneity are so routine now that we take them for granted; when Avril Lavigne released her second album in May 2004, it topped the charts almost immediately, all over the world. The images of terrorists beheading Nick Berg that same month were seen around the world—but more importantly, at the same time, and generating the same types of debates.

We return to globality later in this section. For many, contemporary globalization is primarily about major economic transformations in the last fifty years. First, of course, has been the development of a complex international trading system. After World War II, a host of international institutions and conventions were established to create the beginnings of a true international economic system: the General Agreement on Tariffs and Trade (GATT—now superseded by the World Trade Organization or the WTO), the International Monetary Fund (IMF), the World Bank, and the Bretton Woods agreement on currency transactions. The logic behind these initiatives was twofold: first, to create a set of supranational decisionmaking bodies that would create stable and harmonized international regimes dealing with a host of issues from trade to communications; second, to knock down those major barriers between countries that impeded or prevented interactions or communication. The postwar efforts were largely successful on both counts. Figure 2.1 (page 48) shows the increased volume in global trade from 1950 to 2002. The key point is that, despite dips, the long-term trend for world trade has been steadily upward. In 2001, due in large part to the terrorist attacks on the World Trade Centre, international trade declined and only began to improve after 2002. It is clear that the world economy is subject to turbulence as well, and there may be reversals as well as advances in international economic integration. However, the trend line seems clear: as borders become more porous, goods, services, and information can travel more freely across political lines. As well, in an often-ignored development, people move as well, and immigration is a major component of contemporary globalization (Sassen, 1998). In fact, the process of global economic integration has deepened recently, as **trade liberalization** efforts move from "border barriers to domestic policies. In this new template the major impediments to liberalization, whether of trade or investment, arise from a nation's regulatory and legal system" (Ostry, 1999, p. 2).

In a pre-globalized world, lines on maps mark territories where, through public policy as well as forces of history, society, economy, and governance, "national systems" coincide. At the most elementary economic level, for example, national boundaries marked coherent economic systems. International trade in goods and services could be blocked through public policies that protected domestic markets. The

Figure 2.1   Growth in the Value of World Merchandise Exports, 1950–2002

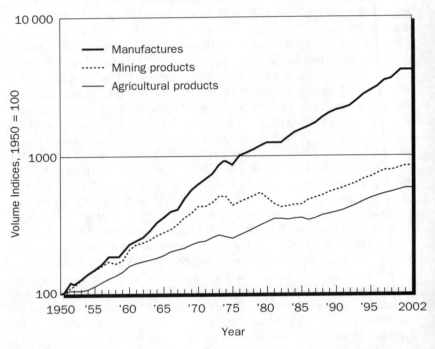

SOURCE: World Trade Organization, *International Trade Statistics 2003*, Chart II.1, p. 30.

whole idea of a national economy presumes that there is more internal than external trade. In a globalized world, as barriers between and within local markets fall, markets get integrated globally. Companies sell locally, regionally, and internationally, wherever anyone is willing to buy the product. Obviously, domestic policies are not the only impediment to world trade: geography and social factors play a role as well. But these too have been affected by technological changes in the past twenty-five years, making it much easier for firms to manage production and sales processes across widely flung international networks. It is important not to overemphasize the degree of economic integration and hence interdependence, even if the broad trends seem clear. Helliwell (2002) points out that statistical analysis of trade patterns and intensities shows that they are not as large as sometimes assumed, and that there are indeed "border effects" that reflect tighter internal structures to national and regional markets.

Canada, always a trading nation, crossed an important threshold in the 1990s. Interprovincial trade through the 1980s was as important to the country as international trade, both growing yearly at about the same rate. In 1990, however, interprovincial trade flattened and increased only slightly each year, while international exports continued to make gains. By 1996, only P.E.I., Nova Scotia, and the Northwest Territories were exporting more to other provinces than to the rest of the world. As Figure 2.2 shows, throughout the 1990s international trade increased significantly more than interprovincial trade. By 2000, however, foreign markets were weakening, and provinces began to rely more on interprovincial trade. In fact, international trade declined 2.1 percent annually in 2000 and 2001. Overall, exports as a proportion of GDP declined between 2002 and 2004. Nonetheless, it is important to remember that the value of foreign exports was almost double that of interprovincial exports (Statistics Canada, 2004).

Figure 2.2 Interprovincial and International Trade, Canada, 1992, 2000, 2002

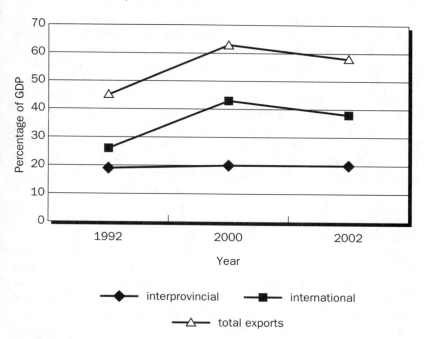

SOURCE: Statistics Canada. (2004). *Interprovincial and international exports by province and territory since 1992.* Catalogue no. 11-621-MIE2004011.

A second economic dimension of globalization is the well-known phenomenon of **transnational corporations** (TNCs). This too has evolved over the postwar period. Multinational companies are not in themselves new—think of the Hudson's Bay Company (chartered in 1670) or the British East Indian Company (founded in 1600 to trade with Mogul kings in what is now India). But these companies were instruments of an imperial system of mercantilism, tools of imperial governments. What is different about modern multinational commercial firms is that their commercial interests are primary, they operate across the globe, and their national home base is relatively unimportant. As was the case with international trade, the 1990s were a boom period for TNCs and foreign direct investment (FDI). In 1998, FDI rose by almost 40 percent to over $640 billion, most of which was in developed countries. The global recession in 2001, however, nearly halved FDI that year. But TNCs continue to be important players in the international economy. There are some 67 000 TNCs controlling 870 000 affiliates, employing 53 million people abroad. FDI is actually more important than trade: in 2002, sales by TNCs accounted for US$18 trillion, whereas world exports were only US$8 trillion (United Nations Conference on Trade and Development 2003, p. xvi). Thus, a good part of what we think of as economic globalization in terms of economic interdependencies among countries is really due to a network of huge corporations and the investments they make and the goods and services they sell.

Country of origin mattered at one time but in the contemporary phase of economic globalization is less and less important. This is because of a shift in the way in which these firms operate. The first phase of multinational development entailed exports to foreign markets of goods produced domestically (e.g., cars made in the United States or Japan exported elsewhere). The second phase was the establishment of production facilities in these foreign markets, facilities that were still quite dependent on the parent corporation for services, inputs, and strategies. A third phase has seen multinational firms begin to operate as transnational firms, that is, to organize their production process globally. What this means is that an "American" car will have parts produced in a variety of countries for final assembly somewhere completely distinct from the production of those parts. This is a significant change in the nature of globalization, since it implies a much more tightly integrated international market. As Thurow (1996) notes, "For the first time in human history, anything can be made anywhere and sold everywhere" (p. 113). Global sourcing means that companies will shift production to the most attractive sites, either in terms of expertise or labour costs. Global sourcing presumes an international or global production market, and by the same token an emerging global consumption market. In other words, if production is organized globally, and consumption is increasingly similar in terms of the goods and services that people buy, then it makes less and less sense to talk about "domestic" and "foreign" markets; what seems to be emerging, at least for some goods and services, is a global market or a single economic space. It is important to remember that local markets continue to exist, and local or national markets have institutional advantages (e.g., similar languages or social customs) over international ones.

A final aspect of economic globalization is the increase in capital flows and mobility. Large financial institutions such as banks, insurance companies, and investment brokers have gradually developed systems to allow virtually instantaneous transfers of capital anywhere in the world. This is based in part on new technology and in part on the emergence of large international institutions and the multinational corporations mentioned above. On top of this are millions of individuals now investing in stocks, bonds, and currencies. In Friedman's colourful phrase, these institutions and individuals together comprise an "Electronic Herd" that stampedes around global markets, often with devastating results. Enormous quantities of liquid capital are shifted from country to country, stock exchange to stock exchange, in response to business opportunities as well as perceived risk. Companies such as Standard and Poor's provide rating services on countries and state enterprises that provide crucial information for international investors. Shifts in capital based on this information have consequences for domestic interest rates, stock prices, and exchange rates. From a policy perspective, clearly the most daunting implication has been for governments that run large deficits. Deficits are covered by borrowing, and with a long enough string of deficits, governments have to go beyond domestic sources of capital to international ones. Reliance on international investors means keeping them happy, and in recent years these investors have not been very happy at all with deficits, what they consider high spending, or indeed anything that undermines their "confidence." The most dramatic recent example of what can happen occurred in 1998 with the capital crisis in Southeast Asia, which soon spread around the world and created what the IMF called "some of the most severe financial market turbulence in the postwar period" (International Monetary Fund 1999, p. 9). The crisis began with weak commodity prices that lowered output in Malaysia, Thailand, and Indonesia, picked up momentum with doubts about the Japanese economy, then spread to Russia once its government decided to unilaterally restructure its domestic debt and depreciate the ruble. External debt for these countries climbed alarmingly, just as international lending dried up. This reduction of lending capital put pressure on indebted Latin American economies, particularly Brazil. By late 1999, markets had stabilized, but the severity of the crisis induced the IMF to think more about monitoring and early intervention when countries are in financial danger. But the interdependencies remain. In 2004 the United States government was running the largest deficit in its history, with implications for domestic savings and interest rates. Changes in American interest rates, of course, can ripple through the world economy, raising rates in Europe and Asia, even if countries in those regions would prefer otherwise.

What does this all this mean? Details will be explored in subsequent chapters, but economic globalization has had several consequences that together change the terrain of modern policymaking and analysis. Primarily, the development of international trading regimes means that governments have fewer policy instruments at their disposal to protect domestic markets, what Porter (1990) calls the "home base." In part this is because governments have deliberately entered into agreements to increase trade and investment that constrain their own powers to discriminate in favour of their domestic industries or workforce. The North American Free Trade Agreement and the GATT (administered by the WTO), along with a host of new international trade agreements on intellectual property and trade in services, are prime examples. Dealing with trade disputes around the clash between domestic law and international agreements is now a small governmental cottage industry. Between 2000 and 2004, for example, Canadian authorities were involved in appeals of the following: a WTO ruling that Canada's patent legislation was inconsistent with the Agreement on Trade-Related Aspects of Intellectual Property Rights (TRIPS); Australian restrictions on the import of Canadian salmon; complaints from Japan and the European Union about the Canadian Auto Pact; and charges by the United States and New Zealand that Canadian dairy milk exports were being subsidized. In some cases, Canadian legislation is a target of other countries under WTO rules; in other cases, Canada uses international agreements as the basis for its own complaints. International agreements of this sort are swords that cut both ways—that is why governments sign them—but they undeniably shift key decisionmaking powers over policy to international organizations. But the reduced capacity of governments is also due to facts on the ground—or on the globe. With current communications and transportation technologies, both companies and people can more easily evade the traditional instruments at the disposal of governments, such as taxation, regulation, and simple surveillance. Moreover, the discipline of the global marketplace, exercised through massive and almost instantaneous capital flows, gives governments (with perhaps the exception of the United States) less and less room to manoeuvre, and less and less capacity to go it alone. It may drive them to a "**race to the bottom**" as they try to attract international capital through lower and lower standards. Yet another reason that governments have a harder time of going it alone is that globalization induces mutual interdependence and integration so that everyone is interested in everyone else's business. The SARS and Mad Cow crises in 2003 and 2004 were stark reminders of that reality. In the case of SARS, "globality" meant that everyone on the planet was aware of its outbreak in Hong Kong and in Toronto. Indeed, SARS spread through the other emblem of globalization—international air travel. Even though the number of cases was tiny, the economic effects in terms of tourism were huge. Isolated cases of Mad Cow in Alberta saw international beef markets clang shut instantaneously.

Does this interdependence and economic integration mean that the state will wither away? For many, the answer is no, because economic globalization is neither desirable nor inevitable. Cameron and Stein argue

> Processes of globalization do pose formidable challenges to the state—and to the citizen. The story is, however, more complicated than the critics suggest. Global markets and global politics are certainly expanding, but they do not constrain the state from fulfilling its social contract with its citizens. States still have real and significant capacity, both to provide public goods to their citizens and to mediate the impact of global economic, social, and cultural forces. While it is true that some postindustrial states have shed some responsibilities, they have also assumed new ones: helping their citizens to acquire the skills and knowledge to become competitive; and innovating in the way they organize and regulate the delivery of public goods. (Cameron and Stein, 2002, p. 8)

The legendary protests in November 1999 against the WTO meetings in Seattle, and similar ones afterward at both WTO and G-8 meetings have become the most powerful symbol of resistance against the blind forces of economic globalization. In Seattle, some 50 000 activists from nongovernmental organizations (NGOs), including labour, women's groups, environmentalists, and church groups, gathered to hold protests, parallel events, and some violent demonstrations that effectively shut down the WTO and much of the city. By the June 2004 G-8 meetings in Sea Island, Georgia, the level of organization and capacity was truly impressive. TOES, or "the other economic summit" was just one of dozens of groups that provided information, a parallel conference, news releases, and media information. The 2001 G-8 Summit in Genoa was marked by street protests and strong police responses—as well as the death of one protester. Subsequently, the G-8 organizers held meetings in remote locations such as Kananaskis, Alberta, and Evian, France. The 2004 meetings in Georgia were also deliberately remote and isolated, to blunt the activities of antiglobalizers. In fact, the coastal city of Brunswick, where protesters were forced to mount their rallies, even passed an ordinance closely regulating the demonstrations. Despite this, organizers hoped for tens of thousands of people to show up. It is important to note that the protests are not merely about the economic dimension of globalization and the role of governments and international organizations like the WTO—as Box 2.1 illustrates, it is a clash of world views that is at stake (O'Brien et al, 2000).

Despite the momentum behind economic globalization, it is unlikely that the state will disappear anytime soon as a prime locus of public power and public policy. Indeed, it is important to recall that many aspects of the global economy have in fact been deliberately created by states, even if at the end of the day they cannot completely control them (Pauly, 1997). Moreover, globalization theorists often assume a hypermobility or hyperfluidity of capital and trade that belies the degree of concentration of material facilities and work processes in territorial sites—globalization is in fact "managed" through a small number of "global cities" or sites such as London, Tokyo, Frankfurt, and New York (Sassen 1998, chap. 10), and these are themselves located in states that still have the capacity to regulate them in various ways.

It is also important to remember the adaptability of states, their differential capacity, and their increased importance in a globalized world. Weiss (1998), for example, highlights the importance of states— particularly strong states—in acting as "facilitators not victims" of globalization, and the emergence of catalytic states—such as Singapore—that consolidate networks of national and regional trade and investment. Observers like Paul Hirst (1997) point out that in fact the "world economy" is largely restricted to the triad of Europe, Japan, and North America, and moreover is an artifact of a relatively small number of transnational corporations operating for the most part within the triad economies. Like Sassen, he notes that these companies are far from rootless, but rather are located in space, and usually in spaces controlled by large states. Policy choices can and should continue to be made to address concerns about public welfare and infrastructure. In Hirst's view, national experiences and performances will continue to diverge, not converge, in a globalized world as governments respond to the challenges but with different mixes of institutional and policy assets.

Box 2.1   FAIR WORLD FAIR

The Fair World Fair is an exposition with forums, speakers with music, food and fun. The only difference between a typical festival and this one is that there will be as much food for thought as there will be food to eat.

CHILDREN'S ACTIVITIES AND CHARACTER-BUILDING WORKSHOPS

- Koinonia Partners will provide workshops on civic responsibility and peace (confirmed)
- Brunswick's the Gathering Place will provide youth workshops (tentative)

ACTIVITIES FOR YOUNG ADULTS IN HIGH SCHOOL AND COLLEGE

- Jubilee USA will bring in speakers and provide exhibits and workshops on globalization issues (confirmed)
- Global Exchange will present their cultural awareness and travel exchange programs with exhibits, speakers and workshops (confirmed) and activities for advanced activists and area educators
- The Other Economic Summit (TOES) will bring in some of the finest academics and activists who work with globalization, social justice and environmental topics into a conference with plenary sessions and workshops (confirmed)

The Fair World Fair (formerly G8 Carnival) in Brunswick, Georgia is to be a model for productive educational alternatives in globalization. Our idea is to educate people, especially the up and coming generation of children, about the legacy they will inevitably bear and how the G8 meeting taking place just miles away will affect parts of that legacy.

Less powerful nations who may be suffering oppression from G8 policies can do little about what we, as a world power, do to them. We, as a nation, have the power and the responsibility to choose leaders who will be accountable and just to the rest of the world. In short, we alone have the power to determine how America wields its power and wealth. Will we raise our toddlers into tyrants who draw their power only from guns and their wealth only from money? Or will we raise leaders who understand strength as power with ethical discretion and wealth not only in terms of money and resources but also in terms of creativity and kindness?

Box 2.1 (continued)

The 3-day G8 Carnival and Sustainable Fair World Exposition will explore these challenges using the practical business environment of the trade show combined with the fun loving games and rhythm of a carnival. Mainstage events will include celebrity performances throughout the day (TBA).

During the night political films will be screened. Vendors utilizing fair trade cooperatives, sustainable living products and practices as well as established organizations who work with social justice issues will be hosted in the vendor expo tent or facility. Films will also be screened and forums held in a smaller forum facility and a fixed, teaching art exhibit will be hosted in a "globalization spook house" tent. Additionally, in honor of this year's "Green Summit" theme, a toxic tour bus will be provided to showcase Brunswick's superfund sites, with enlightening narration by local environmentalists as well as environmentalists who will compare the Brunswick environmental condition with the rest of the world. A large frame tent will serve as a community center and campground space will be provided for tents and RV's.

There will also be a "video soapbox" venue so that people from all over the world can send in their protest message. This will be compiled into a tape that will be presented to the WTO, IMF, World Bank and the G8 organizers with hopefully their promise to set aside time to view it and address the issues and activists directly.

SOURCE: Fair World Fair, Greedy 8 Alternative Coalition (n.d),
http://g8carnival.org/

Finally, in response to the argument that globalization inevitably leads to a race to the bottom, analysts like Vogel (1995) point to the "California effect": trade can lead to higher environmental standards as political jurisdictions with higher standards "force foreign producers in nations with weaker domestic standards either to design products that meet those standards or sacrifice export markets" (p. 261). Foreign producers then have incentives to force their own countries' governments to increase standards.

In short, globalization is not an implacable and impersonal juggernaut. Despite its reality, it is both less extensive and intensive than the globalizers would have us believe. It takes place in real space, often in quite limited spaces, and those spaces are subject to some form of policy intervention. Moreover, globalization itself is not merely an economic phenomenon but in large part is politically driven as countries decide that it is in their interests to integrate more closely. Once more, this is an arena of policy and of choice. Finally, citizens will not soon cease to demand the core services and programs of the contemporary welfare state, nor will they hesitate to demand protection from the worst excesses of globalization. The trajectories of all these forces are difficult to predict, but it seems clear now that states, despite a diffusion of their power, remain important. Globalization has not banished geo-politics, though it has created new channels through which geo-politics might flow. As well, the idea that globalization means relentless and implacable convergence, or a world without policy choices, is without solid foundation. In fact, what is striking is how patterns of convergence and divergence appear simultaneously—even as trade increases and G-8 summits are held, major differences over policy arise between the United States, the European Union, Russia, China, and Southeast Asia. Choices, and consequences, remain.

CULTURAL GLOBALIZATION

Globalization is about more than economics, however. It relies, for instance, on technologies of communication that also have had a dramatic effect on culture. Once again the central issue is the degree to which borders matter less as an element of cohesion in defining national cultures and societies. We have already noted how markets have become uncoupled from territorial boundaries, and the same is increasingly true of culture and communications. One line of argument about this phenomenon is that all around the world people are rapidly becoming the same. The globalization of culture means sameness. To some extent this is true. The massive penetration of American culture through icons such as Coke, McDonald's, Hollywood, and Nike means that there is a pervasive sameness to capital cities no matter where one goes on the planet. Consumers "around the world are beginning to develop similar cultural expectations about what they ought to be able to buy as well as about what it is they want to buy" (Ohmae, 1995, p. 28).

However, local cultures do have a resilience and carve out niches for themselves even in the shadows of what Barber (1995) calls "McWorld." Indeed, the counterargument to this view that globalization means sameness is that it in fact portends a growing awareness of differences and an emphasis on particularities (Cameron and Stein, 2002, p. 12). In this scenario, which seems supported by the tenacity of ethnic differences and conflicts around the world, people retain their local cultural idioms, but globalization no longer makes it possible for them to conceive of their own culture as somehow "natural" and the only single possible world. Communications exposes the differences among peoples everywhere in the world and makes us realize that ours is simply one lifestyle or mode of society.

The telecommunications and information revolution has taken a giant leap forward with the Internet. The Internet cuts through traditional debates about the effects of telecommunications and broadcasting on community and culture because it has the potential to globalize and localize at the same time. Accurate numbers are hard to come by, but estimates for March 2004 were that as many as 605 million people were online around the world (NUA, 2004). North America and Europe accounted for over two-thirds of the total, with only 6.3 million in all of Africa, for example. Whereas traditional broadcasting media such as TV and film did in fact have a homogenizing dynamic since so much of it was produced for American sensibilities and sent around the world, the Internet has at least the potential to permit the development of differences and indeed of new communities of interest and of affinity. Balanced against this of course are the facts that the Internet is increasingly becoming commercialized and that commercialism is coupled with technological changes that will effectively blur video, TV, and Internet communications. In that situation, it is entirely possible that the American cultural dominance in TV, film, and music will come to colour the Web as well—a sort of "McWeb." However, there are signs that the nature of the Internet makes such dominance difficult and perhaps impossible. The music industry, for example, is undergoing a massive shakeup with the arrival of services like Napster, Winamp, and Kazaa, and bands selling their songs directly online for a small fee, or through a service like I-Tunes, which in its first year sold over 70 million songs. No one yet knows where these experiments will go, but they highlight the possibility of both eliminating the middle man and providing direct access to music and culture that in the past would not have got past the major studios and distribution chains. The Internet also is creating the possibility of "we journalism"—a massive global printing press where anyone can share thoughts and ideas through blogs or personal websites (Rheingold, 2004).

The convergence of computers and telecommunications and the plummeting costs of the technology suggest that the "death of distance" has indeed arrived (Cairncross, 1997). This is precisely the policy challenge contemporary states face in the cultural field. Cultural affinity has traditionally tended to coincide with territory, so that people define their relevant communities in terms of the territory defined by the state. Under healthy circumstances (insularity can also be dangerous), this produces a desired degree of **social cohesion** and a foundation for stable community identity and cultural production. Globalization threatens this in a variety of ways. It can annihilate local cultural traditions in favour of some homogenous global standard—McWorld. It can destabilize cultural norms and understandings by "relativizing" them to a host of others and thereby reducing their apparent weight. It can encourage people to define their relevant communities in nonterritorial ways, and thereby weaken national bonds and support for national projects and policies. Governments therefore find themselves with distinctive policy conundrums: while many people welcome increased access to global culture, many resist fiercely and sometimes even violently. This is what Castells means when he refers to the network society and its "systematic disjunction between the local and the global for most individuals and social groups." The effects of globalization are so corrosive that the "search for meaning takes place then in the reconstruction of defensive identities around communal principles" (Castells, 1997, p. 11). Religious fundamentalism, militias, eco-terrorists, deep ecologists—these disparate social movements are symptoms of resistance to the globalized, net-worked society. Even in its less-threatening form, as the fragmentation of identity and community continues in the face of a "500-channel universe," governments have increasingly turned their attention to issues of social cohesion and national identity. At a more mundane level, governments have to also rethink what they understand as cultural policy—it is probably less possible to protect local culture than it is to support and promote it, perhaps through marketing it internationally.

If culture depends on communication, the communications and information revolution mean that communication is now global, suggesting the emergence of certain global understandings or standards. This is the third aspect of globalization, the development of **international standards** of conduct.

INTERNATIONAL STANDARDS

The best example of these emerging standards is the **human rights** conventions that have evolved since 1945. The United Nations came into being on October 10, 1945, and its Economic and Social Council was instructed to establish a commission to draft an international bill of rights. The UN Charter itself referred to the "principle of equal rights" and the importance of universal respect for "human rights and fundamental freedoms for all." The Council established a Commission on Human Rights that produced the Universal Declaration of Human Rights, which was passed in December 1948. The Universal Declaration was nothing more than that—a declaration without force of international law and without any enforcement mechanism. It recognized the "inherent dignity of and the equal and inalienable rights of all members of the human family" and proceeded to list virtually every conceivable human right from traditional civil and political ones to

Box 2.2   THE CULTURAL
                                    GLOBALIZATION INDEX

Culture is the most visible manifestation of globalization, whether
it is the appearance of new cultural forms (such as Disneyland
Paris) or the transformation of traditional cultural expressions
into something a bit different (such as Egyptian McDonald's
restaurants serving their patrons "McFalafel").

While there are ample data to track the cross-border movement
of people, merchandise, and money, it is extraordinarily difficult
to measure the global spread of ideas and trends. However, it is
possible to get a hint of a country's level of cultural integration by
identifying "cultural proxies"—the conduits by which ideas,
beliefs, and values are transmitted. One way to measure the globalization of culture is to chart the movement of popular media,
which have more impact on our thinking than some of the other,
more frequently cited symbols of cultural globalization (such as
the proliferation of Starbucks coffee shops around the world).

We have created a ranking of the 20 most culturally globalized
countries by measuring each nation's exports and imports of books,
periodicals, and newspapers. (The dissemination of movies would
be another ideal indicator. Yet data for films are available only for
a small number of countries. The most recent data on cultural trade
available from the United Nations Educational, Scientific, and
Cultural Organization (UNESCO) date back to 1997). We then
divide those total exports and imports by the nation's population
size. The higher a country is on this index, the more likely an individual in that country is to receive foreign cultural products.

One clear pattern that emerges from this ranking is that the globalization of culture may have a significant linguistic component.
Three of the top five nations (Singapore, Switzerland, and Canada)
have official bilingual policies. English-language permeation also
ties into a country's capacity to absorb international cultural products. Seven of the top 20 nations in this index (United States, United
Kingdom, Canada, Australia, Ireland, Singapore, and Israel) are
among the top 10 English-speaking countries in the world.

However, when we consider the bottom 10 countries (Peru,
Romania, Morocco, Thailand, Turkey, Philippines, Egypt,
Indonesia, China, and Pakistan) [not shown here] we see that multilingual nations are not guaranteed a high degree of cultural
globalization: The Philippines and Pakistan—two countries where

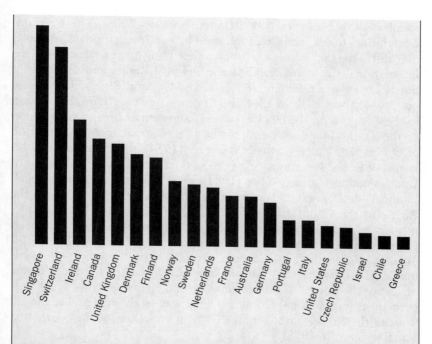

Singapore, Switzerland, Ireland, Canada, United Kingdom, Denmark, Finland, Norway, Sweden, Netherlands, France, Australia, Germany, Portugal, Italy, United States, Czech Republic, Israel, Chile, Greece

English is widespread—still rank near the bottom. The biggest barrier to cultural globalization seems to be poverty, as all of these countries have a per capita gross domestic product of under $8,000, and four of the ten have a literacy rate of less than 60 percent. Also, some countries, notably China and Indonesia, have government policies that restrict the import of foreign books and journals. Poverty, illiteracy, and lack of social openness all are associated with a lack of cultural globalization.

SOURCE: Kluver, R., and Fu, W. (2004). The cultural globalization index. *Foreign Policy*. Retrieved August 5, 2004, from http://www.foreignpolicy.com/story/cms.php?story_id=2494#

newer ones such as social security, work, rest, leisure, the right to an adequate standard of living, education, and free participation in the cultural life of the community. At the time these were lofty ideals indeed, and brought together in one document two sets or generations of rights that coincided with the emerging global divisions around the Cold War: civil and political rights central to liberal democracies and social and economic rights championed by socialist and communist states.

The history of human rights since 1948 has seen the progressive elaboration of both standards and institutions to monitor and enforce those standards (Montgomery, 1999; United Nations, 2003). The Universal Declaration, for example, was followed by two International Covenants that did have the force of treaties rather than mere declarations: the International Covenant on Civil and Political Rights and the International Covenant on Economic, Social and Cultural Rights. These were both passed by the UN in 1966 and came into effect in 1976. In addition to these covenants, the UN has passed Conventions for the Suppression of the Traffic in Persons and of the Exploitation of the Prostitution of Others (1951), the Status of Refugees (1954), the Elimination of All Forms of Racial Discrimination (1969), the Elimination of All Forms of Discrimination against Women (1981), against Torture and Other Cruel, Inhuman or Degrading Treatment or Punishment (1987), and on the Rights of the Child (1990). These UN initiatives have been complemented by similar regional conventions; for example in the European Union with the gradual development of citizens' rights through the 1950 Treaty of Rome, the 1961 European Social Charter, and the 1989 Community Charter. The 1997 Amsterdam Treaty gave the European Court of Justice the power to enforce fundamental rights. On July 1, 2002, a permanent International Criminal Court was established at The Hague (though the Rome Statute, which is the foundation for the court, was actually signed in 1998).

Critics often dismiss this dense system of overlapping covenants and declarations as largely meaningless posturing by governments, many of which are energetic violators of the very agreements they have signed. But events such as the 1993 Vienna World Conference on Human Rights and the 1995 Beijing World Conference on Women demonstrate that a global moral community has emerged from these efforts. Human rights violations will continue but no longer invisibly and without impunity. As noted earlier, modern communications technologies make it more and more difficult for authorities to hide their actions; the worldwide exposure of the torture of Iraqi prisoners in May 2004 was a clear indication that digital evidence of inhumane behaviour has the potential to sweep the planet in a nanosecond. Even Canada is not immune to this process: UN human rights committees have sanctioned Canada, for example, in 1993 for Quebec's Bill 178 restrictions on non-French commercial signs, and again in 1995 for federal cuts to social programs. In short, the most important development is less the absence of enforcement mechanisms than the emergence of standards that millions of people, regardless of place or culture, now accept as worthy of enforcement. In large measure, of course, these standards are Western in origin, and so the call for universalism is in part a call for the universal application of a certain view of individual rights and obligations.

As with the other elements of globalization, the implications of the emergence of international standards, many of them contained in conventions and treaties that Canada has willingly signed, are that the policy process and the principles by which it is made are no longer delimited by purely domestic considerations. In most policy fields—from the environment to Aboriginal affairs—governments have to take note of international standards, international agreements that may bind them to those standards, and international reactions to their behaviour. This does not mean that governments are necessarily at the mercy of these standards and agreements; they can still find ways around them if they need to. The simple point is that these standards have a reality that can no longer be ignored, and when mobilized by international actors or institutions, can have a potentially very powerful effect.

Any policies Canada develops will be measured against what other governments have done. In addition to standards and international institutions to monitor them, of course, is the emergence of what some have called a **"global civil society"** of activist NGOs that can be mobilized quickly around domestic policy issues (Keck and Sikkink, 1998). Canada's environmental policies, for instance, are closely watched by various groups around the world such as the Sierra Club and Greenpeace. The Yearbook of International Organizations conservatively estimates that in 2004 there were some 44 000 international NGOs, up from 7500 in 1991 (Union of International Organizations, 2004).

In short, the traditional association between public policymaking and the territorial boundaries of the nation-state has been severely challenged in the last decade. Both the source of policy problems and their potential solutions now lie as much outside the boundaries of the state as they do within. This is not to say that states are irrelevant or that they cannot tackle major policy issues. The nation-state will remain as a fundamental organizing unit for contemporary industrialized societies, but the sort of control and dominance that they once enjoyed both over the policy process and the intellectual resources required to analyze it is waning. The ways in which policy problems are defined will change, as will the range of instruments and strategies to deal with them.

THE POLITICS OF DIFFERENCE

Globalization helps us conceptualize changes that have occurred at the international level, along with their effects on domestic politics and policymaking. It would be surprising, however, if these international changes were not accompanied with equally significant changes in the ways in which domestic political communities see themselves and their relations to government. For example, how could international human rights regimes strengthen over the past fifty years without human rights simultaneously becoming more important as standards of civil conduct on the domestic level?

Political culture across the industrialized democracies has indeed changed significantly, no less in Canada than elsewhere. Evidence of this abounds: the collapse of communism in Eastern Europe signalled the triumph of liberal individualist values that seem secure even in the face of the resurgence of authoritarian governments in some countries like Belarus, Ukraine, and the Russian Federation; people everywhere seem more prepared to articulate their political concerns in terms of individual rights; even while Western societies have become more materialistic and consumer oriented, social movements have arisen around the globe to press for "postmaterialist" concerns such as the environment, peace, gender relations, and sexual orientation; and along with an emphasis on the universal rights of individuals there has come a greater sensitivity to the issues of identity and diversity. This section will briefly sketch three developments that set the backdrop to important shifts in political culture: the rise of **postmaterialism,** the increased salience of rights, and the new emphasis on "difference." Together, these comprise what some have called the **"postmodern condition"** of contemporary governance: "some state responses to globalization are fashioning a weaker kind of citizenship, because states sometimes act to diminish their own capacities. Indeed, in several ways the key actor in any citizenship regime—that is the state that confers recognition, establishes rights and responsibilities, provides access to political participation and helps fashion feelings of belonging—has withdrawn from centre-stage" (Jenson, 2003, pp. 313–14).

Postmaterialism in the West consists of a shift away from deference, away from concern with material gain, away from economic issues *per se.* These are displaced by lifestyle concerns, social, and even spiritual issues, all conducted in a much more participatory mode than was characteristic of the 1960s. "In this process, an emphasis on economic security gradually fades, and universal but often latent needs for belonging, esteem, and the realization of individual intellectual potential become increasingly prominent. Although individuals still value economic and physical security, they increasingly emphasize the need for freedom, self-expression, and improving the quality of their lives" (Abramson and Inglehart, 1995, p. 9). This is a gradual and long-term process that, according to Inglehart, will become evident through generational replacement. The trend is not inevitable, but there is considerable evidence that it has affected most industrial countries in the world. The consequences of a shift to postmaterialist values are potentially profound: greater support for democratic institutions, and in particular, greater support for participatory democracy and a politics of identity and recognition.

Clearly, the growth of postmaterialism has links to the development of what Mary Ann Glendon has called the dominance of **"rights talk"** as a mode of political discourse. In the previous section we discussed the development of international human rights regimes. This development has been mirrored at the domestic level in the elaboration of human rights documents, institutions, and political discourse. Glendon is careful to point out that the American version of rights talk is only a "dialect" of a form of discourse that has spread rapidly throughout the world since 1945. There is now a universal language of rights, though the American dialect has peculiarities that, she feels, contribute to and are a symptom of "disorder in the body politic." She argues that while rights talk is impervious to other more complex languages whereby we regulate our social and political lives, it "seeps into them, carrying the rights mentality into spheres of American society where a sense of personal responsibility and of civic obligation traditionally have been nourished" (Glendon, 1991, p. x). American commentators on the rise of rights talk have been preoccupied with problems of civic dialogue, compromise, and community within their own society, with the shift to what Sandel calls a "procedural republic": "In recent decades, the civic or formative aspect of our politics has largely given way to the liberalism that conceives persons as free and independent selves, unencumbered by moral or civic ties that they have not chosen" (Sandel, 1996, p. 6). Others argue that in fact the rights revolution of the past fifty years, while it had some negative consequences for social solidarity, has produced a more inclusive and tolerant community (Walker, 1998). Canadian analysis has been driven by the patriation of the Constitution in 1982 and its incorporation of a far-reaching Charter of Rights and Freedoms. Along with the traditional liberal-democratic rights of association, expression, and so on, the new Charter contains modern clauses on equality and group rights. Canadian courts were granted a constitutionally entrenched power to review all federal and provincial statutes to ensure that they do not violate the Charter. Unsurprisingly, constitutional rights–based litigation mushroomed, and Canadian observers have been trying to figure out what this rights revolution means ever since (Ignatieff, 2000).

Alan Cairns has been the pre-eminent thinker on the Canadian equivalent of rights talk (1991, 1992, 1993; for a critique of the Cairns thesis, with rejoinder, see Brodie and Nevitte, 1993). His argument consists of several key points. First, the Charter should not be seen in isolation; it reflects, as Glendon notes, an international movement toward specifying and entrenching individual rights against governments. Second, while the Charter in broad terms was a symptom of this development, it nevertheless has several specific effects on Canadian political discourse and practice. Traditionally, Canadian politics has been organized through and around federalism, and its constitution has been a "government's" constitution in the sense that it was primarily about division of powers with little reference to citizens and their rights. The 1982 Charter for the first time brought citizens' rights into the Constitution, but more importantly articulated many of those rights in terms of minority-group identities (racial, ethnic, gender, Aboriginal, disabled, aged, etc.). Third, it is the combination of these constitutional rights and the demographic realities of ethnic, linguistic, and racial diversity in Canada that give the Charter its explosive power. Fourth, this power is being channelled in ways that undermine the "old constitution" of governments and underscore the importance of rights-based citizens' movements. Cairns and others have noted the process whereby the Meech Lake Accord (1987) and the Charlottetown Accord (1992) both collapsed in part before an onslaught of citizens' groups and rights claims (for similar versions of this argument focusing on the failure of these constitutional adventures, see Pal and Seidle, 1993; Lusztig, 1994).

The third element of the changed political culture in industrialized democracies, especially Canada's, is a tension between individual and group rights. The former consist of the traditional collection of civil and political rights that aim to treat individuals roughly the same, regardless of their social and economic differences. The original objective was to build a political community that, for the purposes of public policy, ignored group differences and concentrated instead on equal rights of **citizenship**. This is a noble political ideal and one that still commands substantial support. However, this type of **liberal individualism** was vulnerable to the argument that differences did matter, particularly economic differences, and they impeded the practical achievement of real political equality.

The contemporary version of the argument about difference shifts ground, however. The old argument with liberalism was that differences mattered but essentially that they should somehow be overcome. The objective for **liberal universalism** was still the same. The modern argument of difference challenges the core assumptions of liberal individualism by insisting that differences matter in a positive way, that equal treatment of individuals as abstract citizens ignores fundamental social and cultural characteristics that define identities. In the words of Iris Young (1990), "To promote social justice, I argue, social policy should sometimes accord special treatment to groups" (p. 158). Kymlicka (1992) describes this position as **cultural pluralism**, and it has fundamental implications for the way we conceive citizenship.

Liberal individualism insists that equality will best be achieved by treating people as individuals under a system of universally applicable and consistent rules. Cultural pluralism insists that equality can be achieved only by treating people on the basis of their group affiliation and in some cases treating them according to different rules. Of course, not every group characteristic is important; blue eyes or left-handedness is something shared by millions of people but it hardly matters as a basis of group affiliation. Kymlicka (1995), for example, distinguishes between national minorities and ethnic groups and grants more rights to the former. Young (1990) argues that only social groups—defined in terms of salient social, cultural, or racial differences—that have experienced oppression qualify for different treatment. Her list, for example, includes racial minorities (in the American context, Blacks and Hispanics), women, gays and lesbians, people with disabilities, and Aboriginals. These differences are basic and powerful enough to define shared interests, world views, and even cultural norms among members of the group. Moreover, these groups exist in a society marked by inequality and oppression. If groups were different, but these differences were already accommodated and addressed through social and political institutions, there would be little to discuss in terms of public policy. But the **"politics of difference"** argues that in fact these differences are routinely and systematically oppressed. Indeed, it is the fact of oppression that gives these groups special claims within the political system. Note that a "difference perspective" emphasizes **collective identities** as a basis for claims, and urges the importance of those identities in making public policy. It explicitly privileges **cultural identity** as a normative base for making specific rights claims on behalf of individuals who are members of specific groups (see Eisenberg, 1994; Fierlbeck, 1996; and Green, 2000).

This cluster of ideas leads to the conclusion that the application of universal rules will serve only to further disadvantage these groups and suppress their legitimate differences. The opposite approach—of different treatment—is evident in policies of employment equity with their differential treatment of women, people with disabilities, visible minorities, and Aboriginals. Multiculturalism policy, though it has had fewer teeth than the equity agenda, has from its beginnings been a program that recognizes and celebrates differences. The whole sorry history of Canadian constitutionalism (and now separatism) is rife with what Charles Taylor (1994) calls the **politics of recognition.** The demand that Quebec be designated a "distinct society" was based on the firm view that people in that province are distinguished from other Canadians in terms of language, culture, and historical experiences, and that those differences matter enough that they should be the basis of real powers and special treatment. Similar if not even more powerful arguments are made on behalf of "nation-to-nation" relations between Canada's First Nations and the federal government.

From a policy perspective, the impact of postmaterialism, rights talk, and cultural pluralism is complex and often contradictory. For one thing, it has contributed to the widely noted **decline of deference** among the Canadian population and democratic citizenry in other countries. Citizens trust their governments and politicians less than they used to. If they trust less, they inevitably demand a different type of policy process. They want to be consulted, they want to participate, and they want their voices to be heard. "The more fundamental complaint about contemporary democracies is that the institutions and elected representatives have become so remote from the public that no real popular choice of policy can be made. Citizens say in surveys that they do not believe that elected politicians do what their constituents want, but rather pursue their own career interests" (Peters, 2003, p. 83). Voter turnout in Canada in the past decade has been declining steadily, and citizens seem to be taking out their frustrations against traditional political institutions. This can make for a more volatile citizenry, since it is less willing to accept "cues" from organized political parties on key public issues. Linked to the issue of "ways of life," these key areas of public policy are thus increasingly controversial and turbulent where once there might have been a greater degree of social consensus: abortion, capital punishment, gambling, drug use, physician-assisted suicide, pornography, and gay and lesbian rights (Mooney, 1999).

Another consequence has been a new emphasis on identity and the politics of recognition. Demographics play an important role in this, and Canadian society is increasingly ethnically and racially diverse. But new sensibilities abound as well, some of them encouraged through government policies like multiculturalism, bilingualism, and equity employment, and recent court decisions (on same-sex marriage, for example). Deeper cultural shifts due to the nature of modernity itself may also be contributing an undertow to an increasing diversity of identities and the notion that people are not bound by destiny to any overriding identity but have choices in defining themselves. "Having discarded, in large measure, their traditional attachments to religious and secular faiths, Canadians have constructed a national identity that consists of flexible, multiple personalities—a sort of synergistic schizophrenia. And although Canadians continue to value their individual linguistic and ethnic roots, fewer and fewer remain prisoners of any one identity that dictates their every thought and action" (Adams, 1997, p. 39). People increasingly identify themselves strongly with nonterritorially based groups—religious, ethnic, gender, linguistic, sexual, generational, or some exotic combination. They identify themselves as members of diverse communities and rely on the integrity and health of those communities for their personal well-being. From a policy perspective, this raises two challenges. One is the potential for **social fragmentation** and the importance of supporting some sort of social cohesion. Pluralism and diversity are certainly to be valued in any society, but by the same token, any society worthy of the name shares things in common. Without that, a pleasing diversity can quickly become a scattered collection of mutually exclusive groups. The idea of social cohesion, "a sense of belonging to a community that shares values and a sense of purpose and commitment" (O'Hara, 1998, p. 7) captures the tension of balancing plurality with difference. The second challenge is dealing with thorny issues of "ways of life" and collective rights. Both citizens and policymakers are often willing to compromise on material interests, but ways of life are intrinsically more precious and less negotiable. The result is new difficulties in dealing with some policy questions that are increasingly posed in terms of preserving, protecting, and promoting a way of life, and a certain prickliness on the part of significant segments of the public who feel that public policy should not merely confer benefits but also afford dignity, recognition, and support. These "ways of life" can be traditional or cultural in the conventional sense of the term—for example, Aboriginal fishing rights and self-government, or heritage language support. They can also involve a sense of local community. The Ontario Healthy Communities Coalition, for example, was established in 1992 as a registered charity to provide an umbrella for a host of provincial, regional, and local coalitions interested in economic, social, and environmental well-being at the community level. The Ontario Ministry of Health and Long-Term Care is a major funder of the organization, and the healthy communities movement began several decades ago as a more locally focused, ecological approach to population health (OHCC, 2000, p. 9). But community development and participation are important means to that end (OHCC, 2004). Ways of life can also be more unconventional, such as the demand for full equality and inclusion of various sexual minorities. The fight for same-sex marriages is part of that, but sexual minorities are also exploring issues of identity and community building that deal, for example, with sexual orientation and cultural communities. In May 2004, for instance, the Canadian Mental Health Association (CMHA) organized a conference to address the intersection of the interests of the lesbian, gay, bisexual, transgendered, or two-spirited (LGBTTS) and cultural communities:

> Organized by the CMHA's Committee for Family and Quality of Life for Gays and Lesbians in collaboration with Egale Canada, Project 10, Gay and Lesbian Asians of Montreal (GLAM), Lesbian Mothers Association of Quebec, Gay Line, and Nice Jewish Girls, Out in Colour will consist of presentations and workshops that delve into four main themes: families; culture, race, and religion; health and well-being; and interacting with the "mainstream" LBGTTS community. The event is intended to bring together LGBTTS people from different cultural backgrounds in order to build community, reinforce self-esteem, and support initiatives to promote inclusiveness in various environments. (EGALE, 2004)

A final and somewhat contradictory consequence of this shift in public values is a growing skepticism of traditional representative institutions. We noted the decline in voting earlier—turnout for the 2000 federal election was at an historic low, with only 61 percent of 21.2 million eligible voters bothering to cast ballots. The decline of deference certainly induces people to be skeptical of politicians, but added to the new emphasis on identity and rights, it makes them suspicious of institutions that represent majoritarian interests. Parliament, political parties, and the electoral system are skewed toward the majority, but the new political culture sees rights as against majority interests, and minority rights as against majority rule. Institutions like the courts, which formally have no representative function, and that appear to be dispassionately concerned only with truth and justice, come off much better in this view (Fletcher and Howe, 2000). It is no coincidence that courts have become much more important in contemporary Canadian public policy just as our political culture has become more rights oriented. This may, however, be a chicken-and-egg issue, since the cultural shifts have themselves coincided with major institutional changes in Canada, such as the adoption and extension of the Charter of Rights and Freedoms, that have given the courts much greater scope for effectively making public policy.

The role of courts in Canadian public policy has not been uncontroversial. Simply because the Charter might have given the courts more scope does not mean that they necessarily had to become major players in policy development. All Canadian legislation must be consistent with the Charter (and the rest of the Constitution), and the courts have the responsibility for adjudicating claims. There are thus three elements at play here: the extent of Charter rights themselves, the willingness and capacity of litigants to take Charter cases to the courts, and the readiness of the courts to make bold decisions. In the conditions of an anemic Charter, supine interest groups, and a somnolent court, constitutional cases would rarely be controversial. In Canada's case, the Charter is robust, interest groups and individual litigants have been active (Brodie, 1997; Mandel, 1994; Hein, 2000), and courts at times have been willing to make bold decisions that increasingly involve "reading in" underlying meaning to constitutional text that does not exist on the surface (Martin 2003), a practice widely supported by a broad constituency of lawyers and policy advocates (Morton and Knopff, 2000). A more activist court changes the policy process significantly, since policy decisions can arise from a different institutional source with different—largely legal—rationales. In June 2004, for example, the Supreme Court of Canada heard a case that claimed that long waiting lists for surgical procedures violated the Charter of Rights and Freedoms. Though unlikely, the Court could conceivably rule that patients have a right to seek private care if the public system cannot provide it—a monumental policy decision that would shake the foundations of the Canadian health care system. The impact of courts on public policy has the collateral effect of elevating the importance of legal analysis in governmental policy work and situates agencies such as the federal Department of Justice at the centre of key policy decisions and processes (Kelly, 2000).

It is important not to exaggerate the impact of the politics of difference on contemporary Canada or other industrialized states. Traditional liberal-democratic institutions continue to exist, there is a continued impulse toward universalism or "cosmopolitanism," and most social and political issues do get addressed in a reasonably civil fashion, even if they are not necessarily resolved. The idea that a heightened politics of difference in the guise of multiculturalism might contribute to social fragmentation has been challenged, for example, in connection with the welfare state. States with the highest incidence of multicultural policy (defined as giving explicit recognition to ethnic groups) are the states generally with the best developed welfare systems (Banting and Kymlicka, 2003). The Charter enjoys strong support among the Canadian public, even if there may be disagreement over specific decisions. Moreover, the courts are not uniformly activist; the boldness of decisions is a reflection of different issues at stake, and the chemistry and personalities of the judges (McCormick, 2000). Kymlicka (2003) even challenges the claim that identity politics makes some policy issues uniquely challenging to resolve: "For those who have been raised on fears about the inherently explosive and irrational nature of identity politics, what is perhaps most striking about identity politics in Canada is its utter banality" (pp. 384–385).

On balance, however, it is clear that things have changed in important ways. The way that Canadians discuss rights, and how they frame policy issues in terms of rights, is vastly different today from a generation ago. There has been an undeniable decline in trust, deference, and engagement with conventional political institutions. Courts have become key policymaking—or at least -interpreting—institutions, to the degree that in 2003 the prime minister referred legislation on same-sex unions to the Supreme Court for an opinion—before that legislation had been introduced in the House of Commons. The shifting patterns of identity and allegiance have become important considerations in policymaking. All of this is new.

GOVERNANCE AND PUBLIC MANAGEMENT

The third major change in the context of policymaking and analysis has been in our concepts of the proper scope of governance by the state and the nature of public management. These are of course entangled with the changes described above in the domestic economy, globalization, and culture shifts, and probably represent the results of outcomes of these changes more than they do independent forces in their own right. Nonetheless, it is a crucial category for policy analysis since it cuts closest to what governments see themselves as properly doing, and the new politics of governance and public management rapidly developed their own dynamics, however much they might be a consequence of deeper factors.

Ideas about governance operate at several distinct levels. The most general is the view of the proper scope and nature of government activity. The 1990s was a decade where policymakers across the ideological spectrum lost confidence in the capacity of government to do things. Conservatives retained less faith than liberals or those on the left, but generally the centre of gravity on these issues shifted perceptibly to the right. In the last two or three years this may have changed, and certainly the 2004 federal election demonstrated that the pendulum had swung back to some extent. All four major parties were willing to countenance substantial new spending and increased government activism. By the same token, the sponsorship scandal in early 2004 (where it was alleged that government grants to Quebec advertising firms had been made improperly), the legendary Canadian gun registry, and consensus that government should not incur deficits all suggest that there remains a heightened emphasis on public management efficiency. And many of the key questions in the debates over governance in the 1990s have not disappeared. Should governments provide services themselves, or should they develop mechanisms for the delivery of these services through either for-profit or nonprofit agencies? Can and should government "correct market failures," or is the medicine worse than the malady? To what extent should government encourage the pursuit of what are basically private interests, such as child-care or a university education, through the public sphere in the form of either services or legal structures that support such pursuits?

Another, more specific level, concerns the tools that governments realistically have at their disposal for policy development and implementation. Can governments control unemployment and inflation through monetary policy? Can they "create jobs?" Can they solve poverty and eradicate racism? Can they provide adequate housing? Obviously, if one believes that the market can and should do this, the question of policy instruments will not arise at all. However, even in cases where one thinks that the role of government should be minimal, there can be disputes about appropriate tools for governance. The final aspect of governance concerns management practices. Given a certain vision of the role of government and the feasible tools at its disposal for dealing with public problems, how best to organize the administrative machinery of government to achieve those ends?

It is clear that ideas about governance and public management have been changing radically in the last two decades. The movement has coincided with the political ascendancy of the right in most liberal democracies, starting with Ronald Reagan in the United States (elected president in 1980) and Margaret Thatcher in Britain (who became prime minister in 1979). In Canada, the Progressive Conservatives were elected for terms in 1984 and again in 1988, before being almost wiped out in 1993. Interestingly, the Liberals accepted many key elements of the Tory agenda: **deficit reduction** and **government restructuring** being most prominent. This mimics a pattern in other countries such as New Zealand, where the change in public administration and management was led by left-wing parties. But the gospel of smaller government, balanced budgets, reduced public debt, and new management practices seems to have gained converts from both left and right.

What are its main features? Primarily, there is a belief that what Barzelay (1992, p. 5) calls the "bureaucratic paradigm" of carefully defined roles, reliance on rules and procedures, line and staff distinctions, tight financial control, and central agency oversight, should be replaced with a more client-focused, service-oriented system. More recently, Bevir, Rhodes, and Weller (2003) highlight the following features of the **new public management (NPM):**

> The term refers to a focus on management, not policy, and on performance appraisal and efficiency; disaggregating public bureaucracies into agencies which deal with each other on a user pay basis; the use of quasi-markets and of contracting out to foster competition; cost-cutting; and a style of management that emphasizes, among other things, output targets, limited term contracts, monetary incentives and freedom to manage. . . . It is said to be a global phenomenon. (pp. 1–2)

One of the most widely read examples of the NPM thinking was in a 1992 book entitled *Reinventing Government*, by David Osborne and Ted Gaebler. The most important aspect of the book's argument was its rejection of the hierarchical architecture of most government bureaucracies. Close accountability requires close scrutiny and a minimum of bureaucratic discretion. This traditional system of public administration has many benefits, but it is also in large part responsible for the stereotypical inflexibility and unresponsiveness of government bureaucracy. The result very often is costly, lumbering organizations that are driven by rules rather than results. Creativity is stifled, problem-solving is discouraged in favour of following routine, and significant resources are devoted simply to managing people within the system, rather than achieving policy goals. Osborne and Gaebler distilled ten principles of reinventing government from the cases they reviewed. These principles are grounded in the assumption that government is necessary, but it does not necessarily have to act like government.

> Most entrepreneurial governments promote *competition* between service providers. They *empower* citizens by pushing control out of the bureaucracy, into the community. They measure the performance of their agencies, focusing not on inputs but on *outcomes*. They are driven by their goals—their *missions*—not by their rules and regulations. They redefine their clients as *customers* and offer them choices—between schools, between training programs, between housing options. They *prevent* problems before they emerge, rather than simply offering services afterward. They put their energies into *earning* money, not simply spending it. They *decentralize* authority, embracing participatory management. They prefer *market* mechanisms to bureaucratic mechanisms. And they focus not simply on providing public services, but on *catalyzing* all sectors—public, private, and voluntary—into action to solve their community's problems. (Osborne and Gaebler, 1993, pp. 19–20)

Kenneth Kernaghan (2000a) provides a useful list that contrasts what he calls "bureaucratic" with "post-bureaucratic" organizations. It is presented in Figure 2.3 (page 76). Note that the characteristics on the post-bureaucratic side lend themselves to a variety of different configurations—decentralized organizations, for example, could be completely privatized ones or public agencies with greater responsibility for their own actions.

In the United States, the Clinton administration launched a **National Performance Review** on government, headed by Vice-President Al Gore, in March 1993. Its first report contained 384 recommendations for improving federal governmental performance, touching on virtually every agency and program in the American federal government (National Performance Review, 1993). Despite criticisms that the process was stalled within months of the release of the report, Kettl and DiIulio (1995) conclude that it led to real change, for example, in governmental culture, procurement practices, and cuts to some government agencies. By the second Clinton–Gore term, the effort had shifted to trying to imbed reinvention as a permanent feature of federal government agencies, and so the NPR was rechristened as the National Partnership for Reinvention in Government. The priorities enunciated at the time included better service delivery, partnerships, and efficiency. These were joined by an emphasis on customer satisfaction and more online services. The election of George W. Bush in 2000 signalled a new direction in public management priorities for the United States government. Bush supported the mantras of efficiency and smaller government, but was much more ideologically enthused by reliance on market mechanisms to achieve public policy goals. Moreover, his one overarching public management initiative in the early part of his first term was more community-based delivery of public services and programs, but, in particular, with an emphasis on faith-based organizations (principally charities, but churches as well). Bush created the White House Office of Faith-Based and Community Initiatives almost immediately on taking office, and it became the centrepiece of his "compassionate conservativism." This was NPM in the sense of community partnerships, and in the sense of a skepticism of traditional government bureaucracy, but with a new focus on charitable organizations. The 9/11 terrorist attacks eclipsed this initiative and indeed put the Bush administration on a completely different track with respect to public sector management. From a champion of small government, Bush was transformed into a champion of strong, robust, and at least in connection with things pertaining to security, muscular and interventionist government. In the largest centralizing move in American peacetime, Bush released the National Strategy for Homeland Security, passed the

Figure 2.3   Bureaucratic versus Post-bureaucratic
Organization/Management

Bureaucratic Organization	*Post-bureaucratic Organization*
Policy and Management Culture	

Organization-centred
  Emphasis on needs of the
  organization itself
	Citizen-centred
	  Quality service to citizens (and
	  clients/stakeholders)

Position power
  Control, command and
  compliance
	Participative leadership
	  Shared values and participative
	  decision making

Rule-centred
  Rules, procedures and
  constraints
	People-centred
	  An empowering and caring milieu
	  for employees

Independent action
  Little consultation, cooperation
  or coordination
	Collective action
	  Consultation, cooperation and
	  coordination

Status quo-oriented
  Avoiding risks and mistakes
	Change-oriented
	  Innovation, risk taking and
	  continuous improvement

Process oriented
  Accountability for process
	Results oriented
	  Accountability for results

Structure	

Centralized
  Hierarchy and central controls
	Decentralized
	  Decentralization of authority and
	  control

Departmental form
  Most programmes delivered by
  operating departments
	Non-departmental form
	  Programmes delivered by wide
	  variety of mechanisms

Market Orientation	

Budget driven
  Programmes financed largely
  from appropriations
	Revenue driven
	  Programmes financed as far as
	  possible on cost recovery basis

Monopolistic
  Government has monopoly
  on programme delivery
	Competitive
	  Competition with private sector
	  for programme delivery

SOURCE: Kernaghan, K. (2000). The post-bureaucratic organization and public service values. *International Review of Administrative Sciences, 66.*

Homeland Security Act, and created the Department of Homeland Security with 180 000 employees. Funding for homeland security tripled in the first two years to US$30 billion. The new department brought together the security services, Coast Guard, border control, emergency preparedness agencies, and immigration, along with several others. From that point on, the demands of fighting terrorism induced large and intrusive government at the national level, as well as massive spending to create the largest deficit in United States history.

The Bush administration has a management agenda, one that was announced before the 9/11 terrorist attacks (Office of Management and Budget, 2002). The agenda laid out five management priorities—human capital development, competitive sourcing, improved financial management, e-government, and integration of budget and performance information. A clear emphasis has remained on performance reporting, and executive agencies are expected to report quarterly on their performance against the five management priorities as well as a series of program initiatives. Box 2.3 shows the March 31, 2004, scorecard. The graphic displays executive agencies, and gives a dark (success), medium (mixed results), and light (unsatisfactory) rating along each dimension.

The British example is perhaps more relevant to the Canadian context because Britain too is a parliamentary democracy, and because it has not mixed NPM principles with religious fervour or a new massive security apparatus. In Britain today, three-quarters of "government employees" do not work for traditional departments but instead for executive agencies that have been contracted to provide certain services. The wide range of reforms has been under way since Margaret Thatcher's prime ministership, but two initiatives, the **Next Steps** program and the **Citizen's Charter,** illustrate the early goals of the organizational revolution that took place in the United Kingdom (Jenkins and Gray, 1993; Doern, 1993). Tony Blair's "New Labour" victory in 1997 carried the government reform agenda forward with even greater vigour.

Next Steps had its origins in the Financial Management Initiative of 1982, which tried to underscore the importance of management in government by introducing better practices and giving managers greater autonomy over budgets and operations as long as they met certain performance and output targets. By the late 1980s the reform had bogged down, and so efforts were redoubled to take the "Next Steps" of the original Financial Management Initiative in decentralizing government services. The plan called for as many agencies as possible to be converted to "departmental executive agencies" that would essentially act as businesses delivering public services. The chief executive officer of each Next Step agency was to negotiate a contract with the department

Box 2.3

Executive Branch Management Scorecard

	Current Status as of June 30, 2004					Progress in Implementing the President's Management Agenda				
	Human Capital	Competitive Sourcing	Financial Perf.	E-Gov	Budget/Perf. Integration	Human Capital	Competitive Sourcing	Financial Perf.	E-Gov	Budget/Perf. Integration
AGRICULTURE	●↑	●	○	●	●↑	●	●	●	●	●
COMMERCE	●	●	○	●	●	●	●	●	●	●
DEFENSE	●	●↑	○	○	●	●	●	●	●	●
EDUCATION	●	●	●	●	●↑	●	○	●	●	●
ENERGY	●↑	●	●↑	●	●	●	●	●	●	●
EPA	●	●↑	●	●↑	●	●	●	●	●	●
HHS	●	●	○	●	●↑	●	●	●	●	●
HOMELAND	○	●	○	●	●	●	●	●	○	●
HUD	●↑	○	○	○	○	●	●	●	●	●
INTERIOR	●↑	●	○	●↑	○	●	●	●	●	●
JUSTICE	○	●	○	●↑	○	●	●	●	●	●
LABOR	●	●↑	●	●	●↑	●	●	●	●	●
STATE	●↑	○	●	●	●	●	●	●	●	●
DOT	●↑	●↑	○	●↑	●↑	●	●	●	●	●
TREASURY	○	○	○	○	○	●	●	●	●	●
VA	●↑	○	○	●	●	●	○	●	●	●
AID	○	○	○	●	●	●	●	●	●	●
CORPS	●	○	○	●	●	●	●	●	●	●
GSA	●	○	○	●	●	●	●	●	●	●
NASA	●	●	○	●	●	●	●	●	●	●
NSF	●	○	●	●	●	●	●	●	●	●
OMB	●	○	○	●	●	●	●	●	●	●
OPM	●↑	●	●	●	●	●	●	●	●	●
SBA	●	●	○	●↑	●↑	●	●	●	●	●
SMITHSONIAN	○	○	○	○	○	●	●	●	●	●
SSA	●↑	●↑	●	●	●↑	●	●	●	●	●

↑↓ Arrows indicate change in status since evaluation on March 31, 2004.

SOURCE: *The President's management agenda: The scorecard.* Retrieved August 6, 2004, from http://results.gov/agenda/scorecard.html

specifying performance goals and targets but would then have substantial freedom to operate the "business" as he or she saw fit.

In a little over a year, eight agencies were created. By April 1993, there were 89 such agencies employing almost two-thirds of the civil service. By 1998, 377 500 civil servants worked in 138 Next Steps agencies and four departments with Next Steps business lines. These are not privatized agencies; they remain part of government and their employees are still civil servants. But they are stand-alone organizations with only loose connections to core ministries. The key change is the introduction of substantial managerial autonomy. Each agency has a framework document or agreement that is negotiated between the parent department and the Treasury and is subject to some renegotiation later by the chief executive officer. The framework document differs for each agency, though all outline the agency's objectives and targets, resource management guidelines, and the pattern of agency–department relations. The result is the provision of government services in markedly new ways. The Next Steps agencies, for example, no longer need to follow general government guidelines on expenditures as long as they work within their framework agreement. Agencies can set salary levels and classify jobs as they see fit. Managers can take risks, be more entrepreneurial, and the agency as a whole can respond more effectively to its "customers." In 1998 the government decreed that for the most part the creation phase of Next Steps agencies was over and that the focus would now shift to performance improvement (Cabinet Office, 1998a, p. 3).

The emphasis on performance and service fits well with the other major initiative, the idea of the Citizen's Charter. The U.K. Citizen's Charter was introduced by John Major in 1991 after he had assumed the prime ministership from Margaret Thatcher. The Charter's principles, however, are entirely consistent with the Next Steps project of remaking the way that government works. Whereas Next Steps introduced fundamental organizational changes, the Charter is designed to alter bureaucratic practices in order to raise the quality of public services. The Charter was launched with a White Paper that laid out four key themes: (1) the improvement in the quality of public services, (2) the introduction, wherever possible, of greater choice through competing providers of public services and consultation with citizens about the type of services they wanted, (3) the clear statement of standards of services, to enhance accountability, and (4) the assurance that taxpayers would receive value for their money. The Citizen's Charter applied across the British government. As a result of consultations in 1997, a new charter program entitled Service First was launched to ensure that it was "driven by the needs of users, and whose aims are shared by all staff, particularly those on the front line" (Cabinet Office, 1998b). This was joined to an experiment with a national People's Panel consisting of 5000 randomly selected citizens who would provide advice and consultation for the government in its public sector reform efforts. There was also an improved **Charter Mark** program. The Charter Mark program is a scheme to judge public sector organizations on their performance with customers and clients. Any agency that provides services directly to the public, and voluntary agencies that receive at least 10 percent of their funds from public sources, may apply to receive a Charter Mark. Applications are made to assessors, based on six service standards (strong performance standards; serving customers; fairness, accessibility, and choice; continuous improvement; effective resource management; and contribution to the quality of life in the community) and empirical evidence that customers agree that those standards have been met (Cabinet Office, 2004). Both the Service First and People's Panel initiatives were phased out in 2002 in favour of yet another set of reform programs, but the Charter Mark was retained.

In 2002 the Blair government launched a host of new spending programs on social services, accompanied by a new framework for the reform of the delivery of those and other government services. The overarching goal of the new strategy was customer satisfaction with the quality and variety of services. The plan is premised on four key principles, which were to be buttressed with a new, more robust performance measurement and standards regime:

- It is the Government's job to set national standards that really matter to the public, within a framework of clear accountability, designed to ensure that citizens have the right to high quality services wherever they live.

- These standards can only be delivered effectively by devolution and delegation to the front line, giving local leaders responsibility and accountability for delivery, and the opportunity to design and develop services around the needs of local people.

- More flexibility is required for public service organisations and their staff to achieve the diversity of service provision needed to respond to the wide range of customer aspirations. This means challenging restrictive practices and reducing red tape; greater and more flexible incentives and rewards for good performance; strong leadership and management; and high quality training and development.

- Public services need to offer expanding choice for the customer. Giving people a choice about the service they can have and who provides it helps ensure that services are designed around their customers. An element of contestability between alternative suppliers can also drive up standards and empower customers locked into a poor service from their traditional supplier. These four principles underpin the entire programme of reform. (Office of Public Services Reform, 2002, p. 10)

Canada did not go as far as the United Kingdom or other leaders in NPM such as New Zealand and Australia, and its administrative practices have diverged sharply from the Bush administration's. At the provincial level, the governments of Alberta under Ralph Klein and Ontario under Mike Harris attracted the most attention, though some important administrative changes to the health and education sectors have also been made in most of the other provinces, such as New Brunswick. The Alberta government passed a Deficit Elimination Act that committed it to that goal for 1996/97 but actually achieved a balanced budget a year earlier through deep spending cuts. It restructured its welfare services, closed hospitals, consolidated school boards, and privatized its liquor stores (Bruce, Kneebone, and McKenzie, 1997). A Conservative government was elected in Ontario in 1995 on the platform of its Common Sense Revolution, which promised virtually the same policy configuration as Alberta's (Ibbitson, 1997). In the words of Mike Harris, "I am not talking about tinkering, about incremental changes, or about short term solutions. After all, the changes we have all experienced in our personal lives have been much more fundamental than that. It's time for us to take a fresh look at government. To re-invent the way it works, to make it work for people" (Progressive Conservative Party of Ontario, 1995, p. 1). The high rhetoric, however, actually reflected massive changes under way in all the provinces. Lindquist and Murray (1994) concluded that all provincial governments had been engaged in downsizing, delayering, and focusing on service quality. While Alberta and Ontario led the way, governments in British Columbia under Gordon Campbell and in Quebec under Jean Charest each implemented NPM principles.

At the federal level, the vehicle of public sector reform was the **Program Review** exercise, launched in 1994. The scope and impact of the review hit home with Canadians only in the February 1995 federal budget statement. The language of that budget was as uncompromising as that in the Common Sense Revolution: "The Program Review will lead to long-standing structural change in what government does" (Department of Finance, 1995, p. 32). Program Review was guided by six tests or questions: "serving the public interest; necessity of government involvement; appropriate federal role; scope for public sector/private sector partnerships; scope for increased efficiency; affordability" (Department of Finance, 1995, p. 34). These tests were explicitly linked to a deficit-reduction strategy that the federal government finally decided to embark upon seriously in 1995 (Greenspon and Wilson-Smith, 1996). Compared to some other countries, Canada's federal public reform effort was at first primarily fiscally driven. This set up two dynamics. The first was directly harnessed to the fiscal program and sought to implement wide-ranging public sector reforms to achieve more effective and efficient governance. The lead agency on this front was the Treasury Board, and it carried forward a program of management reform through the late 1990s under the rubric of "**Getting Government Right.**" The other dynamic was a reactive one, as the public sector sought to implement reforms to deal with the consequences of fiscal cuts; this was spearheaded primarily by the Clerk of the Privy Council, whose efforts under *La Relève* were briefly described in Chapter 1.

The *Getting Government Right* (1997) initiative was organized around several key themes. Together they summarize Ottawa's reform efforts, which, while they were not structurally radical, did have a wide scope in covering both services and programs as well as their presentation to Parliament and to the public:

- *Modernizing program delivery:* This included "service clustering (co-location of referral services as well as actual program delivery), regulatory reform (more transparency, more streamlined and co-operative regulatory procedures), cost-recovery (where appropriate, to charge for government services targeted to very specific groups and businesses).

- *Alternative service delivery:* This included using different organizational forms to delivery services (e.g., a special operating agency, a crown corporation); devolving, commercializing, or even privatizing some services.

- *Partnering with other levels of government and the private sector:* Primarily, this entailed working with other levels of government, the voluntary and private sectors to cut costs, reduce duplication, and bring services closer to the people. The devolution of health and social services to Aboriginal communities was cited as an example.

- *Governance and strategic management:* This involved a number of initiatives to change the way the central agencies in the federal government interact with departments and provide oversight, particularly on management and expenditure issues. The Treasury Board was to become more strategic, focused on results and performance accountabilities.

- *Accountability and the relationship to parliament and citizens:* This embraced a series of changes, which also included a "modern comptrollership function" for the Treasury Board (more flexible oversight coupled with greater responsibilities for managers). It also included a pilot project that soon was mandated for all federal departments and agencies to report in new, more comprehensible formats to parliament and the public. The arcane and unreadable Estimates were to be replaced by annual Departmental Performance Reports in the spring, and annual Plans and Priorities Reports in the fall. These were to be drafted around a department's "business lines" and around explicit performance indicators. This section of the report also highlighted the importance of quality services: "It focuses on ensuring that the principle of delivering quality services to Canadians, appropriate to their needs and within the government's fiscal framework, underlies all government initiatives and priorities as an integral part of day-to-day operations. This strategy encourages government organizations to develop and communicate demonstrable service standards that Canadians can use to assess the government's performance, as well as the feedback systems necessary to maintain that quality."

The next building block for management reform from the Treasury Board was the president's 2000 report entitled *Results for Canadians*. The president pointed out that the management framework articulated in the document did not mark a departure from *Getting Government Right,* but a consolidation. The framework was to be guided by a four-step agenda: recognize that the federal government must build a "citizen focus" into all its activities and services; highlight the importance of public service values; focus on achieving results for Canadians; and promote "discipline, due diligence and value for money in the use of public funds." (*Results for Canadians,* 2000). Despite its length, the following quote illustrates the core of the philosophy behind the approach:

> First and foremost, the Government of Canada must sharpen its citizen focus in designing, delivering, evaluating and reporting on its activities. It must improve service and expand partnerships with other governments, the private sector and voluntary organizations.

> Second, management in the public service must be guided by a clear set of values. Management must respect and reinforce Canadian institutions of democracy and it must be guided by the highest professional and ethical values.

> Third, as an integrating principle, management in all departments, agencies and functions must be focused on the achievement of results and on reporting them in simple and understandable ways to elected officials and to Canadians.

> Fourth, given the limited nature of public funds, the Government of Canada must ensure responsible spending. The costs of initiatives must be linked with results to ensure value for the taxpayer. Existing programs as well as new spending proposals must be systematically assessed and management frameworks

must be in place to ensure due diligence and proper steward-ship of public funds. Activities critical to the public interest must be resourced sustainably, over the long term.

Living up to these commitments requires public service em-ployees at all levels and in all regions who put the interests of Canadians first and who demonstrate daily attention to values and results. Employees are critical to improvement. They must be supported by a working culture that values learning, inno-vation, inclusiveness and diversity, intelligent risk taking and continuous improvement—allowing them to make their best contributions to Canada. (*Results for Canadians*, 2000)

Results for Canadians did not depart markedly from the 1997 approach, except that it emphasized structural changes in the federal government much less. In a sense, Ottawa had undergone whatever organizational changes it was prepared to stomach (indeed, federal employment began to grow again so that by 2003 it was at pre-Program Review levels). What was new was an emphasis on values and democratic accountability. As well, the focus on results was much greater—larger efforts were to go into developing indicators of program performance and reporting on them. In 2001 and 2002, the government produced government-wide performance reports for the country as a whole, taking the process beyond simply reporting at a departmental or agency level.

In its report on its *Plans and Priorities 2003–2004*, the Treasury Board cited the importance of both Getting Government Right and *Results for Canadians* as the core of the federal government's manage-ment framework (Treasury Board of Canada, 2003). It highlighted again the importance of service quality improvements, particularly in reference to the Government On-Line initiative, an $880 million program over six years to make the most commonly used federal government services available and accessible to all Canadians online (Government On-Line, 2003). It also referred to the introduction of a comprehensive package of reforms to the federal public service—the Public Service Modernization Act. The core of this initiative was to encourage all federal managers (deputy heads) to use more flexible definitions of merit in their hiring decisions, and give them wider authorities over hiring and staffing in their organizations. This was intended to streamline the often cumbersome human resource practices in the federal government.

It is clear that NPM in Canada has affected management practices and rhetoric at both the provincial and federal levels. The irony is that in practice, perhaps more at the federal level than at the provincial (cer-tainly in places like Alberta), the bark of NPM may be worse than its bite. The holy grail of Getting Government Right has been pursued for more than a decade, and yet by 2003–2004, there was a sense of malaise in the federal public service. Various scandals and reports kept hitting the news that made it appear that government was not very streamlined, or efficient, or indeed responsive to customers and clients.

This should not be entirely surprising. On the one hand, NPM appeared to be a global phenomenon, celebrated by the OECD, and argued to have similar characteristics no matter what the national context (Kettl, 2000; Lynn Jr., 2001). As Pollitt (1995) put it: "One senses an 'official line' advanced, with local inflections, by most national government leaders" (p. 204). This official line coalesced around a strong political emphasis on certain techniques: decentralization of budgeting, performance indicators, performance-related pay, an emphasis on quality and standards, the contractualization of relationships, and evaluation coupled with a concern about value for money. We should remember, however, that academic versions of the NPM, as well as some practical real-world examples, suggest a variety of sometimes inconsistent models (Peters, 1995). The emphasis on empowerment and the distrust of bureaucracy, for example, is just as likely to lead to a greater emphasis on broad political participation in policy-making as it is market-based prescriptions (Denhardt, 1993). And the enthusiasm with which new visions of governance have been seized by politicians has not been mirrored by analysts. For many students of public administration, wide-sweeping changes were often implemented without public consultation or popular mandates (e.g., New Zealand), and for others the NPM is yet another postwar fad that kowtows to the market as the only credible model for human organization (Savoie, 1995). As well, as more research has been conducted on the actual fortunes of NPM around the world, it is clear that the Canadian experience of variation, differential acceptance, and uneven implementation is true around the world (Bevir, Rhodes, and Weller, 2003; Christensen and Laegried, 2002). Different countries implemented differently, selecting some elements and not others, and the success of implementation depended on a host of institutional and political variables.

CONCLUSION

Are the forces described in this chapter permanent? Yes and no. Globalization, increasing cultural diversity, the decline of deference, and the information revolution are impossible to reverse, and almost impossible to avoid. Governance, or our systems of public policy development and administration, are reactions to these forces, and can be expected to change and vary over time. Governing is about making choices, and choices are still very much available despite the inevitability of these forces. For example, the budget cutting, downsizing, and restructuring that characterized the last few years was indeed compelled by globalization, but governments handled it in different ways. New Democratic governments in Western Canada cut expenditures but also raised taxes. Alberta focused on expenditure reductions. Ontario cut spending and taxes at the same time and also launched a revolution in the organization of government. Federal political parties shifted to the left in 2004, and the Ontario Liberals were elected in October 2003 on a platform substantially different from the ruling Tories. As we noted above, many NGOs and citizens resist globalization and demand that their governments act on their behalf to either block it or ameliorate its worst effects.

The changed context for policymaking does not mean the end of choices, simply different constraints, and different choices within those constraints. Indeed, with the gradual elimination of deficits for most governments in Canada and in the developed world, a whole new set of choices about where to put public resources has arisen, along with a renewed appreciation of the importance of a well-functioning public sector (Kernaghan, 2000b). But those choices will not be made by governments of the type familiar in the 1980s; we have moved and continue to move from a bureaucratic model to something different. Forms and processes of governance have changed, as have the problems they tackle and the means at their disposal. This book is about the new constraints, the new choices, and the new tools available to policymakers. The themes developed in this chapter will weave through the rest as we explore what it means to go beyond policy analysis. The next chapter looks more closely at the first key phase of policymaking, problem definition, and its link to the agenda-setting process.

KEY TERMS

Charter Mark (U.K.)—a scheme to engage independent assessors to judge and certify public sector organizations on their performance with customers and clients

Citizen's Charter (U.K.)—introduced by John Major in 1991 and designed to alter bureaucratic practices by publicly stating government service obligations to citizens

citizenship—traditional collection of civil and political rights that aim to treat individuals roughly the same, regardless of their social and economic differences

collective identities—widely shared characteristics such as race or language that are politically salient as a way of orienting oneself in politics

cultural identity—a normative base for making specific rights claims on behalf of individuals who are members of specific cultural groups

cultural pluralism—the condition wherein a political community is marked by a wide variety of cultural groups, and for whom those cultural differences are salient as a basis of claim or grievance

decline of deference—the decline in citizens' trust and confidence in their governments and increasing desire to be consulted, to participate, and to be heard in policy development

deficit reduction—a fiscal policy to reduce and eventually eradicate the budget deficit

free market capitalism—a type of capitalism that emphasizes smaller government, the minimum of controls and regulations, and wide scope for markets in the delivery of goods and services

Getting Government Right—a program of federal management reform led by the Treasury Board Secretariat through the late 1990s, which sought to implement wide-ranging public sector reforms to achieve more effective and efficient governance

global civil society—an emerging series of networks of activist NGOs and connected nongovernmental institutions that can be mobilized quickly around policy issues

globality—the sense that the entire planet is a single social space, that people carry on conversations in that space irrespective of territoriality, that they pay collective and simultaneous attention to "global events"

globalization system—the idea that globalization is not simply a matter of greater interdependence but is also a system with its own dynamics and logic

government restructuring—substantial and wide-reaching structural change in public administration and management, usually intended to reflect new public management objectives of efficiency and effectiveness

human rights—the recognition of the inherent dignity and of the equal and inalienable rights of all members of the human family

international standards—either formal or informal standards developed by the international community that are intended to supplement and sometimes override domestic standards

liberal individualism—insists that equality will best be achieved by treating people as individuals under a system of universally applicable and consistent rules

liberal universalism—the preference to treat individuals according to a universally applicable set of rules, not those tailored to specific group differences

National Performance Review (U.S.)—a program of public sector reform of Clinton administration, headed by Vice-President Al Gore, in March 1993, touching on virtually every agency and program in the American federal government

new public management—focus on performance appraisal and efficiency; disaggregating and decentralizing public bureaucracies; the use of market mechanisms and of contracting out to foster competition; financial management; partnerships

Next Steps (U.K.)—the plan in the late 1980s to convert many traditional departments into "departmental executive agencies" that would essentially act as businesses delivering public services

policy reversal—the changes in key policies during the early 1990s that have altered key social and political systems built up in the postwar period in both the developed and developing world

political culture—people's orientations of support and trust toward the political system

politics of difference—an emphasis on rights, discourse, culture, and group-specific differences as the foundation of politics and policy

politics of recognition—the recognition and celebration of "difference" and the view that differences must be recognized and validated

postmaterialism—the broad cultural shift around the world but particularly in the West away from material concerns to questions of identity and lifestyle

postmodern condition—term used to describe the amalgam of conditions consisting of the rise of postmaterialism, the increased salience of rights, and the new emphasis on "difference"

Program Review—the federal Liberal government's policy in the mid-1990s of management reform and program-by-program assessment according to six criteria as a means for reducing the deficit and enhancing efficiency

public management—the process of directing the public sector as a whole as well as the specific agencies within it

race to the bottom—competition among countries for investment by lowering of standards

rights talk—a mode of political discourse that emphasizes the salience of individual and group rights

social cohesion—a sense of belonging to a community that shares values and a sense of purpose and commitment

social fragmentation—the process of losing social cohesion

trade liberalization—the process of lowering trade barriers of every sort such as duties and nontariff barriers, to encourage trade and investment flows

transnational corporations—commercial firms that operate in numerous countries, not simply for the sale of their products, but to organize production itself

Weblinks

Europa (the European Union website)
http://www.europa.eu.int

Globalization and Autonomy
http://www.humanities.mcmaster.ca/~global/globalizationautonomy.htm

Treasury Board Secretariat (Canada)
http://www.tbs-sct.gc.ca

World Trade Organization
http://www.wto.org

World Values Survey
http://wvs.isr.umich.edu
http://www.worldvaluessurvey.com

Further Readings

Barzelay, M. (2001). *The new public management: Improving research and policy dialogue.* Berkeley: University of California Press.

Inglehart, R. (Ed.). (2003). *Human values and social change: Findings from the values surveys.* Leiden, Netherlands: Brill.

Kettl, D. F. (2000). *The global public management revolution.* Washington, DC: Brookings Institution.

Scholte, J. A. (2002). *Globalization: A critical introduction.* Basingstoke, UK: Palgrave.

Stiglitz, J. E. (2003). *Globalization and its discontents.* New York: W. W. Norton.

REFERENCES

Abramson, P. R., and Inglehart, R. (1995). *Value change in global perspective*. Ann Arbor: University of Michigan Press.

Adams, M. (1997). *Sex in the snow: Canadian social values at the end of the millennium*. Toronto: Viking.

Banting, K., and Kymlicka, W. (2003). Multiculturalism and welfare. *Dissent* (Fall), 59–66.

Barber, B. R. (1995). *Jihad vs. McWorld*. New York: Times Books.

Barzelay, M. (1992). *Breaking through bureaucracy: A new vision for managing government*. Berkeley: University of California Press.

Bevir, M., Rhodes, R.A.W., and Weller, P. (2003). Traditions of governance: Interpreting the changing role of the public sector. *Public Administration* 81 (1), 1–17.

Brodie, I. (1997). *Interest groups and the Supreme Court of Canada*. Ph. D. dissertation. University of Calgary.

Brodie, I., and Nevitte, N. (1993, June). Evaluating the citizens' constitution theory. *Canadian Journal of Political Science*, 26, 235–59.

Bruce, C., Kneebone, R. D., and McKenzie, K. J. (Eds.) (1997). *A government reinvented: A study of Alberta's deficit elimination program*. Toronto: Oxford University Press.

Cabinet Office (United Kingdom). (1998a). *Next Steps briefing note*. (September). Retrieved September 1, 1998, from http://www.cabinet-office.gov.uk/civilservicerecruitment/1998/admin/next%20steps.pdf

Cabinet Office (United Kingdom). (1998b). *Service First: The new Charter programme*. Retrieved September 1, 1998, from http://www.cabinet-office.gov.uk/servicefirst/1998/sfirst/bk1toc.htm

Cabinet Office (United Kingdom). (2004). *Chartermark standard*. Retrieved August 6, 2004, from http://www.chartermark.gov.uk/apply/CharterMarkStandard.pdf.

Cairncross, F. (1997). *The death of distance: How the communications revolution will change our lives*. Boston: Harvard Business School Press.

Cairns, A. C. (1991). *Disruptions: Constitutional struggle, from the Charter to Meech Lake*. (D. E. Williams, Ed.). Toronto: McClelland and Stewart.

Cairns, A. C. (1992). *Charter versus federalism*. Montreal: McGill-Queen's University Press.

Cairns, A. C. (1993). The fragmentation of Canadian citizenship. In W. Kaplan (Ed.), *Belonging: The meaning and future of Canadian citizenship* (pp. 181–220). Montreal: McGill-Queen's University Press.

Cameron, D. R., and Stein, J. G. (2002). Street protests and fantasy parks. In D. R. Cameron and J. G. Stein (Eds.), *Street protests and fantasy parks: Globalization, culture, and the state* (pp. 1–19). Vancouver: UBC Press.

Castells, M. (1997). *The information age: Economy, society and culture. Vol. II: The power of identity.* Oxford: Blackwell.

Christensen, T., and Laegried, P. (Eds.) (2002). *New public management: The transformation of ideas and practice.* Hampshire: Ashgate.

Clarkson, S. (2002). *Uncle Sam and us: Globalization, neoconservatism and the Canadian state.* Toronto: University of Toronto Press.

Courchene, T. J., and Savoie, D. J. (2003). Introduction. In T. J. Courchene and D. J. Savoie (Eds.), *The art of the state: Governance in a world without frontiers* (pp. 1–27). Montreal: Institute for Research on Public Policy.

Denhardt, R. B. (1993). *The pursuit of significance: Strategies for managerial success in public organizations.* Belmont, CA: Wadsworth Publishing Co.

Department of Finance (Canada). (1995). *The federal budget.* Ottawa: Ministry of Finance.

Doern, G. B. (1993). The UK citizen's charter: Origins and implementation in three agencies. *Policy and Politics, 21,* 17–29.

EGALE. (2004). *Out in colour: Showing the true colours of Montreal's gay, lesbian, bisexual, and transgendered community: Conference to focus on issues of diverse cultures and sexualities.* Retrieved September 4, 2004, from http://www.egale.ca/index .asp?lang=E&menu=1&item=977

Eisenberg, A. (1994, March). The politics of individual and group difference in Canadian jurisprudence. *Canadian Journal of Political Science, 27,* 3–21.

Fierlbeck, K. (1996, March). The ambivalent potential of cultural identity. *Canadian Journal of Political Science, 29,* 3–22.

Fletcher, J. F., and Howe, P. (2000, May). Public opinion and the courts. *Choices, 6.*

Friedman, T. L. (1999). *The Lexus and the olive tree: Understanding globalization.* New York: Farrar, Straus, Giroux.

Getting Government Right. (1997). Ottawa: Minister of Public Works and Government Services Canada.

Glendon, M. A. (1991). *Rights talk: The impoverishment of political discourse.* New York: The Free Press.

Government On Line (2003). *2nd Annual Report.* Retrieved August 6, 2004, from http://www.tbs-sct.gc.ca/report/gol-ged/2003/gol-ged02_e.asp

Green, J. (2000, March). The difference debate: Reducing rights to cultural flavours. *Canadian Journal of Political Science,* 33, 133–44.

Greenspon, E., and Wilson-Smith, A. (1996). *Double vision: The inside story of the Liberals in power.* Toronto: Doubleday.

Hein, G. (2000, March). Interest group litigation and Canadian democracy. *Choices,* 6.

Helliwell, J. F. (2002). *Globalization and well-being.* Vancouver: UBC Press.

Hirst, P. (1997, July). The global economy—myths and realities. *International Affairs,* 73, 409–25.

Ibbitson, J. (1997). *Promised land: Inside the Mike Harris revolution.* Scarborough, ON: Prentice-Hall.

Ignatieff, M. (2000). *The rights revolution.* Toronto: House of Anansi.

International Monetary Fund. (1999). *International capital markets: Developments, prospects, and key policy issues.* Retrieved August 6, 2004, from http://www.imf.org/external/pubs/ft/icm/1999/index.htm

Jenson, J. The frontiers of citizenship: Reflections. In T. J. Courchene and D. J. Savoie (Eds.), *The art of the state: Governance in a world without frontiers* (pp. 311–21). Montreal: Institute for Research on Public Policy.

Jenkins, B., and Gray, A. (1993). Reshaping the management of government: The Next Steps initiative in the United Kingdom. In F. L. Seidle (Ed.), *Rethinking government: Reform of reinvention?* (pp. 73–109). Montreal: Institute for Research on Public Policy.

Keck, M. E., and Sikkink, K. (1998). *Activists beyond borders: Advocacy networks in international politics.* Ithaca: Cornell University Press.

Kelly, J. B. (2000, Winter). Bureaucratic activism and the Charter of Rights and Freedoms: The Department of Justice and its entry into the centre of government. *Canadian Public Administration,* 42, 476–511.

Kernaghan, K. (2000a, March). The post-bureaucratic organization and public service values. *International Review of Administrative Sciences,* 66, 91–104.

Kernaghan, K. (2000b). *Rediscovering public service: Recognizing the value of an essential institution.* Toronto: Institute of Public Administration of Canada.

Kettl, D. F., and DiIulio, Jr., J. J. (Eds.). (1995). *Inside the reinvention machine: Appraising governmental reform.* Washington, DC: The Brookings Institution.

Kettl, D. F. (2000). *The global public management revolution.* Washington, DC: Brookings Institution.

Kymlicka, W. (1992). *Recent work in citizenship theory.* Ottawa: Multiculturalism and Citizenship Canada.

Kymlicka, W. (1995). *Multicultural citizenship: A liberal theory of minority rights.* Oxford: Clarendon Press.

Kymlicka, W. (2003). Being Canadian. *Government and Opposition,* 38, 357–85.

Lindquist, E. A., and Murray, K. B. (1994, Fall). Appendix: A reconnaissance of Canadian public administrative reform during the early 1990s. *Canadian Public Administration,* 37, 468–89.

Lusztig, M. (1994, December). Constitutional paralysis: Why Canadian constitutional initiatives are doomed to fail. *Canadian Journal of Political Science,* 27, 747–71.

Lynn Jr., L. E. (2001). Globalization and administrative reform: What is happening in theory? *Public Management Review,* 3, pp. 191–208.

Mandel, M. (1994). *The Charter of Rights and the legalization of politics in Canada.* Rev. ed. Toronto: Thompson Education Publishing.

McCormick, P. (2000). *Supreme at last: The Evolution of the Supreme Court of Canada.* Toronto: James Lorimer.

Martin, R. I. (2003). *The most dangerous branch: How the Supreme Court of Canada has undermined our law and our democracy.* Montreal and Kingston: McGill-Queen's University Press.

Montgomery, J. D. (1999). Fifty years of human rights: An emergent global regime. *Policy Sciences,* 32(1), 79–94.

Mooney, C. A. (1999). The politics of morality policy: Symposium editor's introduction. *Policy Studies Journal,* 27(4), 675–80.

Morton, F. L., and Knopff, R. (2000). *The Charter revolution and the Court Party.* Toronto: Broadview Press.

National Performance Review. (1993). *From red tape to results: Creating a government that works better and costs less.* Retrieved September 5, 2004, from http://acts.poly.edu/cd/npr/np-realtoc .html

NUA Internet Surveys. (2004). *How many on-line?* Retrieved August 6, 2004, from http://www.nua.com/surveys/how_many_online/

O'Brien, R., Goetz, A. M., Scholte, J. A., and Williams, M. (Eds.). (2000). *Contesting global governance: Multilateral institutions and global social movements.* Cambridge, MA: Cambridge University Press.

Office of Management and Budget (USA). (2002). *The President's management agenda.* Retrieved August 6, 2004, from http://www .whitehouse.gov/omb/budget/fy2002/mgmt.pdf

Office of Public Services Reform. (2002). *Reforming our public services: Principles into practice.* Retrieved August 6, 2004, from http://www.pm.gov.uk/files/pdf/Principles.pdf

O'Hara, K. (1998). *Securing the social union.* CPRN Study No. 02. Ottawa: Canadian Policy Research Networks.

OHCC (Ontario Healthy Communities Coalition). (2000). *Inspiring change: Healthy cities and communities in Ontario.* Toronto: OHCC.

OHCC (Ontario Healthy Communities Coalition). (2004). *Community stories.* Retrieved August 6, 2004, from http://www .healthycommunities.on.ca/community_stories/index.html

Ohmae, K. (1995). *The end of the nation state: The rise of regional economies.* New York: The Free Press.

Osborne, D., and Gaebler, T. (1993). *Reinventing government: How the entrepreneurial spirit is transforming the public sector.* New York: Penguin.

Ostry, S. (1999). *The deepening integration of the global economy.* Retrieved August 6, 2004, from http://www.utoronto.ca/cis/cuba.pdf

Pal, L. A., and Seidle, F. L. (1993). Constitutional politics 1990–92: The paradox of participation. In S. Phillips (Ed.), *How Ottawa spends, 1993–94: A more democratic Canada?* (pp. 143–202). Ottawa: Carleton University Press.

Pauly, L. W. (1997). *Who elected the bankers? Surveillance and control in the world economy.* Ithaca: Cornell University Press.

Peters, B. G. (1995). The public service, the changing state, and governance. In B. G. Peters and D. J. Savoie (Eds.), *Governance in a changing environment* (pp. 288–320). Montreal: Canadian Centre for Management Development and McGill-Queen's University Press.

Peters, B. G. (2003). Democracy and political power in contemporary western governments: Challenges and reforms. In T. J. Courchene and D. J. Savoie (Eds.), *The art of the state: Governance in a world without frontiers* (pp. 81–108). Montreal: Institute for Research on Public Policy.

Pollitt, C. (1995). Management techniques for the public sector: Pulpit and practice. In B. G. Peters and D. J. Savoie (Eds.), *Governance in a changing environment* (pp. 203–38). Montreal: Canadian Centre for Management Development and McGill-Queen's University Press.

Porter, M. E. (1990). *The competitive advantage of nations.* New York: Free Press.

Progressive Conservative Party of Ontario. (1995). *The common sense revolution.* Toronto: Progressive Conservative Party of Ontario.

Results for Canadians. (2000). Ottawa. Retrieved August 6, 2004, from http://www.tbs-sct.gc.ca/res_can/rc_1_e.asp#pre

Rheingold, H. (2003) *Smart mobs: The next social revolution.* Cambridge, MA: Perseus Publishing.

Rheingold, H. (2004). From the screen to the streets. *In these times.* Retrieved August 6, 2004, from http://inthesetimes.com/comments .php?id=414_0_1_0_M

Sandel, M. J. (1996). *Democracy's discontent: America in search of a public philosophy.* Cambridge, MA: Harvard University Press.

Sassen, S. (1998). *Globalization and its discontents.* New York: The New Press.

Savoie, D. J. (1995, Spring). What is wrong with the new public management? *Canadian Public Administration, 38,* 112–21.

Scholte, J. A. (2003). *What is globalization: The definitional issue—again.* Institute on Globalization and the Human Condition, McMaster University, Working Paper Series.

Statistics Canada. (2004). *Interprovincial and international exports by province and territory since 1992.* Catalogue no. 11-621-MIE2004011. Retrieved August 6, 2004, from http://www.statcan.ca:8096/bsolc/english/ bsolc?catno=11-621-MIE2004011#formatdisp

Taylor, C. (1994). *Multiculturalism: Examining the politics of recognition.* Princeton: Princeton University Press.

Treasury Board of Canada. (2003). *Plans and priorities. 2003–2004.* Ottawa. Retrieved August 6, 2004, from http://www.tbs-sct.gc.ca/ est-pre/20032004/TBS-SCT/TBS-SCTr34_e.asp#1A

Thurow, L. C. (1996). *The future of capitalism: How today's economic forces shape tomorrow's world.* New York: William Morrow and Co.

Union of International Organizations. (2004). *International organizations and NGOs project.* Retrieved August 6, 2004, from http://www.uia.org/organizations/home.php

United Nations. (2003). *The globalization of human rights.* Geneva: United Nations University Press.

United Nations Conference on Trade and Development. (2003). *World investment report 2003: FDI policies for development: National and international perspectives.* New York and Geneva: United Nations. Retrieved September 14, 2004, from http://www.unctad .org/templates/webflyer.asp?intitemID=2979&lang=1

Vogel, D. (1995). *Trading up: Consumer and environmental regulation in a global economy.* Cambridge, MA: Harvard University Press.

Walker, S. (1998). *The rights revolution: Rights and community in modern America.* New York: Oxford University Press.

Weiss, L. (1998). *The myth of the powerless state.* Ithaca, NY: Cornell University Press.

Young, I. M. (1990). *Justice and the politics of difference.* Princeton, NJ: Princeton University Press.

Chapter 3

Problem Definition in Policy Analysis

Policymaking is in large measure about trying to solve problems, and so the nature of those problems—how they are defined—is central to the entire process. But defining problems is not merely a technical exercise; it entails political and strategic manouevres, insofar as problem definition sets the tone for successive stages in the process. Framing problems draws on a wide variety of ingredients, from scientific expertise to conventional wisdom and rhetoric. In a democracy, it always means shaping arguments in ways that capture public attention and support. This process is connected to interests and institutions, of course, but the study of problem definition and framing clearly underscores the importance of ideas in policymaking. The second part of the chapter explores ways in which both the substance and the process of problem definition are changing in the face of the forces described in Chapter 2.

The core of any public policy is the triad of problem definition, goals, and instruments. Know them, and you know the policy. But if we view policy more dynamically, which of these elements comes first, or what is the prime mover in the policy response? There is universal agreement that the key factor is the problem or at least the definition of a situation considered problematic (Geva-May and Wildavsky 1997, p. 1). As Dunn puts it: "Problem structuring is a central guidance system or steering mechanism that affects the success of all subsequent phases of policy analysis. The reason problem structuring is so important is that policy analysts seem to fail more often because they solve the wrong problem than because they get the wrong solution to the right problem" (Dunn, 2004 p. 72). Policies are responses to problems, and so the character and shape of the problem will deeply affect the nature of the response. At the most extreme, if a problem is not widely recognized at all, there will be little or no policy response. The existence of widespread and systematic poverty in the United States in the late 1950s was largely ignored, for example, until the publication of Michael Harrington's *The Other America: Poverty in the United States* (1962). The same could be said of modern environmentalism; until Rachel Carson's *Silent Spring* (1962), the notion that what we were doing to the environment was a problem simply did not occur to many people. A striking Canadian example comes from research conducted by the Canadian Advisory Council on the Status of Women in 1987 on domestic abuse: the study entitled *Battered but Not Beaten* by Linda MacLeod took something from the shadows of private family life and exposed it as a major social problem. In 2004 there was a sudden burst of reports across North America about the looming "crisis" of obesity. While fat and dieting have been features of contemporary culture for years, obesity suddenly emerged as a policy problem whereas before it had been visible only as a personal issue. In March 2004, for example, the American Centers for Disease Control and Prevention announced that obesity would soon overtake smoking as the leading cause of preventable death, and media were festooned with stories about the connections between obesity and diabetes, the impact on the elderly, and the rising "epidemic" of obesity among the young (linked to sedentary lifestyles, fatty foods, and video games). All of these cases illustrate the fact that policy problems do not simply "exist out there"—they have to be recognized, defined, structured, and made visible.

It would seem that there should be another end of the continuum to complement problem invisibility, a point where problems are so well defined and understood that the policy response seems obvious and uncontroversial. In fact, there are very few of these, at least with respect to proposed solutions. On some issues, such as child pornography, consensus appears overwhelming about both the character of the problem (universally despised) and the solution (a strong prohibition). However, in concrete cases there is still lots of room for debate. For example, in January 2000 the Supreme Court of Canada heard a case involving the possession of what qualifies under the law as child pornography. John Robin Sharpe had been charged with possession of fictional stories and sketches involving minors and sex, had argued his own case in the British Columbia lower courts, and had been acquitted. The Supreme Court listened to arguments in his defence that these materials did no harm to real children and that Canada's child pornography laws were too broad, and in February 2001 basically upheld the law, though with some reservations. So it is clear that problems are not simply either recognized or not: they have to be discerned, shaped, articulated, and defended. There are so many different elements that can conceivably go into a problem definition—including both facts and values—that people may see the same situation quite differently, even if they agree on its general aspects, and so will offer very different solutions.

The idea that people disagree in their perceptions of problems and solutions is hardly news, so it may come as a surprise to learn that until the last decade, policy analysis held out the hope of trying to "get it right," in other words, to achieve the correct definition of the problem. As Rochefort and Cobb (1994) describe it:

> Through the accumulation of information, a troubling social condition comes to light and is documented. Next it is the job of public officials to assess that problem and its causes and to respond as efficiently as possible through such means as new legislative enactments. Attention continues until the distressing concern is alleviated. (p. 56)

As Stone (2002) puts it:

> In conventional policy analysis textbooks, as well as in the larger rationality project, a problem definition is a statement of a goal and the discrepancy between it and the status quo. In this conception, problem definition is a matter of observation and arithmetic—measuring the difference between two states of affairs" (p. 133).

Almost twenty years ago, a leading text could refer to the possibility of making "mistakes" in the problem definition or initiation phase of policy design (Brewer and deLeon 1983, p. 35). The idea of "making mistakes" would strike Stone (2002) as very odd since, to her, problem definition "is a matter of representation because every description of a situation is a portrayal from only one of many points of view . . . [and it] is strategic because groups, individuals, and government agencies deliberately and consciously fashion portrayals so as to promote their favored course of action" (p. 133). When everything is open to interpretation, there is no clearly superior way of discerning a situation, and so all interpretations are equally valid. This explains the problem-saturated policy environment within which we live. The media, interest groups, experts, analysts, think-tanks, and political parties subject us to a constant barrage of crises and problems. Not only is the number of problems apparently large, but also the range of solutions seems bewilderingly wide.

Governments do not have infinite resources or time, however, and every government faces the ultimate test of having to choose among definitions and solutions and doing what it was elected to do—govern. It is this combination of epistemological variety and political reality that shapes the agenda of questions that occupy the literature on problem definition: (1) by what political and intellectual processes are problems defined, (2) what are the generic elements of a problem definition, (3) how are some problems chosen to be on the political/policy agenda while others languish in obscurity, and (4) what impact does problem definition have on subsequent stages of the policy process? The good news is that most of the answers to these questions are interesting and insightful. The bad news is that they are not systematic nor could they really be expected to be. Problem definition has a strong socio-psychological dimension; it is one component in the imaginative construction of reality, with heavy doses of professional skill, creativity, intuition, and serendipity. Moreover, problem definition is embedded in fluid political and policy processes, where accident and luck play a great role. It is not surprising, therefore, that the literature is dominated by case studies that, while interesting themselves, often conclude that "it all depends."

However, the questions, and some of the general answers to them, are worth exploring, if only because they do provide an organized way of thinking about problem definition and formulation. Contemporary policy analysis needs to go beyond this to recognize that some key elements of both the substance and process of problem definition have changed dramatically in the last decade in response to the forces described in Chapter 2. In terms of the substance of public policy problems, **globalization**, diversity, and the role of government in actually causing problems rather than solving them are new parameters within which any policy analysis will have to take place. Recently, some new frames of reference, or what we will term below "**ideas in good currency**" seem to have made inroads in policy debates. The tools needed to deal with policy problems in this new environment are different from those in the past, and this chapter closes with a consideration of the demands this places on analysts.

PROBLEM DEFINITION: KEY ISSUES

What constitutes a problem? The most common definition in the field is that a problem is a "substantial discrepancy between what is and what should be" (Dery, 1984, p. 17), or to put it another way, policy "problems are unrealized needs, values, or opportunities for improvement that may be pursued through public action" (Dunn, 2004, p. 72). There are three components to these definitions: reality (what is, the unrealized needs or values), a desired state of affairs (what should be, the improvement), and the gap between them (the discrepancy). But why should the simple fact of a discrepancy or gap between reality and the ideal constitute a problem? Clearly it does not, and note that the definitions address what should be, and not what could be. There have to be realistic opportunities for improvement. So this is a first clue on the nature of problem definition—it is incomprehensible without some understanding of the goals being pursued or the standards being used to judge "what should be."

If standards are always involved in defining the desired state of affairs, the other key ingredient is discerning the gap or discrepancy. Indeed, this is the first phase in the process of problem definition. Before problems can be defined they have to be recognized or sensed. This is a primordial stage in problem definition in that it usually involves just a first tremor that something is wrong, a sense of unease, that there is a difference between reality and our preferred standard. Strict constructionists (in the sense that all problems are socially constructed) like Deborah Stone (2002) see this as a highly unpredictable and strategic process and, moreover, one that is contingent on core assumptions, world view, and social location. It is widely agreed, however, that values, perceptions, and interests play a huge role in this phase, since recognition depends on attention, and attention depends on relevance and an ability to notice and care about signals coming in from the environment around us. How likely is someone with a secure job who lives a middle-class lifestyle to notice or care about urban homelessness or Aboriginal suicide?

While the role of selective perception has a measure of truth to it, too strong an emphasis on mutually exclusive values tends to underestimate the degree to which some standards whereby we recognize nascent problems and public issues are in fact widely shared and hard-wired into the political process itself. **Problem recognition,** according to Kingdon (1995), is often stimulated by widely agreed-upon **indicators** and routine monitoring that turns up discrepancies or patterns that hint that something is amiss:

> Fairly often, problems come to the attention of government decision makers not through some sort of political pressure or perceptual sleight of hand but because some more or less systematic indicator simply shows that there is a problem out there. Such indicators abound in the political world because both governmental and nongovernmental agencies routinely monitor various activities and events: highway deaths, disease rates, immunization rates, consumer prices, commuter and intercity ridership, costs of entitlement programs, infant mortality rates, and many others. (p. 90)

Kingdon goes on to say that while pressure campaigns and dramatic events are certainly important in attracting notice to a problem, in fact people pay attention "rather straightforwardly because there actually is a demonstrable problem that needs their attention" (p. 93). This occurs in those instances where there is a reasonable degree of consensus about the indicators and what they mean. Canadian debates about poverty, for example, are normally based on the low income cutoffs (LICO) developed by Statistics Canada. These cutoffs, however, were never intended to be a measure of poverty but rather an indicator of when the consumption of an "average" package of goods would become difficult (Sarlo, 1996, chap. 2). Moreover, the LICO is a relative measure—it measures low income as a proportion of income spent on certain goods (food, shelter, and clothing) above what other Canadian families of the same size spend. Another approach is an absolute measure of low income or poverty, which tries to determine what it would take at a minimum to survive. But even here, the definitions of these "market basket measures" can vary from bare necessities to something more elaborate (National Council of Welfare, 2004). Nonetheless, despite debates and a variety of measures, when the numbers of Canadians who fall below the LICO increases, there are immediate concerns about possibly rising poverty in the country. Changes in other indicators such as the gross national product (GNP), the exchange rate, crime statistics, productivity rates, literacy, aging, teenage pregnancies, and smoking (to choose just a few), also convey messages. When the indicator shows a positive development, there is a general sense that "things are going well" (e.g., increases in GNP, productivity, and literacy). When the indicator shows a negative development, this signals that perhaps there is a problem that needs attention (e.g., increases in crime, pregnancies, and smoking).

Indicators come in various forms. Sometimes they are simply routinely produced by programs and government departments—annual reports, unemployment statistics, Statistics Canada data, and government-sponsored research reports and studies. Interest groups, think-tanks, and foundations of course have an interest in either highlighting indicators that support their cause or their orientation or in developing research that casts light on suspicions they have about a given issue or problem. These types of indicators are different from what Kingdon calls "**focusing events**," which can be sudden catastrophes or crises that grab attention. One of the most chilling of these was the SARS (Severe Acute Respiratory Syndrome) epidemic. The first known outbreak occurred in Foshan City, Guangdong Province, China, on November 16, 2002. At that time it was not recognized as SARS, but simply as an unusual respiratory ailment. Almost two months later, the World Health Organization (WHO) received an e-mail describing an unusual contagious disease that had left more than 100 people dead in Guangdong Province. In the next few days, Chinese authorities revealed that some 300 people were ill, and five had died, but that this was simply a case of atypical pneumonia, and that the outbreak was under control. Then followed a series of deaths and illnesses in Hong Kong that were ascribed to avian flu. By the end of the month, there were reports and rumours of as many as fifty hospitals in Guangzhou (in Guangdong Province) with ill patients. The mystery disease began to spread beyond China, as a Canadian woman and an American man both made their way homeward. The American man stopped over and became ill in Hanoi, and by March 5 the Canadian woman was dead in Toronto and five relatives were hospitalized. Still no one knew precisely what the disease was or where and how it was spreading. By mid-March the WHO had given SARS its name and issued a travel advisory on the suspicion that the disease was spreading through international flights. It was not until mid-April that the causative agent in SARS was identified—a completely new coronavirus, unlike any other human or animal member of the coronavirus family (World Health Organization, 2003). The 2003 epidemic affected 8098 people worldwide, of whom 774 died.

SARS was unusual in that it attracted worldwide attention very quickly. By themselves, most focusing events are not so mysterious and dramatic, and usually have to be supplemented by other factors such as a receptive public mood, energetic politicians, interest groups willing to push the issue, or some sense that trends are developing beyond acceptable thresholds. It is in the character of focusing events that they galvanize debate and discussion, but the most that happens at this stage is the development of a sense that there may be a problem that needs attention. Beyond problem recognition or sensing there has to be a phase of problem definition. In the SARS case, this had to be undertaken with a vengeance since the focusing event itself—the spreading illness and death—was completely mysterious. Networks of laboratories were established around the world to develop diagnostics as well as causative agents, so that a cure could be found.

So, as Kingdon and others have pointed out, indicators or events— whether in the form of routine reports or focusing events—have to be interpreted. In themselves they mean relatively little. Another good example is the evolving debate over government deficits and what they meant. The numbers were indisputable and widely accepted—the issue was what those numbers meant, what the underlying causes of deficits were, and what might be done about them. To simplify only slightly, the argument gradually emerged in the 1980s and 1990s that deficits were caused by overspending, were a drag on the economy, and were reaching unsustainable levels. The counterargument—that deficits were an occasionally necessary instrument to stimulate the economy and would self-correct once economic activity took off again—gradually lost force. There now appears to be a broad consensus on both left and right—as demonstrated by Canadian party positions in the 2004 election—that deficits are unacceptable and economically counterproductive. But this consensus, fragile as it is, took almost two decades to develop. The U.S. deficit in 2003 was US$340 billion, the largest in its history. Even while it had been deliberately created in part by Iraq war expenditures and tax cuts, the Administration promised to halve it in five years, while opposition Democrats took it as a symbol of economic mismanagement. A similar process may be under way with respect to debates about Canadian economic productivity and living standards, and the right policies to tackle the problem. Again, the numbers are not in dispute. In 1998 the OECD released a country report on Canada that showed that living standards had deteriorated in comparison with the European average, due largely to lagging productivity rates. Another report showed that the average Canadian worker is only four-fifths as productive as the average American worker (Centre for the Study of Living Standards, 1999). Moreover, the trends indicate that Canadian productivity growth has lagged the United States as well: in the 1990s it was 0.8 percent per year compared to the U.S. rate of 1.0 percent. The pattern was even worse between 2000 and 2004, with productivity in the United States rising to record levels, while in Canada the rate of growth was actually declining (Sharpe, 2004, p. 18). Productivity is the foundation for incomes, and so a debate has been emerging around the causes of this productivity gap and the best ways of addressing it—leading many analysts to argue that investments in human capital, innovation, and technology are the right path.

Problem definition or structuring is the arduous process of taking some indicator that a problem exists—such as lagging productivity or average income—and answering three fundamental questions. The first question is about the indicator itself. Respiratory problems or low productivity rates both indicate a problem, but in each instance the first step is an investigation of the event or the numbers. As we noted above, in the case of a potential epidemic, one might ask questions about patterns of infection, means of transmission, and characteristics of the disease itself. The same is true of productivity rates—do the aggregate rates mask any important trends or differences in different economic sectors? The second question is also about the indicator but now shifts to causality. Why did this happen and how? What matrix of cause and effect is at work? In both of our examples, the central question is why? What is the cause of SARS or low productivity? In the SARS case it might be atypical pneumonia or a completely new strain of a pathogen. In the productivity case, it might be low rates of capital investment, high taxes, cyclical variations, or low levels of innovation and scientific research. Each one of these hypotheses would have to be considered and tested in some fashion. The third question is about what action to take in the event that there is a "real" problem at stake. Is this a problem that can be solved, and who should solve it? Most importantly, is this a problem that government should solve? Is it in the public sphere, or is it a matter either for private initiative or nongovernmental collective action? The answers seem obvious in the case of SARS but perhaps less so in the case of productivity.

It is rare for these questions—particularly the first two on the nature of the indicator and the causal matrix that might underlie it—to be answered in detail except by specialists. The range of specialists that will be engaged in a policy issue will vary with the substance of that issue; economic problems will engage economists, environmental problems will engage experts in biology and environmental sciences, and so on. But policy problems are different from more general research problems in that the objective is to address and if possible solve the problem in some practical way. Accordingly, a key aspect of determining these questions and developing answers to them is what Dunn (2004) calls **"problem structuring"** (p. 72). He points out that some problems are well structured (few decisionmakers and a small set of alternatives), while some are moderately or ill-structured. Ill-structured problems are marked by high levels of uncertainty and competing objectives and alternatives (p. 79). In this case, policy analysis must rely on creativity, insight, and judgment in helping to shape a workable understanding of the problem. Nonetheless, there are generic techniques that can be used to help scope out the nature of a policy problem. Box 3.1 (page 106) outlines some of the major ones described by Dunn. Box 3.2 (page 108) provides a summary of the basic considerations generally defined in the policy literature in addressing problem definition. These techniques and steps are far from infallible, but they do provide some conceptual tools to help move beyond the recognition stage to problem definition and problem structuring, particularly when there are a large number of stakeholders and a variety of different views, assumptions, and arguments about the nature of the problem.

Few of us, however, have the time to be that well acquainted with a problem definition or to apply these techniques independently. Most of us, even in cases where we are quite interested in a given policy issue, will tend to summarize it in what Baumgartner and Jones (1993) call **"policy images."** Policy images are a "mixture of empirical information and emotive appeals" that explain the issue and justify the public policy response (p. 26). Moreover, since these images are shorthand, they convey more than information; they give a sense of the tone of the issue

Box 3.1	METHODS OF PROBLEM STRUCTURING

METHOD	DESCRIPTION
Boundary analysis	This is a technique to canvass the whole range of existing definitions and conceptualizations of a given problem. Involves: (1) saturation sampling: multi-stage process of contacting or canvassing all stakeholders involved in an issue, until no new stakeholders can be added or named, (2) problem representations: develop a full list of all problem representations held by stakeholders, (3) boundary estimation: plot the frequency of new elements added to the problem definition until the frequency of additions approaches zero.
Classification analysis	This involves breaking down the problem phenomenon into logically distinct categories or classes. There is no clear rule about this, but, for example, in addressing the problem of poverty, one would want to go beyond just two classifications (those who fall below the poverty line, and those who do not) to include gender, race, disability, age, and so on. The problem might appear quite differently for different groups (and hence invite different solutions), but we also get a better sense of the causal factors at work with a more complex classification scheme.
Hierarchical analysis	This is a technique for identifying possible causes of a problem. Three classes are used: possible causes, plausible causes, and actionable causes. Possible causes are factors, that, however remote, may have some bearing on the problem. Plausible causes are ones that are more conventionally highlighted in the research or debates on the issue. Actionable causes are ones that can be addressed by governments.

Synectics	This technique relies on the use of analogies to see if new policy problems have sufficiently similar characteristics to older ones that the previous problem definitions and solutions can provide some guidance. For example, in thinking about the legalization of marijuana, one might consider the analogy of Prohibition policies against alcohol in the 1930s.
Brainstorming	A family of techniques, more or less formal, to generate ideas, goals and strategies. Can involve informal and unstructured exchange to scenario writing.
Multiple perspective analysis	Deliberately review the problem situation from three perspectives: (1) the technical perspective: cost-benefit analysis, econometrics, systems analysis, (2) organizational perspective: focus on institutional rules and processes, and the following of standard operating procedures, (3) personal perspective: view problems and solutions in terms of individual perceptions and values.
Assumptional analysis	Aims at developing a synthesis of the different assumptions that stakeholders have about the issue or problem. Involves canvassing the full range of solutions proposed for the issue or problem, and using that as a vehicle for analyzing and challenging the assumptions that underlie the problem definition.
Argument mapping	A technique to map and classify the different components of policy arguments made by stakeholders—components such as arguments based on statistics, on authority, on values, on intuition or judgement.

SOURCE: Dunn, W. N. (2004). *Public policy analysis: An introduction,* 3rd ed. Englewood Cliffs, NJ: Prentice Hall, chap. 3.

Box 3.2

MAJOR CONSIDERATIONS IN PROBLEM DEFINITION

Define the Process
- Regard problem definition as an iterative process;
- Be inventive;
- Work with the client to formulate the problem;
- Don't believe that problems can define all solutions;
- Adopt backward problem definition.

Identify Context and Actors
- Develop an understanding of the decision making context;
- Identify the actors involved;
- Identify your client's needs;
- Consider the public's concerns;
- Consider the values that raise the concern;
- Probe the assumptions implicit in your client's statement;
- Encourage being questioned by the client;
- Be aware that a politician's definition differs from yours.

Identify Variables
- Look for experts' help;
- Search for historical analogies;
- Draw from contemporaneous analogies;
- Package them into 'range of feasible manipulations';
- Limit the number of policy variables.

Identify Policies and Goals
- Differentiate between the two;
- Be explicit about the relevant goals;
- Consider whether implicit goals need to be brought to light.

Decide upon Degree of Complexity
- Examine general as well as specific views;
- Use a mix-scanning technique;
- Avoid forcing problems into generic classifications.

Consider Gathering Data Skills & Strategies	• Develop a data base; • Collect any data that come your way: they may come in handy later; • Be aware that most data are derivative rather than original; • Check your sources of information; • Be cautious of monetary or time baselines, ratios, etc.

SOURCE: Geva-May, I., and Wildavsky, A. (1997). *An operational approach to policy analysis: The craft.* Boston: Kluwer Academic Publishers, p. 37.

in positive or negative terms. Baumgartner and Jones cite the changing tone in the policy image surrounding civilian nuclear power from a largely positive association with economic progress to a negative connotation linked to environmental damage. A policy issue may be framed in various images, depending on the interests and actors in the field. Stable policy fields tend to coalesce around one dominant policy image, and policy challenge and change is largely about mobilization through the "redefinition of the prevailing policy image" (p. 239). We mentioned attitudes toward deficits earlier: it seems likely that a stable policy image has coalesced around the question of deficits in that they are now almost universally considered undesirable.

Problem structuring or definition therefore involves various techniques aimed at probing an issue that has been signalled in some way as a possible policy problem. The process of problem definition is one of shaping a persuasive argument about the nature of the problem and, of course, the solution. Of what does that argument and persuasion consist? Rochefort and Cobb (1994) offer a scheme that captures some of the key elements, summarized in Box 3.3 (page 110).

Not every problem definition or **policy argument** will contain all these characteristics, but most will be present. The definer has to deal with the question of causation. Without an idea of why the problem exists there is no way to figure out what to do about it. The "**causal images**" we use can differ in their emphasis on individual responsibility or systemic sources. Is poverty a result of individual decisions and choices or of large economic forces? Definitions can also differ in the degree of complexity of their causal portraits. Inevitably, however, policy action can be taken only across a narrow range of factors so that the causal assumptions in most policy-relevant problem definitions are usually limited. The severity of the problem is another important

Box 3.3	ASPECTS OF POLICY ARGUMENTS AND PROBLEM DEFINITION
Causality (what kinds of causal factors lie behind the problem?)	• Individual causation versus systemic (the former stresses choices and culpability; the latter stresses impersonal and unavoidable forces). • Intentional versus accidental causes. • Causes due to the nature of values systems. • Complex causal systems versus simple causal agents
Severity (How bad is the problem, and how bad is it likely to get?)	• This distinguishes between the acknowledged existence of a problem (e.g., recession) and how serious it is likely to become. • Severity is usually measured against some backdrop or context, such as trend lines ("this will soon go away" or "this is getting worse"), specific populations ("this is a big problem only for group X"), or what is considered normal or deviant.
Incidence (What is the scope and impact of the problem?)	• Who is affected generally? • What subgroups are affected and how? • What patterns of incidence are most important?
Novelty (Is this new?)	• Is the issue or problem new? • Is it unexpected?
Proximity (How "close" is the problem?)	• This refers to how close a problem "hits home." • Depends on how "home" is defined (i.e., children are valued for any social group's survival, so by definition anything that affects children negatively is bad).

Crisis (How pressing is the problem?)	• Largely a rhetorical device to signal severity and proximity.
Problem populations (Who will be targeted in the policy response?)	• Problem definitions can also define the people who are potential targets of policy interventions. • Deserving vs. undeserving of assistance. • Sympathetic vs. deviant definitions of groups. • Definitions that emphasize capacities vs. those that emphasize dependency.
Instrumental vs. expressive orientations (How important is the process of solving the problem in comparison to the solution itself?)	• Difference between focusing on ends (the instrumental intent to solve the problem) and the means (the degree to which what you do expresses an important symbol or value—e.g., refusing to negotiate with terrorists even if it harms hostages).
Solutions (What can be done?)	• Solutions sometimes actually precede the problem and help shape it (e.g., a commitment to vouchers as a policy instrument to deal with a host of problems). • Are solutions available—can something actually be done to solve a problem, or is action taken merely for its own sake or for symbolism?

SOURCE: Adapted and amended from Rochefort and Cobb. (1994). Problem definition: An emerging perspective. In D. A. Rochefort and R. W. Cobb (Eds.), *The politics of problem definition: Shaping the policy agenda* (pp. 1–31). Lawrence: University of Kansas Press.

characteristic. A problem may be acknowledged, but it might be innocuous enough not to matter in policy terms (e.g., physical fitness of the general population). This often gets connected to the incidence of the problem in the sense of how different groups in the population are affected. Concerns about violence against women or date rape focus on the incidence and severity of these phenomena on women.

Novelty, proximity, and crisis are all elements that help heighten the urgency of a problem. The way in which a problem definition portrays potential target populations of policy interventions has received more attention in recent years (Schneider and Ingram, 1997) on the sound assumption that policies are more than just instruments for solving problems. Policies also convey signals about how policymakers picture recipients of government programs. Welfare programs are typically paternalistic, conveying the image that welfare recipients cannot plan their own lives and must be watched carefully for fraud. Premier Mike Harris once famously defended his welfare reforms on the grounds that they would ensure that welfare moms would not spend their cheques on beer. This is another aspect of the symbolic or expressive dimension of policy. Often what matters most about a problem is not whether it *can* be solved or managed but *how* it will be solved or managed. This is because of the simple fact that what we do (in this case, collectively as a political community) says much about who we are.

We can apply some of these categories to our two earlier examples of SARS and productivity rates. Obviously, causality is a key element in both, though it remains murky. This may seem odd in the SARS case, since the virus was eventually identified. But this is an epidemiological cause; the problem of the *epidemic* was due to how it was contained and dealt with, and this was more a matter of hospital, health, and immigration organization. China, for example, was widely blamed for not reporting the first cases for months. In Toronto, there were complaints about the emergency response system and the practice of rotating nurses among hospitals (thus potentially spreading the disease). The severity of SARS was acutely high, since people died and the economic impact was devastating; the productivity question is less immediate even though it might be of fundamental economic importance. The incidence of SARS in North America was limited to Toronto in the end, but the fear at the time was that it might spread, and spread rapidly. Thus while it remained a local problem, it had national and even international dimensions. The productivity and wealth question affects the whole of society. In terms of novelty, the SARS tragedy was unexpected and frightening. This added to the sense of crisis. The productivity question has been building for some time, and enjoyed a spike in news coverage and attention around 2001–02, but since then has not been prominent, despite discouraging trends. Neither of these issues hinges on a problem population, though the elderly were more at risk with SARS. The SARS issue forced consideration of procedural questions—testing and the appropriate protocols for health authorities and the WHO. There is no expressive dimension to the productivity puzzle. Finally, SARS was susceptible to a "solution" for two reasons. First, the pressure was intense because of the nature of the epidemic. The fact that it was an international crisis mobilized international resources through the WHO to track its source. Second, quarantine and immigration controls could plausibly contain the epidemic, even if they could not cure the disease. In the case of productivity, the causal matrix is so complex that ready solutions are hard to come by.

There is no science of problem definition, and providing the sort of checklist found in Box 3.3 is at best an approximation of the elements that go into the process of persuading others that a problem exists and that it should be addressed. What is clear, however, is that much of the time the process of problem recognition and definition is one of making arguments and persuading others (Majone, 1989). **Constructivists** emphasize that there can be no absolutely conclusive proof of anything outside a shared paradigm of understandings. Within those worlds, of course, according to their own canons, it is possible to make a case that will be widely judged as "more true" than the next. Across those worlds, different values and standards of evidence and persuasion will make it difficult to come to firm and widely accepted conclusions. However, there is neither an infinite variety of conceptual paradigms nor of standards of what constitutes good argument. While rhetoric and presentation are always important, there are both inherent constraints within issues themselves, as well as broadly shared understandings at any given point in time that form a common backdrop for the debate about public policy issues. Dunn's (2004) illustrations of boundary analysis show that, for example, in asking a group of twenty people what criteria they use to judge the severity of a problem (e.g., cost, social impact), the number of criteria are not infinite. The first person asked might list a dozen criteria. The second person, in adding new ones, might offer eight. And so on, until no one can think of any more to add. The "boundary" or complete set of criteria is reached fairly quickly. People will still disagree over weights and interpretation, but they do so on a foundation of commonly agreed criteria, which is an important first step.

In another example, Milward and Laird (1996) examined five cases of agenda-setting (supply-side economics, the greenhouse effect, child abuse, drunk driving, and comparable worth) and argued that the way in which an issue is framed is "critically important to the success of the issue on the public agenda" (p. 63). Some of these issues, such as child abuse and drunk driving, were clearly framed, and this clarity contributed to their success on the public policy agenda. "A clearly framed issue is one that succinctly states what the problem is in plausible terms and embodies an easily understood solution" (p. 64). Moreover, issues are not infinitely malleable but have characteristics that make them more or less amenable to clear framing. Supply-side economics, for example, is difficult to personalize, but child abuse and drunk driving both leave victims that can put a human face directly onto a policy problem. Issues that are driven by powerful underlying demographics, such as pensions today because of the greying of the boomers, develop an urgency that can move them up the agenda quite rapidly. The same is true of issues that have no credible opposition. As Milward and Laird argue, there are no "spokespersons for 'killer drunks' or child abusers" (p. 70).

Issue framing or problem definition consequently has two dimensions. The first is analytical and emphasizes the logical elements that make up an argument or claim. William Dunn (1993; 2004, chap. 1, 8), for example, offers a schema to decipher the different statements that comprise any policy argument. *Policy-relevant information* (I) is the data or evidence at the policy analyst's disposal. A *policy claim* (C) is the conclusion of the policy argument, usually in the form of a recommendation on how to tackle the problem. A *warrant* (W) is an assumption that permits the analyst to move from the information to the claim. Warrants come in different forms—appeals to authority, to intuition, to values, and so on. *Backings* (B) are statements that provide support for warrants or neutralize possible criticisms or objections. Finally, *qualifiers* (Q) are statements that express the degree of confidence or certainty in the policy claim (e.g., "very likely" or "probably").

Take the question of legalization of marijuana, possession of which is currently a criminal office in Canada and the United States. The policy-relevant information (I) in this instance would consist of medical evidence on the impact of marijuana use, the costs of enforcement, the rate of arrests for different groups, the effect of criminal records, number of illegal grow houses and so on. Those in favour of decriminalization would make that policy claim (C), based on several possible warrants (W): everyone uses it, whether it is legal or not; recreational use does not lead to addiction or impaired health, at least not any more than reasonable alcohol consumption; government has no role in regulating a substance like this. Backing (B) would come from statements producing evidence or arguments to support the warrant in question, and qualifiers (Q) would indicate the likelihood of a surge in addictions or drug use. Those opposing decriminalization would begin with much the same information (I), but of course make a completely opposite policy claim (C). The warrants (W) might be empirical (e.g., relaxation of controls will lead to a surge in use; the negative health effects are not negligible; the difficulty of enforcing regulations), or moral (e.g., society is already too hedonistic). Backing (B) and qualifiers (Q) would be adduced to make the case stronger. As Dunn points out, understanding the structure of policy arguments helps us understand that often the same policy-relevant information (I) can lead to very different claims (C), based on different assumptions, values, and perspectives on the evidence (W). This is precisely what happened when a study was released in Canada in 2004 recommending the legalization of marijuana and its taxation to generate some $2 billion in revenues (Easton, 2004).

Policy arguments can also be viewed from the perspective of rhetoric. In this view, the analytical statements are less important than structural elements of language that stimulate almost unconscious reactions to the argument. For example, there is growing interest in the way in which policy arguments are actually framed as narratives or as stories. We are all familiar with certain archetypal "story lines," and a policy argument that can tap into one of these draws on the power of the narrative structure itself. Arguments about social policy and the deficit, for example, can be seen as "redemption stories." In the past, goodwill and good intentions built a welfare state to meet important needs, but then temptation led us astray and we indulged in excesses and financial debauchery. Our problems got worse, but we ignored them and continued our profligate ways. Now the only option is a complete renunciation of our past sins, and with much pain and suffering we will be redeemed. No wonder finance ministers have sounded like preachers in recent years. Their "narrative line" has been about nothing less than weakness, temptation, and eventual, if painful, redemption. In the new millennium, the story line is shifting from punishment to reward. After years of sacrifice and high taxes, now that the deficit has been eliminated, ordinary citizens deserve rewards for their suffering. Part of this reward story—as told by critics of government—is that those governments would rather hold back the reward and spend the money themselves for political gain. Demands for tax cuts coming from the right depend on policy-relevant information and good argumentation, but this rhetorical narrative gives their policy claims a considerable boost.

Consider the way in which certain words are used to tilt meaning and stimulate reactions. **Labels** are summary words that convey subtle but powerful meanings: "axis of evil" versus "enemies," "gay" versus "homosexual," "homeless" versus "vagrant," "user fee" versus "tax," "sex-worker" versus "prostitute," "pro-life" versus "anti-abortion." Intense policy battles are often fought over labels, because labels are often the first way in which the public is acquainted with a policy issue. **Metaphors** are another weapon in the linguistic arsenal. Consider some of the most famous: Cold War, Iron Curtain, Third World, pork barrel, social safety net, spaceship Earth, global village, and of course, war metaphors such as the War on Poverty, line in the sand, and so on—and these do not even include the ubiquitous sports metaphors! What Dunn calls synectics (see Box 3.1)—the use of analogies to think through the nature of policy problems—also has its rhetorical dimension in the use of metaphors. If people accept that spanking "is *like* child abuse," a good deal of the policy argument has been won. To return to marijuana, whether it is "*like* alcohol" or "*like* cocaine" will tilt the policy argument in very different directions. Medical analogies also can sway thinking: epidemic, quarantine, virus, infection, health.

As Kingdon (1995) points out, getting people to see new problems or see old ones in new ways, "is a major conceptual and political accomplishment" (p. 115). At any given time, there is a host of problems competing for public attention. Some are old and familiar, some are new twists on old issues, and a very few are completely new. The first hurdle is the one mentioned earlier, of providing persuasive indicators that something of importance is actually going on. The next step is a fuller description or definition that will likely take into account some or all of the elements outlined in boxes 3.1, 3.2, and 3.3. A critical aspect of this process is one that was briefly alluded to earlier: defining the problem as one that falls in the public sphere, and indeed as a problem to which the government can offer a credible and feasible response. Even if successful in all this, however, the problem still has to be positioned high enough on the public agenda to receive attention. This is the process of **agenda-setting.** Why do some problems or issues get onto the agenda when others do not, and what explains the relative positions of issues on that agenda?

We already have referred to the importance of issue-framing, and to the vague but important principle of some broad public consensus that determines which ideas (and issues) are plausible and important. At any given time, the number of such "ideas in good currency" as Donald Schon (1971) termed them, is quite limited. They change slowly, and lag behind present circumstances, but provide a point of reference for policy debates. According to Schon, beneath every policy debate "there is a barely visible process through which issues come to awareness and ideas about them become powerful" (p. 123). Some examples of ideas in good currency from the 1950s included competition with the Russians, the space race, and basic research. Certainly the 1990s list would have included competition, sustainable development, and fiscal prudence. The new millennium seems to have generated a few of its own ideas in good currency: tax cuts, investment in health care, and the idea of social capital (relations of trust and reciprocity in society that provides the underpinning for economic performance and social cohesion) security. Kingdon (1995) captures much the same idea with the notion of the **"national mood"**:

> People in and around government sense a national mood. They are comfortable discussing its content, and believe that they know when the mood shifts. The idea goes by different names—

the national mood, the climate of the country, changes in public opinion, or broad social movements. But common to all of these labels is the notion that a rather large number of people out in the country are thinking along certain common lines, that this national mood changes from one time to another in discernible ways, and that these changes in mood or climate have important impacts on policy agendas and policy outcomes. (p. 146)

Baumgartner and Jones (1993; also see True, Jones, and Baumgartner, 1999), while emphasizing the turbulence and change in American politics, note also that periods of policy stability are marked by substantial consensus over policy images: "One of the clearest findings from our research is the extent to which a prevailing conception of a policy issue dominates both press coverage and official behavior during periods when policy subsystems are especially strong" (p. 238).

Ideas in good currency and the policy images that dominate a given policy field at any given time help clarify the boundaries and constraints in agenda-setting. The political system as a whole can handle only a limited number of ideas at one time. It is rare for new ideas to come out of nowhere. Fresh policy proposals typically are framed in ways that resonate with existing ideas in good currency, but, if they fail, they drop off the agenda into a sort of twilight zone for policy innovations that might be mobilized again later, when the opportunity affords itself. This process of ideas struggling for attention and then fading away has supported the image of an agenda-setting cycle where issues arise, enjoy some intensive debate and perhaps success, and then gradually fall off. An early and influential example of this image was Anthony Downs's "issue attention cycle" (1972), but a cyclical image underpins most discussions of agenda-setting. Baumgartner and Jones (1993) have borrowed the idea of "punctuated equilibrium" to convey a process that simultaneously combines long stable periods of policy consensus followed by bursts of change around new issues and new policy images. Research on Canadian data shows little evidence for either an issue attention cycle or for punctuated equilibria, possibly because the parliamentary system gives "extensive agenda-setting powers to governments by, among other things, curtailing public and media access to information" (Howlett, 1997, p. 27; also see Soroka, 2002).

A great deal of the agenda-setting process is contingent on unpredictable factors and personalities, or as Kingdon puts it, the "opening of policy windows." Windows sometimes open regularly (e.g., cabinet shuffles and budget speeches), but who jumps through successfully or not is still a matter of chance and skill. It is clear that some issues are driven onto the agenda by fundamental characteristics of a political community and economy itself: in Canada, for example, the perennial questions of Quebec and of our relationship to the United States. Modern welfare states have a wide range of important redistributive social programs that are of vital importance to recipient groups (e.g., pensions and the elderly), and so issues of this type are usually high on the public agenda. Massive changes in economic circumstances, or powerful shifts in technology, also have a way of rippling through the political system and generating issues for public discussion. But these structural explanations can illuminate only the broad shape of the public agenda. Much depends on political jockeying, **policy entrepreneurs,** and combinations of complex and unpredictable forces. The best that one can hope for in this field is a grasp of the institutions and the routines they generate (Howlett, 1998), the actors, and the opportunities, as well as the importance of shaping a coherent problem definition. As we will argue shortly, however, the dynamics and circumstances of problem definition have changed significantly in the last decade, and some of the old assumptions no longer apply.

What is the relation of problem definition to policy solutions? The conventional argument in the literature is that the way in which a problem is defined has a dramatic impact on the proposed solutions. At one level this makes sense: if you have to hit a nail, use a hammer, or something that hammers, which could just as easily be a shoe or a brick. Problem definition shapes solutions primarily because of the causal explanations that are its heart. Unemployment, for example, is a problem, but to deal with unemployment we need to know what causes it. If it is due to an international recession, there is not much the government can do to insulate the economy. If it is due primarily to a skills shortage, then the answer may be training programs. According to Statistics Canada (1996) 22 percent of Canadian adults fall in the lowest category of literacy (defined as having difficulty reading a product label), but how to deal with this? Better early education? Better diagnosis of persons with reading disabilities? Adult literacy programs? The solution would depend on the fundamental causes at work.

There are, nonetheless, important variances between problem definition and solutions. First, problems are not always so easily defined. Many social problems are "squishy" in that they don't lend themselves to mathematical formulation and are politically controversial (Strauch, 1976, p. 134), or "messy" in that they are deeply entangled with other problems (Ackoff, 1976, p. 21). The less clear the causal underpinnings of a problem, or the more irreducibly complex a problem appears, the less likely unique solutions can be derived from the definition. Second, even if the causal connections are clear, it is not always feasible to deal with "root" causes. Sometimes, Band-Aid solutions are all that we have. Third, most problem definitions deal with clusters of issues and raise questions about what governments should do across a range of options. This poses the question of what combination of solutions to apply and what emphasis government should place on any single solution. Just as there is no science of problem definition, there is no clear science of solutions.

PROBLEM DEFINITION: BEYOND OLD CATEGORIES

The preceding section sketched out the conventional theories of problem definition and agenda-setting. But, as Chapter 2 argued, the context within which policy analysis is practised today has changed substantially, and some of the key assumptions about the reality to which these theories apply—the substance as well as process of problem definition and agenda-setting—need to be re-examined. This section comes at problem definition and agenda-setting from this angle: what are the implications of globalization, culture shift, and governance for the ways in which we define public policy problems? Problem definition cannot be easily disentangled from the other phases of the policy process, but this chapter will concentrate on the emerging societal policy agenda and ideas in good currency. More detailed aspects of policy design, implementation, and evaluation will be taken up in subsequent chapters.

THE EMERGING POLICY AGENDA

With a new context for policymaking, we should expect both a new agenda and a new sense of the sources of policy problems. One of the most important changes in the sources of policy problems is that many of them are now generated beyond our borders due to the phenomenon of globalization. As was argued in Chapter 2, the dynamics of globalization and internationalization mean that borders are much more permeable. But that permeability is coupled with a new level of integration in the international political economy. It is important not to exaggerate this phenomenon. There have been many areas of public policy in the past—finance, communications, foreign policy, agriculture, trade, to name a few—that have traditionally been highly exposed to international forces and tightly integrated into international systems. By the same token, there remain many policy areas today that will continue to be insulated from the direct influence of these international forces or systems, for example, health care, social security, or overland transportation. Rather, what has happened is that the intensity of international exposure has increased in many policy fields traditionally marked by global influences, and a host of other areas have been indirectly affected by these wider forces. Policymaking systems have essentially shifted away from a preponderant concern about problems generated domestically within national borders to problems generated internationally. The policy challenge is how to respond to these new types of problems. While globalization takes pride of place in the new pantheon of sources of policy challenges, it is not alone. Technology is another obvious candidate, both in its own terms and because of its close connection to globalization. And most recently, the issues of international terrorism and epidemics are much on the public mind.

One window on the range of policy challenges posed by these and other phenomena is the Policy Research Initiative (PRI) discussed in Chapter 1. The PRI was launched in 1996 as a network of over thirty federal government departments and agencies that would reach out to the wider policy research community and identify key pressure points most likely to create policy challenges in the future. Four research networks were then established, and two reports emerged from this early work. The first report was on *Growth, Human Development, and Social Cohesion* (Policy Research Initiative, 1996) and emerging challenges to the year 2005. It set the context by noting that Canada might very well be entering a new postwar phase of economic development:

> The period after the early 1970s, which could be called the era of globalization, has been much less felicitous for Canada. It has been characterized by two trends: increasing international integration and declining public expectations because of weakening economic performance. First, the oil crises brought home the growing interdependence of nations, economies and societies, and the inability of any one nation to insulate itself from outside shocks. Inexplicable then, and still not well understood, an abrupt decline occurred in most western economies in the productivity growth that had led postwar expansion. At the same time, international competition proved relentless; individuals, firms and governments found themselves compelled to adapt to new pressures. . . . Based on the expectations of the first postwar period, countries undertook bold experiments in public policy to try to maintain an expected rate of progress. But the underlying economic performance did not sustain these expectations. . . . As this century draws to an end, Canadian expectations seem to be painfully falling in line with the ability of the economy to support them. Apart from unemployment, the other symptoms of the failures of the period—inflation, deficits and debt—are being brought under control. The private sector is adapting, if still somewhat grudgingly, to technological and competitive pressures. The appetite for the kind of bold

policy initiatives that were common earlier in the period appears to have been lost. . . . Some evidence gives reason to believe that the difficult growth-slump period may be coming to a close. A knowledge-based change in the economy appears to have begun. Knowledge-based growth, with its dependence on highly educated and adaptable workers, will have an impact on future economic and social development. Whether it will be the key to reversing the trends in economic performance, or just a change which fails to live up to its billing, is still to be determined. (Policy Research Initiative, 1996)

The report then went on to identify five underlying forces that will drive change in the Canadian economy and society over the medium and long term. Three of them are international in scope, and while public policy may help Canadians respond, for the most part it "will do little to shape the underlying forces themselves." The first key factor was globalization and North American integration. As we noted in Chapter 2, economic globalization means a wider scope and depth of global economic transactions and pressures, but the primary manifestation of globalization for Canada is increasing economic integration with and dependence on the American market. The second factor was technological change and the information revolution. The third factor was environmental pressures. The collapse of the Atlantic cod fishery, the threats to the Pacific salmon fishery, and global warming are just three examples of a heightened sense that the planetary ecology is more fragile than we once thought. The fourth factor was demographic. The Canadian baby boomers account for almost two-thirds of the population, and they are aging. Fertility rates have plummeted, and the overall growth of the population has declined to 1 percent per year. Net population growth now depends exclusively on immigration, and immigration patterns have shifted from a reliance on Western Europe to Asia and the Middle East (accounting in 1994 for 64 percent of immigrants). If these trends continue, by 2016 one in five Canadians will be a visible minority. The fifth factor was the fiscal context, though more in terms of the level of public debt than of the deficit.

The second report produced by the PRI networks (1997) was *Canada 2005: Global Challenges and Opportunities;* in twelve chapters it provided an overview of the changing international context and the domestic and foreign policy challenges they pose. The end of the Cold War completely reconfigured the international balance of power, leaving the United States as the only superpower but one increasingly surrounded by a more complex array of states and regions exercising influence—and sometimes threats—through military and economic means. Global markets, population movements, international crime, terrorism, climate change, ethnic conflicts—the potential stew of pressures is a daunting one. In addition, the report highlighted two cross-cutting issues with potentially "deadly" consequences for Canada: the gradual decline in sovereignty and state power and the continued integration of the North American economy.

By 2004 the PRI research agenda had evolved to focus on five broad themes, themes that built to a large extent on the ones identified earlier in its mandate: population aging and life-course flexibility, poverty and exclusion, social capital, North American linkages, and sustainable development. The next four pages provide a flavour of each of these research themes with direct excerpts (Policy Research Initiative, 2004):

Population Aging and Life-Course Flexibility

For decades, there has been much apprehension about the negative effects of aging populations. Around the world, headlines have warned that we will not be able to afford the growing costs of pensions and health care.

And, indeed, deep change can be expected in the coming years. For decades now, the proportion of the total Canadian population that is employed has been growing. That, along with productivity growth, has contributed to our increasing levels of material well-being. In five to ten years time, that will change when the baby-boom generation starts retiring in earnest . . . [at that time] the proportion of the population employed will then flatten out or fall.

If left unchanged, social policies are likely to re-enforce the negative effects of that exodus from the labour market—reducing the growth of material well-being, adding to labour shortages and placing even greater pressures on the time available for mid-career learning, child-care and elder care. Current social policies have, on balance, favoured more time in schooling, more time in retirement, and less time in work. They have helped squeeze work into the middle years of life. In other words, the potential challenge is easy to see. . . .

However, in the last few years, countries around the developed world are beginning to understand that the policy changes that are required to prevent a shrinking labour supply do not have to be painful. If well designed, they could bring many social as well as economic benefits. Win-win gains are possible by tapping into a huge pool of under-used time. There has been a dramatic growth in recent decades in the time that is spent in leisure among older people, where it is mainly passive and often unwanted. People have been retiring earlier and, once retired, are living much longer and healthier lives.

New Approaches to Addressing Poverty and Exclusion

As in all developed countries, Canada's policies for tackling poverty and exclusion consist of a mix of taxes, transfers and services aimed at the population as a whole, supported by special measures aimed at those who are unemployed, or who are unable or not expected to work. Governments at all levels play an important role. Taken as a whole, and compared with many other countries, the Canadian system works well. The system has evolved gradually towards the traditional goal of a guaranteed annual income, using a targeted approach that encompasses both transfers and the tax system—along with a strong system of public health care and education. In terms of poverty, that evolution is perhaps most advanced for retired people, where Canada has one of the best—perhaps the best—systems in the world for addressing low incomes among seniors.

Progress has, of course, been uneven. And, since poverty and exclusion are relative concepts, policy will always have to deal with the most disadvantaged groups in society. The Government of Canada, for example, currently places high priority on addressing challenges in the Aboriginal communities and among poor children . . . [because] persistent low-incomes are highly concentrated in high at-risk groups. These are people with work-related disabilities, recent immigrants, single mothers, unattached older people (until they reach pension age), and Aboriginal peoples.

Throughout the OECD world, there has been much new thinking about policies that could address poverty and exclusion in a more effective manner.

Increasingly, the problem has been formulated not only as the lack of income at a single point in time in a person's life, but rather in terms of persistent lack of income and other resources that are needed to enable people to participate in mainstream economy and society. This perspective is often reflected in the greater use of the terminology of social exclusion, rather than of more traditional concepts of poverty that were based on income alone.

Social Capital as a Public Policy Tool

People and communities with good access to a diverse mix of social capital tend to be more 'hired, housed, healthy and happy.' Although views about the precise definition of social capital differ, social capital is essentially about the ways in which one's social relationships provide access to needed information, resources and supports.

Public policy interest in social capital has grown worldwide in recent years. The concept has been linked to a broad range of issues including health, labour market outcomes, immigrant integration and diversity management, poverty and social exclusion, crime and safety, neighbourhood revitalization and civic renewal.

Efforts to harness the concept of social capital for policy and program development have been limited by conceptual ambiguities and measurement difficulties. If social capital is to become a practical concept for policy use, we need to operationalize it in a way that allows us to concretely identify what it is, explore its productive potential in achieving broader policy objectives, and identify policy levers for affecting the way it is accumulated and utilized.

North American Linkages

Maximizing the benefits associated with being a part of the North American economic space, while simultaneously safeguarding the Canadian "way," has been a key policy concern for Canada in recent decades. This challenge has become central to Canada's policy agenda since the implementation of the Canada–U.S. Free Trade Agreement (FTA, 1989), and the North American Free Trade Agreement (NAFTA, 1994), and continues to dominate the policy agenda today.

To help define and understand the challenges and opportunities associated with the evolving economic integration of Canada and the United States, the PRI is conducting four inter-related research projects.

- International Regulatory Co-operation
- Moving Toward a Customs Union
- Cross-Border Regions
- North American Labour Mobility

Sustainable Development

More than 15 years after the phrase sustainable development (SD) was first coined, and ten years after Canada and the international community made strong commitments to SD at the Rio Earth Summit, little progress has been made. At the domestic level, research suggests most large Canadian cities are maladapted to newer realities, production and consumption patterns are unsustainable, freshwater issues pose serious challenges, and market signals need to be improved to reflect the environmental and social impacts of economic activity.

The PRI is working with federal government departments and other partners to complete a first round of projects on governance, trade and environment, and corporate social responsibility. Simultaneously, the PRI has embarked on a process of redefining the federal government's medium-term research priorities on sustainable development.

The PRI teamed with the International Institute for Sustainable Development (IISD) in 2002 to conduct a scanning exercise that identified SD issues (other than climate change) in greatest need of policy research. Seven key areas were identified as having particular importance for Canada. The publication of the PRI-ISSD report marks the completion of the first phase of our SD project. Consultations are underway on a proposal to study how the federal government could best implement and promote integrated freshwater management policies in Canada.

It is clear that the core preoccupations remain much the same: human capital, demographics, globalization/North Americanization, and the environment, but in a more focused form. It is important to realize that the PRI addresses the non-security, non-defence policy agenda; these latter areas are covered by specialized agencies dealing with international affairs. Nonetheless, the PRI provides one lens on the emerging and long-term policy issues that face the country.

IDEAS IN GOOD CURRENCY

We noted in the first section of this chapter that problem definition is a crucial phase in the policy process but that it is not unconstrained. Better or worse arguments can be made, and not all issues can be addressed simultaneously. Moreover, there is a rhythm to the agenda-setting process wherein issues rise and fall (and maybe rise again!) and jostle for position. A good deal of the success of policy entrepreneurs and policy communities in getting their issues on the agenda depends on good luck and political skill, but luck and skill have to be placed against the backdrop of what Schon calls "ideas in good currency" or others term the "public mood." The two are not quite the same, since ideas in good currency may not necessarily reflect (at least in the first instance) a groundswell of public opinion. Indeed, the public mood might be influenced by a sense of changes in important structuring ideas, ideas that many people might at first find unfamiliar or even disagreeable, but that over time they will come to accept as a standard of importance and plausibility. The evolution of the sense of what constitutes "national security" in the face of terrorism since 9/11 is a case in point.

Any list of such core ideas will have a strong dose of subjectivity to it, but at the same time, if the concept of ideas in good currency has any validity at all, a well-constructed list should "sound right" to most people who hear it. First, consider what might plausibly have been a list from the 1970s and early 1980s, before the influence of the Reagan revolution in the United States and its echo in the Mulroney regime, and just around the time of the passage of the Canadian Charter of Rights and Freedoms. Its central tone or themes were equity, cooperation, a strong national government, "made in Canada" solutions, social justice, and social needs. While being careful not to exaggerate—after all, despite their conservative sabre-rattling, the Mulroney Conservatives passed employment equity legislation and more than doubled the federal debt—it is clear that the mid-1980s was a transition period to something with a different emphasis. Certainly, from the vantage point of 2005, the flavour and tone of what counts as "common sense" in public policy has changed dramatically. Note, however, that it is a matter of tone and emphasis and not of a complete sea change in public discourse. As most analysts cited in the first section of this chapter argue, new ideas do not completely displace old ones in public discourse, and indeed some of the older ones float in a purgatory of lost causes, to ascend again to political heaven when the time is propitious.

While these major changes have affected almost everything that governments do (and we will be looking at these effects in later chapters), at the level of ideas in good currency, the single most important change has been in the perceptions surrounding the fiscal capacities of government. In policymaking, of course, as in most things, bucks always matter. But what has changed dramatically is the sense of how many bucks governments have and what they should do with them. It has been a change, however, not simply in rhetoric, but in reality as well. Canadian governments since the mid-1960s, when they launched major, expensive social programs such as Medicare and the Canada Pension Plan, and certainly since the oil crisis and inflation of the mid-1970s, have constantly wrung their hands and worried publicly about rising deficits and overspending. While they took periodic and often quixotic action on the budgetary front—with perhaps first prize for budgetary bluster going to the Mulroney Conservatives in their almost decade-long, and ultimately futile fight against the deficit—deficits continued to rise. The last time the total government sector in Canada (on a national accounts basis) was in surplus was in 1974 (Doern, Maslove, and Prince, 1988, p. 17). By 1992, Canada had the second-highest level of total government debt as a percent of gross domestic product (GDP) after Italy (Purchase and Hirshhorn, 1994, p. 29). Through the 1980s, Canadian governments continued to borrow to cover their deficits, piling up the public debt (even as they raised taxes) as interest rates began to climb and economic performance slowed. In this sense, the deficit was "structural" rather than "cyclical" in that the debt itself was so large that not even an economic upturn would do much to reduce interest payments. The key policy consequence of a willingness to run deficits was the absence of a need to make hard choices among programs, or cut ones that did not seem to work.

That, at least, is the narrative that now suffuses public opinion on government spending and certainly has been the leitmotif in budget-cutting exercises at the provincial and federal levels since the early 1990s. While in the 1980s there used to be debate about whether the deficit was a "real problem" or whether it was merely an artifact of high interest rates, a sluggish economy, and tax privileges for the wealthy, by the late 1990s all political tendencies, both left and right, agreed that deficits were bad. The debate then shifted to ways of dealing with it, either on the expenditure side (which most governments have done), the revenue side (some arguing for higher taxes on corporations and the middle class, while most governments have opted for revenue generation through various fees and charges), or lower interest rates. The shift in what Kingdon calls the "national mood," along with government determination to reflect that mood (or lead it), has been remarkable. By mid-1996, seven of ten provinces had balanced budgets. Saskatchewan and Alberta led the way, and the first Ontario budget in 1996 echoed the importance of deficit elimination (the Harris government cut the provincial deficit by $3 billion or 27 percent in its first year in office). The picture was broadly similar in 2004. The federal government, and all provinces except Ontario, Newfoundland, and P.E.I. announced balanced or surplus budgets. The idea of "fiscal prudence" was in such good currency that all four major national political parties pledged during the 2004 election campaign that they would not run deficits.

The effects of this new emphasis on the fisc, or the national treasury, in problem definition have been profound (we will revisit the effects on other stages in the policy process in later chapters). If the deficit is the problem, then it implies the government itself is a problem, since the deficit is a reflection of government activity and management. No ministerial musings on the deficit, from Canada to the United Kingdom to New Zealand, have been complete without an explicit attack on the style of government that produced it. The ferocity with which government itself is attacked as a source of problems varies from conservatives to liberals, but the general view is that at a minimum, government should "get itself right," and in doing so will provide the best "solution" to its own negative impact on the economy and society.

With the virtual elimination of deficits across the country (though they may return with a vengeance, as they did for Ontario in its 2004 budget), the nature of policy debate changed as well. In an era of surpluses, the issue became whether these surpluses should be "invested" in new programs or returned to taxpayers through tax cuts. Predictably, the right urged tax cuts, while the left urged new spending, and the national Liberals did a little of both. By 2004 the nature of debate changed again, as the newly formed Conservative Party of Canada claimed that federal budget projections actually hid the true size of the surplus, and so there was additional fiscal room for more spending (Conservative Party of Canada, 2004). It promised a combination of tax cuts and new spending that amounted to $57.8 billion, including $7 billion to the military, $10.2 billion in transfers to the provinces for health care, and even $2.8 billion for a new national pharmacare program. This combination of new spending with tax cuts was new for the right, though routine in the previous national budgets. Whereas the deficit issue in the late 1990s drove a focus on spending cuts and government efficiency, the situation only five years later was more forgiving, and governments do feel some scope for program spending. But the key idea that governments should not go into deficit remains a strong one, and was reinforced in early 2004 with allegations of spending scandals and out-of-control programs such as the national gun registry. If anything, these probably reinforced the public mood in favour of fiscal prudence, efficiency, and program effectiveness.

It is in the nature of democratic governance that there will typically be differences in opinion about public policy and hence relatively few ideas or policy images that command wide consensus. However, we might mention five others that approach the solidity of support enjoyed by the idea of fiscal prudence among the public. The first is perhaps the most obvious—globalization. The consensus here is not on the desirability of convergence or integration—there is sensible disagreement about how far Canada should go in accepting globalization—but rather with respect to the inevitability of global pressures and the sense of a multipolar and multithreat world. Canadians know that globalization is a powerful reality and has to be dealt with across a variety of policy fronts, from defence to peacekeeping to working with the United States. The second is the importance of health care. Every poll in recent years has shown that health care is a top concern for most Canadians. Again, there is room for legitimate disagreement over how to deliver health care services, but health care itself is a major priority. The third is the importance of reform to our democratic institutions. At both the national and provincial levels, there has been a wave of small and large reforms, as well as rhetoric about more to come. British Columbia has experimented with open Cabinet meetings and is considering proportional representation, as is Quebec. In June 2004 Ontario announced that it was moving to fixed election periods (the first Thursday in October every four years), and even has a minister responsible for democratic renewal. All major federal parties have pledged institutional reforms as well. The fourth is the importance of the environment. Public support for environmentalism waxes and wanes, but it is clear that there has been a secular increase in sensibility toward ecological damage and the responsibility that citizens and governments have toward protecting the environment. The final one is a new consensus around the need to deal with security issues and international terrorism. Again, there is room for disagreement, for example, on the war in Iraq, but most Canadians acknowledge that government has to focus on internal security threats, deal with the border in new ways, and maintain a vigilance that even a few years ago would have seemed extreme.

CONCLUSION

No one should read this chapter as claiming that everything about our processes of problem definition and framing has suddenly shifted to the United Nations or consists of nothing more than carping about money. There are still plenty of policy problems bubbling at all levels that are primarily domestic in origins and solutions: drugs, petty crime, literacy, pollution, housing, waste disposal, prostitution—in short, things that matter to people on a daily basis. The simple point of this chapter is that the context and processes of problem definition are never set in stone and that they have changed in important ways in the last decade. Some of the sources of policy problems have a completely different character today: globalization, technology, and the environment, for example.

Others are quite new: the aging of society and dropping productivity. Still others have affected the nature of traditional domestic problems, for example, international terrorism and epidemics. And as we argued in Chapter 2, there has also been a change in approaches to governance, in what we consider possible and acceptable for governments to do in addressing these problems.

And yet there are several paradoxes at the heart of these changes. One is that the nature of these issues (e.g., globalization and technology) is such that they are closely entangled with each other. This has led to laudable demands that policy thinking today be more "horizontal" and cross-cutting, since the issues are more diffuse and interconnected. The aging of the population, for example, is linked to economic issues (productivity and training), to social programs (pensions), and to immigration. The danger, however, is that problem definition will become an exercise in thinking about everything at once. In addition to horizontality, there is also pressure on how to maintain both coherence and focus in problem definition. This is reflected in an almost limitless range of problems and issues that governments could conceivably address. While on the one hand governments are challenged to connect the dots between issues like human capital, early childhood education, and immigration, or between terrorism, security, privacy, and border controls, on the other hand there remains general skepticism about how effective government in general and in particular can actually be.

In practical terms, what does this all mean for doing policy work and developing coherent and workable policy problem definitions? It is important to re-emphasize the distinctions between problem recognition and problem definition. In countries like Canada, even though there is likely a greater degree of agenda control by government, there is a constant stream of data, information, and arguments about the range of existing and emerging problems that require a policy response. A crucial part of good policy work remains the analysis and development of those data into something more detailed—a problem definition that brings together data, research, analysis of causal links, and logical arguments. Moreover, there are techniques and guides (as described in the first part of the chapter), to help this process along. However, the contemporary policy analyst must at the same time be aware of the changed context within which that work takes place. She requires an appreciation of existing research and the broad societal policy agenda (e.g., as described by PRI and in political party platforms). She must have a grasp of "ideas in good currency" and contemporary sensibilities about the nature of the "public" and the "private" and the appropriate role for government. She needs an understanding of the complex matrix of cause and effect that infuses almost any policy issue and in particular the nature of global forces and their effects on local problems. Finally, she has to be able to take her work beyond problem definition to policy design. That is the subject of the next chapter.

KEY TERMS

agenda-setting—the social and political process of determining what issues to address and in what priority

argument mapping—a technique to map and classify the different components of policy arguments made by stakeholders, such as arguments based on statistics, authority, values, intuition, or judgment

assumptional analysis—aims at developing a synthesis of the different assumptions that stakeholders have about the issue or problem. Involves canvassing the full range of solutions proposed for the issue or problem and using that as a vehicle for analyzing and challenging the assumptions that underlie the problem definition

boundary analysis—a technique to canvass the whole range of existing definitions and conceptualizations of a given problem

brainstorming—a family of techniques, more or less formal, to generate ideas, goals, and strategies; can involve informal and unstructured exchange to scenario writing

causal images—a shorthand conceptualization of complex cause-and-effect relationships

classification analysis—breaking down the policy problem phenomenon into logically distinct categories or classes

constructivism—philosophical position that there can be no absolutely conclusive proof of anything outside a shared paradigm of understandings

focusing events—sudden catastrophes or crises that grab attention

globalization—the progressive exposure of domestic economies and polities to a wide range of international forces, and the increased interdependence that comes with it

hierarchical analysis—a technique for identifying possible causes of a problem by classifying causes as possible causes, plausible causes, or actionable causes

ideas in good currency—broad ideas about public policy that are widely shared without much commentary or debate and that change slowly over time but form the backdrop for policy discussion

indicators—atypical or routine monitoring that turns up discrepancies or patterns that hint that something is amiss and lead to further development and analysis of the problem definition

issue attention cycle—a portrayal of public policy going through cycles of attention, reaction and action, and quietude

issue framing—a way of depicting a policy issue or problem in broad, understandable if somewhat simplified terms

labels—summary words that convey subtle but powerful meanings: "homosexual" versus "gay," "vagrant" versus "homeless," "tax" versus "user fee"

metaphors—in a policy context, words or phrases that convey powerful meanings through an implicit comparison, such as the "Cold War," "Iron Curtain," or "social safety net"

multiple perspective analysis—a technique to review the problem situation from three perspectives: (1) the technical perspective: cost-benefit analysis, econometrics, and systems analysis; (2) the organizational perspective: focus on institutional rules and processes, and following standard operating procedures; and (3) the personal perspective: viewing problems and solutions in terms of individual perceptions and values

national mood—an inchoate, broad, but nonetheless real consensus among the population around some national issue

policy argument—an organized set of claims about a policy problem and recommended solutions that include such characteristics as causality, severity, novelty, crisis, instruments, and solutions

policy entrepreneurs—actors who shape the public agenda and can quickly and effectively mobilize around a policy issue when they see or sense an opportunity

policy images—a mixture of empirical information and emotive appeals that explain the issue and justify the public policy response

policy windows—unpredictable openings in the policy process that create the possibility for influence over the direction and outcome of that process

problem recognition—the stage at which there is an emerging sense that there may be a problem that needs attention and further analysis, usually based on indicators or some event that signals an issue

problem structuring—the intellectual process of shaping the problem definition

punctuated equilibrium—a process that simultaneously combines long stable periods of policy consensus followed by bursts of change around new issues and new policy images

synectics—a technique that relies on the use of analogies to see if new policy problems have sufficiently similar characteristics to older ones that previous problem definitions and solutions can provide some guidance

Weblinks

Conservative Party of Canada (2004 Election Platform)
http://www.conservative.ca/platform/english/index.htm

Institute for Research on Public Policy
http://www.irpp.org

Liberal Party of Canada (2004 Election Platform)
http://www.liberal.ca/platform_e_1.aspx

New Democratic Party of Canada (2004 Election Platform)
http://www.ndp.ca/uploaded/20040527091443_Fed.NDP.Platform.eng.sm.pdf

Policy Research Initiative
http://policyresearch.gc.ca/page.asp?pagenm=root&langcd=E

Further Readings

Baumgartner, F. R., and Jones, B. D. (1993). *Agendas and instability in American politics.* Chicago: University of Chicago Press.

Dery, D. (1984). *Problem definition in policy analysis.* Lawrence: University Press of Kansas.

Dunn, W. N. (2004). *Public policy analysis: An introduction.* 3rd ed. Englewood Cliffs, NJ: Prentice Hall.

Kingdon, J. W. (1995). *Agendas, alternatives, and public policies,* 2nd ed. New York: HarperCollins.

Soroka, S. (2002). *Agenda-setting dynamics in Canada.* Vancouver: UBC Press.

REFERENCES

Ackoff, R. L. (1976). *Redesigning the future: A systems approach to societal problems.* New York: John Wiley and Sons.

Baumgartner, F. R., and Jones, B. D. (1993). *Agendas and instability in American politics.* Chicago: University of Chicago Press.

Brewer, G. D., and deLeon, P. (1983). *The foundations of policy analysis.* Homewood, IL: The Dorsey Press.

Carson, R. (1962). *Silent spring.* Boston: Houghton Mifflin.

Centre for the Study of Living Standards. (1999). *Productivity trends: A Canada–U.S. comparison.* Retrieved September 2000 from http://www.csls.ca/pdf/lanc.pdf

Conservative Party of Canada. (2004). *Platform 2004.* Retrieved August 6, 2004, from http://www.conservative.ca/platform/english/sp_plan/sp_plan_1.htm

Dery, D. (1984). *Problem definition in policy analysis.* Lawrence: University Press of Kansas.

Doern, G. B., Maslove, A. M., and Prince, M. J. (1988). *Public budgeting in Canada: Politics, economics, and management.* Ottawa: Carleton University Press.

Downs, A. (1972). Up and down with ecology: The issue attention cycle. *Public Interest,* 28, 38–50.

Dunn, W. N. (1993). Policy reforms as arguments. In F. Fischer and J. Forester (Eds.), *The argumentative turn in policy analysis and planning* (pp. 254–90). Durham, NC: Duke University Press.

Dunn, W. N. (2004). *Public policy analysis: An introduction.* 3rd ed. Englewood Cliffs, NJ: Prentice Hall.

Easton, S. T. (2004). *Marijuana growth in British Columbia.* Vancouver: Fraser Institute.

Geva-May, I., and Wildavsky, A. (1997). *An operational approach to policy analysis: The craft.* Boston: Kluwer Academic Publishers.

Harrington, M. (1962). *The other America: Poverty in the United States.* New York: Macmillan.

Howlett, M. (1997). Issue-attention and punctuated equilibria models reconsidered: An empirical evaluation of the dynamics of agenda-setting in Canada. *Canadian Journal of Political Science,* 30(1), 3–30.

Howlett, M. (1998). Predictable and unpredictable policy windows: Institutional and exogenous correlates of Canadian federal agenda-setting. *Canadian Journal of Political Science,* 31(3), 495–524.

Kingdon, J. W. (1995). *Agendas, alternatives, and public policies,* 2nd ed. New York: HarperCollins.

MacLeod, L. (1987). *Battered but not beaten: Preventing wife battering in Canada.* Ottawa: Canadian Advisory Council on the Status of Women.

Majone, G. (1989). *Evidence, argument, and persuasion in the policy process.* New Haven: Yale University Press.

Milward, H. B., and Laird, W. (1996). Where does policy come from? In B. G. Peters and B. A. Rockman (Eds.), *Agenda for excellence 2: Administering the state* (pp. 38–75). Chatham, NJ: Chatham House Publishers.

National Council of Welfare. (2004). *Income for Living?* Ottawa: Minister of Public Works and Government Services Canada. Retrieved August 6, 2004, from http://www.ncwcnbes.net/

Policy Research Initiative. (1996). *Report on growth, human development and social cohesion.* Retrieved September 2000 from http:// policyresearch.schoolnet.ca/keydocs/oct96rep/oct96rep-e.htm

Policy Research Initiative. (1997). *Canada 2005: Global challenges and opportunities.* Retrieved September 2000 from policyresearch .schoolnet.ca/keydocs/global/index-e.htm

Policy Research Initiative. (2004). Retrieved August 6, 2004, from http://policyresearch.gc.ca/page.asp?pagenm=root&langcd=E

Purchase, B., and Hirshhorn, R. (1994). *Searching for good governance.* Kingston, ON: Queen's School of Policy Studies.

Rochefort, D. A., and Cobb, R. W. (1994). Problem definition: An emerging perspective. In D. A. Rochefort and R. W. Cobb, (Eds.), *The politics of problem definition: Shaping the policy agenda* (pp. 1–31). Lawrence: University of Kansas Press.

Sarlo, C. A. (1996). *Poverty in Canada.* 2nd ed. Vancouver: The Fraser Institute.

Schneider, A. L., and Ingram, H. M. (1997). *Policy design for democracy.* Lawrence: University of Kansas Press.

Schon, D. A. (1971). *Beyond the stable state.* New York: W. W. Norton and Company.

Sharpe, A. (2004). Recent productivity developments in Canada and the United States: Productivity growth deceleration versus acceleration. *International Productivity Monitor, 8,* 16–26. Retrieved August 6, 2004, from http://www.csls.ca/ipm/8/sharpe-e.pdf

Soroka, S. (2002). *Agenda-setting dynamics in Canada.* Vancouver: UBC Press.

Statistics Canada. (1996, September 27) *International adult literacy survey.* Retrieved August 6, 2004, from http://www.nald.ca/nls/ials/ introduc.htm

Stone, D. (2001). *Policy paradox: The art of political decision making.* Rev. ed. New York: W. W. Norton and Company.

Strauch, R. E. (1976, Winter). A critical look at quantitative methodology. *Policy Analysis, 2,* 121–44.

True, J. L., Jones, B. D., and Baumgartner, F. R. (1999). Punctuated-equilibrium theory: Explaining stability and change in American policymaking. In P. A. Sabatier (Ed.), *Theories of the policy process* (pp. 97–116). Boulder, CO: Westview Press.

World Health Organization. (2003). *SARS: Chronology of a serial killer.* Retrieved August 6, 2004, from http://www.who.int/csr/don/2003_07_04/en/

Chapter 4

*Policy
Instruments
and Design*

Policy design is a mix of inspiration and technique. The inspiration comes in framing the policy issue (discussed in Chapter 3) in ways that make sense of the problem and provide a broad sketch of how to tackle it. The technique (though not without its creative side either) comes in the detailing of what tools to use, and in what combination, to achieve a given end. The tools will vary with the task at hand, sometimes involving expenditures, sometimes regulation, partnerships, or the exchange of information. Policy design usually will draw on all of these and more, and then be bundled into programs. The conventional discussion of policy instruments usually proceeds by laying out the basic categories and outlining some of the objective characteristics of each of the instruments; when and why, for example, regulation makes more sense than direct program provision by government. This chapter will honour that format in briefly describing the main categories, but it will also show how the menu of choices has changed in recent years. While the reality of instrument choice has always been more constrained than theory might suggest, the old, full menu of the past has been replaced with something closer to a table d'hôte with a more limited, but in some respects more novel, range of items. At the same time, there are continued pressures on the one hand for governments to do many of the traditional things with the traditional instruments, and on the other, to forego many of these traditional activities in favour of a leaner and less intrusive state. Choosing what to do, why to do it, and how, has never been more interesting.

Policies are best thought of as creative solutions to challenging puzzles rather than just dry legislation and programs. The creative dimension breaks through conventional definitions of the issue and comes up with something people had not thought of before. This does not mean, of course, that those creative solutions are the correct ones, only that they offer an unanticipated or surprising approach. For example, some American states have added a new tool to deal with delinquent taxpayers. The normal approach around the world is fines and punishments, but these can be both time consuming and expensive. A new approach is to publicize the names of taxpayers who have outstanding tax bills on the Internet. Going by names like "CyberShame, DelinqNet, Project Collect Tax, Debtor's Corner, and Caught in the Web, delinquent taxpayer lists now appear on the revenue department websites of Colorado, Georgia, Louisiana, Maryland, Minnesota, North Carolina, Rhode Island and South Carolina" (Perry 2004). Remarking that "it is amazing what a little embarrassment will do," one tax official noted that her state had cleared up 1,800 of 2,200 outstanding accounts, collecting US$161 million in owed taxes.

Policy design is about choosing the most appropriate instrument to deal with the policy problem as it has been defined in order to achieve a given policy goal. This implies that a key criterion in instrument choice and policy design is effectiveness—getting the job done. Efficiency—getting the job done with the least resources—is typically considered another key criterion. The reality of politics means that popularity and re-election cannot be left out of the mix of motives; indeed, they may be overpowering at times. But if one adds the inevitably creative aspect of policy design to the range of criteria by which that design might be judged, it is clear that coming up with a list of tools is no easy task. In fact, while lists abound, and while there is some agreement on at least the major policy instruments and their characteristics, there is little agreement (or knowledge) of how and when particular mixes of instruments should be used in policy design. Like a list of the letters in the alphabet, the keys on a piano, or all the possible ingredients in five-star French cooking, the best that an inventory could provide is a sense of the possibilities of language, music, or cuisine. Choice and design are marked as much by art and circumstance as they are by technique.

Nonetheless, thinking through at least the major categories of ingredients is a useful exercise. The first section of this chapter will do this with brutal economy, splitting only enough hairs to make sense of major alternatives and some of the broad dynamics of choice. Policy instruments will be distinguished here from implementation, which we take up in Chapter 5. There is an overlap between the two, of course, but policy instruments usually refer to the technical means of achieving a goal, such as a **tax** or a **regulation,** while implementation refers to the organizational structure and processes to execute that instrument. Policy instruments and implementation overlap most obviously in cases where a particular organizational format is the technical means of achieving the policy goal, such as a **partnership** between a nongovernmental agency and a government department. But we will leave this for Chapter 6.

The theme of this book is that the world of policymaking is changing, and so the bulk of the chapter will take up these new dynamics and also link the question of **instrument design** to a question that increasingly troubles policymakers: how to fashion democratic and cooperative social institutions as a bedrock for most of the other things a people might wish to accomplish collectively.

INVENTORY AND THE DYNAMICS
OF INSTRUMENT CHOICE

The technical means whereby we pursue goals are a reflection of the ways in which we perceive problems and the goals that we are pursuing. For example, income security programs made their appearance as full-blown policy instruments only when Western governments (grudgingly) came around to the view, during the Great Depression in the 1930s, that income inequality was a problem and that it was a legitimate goal of government to try to redistribute income. Any inventory of policy instruments will therefore be a snapshot of what is considered legitimate and efficacious at any given time. There is a sense of appropriateness or legitimacy to the use of policy instruments that varies in much the same way as Chapter 3 argued that "ideas in good currency" will change from time to time. This sense of what is legitimate rests on several ethical foundations, and in a country like Canada, principally on a cluster of ideas such as equality, equity, liberty, and rights. There is no point in trying to define these ideas, since they are constantly contested, but it is fair to say that at this point in Canadian history, most of us look to the Charter of Rights and Freedoms and the courts for inspiration as to the proper scope and limits of government action in our lives. Policy analysts have to know which way the wind is blowing in these areas, or instruments that they may recommend for good policy reasons may turn out to have little or no legitimacy among the wider public. The government of Singapore, for example, has had a ban on chewing gum for the past twelve years, which it partially lifted in May 2004. Certain types of chewing gum were now permitted, but they can be purchased only if buyers submit names and identity cards. This would be considered outrageous in Canada. Context matters.

The history of attempts to classify governing policy instruments begins with Kirschen (1964). His system presented sixty-two different types of economic policy instruments, and the various contributors to the field since have tried various ways of combining aggregate categories with the more finely grained instruments within them. Doern and Phidd (1992, p. 97), for example, argue that there are really only five broad categories: (1) **self-regulation,** (2) **exhortation,** (3) **expenditure,** (4) regulation (including taxation), and (5) public ownership. Based on earlier work by Doern and Wilson (1974), this typology assumed that as one moves from the first category to the last, one moves roughly along a continuum of **legitimate coercion.** The argument was that all government in a liberal democracy involves some degree of imposition or coercion and that politicians generally prefer to use the least coercive instrument possible. Within these broad categories, Doern and Phidd (1992) identify as many as twenty-six finer "graduations of choice" such as grants and subsidies, **guidelines,** and speeches (p. 112).

Another well-known typology by Hood (1984) developed what he called the "NATO scheme," standing for the different resources that governments have at their disposal to effect policy change. N stands for **nodality** or information resources, A for authority, T for treasure or money, and O for organization or personnel. These struck Linder and Peters (1989) as too broad, and in their article on the question, they developed their own schema that tries to draw on several existing schemes, including Hood's. Four basic classes appeared over and over again in the literature they reviewed, but not always the same four, and so they combined them into a group of seven major categories of policy instruments: "(1) direct provision, (2) **subsidy,** (3) tax, (4) contract, (5) authority, (6) regulation, (the only consensus class), and (7) exhortation" (p. 44). They too provide a finer gradation of choice, based on their view that what really matters is the way in which policymakers themselves subjectively perceive the choices that they have before them. The problem is that this gradation does not mesh very well with other attempts at classification (e.g., McDonnell and Elmore, 1987; Schneider and Ingram, 1990; Howlett and Ramesh, 2003), all of which adopt a different classificatory principle (e.g., government resource versus impact or ends).

Another recent and elaborate classification system for policy tools or instruments comes from Lester Salamon (2002). He defines a policy tool or instrument as "an identifiable method through which collective action is structured to address a public problem" (p. 19). Salamon is particularly interested in the degree to which modern governments are in fact "third-party" governments. "What is distinctive about many of the newer tools of public action is that they involved the sharing with third-party actors of a far more basic governmental function: the exercise of discretion over the use of public authority and the spending of public funds" (p. 2). Box 4.1 provides a list of the policy instruments highlighted by Salamon and his colleagues.

Given this rich variety of classifications and lists, how to proceed? Vedung (1998) defines policy instruments as the "set of techniques by which governmental authorities wield their power in attempting to ensure support and effect or prevent social change" (p. 21). The important thing about this definition is that it reminds us that policy, programs,

---

Box 4.1 | **TOOLS OF GOVERNMENT**

GOVERNMENT CORPORATIONS AND GOVERNMENT-SPONSORED ENTERPRISES

A government corporation is a government agency, owned and controlled by government, which is set up as a separate corporate entity legally distinct from the rest of the government of which it is a part. This form is often used for activities that are expected to be revenue producing and potentially self-sustaining; however, this need not be the case.

ECONOMIC REGULATION

Economic regulation controls the entry and exit of firms (entry controls), prices (price controls), and/or output (production controls). . . . economic regulation is aimed at ensuring competitive markets for goods and services and at avoiding consumer and other harms when such markets are not feasible. Economic regulation addresses the behaviour of firms.

SOCIAL REGULATION

Social regulation is aimed at restricting behaviours that directly threaten public health, safety, welfare, or well-being. These include environmental pollution, unsafe working environments, unhealthy living conditions, and social exclusion.

GOVERNMENT INSURANCE

Government insurance is a tool through which governments agree to compensate individuals or firms for losses from certain specified events. Eligible recipients are typically charged a fee, or premium, for participation in the insurance program, and participation is often mandatory. Government insurance programs can be operated directly by government agencies or indirectly with the aid of private insurers. In either case, government typically bears the financial responsibility for covering any claims that exceed the pool of resources assembled in the program. Government insurance programs differ from private sector ones in two ways: government insurance tends to be offered for risks that the private sector would

---

Box 4.1 (continued)

be unwilling to cover, and government insurance is not usually designed to make a profit (it has social or economic objectives).

PUBLIC INFORMATION

Information is a tool for eliciting desired policy outcomes. Policy-makers inform an audience of target actors about a policy issue or pattern of behaviour to influence what people think, know, or believe when they engage in target behaviour. People change what they do because public policy has changed what they think or has changed what they think about, without necessarily changing anything else about the situation.

CORRECTIVE TAXES, CHARGES AND TRADABLE PERMITS

Corrective charges and tradable permits are a class of policy tools that involve using prices and other market mechanisms to create financial incentives for individuals to change their behaviour in ways that reduce social harms or secure benefits for society at large. In contrast to social regulation, which uses a command and control approach, taxes and charges rely on financial penalties or rewards—it alters the costs and benefits of targeted behaviours, and lets individuals or firms make their own choices.

PROCUREMENT CONTRACTING

Procurement contracting, as a tool of government, is a business arrangement between a government agency and a private entity in which the private entity promises, in exchange for money, to deliver certain products or services to the government agency. The private entity may be a for-profit or a non-profit agency.

PURCHASE-OF-SERVICE CONTRACTING

Purchase-of-service contracting essentially involves an agreement under which a government agency enlists a private organization to deliver a service to an eligible group of "clients" in exchange for money. This type of contracting differs from procurement contracting since the good or service is being purchased for third parties, not for the government itself.

GRANTS

Grants are payments from a donor government to a recipient organization (typically public or nonprofit) or an individual. More specifically, they are a gift that has the aim of either "stimulating" or "supporting" some sort of service or activity by the recipient, whether it be a new activity or an ongoing one. Through this device, a governmental agency (the "grantor") participates in the provision of a service, while leaving to another entity (the "grantee") the task of actual performance.

LOANS AND LOAN GUARANTEES

In a direct loan, the government itself lends money directly to borrowers. It then services that loan (i.e., collects scheduled repayments from the borrowers) and forecloses or otherwise attempts to collect on the loan if a borrower cannot make scheduled payments. When the government guarantees a loan, a private lender, such as a commercial bank or mortgage lender, makes the loan to the borrower. The government enters into a contractual agreement to make full or partial payment to the lender in case the borrower defaults on the guaranteed loan. The private lender originates the loan, secures the government guarantee, and services the loan according to government regulations or minimum standards.

TAX EXPENDITURES

A tax expenditure is a provision in tax law that usually encourages certain behaviour by individuals or corporations by deferring, reducing, or eliminating their tax obligations.

VOUCHERS

A voucher is a subsidy that grants limited purchasing power to an individual to choose among a restricted set of goods and services (e.g., food vouchers, educational vouchers).

TORT LIABILITY

Tort liability, as a tool of government, is the establishing of a right of persons or other entities to seek compensation or injunctive relief through the judicial system for harm that they have experienced caused by the negligence or other wrongful conduct of other persons or entities. This right is ordinarily established in court-recognized

> **Box 4.1 (continued)**
>
> common law, but may also be created by statutory law or by administrative regulation. Tort law is thus an alternative to administrative regulation and other tools as a mechanism for preventing harm. Tort law relies on court actions brought by injured parties to seek remedies for harms that they have suffered.
>
> **SOURCE:** Salamon, Lester M. (Ed.). (2002). *The tools of government: A guide to the new governance.* Oxford: Oxford University Press.

and ultimately the policy instruments that give them effect are about *deliberately achieving some desired outcome,* and that moreover, "social change" is ultimately a result of human behaviour. The question of instruments therefore is really about the resources and techniques that governments have at their disposal to achieve certain outcomes through affecting human behaviour. In a phrase, it often involves making people do things or stopping them from doing some other things. It is for this reason that most classifications of policy instruments stress the degree of coercion that is involved. Salamon (2002) defines coercion as the most salient dimension in understanding policy tools, and suggests that it "measures the extent to which a tool restricts individual or group behaviour as opposed to merely encouraging or discouraging it" (p. 25). The state, even the downsized and globalized one discussed in Chapter 2, has the monopoly of legitimate force in most societies, as well as the capacity to issue **binding rules** and **prohibitions.** It is useful therefore to consider the degree of state involvement and the degree of state coercion embedded in any policy instrument, as long as we understand that the choice of instrument assumes some grasp of what level of coercion will be accepted as legitimate in society. For example, as a general trend, it seems that public opinion in most Western countries is increasingly skeptical of "high-end" coercive policy instruments such as state monopolies or detailed regulation. On the other hand, in Canada at least, there appears to have been a trend favouring more coercive instruments being used against sex offenders or those who violate speech and equity codes.

Since there is no universally accepted typology, and since most typologies of instruments emphasize different criteria, the one offered in this chapter (see Figure 4.1) is deliberately eclectic. We begin by presuming that the policymaker's purpose is to achieve an outcome in terms of (1) the behaviour of individuals; (2) political, social, or economic conditions; or (3) services provided to the public. It would be possible to state

Figure 4.1   Policy Instruments: A Classification

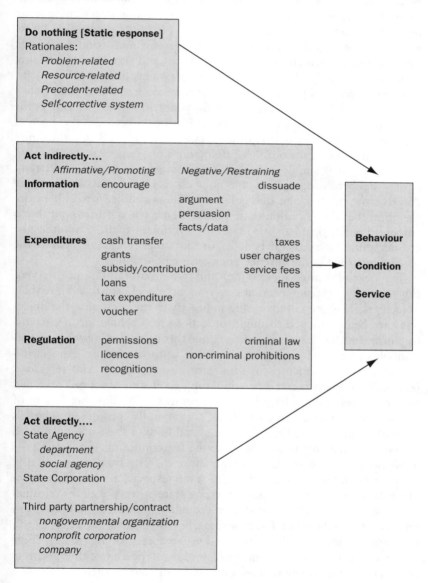

GOVERNMENTS CAN...

Do nothing [Static response]
Rationales:
> *Problem-related*
> *Resource-related*
> *Precedent-related*
> *Self-corrective system*

Act indirectly....
> *Affirmative/Promoting*   *Negative/Restraining*

Information   encourage   dissuade
                     argument
                     persuasion
                     facts/data

Expenditures   cash transfer   taxes
                     grants   user charges
                     subsidy/contribution   service fees
                     loans   fines
                     tax expenditure
                     voucher

Regulation   permissions   criminal law
                     licences   non-criminal prohibitions
                     recognitions

Behaviour

Condition

Service

Act directly....
State Agency
> *department*
> *social agency*
State Corporation

Third party partnership/contract
> *nongovernmental organization*
> *nonprofit corporation*
> *company*

the latter two in terms of behavioural changes as well; for example, the desired outcome of reducing poverty could be achieved through changed behaviours such as employers paying higher wages due to increased minimum wage levels or the poor themselves being able to purchase more necessary goods and services because of tax breaks or subsidies. However, since much policy discussion takes place around conditions (e.g., poverty, unemployment, productivity, crime) and services (e.g., health, education, water quality monitoring), there seems little benefit in jettisoning the terms. Now, given the fact of some desired outcome or policy objective (based on an assessment of the problem), what tools are at the policymaker's disposal for achieving it? Figure 4.1 provides three broad categories. The first is to do nothing. This choice is shaded in the figure because, in a sense, the option of doing nothing is not really a choice of instrument—it is simply inaction. As we noted in Chapter 1, we refer here to deliberate inaction, a conscious choice. We discuss this in more detail below, but the logic of highlighting this as a choice is to underscore the point that doing nothing often makes sense when it turns out that a perceived policy problem was not really a problem at all, or that the cost of intervention exceeds the benefits, or that other forces will achieve the desired outcome in the absence of government action.

The next two categories contain the two broad families of interventions or policy instruments that governments can choose to achieve their objectives. The first entails acting indirectly in the sense that the objectives are being pursued through the actions and behaviour of citizens, organizations, or firms. This can be done through affecting the information or values that underpin behaviour (information or exhortation instruments); the calculus of monetary costs, benefits, and resources (expenditure instruments); or stipulating rules and sanctions attached to certain behaviours (regulatory instruments). Within this family of instruments, information-based tools are generally considered to be less coercive than expenditure-based tools, and both of these are considered less coercive than regulation-based tools. The continuum is not perfect—as we note below, taxes are probably more coercive than self-regulation through **voluntary codes**. As well, in some respects, acting indirectly in our sense actually involves quite coercive state powers (e.g., the criminal justice system). However, it captures a rough scale effect as we move from one category to the other. The other axis, borrowing from Vedung (1998), is between affirmative/promoting and negative/restraining (p. 26). Tools drawn on information, expenditures, and regulation can either promote certain behaviours or outcomes, or prohibit or restrain them.

In the second family of instruments, the state acts directly and is ultimately accountable for achieving its objectives. The most obvious and conventional way to do this is through the use of the state's own resources to change conditions or provide services. For example, Revenue Canada, as a department, used to collect taxes for the federal government. Now taxes are collected through the Canada Revenue Agency, which, however, is still an agency (though at arm's length) of government. Many provincial and municipal governments, in dealing with the housing problems of poor people, directly provide social housing through special agencies. Canada used to be rife with public enterprises or state corporations, most notably Air Canada and Petro Canada before they were privatized but also the still-surviving Canadian Broadcasting Corporation. Whatever the form—a department, agency, or corporation—in all three instances the government is achieving its policy objective through the marshalling of its own resources and organizational capacity and not working through citizens, nongovernmental organizations (NGOs), or the private sector. It is doing it itself. However, another form of direct action is through partnerships or **contracts** with third parties such as NGOs, nonprofit agencies, or companies. This subcategory admittedly stretches the definition of direct action slightly, but it is included here because the state is still formulating its objectives, determining acceptable outcomes, signing the contract for service delivery, providing the funds, and monitoring performance. It is also ultimately responsible for those outcomes.

It is important to understand that in the run of normal or routine politics, the range of instrument choice is generally limited by the existing array that is already embedded in the policy field. Policymakers think through their options on the basis of what is currently in the field or underpinning policy efforts. If evaluation shows that some instruments are not working, they can be amended, but as long as normal politics is incremental politics, the temptation is to build upon already existing and fairly finely graduated policy instruments. In periods of greater policy turbulence, policymakers will actually begin to think in broader instrument categories, because in turbulent times policies are often fundamentally restructured, forcing a consideration of instrument types. We discuss the new dynamics of instrument choice in the second half of this chapter; the changes in governance in the past decade have indeed been turbulent, and with them have come new debates and new approaches to instrument choice. In the sections below, we briefly outline the key characteristics of each instrument. We begin, however, by briefly outlining the logic of "doing nothing."

DOING NOTHING

"Doing nothing" may appear as a "nondecision," which indeed it is if it has no rationale beyond either ennui or a simple desire to remain unengaged. As we argued in Chapter 1, however, a deliberate choice not to intervene, made after an analysis of the problem, should be considered a policy decision—what we will call here **"static response."** There can be several good rationales for declining to intervene. Together they comprise a coherent set of considerations that should be part of any systematic process of instrument choice, even though "doing nothing" does not seem intuitively to fit the notion of an "instrument" or tool. The four rationales that follow presume that a potential problem or opportunity has presented itself to policymakers in some fashion, and that a careful analysis was undertaken about the nature of the problem and the appropriate response.

Problem-related rationales: The analysis indicates that in fact there is either no problem after all or a problem that is not within the government's current priorities or its jurisdiction. In May 1999, for example, the CRTC announced that it would not extend its regulation to the Internet because it "concluded that the new media on the Internet are achieving the goals of the Broadcasting Act and are vibrant, highly competitive and successful without regulation" (CRTC, 1999).

Resource-related rationales: The analysis indicates that there is indeed a problem, and that it falls within the government's general priorities and its jurisdiction. Nonetheless, given current resource constraints and other more pressing demands, the government cannot allocate resources for this problem. The prime example of this through the late 1990s was the federal government's acknowledgment that the health care system was in trouble but that it could not afford to put more money into it. This changed dramatically by 2004, when all governments were vying to put more money into health care. At that point, defence was a good candidate for resource-related rationales: while everyone recognized that more money needed to go into the Canadian military, the sheer magnitude required made some decisionmakers balk.

Precedent-related rationales: A problem exists, but the analysis raises the concern that a policy intervention might set a precedent that could place unmanageable demands on government. In the tainted blood scandal, for example, Ottawa refused to compensate hepatitis-C victims who had contracted the disease from blood products before 1986 in the fear that this would open a floodgate of compensation claims that would go beyond the $1.1 billion the federal and provincial governments were already paying out (Orsini, 2002).

Self-corrective system rationales: In this case, while it is accepted that there may be a problem, it is also assumed that there is also a coherent system (e.g., social, cultural, religious, economic) at work that over time may correct it spontaneously, without the need for government intervention. Market-based rationales are the most familiar example of this these days;

in cases of high prices, monopoly power by single firms, etc., the argument is that market competition over time will correct the problem.

Static response appears like an empty category, a nullity or absence of action, but is increasingly important at least as part of the instrument selection/policy analysis process. In an era that remains skeptical of excessive government intervention and more attuned to the efficacy of markets and civil society, it is no longer assumed that as soon as a problem presents itself that government should reach for active policy instruments. We should also note that the term is slightly misleading—"doing nothing" does require analysis and a decision not to respond directly. This itself sends out information to citizens and organizations and may change the way that they behave and interact.

INFORMATION-BASED INSTRUMENTS

Information-based policy instruments cover government-directed "attempts at influencing people through transfer of knowledge, communication of reasoned argument, and **moral suasion** in order to achieve a policy result" (Vedung and van der Doelen, 1998, p. 103). These policy instruments can include flyers, pamphlets, booklets, training, advertisements, and reports. Information-based instruments are considered the least coercive of all policy instruments since there is no obligation to act on the information and no supplementary inducement or penalty. Some forms of information can be designed to dissuade behaviours—a sterling example is the health warnings on cigarette packages—while others are designed to encourage or promote certain behaviours—for example, the *Canada Food Guide* helps us know how many legumes to consume per week. Of course, all serious policies and programs depend on information in the minimal sense of making people aware of their existence, but Vedung (1998) makes the useful distinction between information *as* an independent policy instrument and information *on* a metapolicy instrument that supports others (p. 49).

A key principle behind information-based instruments is that behaviour is based on knowledge, beliefs, and values. Assume that the government's policy objective is to reduce smoking. If knowledge, in the sense of facts at the smoker's disposal, is incorrect or incomplete (e.g., the addictive qualities of nicotine), or beliefs are wrong (e.g., that smoking has no ill-health effects), or values are counterproductive (e.g., it's "cool" to smoke), then smoking behaviour will continue unabated. Presumably, an information campaign that would enlighten smokers would change their behaviour, since it would appear to be manifestly in their interest to reduce or quit smoking. But of course we know that this is not always the case, and it alerts us to the fact that information-based policy tools work best when knowledge, beliefs, and values are consistent with direct and immediate self-interest. Even when "enlightened" by government information campaigns, smokers may continue to smoke because they like it, because they discount the negative health effects far into the future, or because they want to defy what they perceive as a hectoring, paternalistic government program (the boomerang effect).

There is a paradox about information-based instruments—as benign as they might appear, the most powerful way to change behaviour is to change the knowledge, beliefs, and values upon which it is based. The former communist regimes in Europe and every existing authoritarian government in the world understands that very well. So did Plato in *The Republic*. The use of information/exhortation in democratic states can seem much less objectionable; it is remarkable, for example, how public attitudes toward the environment have changed in only one generation and have become the foundation for acquiescence to blue-box programs, anti-littering campaigns, and even picking up after your own dog in the park. This is all to the good. But there can be concerns. In Canada, the federal government has for decades been the country's single largest advertiser. There is a fine line between promoting public policies and programs, and self-promotion for the government of the day. Other levels of government in Canada have not been left behind. And as the opening example from this chapter indicated, information can be used in a somewhat discomfiting way as a "**shaming**" instrument—in a sense, this is the use of information *about* rather than information *for*. Our behaviour might be changed not because our beliefs have been affected by an information campaign but because of information about us that has been provided to others. The use of shaming as a policy instrument is more widespread than we might assume. Product labelling, for example, can be used to induce companies to remove ingredients that are deemed harmful to the consuming public. Regulatory agencies can issue lists of "worst offenders" (for example, polluters), deliberately using the publicity as a way of inducing change. Graham describes this as "democracy by disclosure": "Stated simply, such strategies employ government authority to require the standardized disclosure of factual information from identified businesses or other organizations about products or practices to reduce risks to the public" (Graham, 2002, p. 138). The interesting thing about the new disclosure instruments is that unlike warning labels that tell people what to do or articulate a harm or risk, mandatory disclosure simply puts factual information in the public domain (e.g., nutritional labelling), and lets people make up their own minds about risk. The combination of public disclosure laws (and the United States is considerably ahead of Canada in this respect), assiduous researchers and critics, and modern media, give information a potency that is sometimes underestimated. We address some new aspects of information/exhortation in the second part of the chapter.

EXPENDITURE-BASED INSTRUMENTS

From the policymaker's point of view, virtually every policy instrument involves expenditure—even giving a speech will entail the cost of speechwriters and distribution of materials. So money is a ubiquitous and universal resource that governments use to affect policy, and rarely, if ever, can expenditure as an instrument be avoided. The point about expenditure-based policy instruments, however, is that it is money itself that is the direct instrument. In this instance, governments are not trying to achieve their objectives or outcomes by changing the information that undergirds behaviour, but rather the calculus of costs, benefits, and financial resources that individuals or organizations undertake before they do something. Producing Canadian films, for example, is risky because of the high probability of not making a profit. Government subsidies can change that equation and induce more Canadian filmmaking. Canadians who live in poverty and who might not be able to afford a proper diet or housing can be aided through **cash transfers** in the form of income security or assistance payments.

In 1998 the auditor general of Canada undertook a special audit of the **grants** and **contributions** practices of several departments, primarily Industry Canada and Heritage Canada. As the report pointed out, the "provision of grants and contributions to individuals, businesses and not-for-profit organizations is one of the most important ways that the Government of Canada pursues its program objectives" (Auditor General of Canada, 1998). The report provided a useful definition of grants and contributions:

> Grants are unconditional transfer payments for which eligibility and entitlement may be verified. If an individual or organization is eligible for a grant, the appropriate payment can be made without requiring the recipient to meet any future conditions. In contrast, the payment of a contribution is subject to performance conditions that are specified in a contribution agreement. The recipient must continue to show that these conditions are being met in order to be reimbursed for specific costs over the life of the agreement. The recipients' use of contributions can also be audited by the government, whereas this is usually not a requirement for a grant. (Auditor General, 1998)

In Figure 4.1 we have distinguished between cash transfers, grants, and subsidy/contributions. In Canadian usage, transfers usually apply to payments by government to individuals or other governments that do not involve any form of exchange and have only minimal conditions attached to them. Equalization payments and the Canada Health and Social Transfer (CHST) are prime examples of cash transfers from the federal government to the provinces. Provincial governments also transfer cash to their municipalities to support a wide range of programs. Old Age Security and the Child Tax Benefit are examples of transfers to individuals. The key point is that a cash transfer tends to be provided for broad support rather than in connection with a specific project or endeavour. Grants, even while they have few if any performance conditions attached, are usually provided in connection with a more specific endeavour (e.g., student educational grants). However, in a technical sense grants tend not to be too closely calibrated to the actual costs of engaging in that endeavour. Contributions and subsidies, on the other hand, have more numerous and detailed conditions, usually demand some measure of performance, and are more carefully calculated to defray some specific proportion of the cost of the endeavour. They differ from **loans** in that the latter must be repaid. **Tax expenditures** accomplish much the same thing as contributions or subsidies, but through the mechanism of reducing taxes for specific activities and thereby increasing the benefits. Perhaps the most publicly visible tax expenditure in Canada is the Registered Retirement Savings Program (RRSP) where interest in special accounts is tax free, though the device is used routinely to support everything from small businesses to investments in high technology and research. **Vouchers** are simply "coupons" for stipulated amounts of money that may be redeemed under certain conditions—the most notorious example is Food Stamps in the United States, although vouchers are increasingly being used to provide educational services, housing, child care, transportation, and health care (Steuerle and Twombly, 2002). While the United States probably leads the world in reliance on vouchers, they are routinely used around the world: Accor Corporate Services, for example, operates in 32 countries and distributes vouchers to over 13 million users per year (Accor Services, 2004).

Expenditure instruments pose substantial management challenges in terms of ensuring that conditions are met and monies are spent appropriately, with some result. The auditor general has been evaluating grants and contributions by the federal government for over twenty years, and in 1984 identified eight critical management processes for grant and contribution programs: "stating objectives clearly; establishing unambiguous terms and conditions; informing potential applicants of program guidelines; reviewing and approving applications diligently;

making payments properly; monitoring individual grants and contributions appropriately; providing good information to management; and assessing program effectiveness" (Auditor General, 1998). Despite this, the government's record on grants and contributions has been marked by consistent problems:

> In summary, our audits of the management of grant and contribution programs over the past 21 years have produced a long series of consistent observations. Our 1977 audit found problems in compliance with program authorities, weaknesses in program design, instances of poor controls, and insufficient performance measurement and reporting. Subsequent audits have made similar observations. While we have found signs of specific improvements in some areas when we followed up on these audits, overall we have continued to find the same problems each time we have audited grant and contribution programs. (Auditor General, 1998)

The so-called sponsorship scandal in early 2004 involving the Ministry of Public Works and contracts with the Quebec communications firm Groupaction simply illustrated that the government still was challenged in handling the spending instrument. As the auditor general noted in her first report on the issue: "Our audit found that senior public servants responsible for managing the contracts demonstrated an appalling disregard for the Financial Administration Act, the Government Contracts Regulations, Treasury Board policy, and rules designed to ensure prudence and probity in government procurement" (Auditor General, 2002, p. 1). Many of the challenges to managing large spending programs are systemic—ironically, in 2000, in the Human Resources and Development Canada "scandal" about a billion dollars lost in employment training funds (eventually it was determined that it was only $85 000) might have been in part caused by new public management practices that led to decentralized decisionmaking and little oversight and information (Good, 2003).

The negative/restraining side of expenditures is to increase the costs of some activities. Governments tax, of course, to get revenue. They can have policies about taxation, in terms of the fairness and incidence of the tax regime. They can also use taxes as deliberate policy instruments. For example, "**sin taxes**" on alcohol and cigarettes are a means of discouraging their use. The distinction between taxes and other types of government levies such as **user charges** or fees is increasingly blurred, but in principle taxes have a compulsory aspect and generally are not connected to any specific service. Income and property taxes do have a discretionary component in that if someone decided not to work or live in a dwelling, he or she would not be liable for those taxes—but in practice, of course, they are almost unavoidable. Nonsmokers do not pay cigarette taxes, but smokers who do pay those taxes do not receive any specific government service in return. Both user charges and **service fees** have a service component in them and so are not usually viewed as taxes. In the case of user charges, the service component is quite general and the charge therefore is levied on a category of person or user. Examples include access to and use of facilities such as airports (many now levy an "improvement charge") or municipal dumps. A service fee usually is connected to some specific service rather than general use; for example, receiving a passport. In practice, the terms are often interchangeable, and for cosmetic reasons policymakers often prefer to use the term "fee" rather than "tax." Whatever term is used, the precise amounts of any levy and its attendant conditions (e.g., when, how, and on which payers) are complex questions of public finance.

REGULATION

Regulation draws on the most fundamental resource a government has, its capacity to command and prohibit. "Regulatory instruments are used to define norms, acceptable behavior, or to limit activities in a given society. The law, backed up with the threat of sanction, represents the 'stick' used to prescribe or prevent certain types of human behavior" (Lemaire, 1998, p. 59). That capacity depends on a blend of legitimacy and effective sanctions for disobedience, with the greatest weight on legitimacy. If governments merely have power without authority, they will have little capacity to command. It is the legitimacy of their commands as perceived by the majority of citizens that permits them to efficiently use sanctions against the minority that disobey. A great deal of public policy is about achieving outcomes through ensuring certain actions or behaviours. Regulatory instruments rely on rules to prohibit or promote selected actions or behaviours. This has an admirable directness to it—"thou shalt" or "thou shalt not"—but we have classified them here under "indirect" instruments since in most cases, regulation is understood to involve government rules aimed at certain activities undertaken by individuals, organizations, or firms to achieve certain outcomes.

It is important to understand that what we conventionally define as regulation is actually "**secondary legislation,**" a form of law. To understand regulation, we need first to understand the nature of law. Most of what government does gets embodied in law in one way or another. The issue here is the use of law or rules themselves to achieve policy objectives. Stipulating rules to achieve those objectives seems both reasonable and effective. The use of criminal law prohibitions against murder or child abuse, or even noncriminal prohibitions such as driving on the left side of the road, are simple and clear. There are several considerations however, that, while fundamental, are often overlooked in the policy literature. The first is that there are different types of legal instruments (Keyes, 1996). It is possible to distinguish among

- *Legislation or statute* (including delegated legislation—or regulation—based on statute);
- *Decisions* (legal ones about what a statute means);
- *Contracts* (applicable to the parties and legally binding);
- *Quasi-legislation* (issued by administrative authorities in the form of internal or nonbinding rules, policies, and guidelines); and
- *Incorporation by reference* (bringing another instrument such as a code of conduct into a statute and giving it the force of law).

Distinctions can be made among these in terms of (1) their legal effect and (2) the procedures used to formulate them. Legal effect has two dimensions: generality (number of people it is directed to) and degree of binding (imposition of some threat or sanction). **Statutes** affect large numbers of people and are binding. This is also true of delegated **legislation** or regulatory authority, but there is a constraint in that courts will demand a clear legal authority for making it. **Decisions** are instruments that apply law, not make it. They are specific rather than general. Contracts are even narrower, binding only on the parties to the contract. Quasi-legislation has no binding legal effect generally—but, for example, Canada Revenue Agency bulletins interpreting the meaning of legislation can have practical effect and can be authoritative to the degree that they are accepted by the courts. Ganz (1987) defines **quasi-legislation** as "a wide spectrum of rules whose only common factor is that they are not directly enforceable through criminal or civil proceedings" (p. 1). She points out that the lines between these two categories are increasingly blurred and that it does not depend on form—a circular may be legally binding but a "law" may not. There has been huge growth in statutory and extrastatutory rules in a plethora of forms: codes of practice, guidance, notes, guidelines, circulars, white papers, policy notes, development briefs, tax concessions, notices, codes of conduct, codes of ethics, and conventions. The main reasons for the use of quasi-legislation are always the same: flexibility and lack of technicality (Baldwin, 1995, p. 4). Flexibility means that rules can be changed easily and quickly. Of course, what appears as flexibility and simplicity from one perspective can seem like "back-door legislation" and confusion from another.

Finally, **incorporation by reference** is quite a powerful and flexible form of rule-making because it can combine instruments that would otherwise stand separate and give them the force of law. A statute that incorporates a regulatory code of conduct developed by an industry association, for example, takes the privately developed code and gives it the force of law. Moreover, depending on drafting, the incorporation can be dynamic in the sense that any amendments made to the code subsequent to the passage of the legislation also automatically get reflected in the legal instrument (there is, for obvious reasons, some debate over this). The law without the code is one instrument, and the code without the law is another. Combined, they form a hybrid that is more than the sum of its parts.

The type of instrument can be linked to the procedure for making it. The reason is that the characteristics of the body making a legal instrument determines how well suited it is to making it. For example, strong compliance with a rule usually depends on people knowing and accepting it, and this knowledge and acceptance improves when people have a chance to participate in the making of the rule. Some types of decision-making bodies are better at involving certain groups of people than others. The logic is that the wider the legal effect and more binding the nature of the rule, the closer one gets to authoritative and generally representative institutions such as Parliament. Delegated legislation and quasi-legislation usually do not bring people into the decisionmaking process as effectively as Parliament potentially can. The narrower the legal effect, and the more valued consensus is among a small group of participants, the more one will rely on forms of rules approaching the quasi-legislative, or discretionary end of the continuum.

Regulation is therefore a distinct type of rule-making available to governments. It is termed "secondary legislation" because, unlike quasi-legislation, it requires a statutory basis. As the 2003 Cabinet Directive on Law-Making makes clear,

> Canada's system of responsible parliamentary government is based on the rule of law. This means that laws must be made in conformity with the Constitution. The Crown retains very few regulatory powers that are not subject to the legislative or law-making process. For example, regulations governing the issuance of passports or medals and honors are still made under the royal prerogative. Parliament may delegate regulatory authority to Cabinet (the Governor in Council), a person (such as a Minister of the Crown) or a body (such as the Atomic Energy Control Board). However, this authority remains subject to the will of Parliament and regulations made under this delegated authority are referred to as subordinate legislation. (Privy Council Office, 2003)

Affirmative/promoting uses of regulation include permissions, licences, recognitions, and self-regulation. **Permissions** are simply permits or enablements with few if any conditions attached—for example, a hunting permit or a city declaration that bars can stay open later for a special event. **Licences** are more complicated in that they involve a mix of prohibition, permission, and condition. This is the classic formula of the regulator: first, generally prohibit some action (e.g., broadcasting TV signals, driving a vehicle, fishing for salmon, doing brain surgery); second, specifically permit that action for individuals or organizations who will respect some pre-defined criteria or conditions. The licence conditions can be as detailed or as scant as the regulator likes. Of course, a key ingredient is defining sanctions for the unlawful (i.e., unlicensed) practice of the regulated act. Use of "regs," as seasoned policy analysts like to call them, is a marvelously flexible instrument in that it can define prohibited acts quite precisely and can attach equally precise conditions to the licensee.

Regulation can also entail "**recognition**" or defining the *bona fide* actors in a policy field. The most benign is simply to recognize certain individuals or organizations for some policy-relevant quality that they have or have achieved. Under the Indian Act, for example, the federal Department of Indian Affairs and Northern Development keeps a registry of all Indians so defined for purposes of the legislation (essentially those individuals descended from Indian bands with whom the federal government struck treaties in the nineteenth and twentieth centuries). Appropriately enough, they are known as status Indians, and other Indians are described as non-status or non-treaty Indians. For the purposes of the Indian Act and what it permits, prohibits, and provides, it matters a great deal if one is status or non-status. Another example is the Green logo designed by Environment Canada or the U.K. Charter Mark discussed in Chapter 2. Products or services that meet certain standards can display the logo and thereby send a signal to consumers. Government is simply lending its authority to designate some actors as complying with the larger policy purpose. That designation carries a certain advantage to its recipients but not much else.

A species of regulation is government-sanctioned self-regulation, where the state delegates its regulatory power not to a state agency but to a nongovernmental organization or association. The professions (medicine, law, engineering) are the main examples and involve the delegation of government powers to set mandatory standards and discipline infractions. The assumption policymakers have made is that these professions can be trusted not to take the short-term view or operate primarily for economic gain. In other cases, government accredits organizations to conduct official activities, and may incorporate the results into legislation, thereby giving those activities the force of law. A good example is the National Standards System, which is managed by the Standards Council of Canada, a crown corporation. The Council accredits over 400 organizations to develop, test, and apply standards. Most standards (and there are thousands, covering almost every conceivable product and many services) are voluntary, though some are incorporated by reference into international law. In another strategy, government can help organizations develop their own voluntary codes of conduct. Voluntary codes also go by other names: codes of conduct, codes of practice, voluntary initiatives, guidelines, and nonregulatory agreements. Successful codes are said to have the following characteristics: (1) buy-in from leaders of the relevant organizations; (2) rank and file support; (3) a clear statement of objectives, obligations, and rules; (4) transparent development and implementation; (5) regular flow of information; (6) an effective dispute-resolution system; (7) meaningful incentives to participate; and (8) negative repercussions for failure to join or comply (Industry Canada, 1998, pp. 7–8). The government's role in voluntary codes is that of a catalyst, facilitator, and sometimes endorser. In those cases where volunteer codes affect business or industrial sectors, government is also interested in the degree to which the codes may impede competition.

Regulations can broadly be classed as economic, social, or environmental, though each of these will have subsets based on the object (e.g., prices, safety) or targets (e.g., specific industries). Economic regulation typically addresses such factors as pricing, advertising, and labelling, competition, some aspects of production, profits, and disclosure of financial information. The classic rationale for economic regulation is that markets are not working efficiently. This may be due to monopolies (the historical case for public utility regulation), oligopolies (hence competition regulation), or the simple occurrence of various forms of behaviour designed to maximize profits at the expense of workers and consumers (e.g., collusion, false advertising, union busting). Social regulation is designed to protect us less as consumers than as persons or citizens. This somewhat vague formulation is fairly clear when it comes to health and safety standards such as fire regulations. Though these frequently apply to products and services, they also affect our use of spaces and buildings as citizens. It is a lot less clear what criteria regulators have in mind as they move into the cultural realm with broadcasting regulations (e.g., Canadian content, nonstereotyping), and social justice regulations such as employment equity or speech codes. Environmental regulation struggles with the standards issue as well, since the science is often not precise enough to determine what the allowable limits of many toxic substances might be. Nor can we easily know the effects of the interaction of hundreds of thousands of substances in the air, land, and water.

ACTING DIRECTLY

The preceding categories of instruments are indirect in that they involve working through citizens or organizations to achieve public goals. Governments can sometimes decide to achieve the conditions or service goals they have in mind by marshalling their own resources toward those ends. A good example is education. Parents need to have their children educated, but governments can elect to provide that education directly themselves, or they may provide parents with the funds (usually through some form of voucher) that they could then redeem for services as they see fit, from either government providers, the private sector, or some mix. Any service directly provided by government, from garbage collection to education, will involve the expenditure of often very substantial amounts of money. In 2003, for example, provincial and territorial governments spent a total of $174 billion on health ($79.1 billion), social services ($40.7 billion), and education ($54.7 billion). This represented 72 percent of total expenditures in that year (Statistics Canada, 2003). So "direct provision" is less an alternative to spending money than it is a means of spending money that reflects a different policy logic. It is a logic reflected in the questions listed in Box 4.2 (page 160). Take municipal garbage collection as an example. The need in this case is the removal of refuse, and municipal governments have traditionally provided this service directly by raising general tax revenues to cover the cost. Traditionally no fees have been attached. Municipal governments have had both the authority and the fiscal capacity to deliver the service. The nub of the issue is in questions 4 and 5. Are there alternative service providers? Absolutely. The garbage business in North America is huge. What is the compelling policy reason to directly collect garbage with city workers rather than through a contract for service with a private company? Typically, the argument from public sector unions has been that the level of service (and the wages and working conditions of sanitary workers) will decline if private companies get into the act. Apart from that, most people care only that the can at the curbside is emptied weekly. This is essentially a question of efficiency. If public sector workers can collect the garbage as efficiently as a private sector company can, there usually is little reason to change. Question 6, however, has risen with a vengeance in recent years. As the costs of garbage collection and recycling have increased dramatically across North America, and as pressure to hold the line on taxes has mounted, more and more municipal governments have decided to charge some sort of fee for collection. This can get quite creative, from charges per can or bag to limits on the number of bags one can put out. The logic in both cases is the same: what was once a "free" service now has a direct cost attached to it. The

---

Box 4.2   QUESTIONS TO ASK ABOUT DIRECT
PROVISION OF SERVICE INSTRUMENTS

1. What is the need or the problem, and what service or bundle of services will meet that need?
2. Do we have the legal capacity to provide the service?
3. Do we have the resources to provide the service?
4. Are there alternative service providers?
5. Is there a compelling policy reason to provide the service directly (e.g., safety, uniformity of standards, recipients cannot choose appropriate service levels, retaining agency capacity in the program field)?
6. If the service is provided publicly, should there be fees attached?
7. If the service is provided privately, will recipients be able to pay for it, or should there be some subsidy?
8. If there is a subsidy, should it be paid to providers or recipients?
9. If the service is provided privately, by what sort of entity (e.g., for-profit or nonprofit).
10. If the service is provided privately, what oversight/regulation should government provide?

---

other questions deal with the ways in which government can either support or regulate the private provision of services. As we shall see in Chapter 5, "alternative service delivery" has become a central issue in the implementation of public policy. More and more jurisdictions are answering question 4 in the affirmative, but question 5 in the negative, and then the game turns into one of deciding how to structure a private sector/public sector partnership. Another implementation issue is, if the service is to be provided through a public agency, how should that agency be designed? Should it be a direct-line department, or an arm's-length entity like a public or Crown corporation?

As the list of questions on service delivery suggests, governments can either provide the service directly or regulate the provision of the service by third parties, or they can do a mix of both. Policy instruments are not mutually exclusive but are usually combined in packages to deal with the different dimensions of the problem.

The preceding has covered most of the major categories of instruments. What can we conclude from the discussion? First, no list is ever complete, and there are some instruments that some authors would include as separate categories (e.g., Crown corporations) and others would place under a broad category such as direct provision. Second, the sliding scale of authority idea is only moderately helpful in distinguishing these instruments. A high government charge on a service I need to use regularly will seem a lot more coercive to me than even the most detailed regulations covering a service I rarely access. Equally, a persistent series of hectoring ads about what the government believes to be naughty behaviour may seem more paternalistic than the income tax I am forced to pay once a year. This point takes on even greater force when we consider a third conclusion: no instrument is an island. Since they tackle clusters of problems, government policies use clusters of programs. These program clusters in turn bundle together groups of instruments. Education, for example, mixes big spending, direct service delivery, taxation (special education taxes), and lots of regulations.

This crude inventory has shown us what instruments we can choose and some of the rationales behind their choice. But what actually explains instrument choice? Theoretically, some instruments are substitutable, meaning that from the point of view of cost and at least the major outcome desired by policy, it makes little difference which instrument you use. Postsecondary education is currently funded in part by federal government transfers to the provinces. For years, federal ministers have mused about converting that transfer to vouchers that would go directly to students. The money would be exactly the same, and it could flow only into postsecondary institutions. The big difference would be the change from a cash transfer to governments to a voucher for students. The other aspect of this issue is comparing the pattern of instrument choice across governments. Expenditures across the OECD countries on health, education, and income security are much closer than the means used to provide these services.

Linder and Peters (1989) provide a model for understanding the links between the broad policy system variables and decisions that policymakers themselves undertake in given situations. They emphasize the importance of systemic variables, organizational characteristics, problem features, and the profile of individual decisionmakers. Systemic variables include such broad factors as national policy style, political culture, and prevailing social cleavages. Organizational variables include the way that the sponsoring department is structured, its history, and its connections with its relevant policy communities. The problem context embraces questions such as how crowded the policy domain is, the political constraints of using a specific instrument, and the requirements of political support. Finally, individual level variables comprise perceptions, values, and experience of the policymaker. This schema operates almost like a funnel, channelling these larger forces down from the systemic level to the individual decisionmakers. Of course, national policy style and political culture are not actors on the policy stage; they have influence only through the decisionmaker's implicit or conscious application. The current debate in some provincial jurisdictions over the use of private management companies to run public hospitals is an interesting illustration. This is contracting out to a third party in a policy area that jealously protects its public character. The decision to use this instrument will certainly depend on cost considerations and effectiveness (the problem context), but also on what is feasible or acceptable in that political regime (style and political culture).

NEW DYNAMICS

As we have argued throughout this book, the nature of governance is changing because of globalization, technology, culture, and new approaches to public management and statecraft. While the impacts on problem definitions are powerful, as we saw in Chapter 3, they are still somewhat difficult to conceptualize because problem definition and agenda-setting are such complex processes in their own right. In this chapter and in Chapter 5, we see clear evidence for new ways of making policy.

SPENDING INSTRUMENTS

The first edition of this book appeared in 1997, when governments across Canada were in the midst of seriously attacking deficits that had built up over almost a quarter century. By late 2000, the federal government was running its third consecutive surplus, paying down the debt, spending on new programs and increasing its expenditures on old ones, and even reducing taxes. By the end of the 1999 fiscal year, only Ontario, Quebec, and British Columbia were running deficits. By summer 2004, as we noted in Chapter 3, the federal government and all but three provinces ran either balanced budgets or surpluses. All of this has been achieved through a mix of deliberate policies of fiscal restraint and pure blind luck—the U.S. economy has had the longest sustained boom in its history, and Canada has benefited enormously. It might seem that the pain of the last decade is now behind us and that governments can once again spend. To some extent this is true, but we need a more nuanced assessment of the effects of cuts and fiscal restraint.

Fiscal restraint of the magnitude that we have experienced in the past decade was not simply about money—it had deep policy impacts as well. At the federal level, Program Review forced policymakers to ask six fundamental questions (see Chapter 2) about each program they administered and to reconsider modes of delivery (i.e., their instruments). Provincial governments went through similar exercises, under different guises. At the federal level, total expenditures in 1992–93 were $161 billion; by 1997 they dropped to $149 billion. Much of that drop was achieved through cuts in transfers to the provinces, particularly in health and social services, with predictable results across the country. Federal spending started to increase again after 1997, but Ottawa has enjoyed an unbroken string of surpluses.

During the period of restraint, the magnitude and unavoidability of the cuts faced by most spending departments in most jurisdictions across Canada demanded a fundamental re-evaluation of lines of business. When funding drops by 20 percent or 30 percent in two years, something has to change, and that change cannot be incremental. Another consequence of fiscal restraint has been greater interlinkage in designing policy. In part, this stems as well from the growing appreciation of the interconnectedness of policy fields. Sustainable development, for example, can be defined to include health and social stability, in which case almost anything becomes relevant as "environmental policy." And as fiscal concerns permeated policymaking in recent years, almost everything came under the purview of departments of finance. Added to this were shifts in economic theory that highlighted the importance of human capital for competitiveness in high-technology, information-based industries—encouraging social policy to merge to a large extent with economic policy. Nonetheless, reduced spending capacity has helped this new appreciation of linkages and leverage to emerge as well.

During the period of restraint, most government departments had to reassess their priorities, cut some programs, reduce spending on others, and downsize their staff and other resources. They had to focus their programs more tightly, budget carefully, and try to demonstrate results. Now that good times appear to be here again, will these disciplines disappear under the political pressure to spend, or has something fundamental changed in the way in which governments view the "spending instrument"? Once surpluses appear, of course, the political pressure to spend increases dramatically. The policy advantage governments had during deficit days was that they would quite plausibly argue that they could not afford new programs. Balanced budgets, and particularly surpluses, demolish that riposte and force policymakers once again to make choices about how to respond to new demands. As well, the natural tendency of any elected politician is to respond positively to demands for new programs and expenditures. Despite these pressures, however, it appears that the experience of the past decade has had an effect on how the Canadian public and their elected governments view spending.

It seems clear that while there is no consensus on the economic theory that should underpin government budgeting, there is an emerging orthodoxy that cuts across political lines that disparages spending *per se* as a policy instrument and that rejects deficits as an appropriate way to stimulate the economy (Campbell, 1999, p. 141). In the June 2004 federal election, the Liberals, Conservatives, and NDP all pledged not to run deficits. Equally significant, while the newly elected McGuinty government in Ontario brought down a deficit budget in May 2004, it also committed itself to a four-year plan to reach balance. Nonetheless, there continues to be an appetite among the Canadian public for focused spending in various areas, particularly in health care, and governments cannot be blind to spending pressures that are associated with changing demographics and a certain minimum maintenance of infrastructure and core services. As we noted earlier, about 70 percent of all provincial government spending is on health, education, and social services, and not surprisingly, these are the top priorities for citizens as well. Indeed, it is remarkable how important health care has become to Canadians and to governments. After the shocks of transfer cuts in the mid-1990s, and facing a constant barrage of criticism from provincial leaders and rising concerns from ordinary Canadians about the quality of health care, the federal government began to respond in various ways. It started to put money back into the system: in 2001 Ottawa established the Commission on the Future of Health Care in Canada (the Romanow Commission), which paved the way for the Health Care Renewal Accord of February 2003. The Accord would transfer $34.8 billion from Ottawa to the provinces over five years for health care. In the June 2004 election, all three national parties pledged to support the Accord and to add even more money.

The issue therefore is not spending *per se*. Even the allegedly fiscally phobic Conservative Party of Canada, in its 2004 election platform, promised to increase federal spending by almost $30 billion per year over seven years. But it promised to do so within a balanced fiscal framework, and that is what seems to have changed. Another interesting indication that spending is viewed more carefully these days is the emphasis on making "investments." Almost all major government spending initiatives are now described as investments. An **investment** implies a return of some sort, a benefit or a profit, and so is rhetorically more useful to contemporary policymakers. As well, we can expect these investments to be relatively modest in scope. While governments will continue to use the expenditure instrument, it is not likely that—

aside from health and perhaps defence/security—they will embark on huge spending programs reminiscent of the 1960s and 1970s. Smaller "boutique" programs are likely to be more prevalent. If the programs are large by contemporary standards, they will have to be justified as being solidly within the government's fiscal framework. Of course, if that framework balloons out with sustained projected surpluses, there will be much more scope to spend on new programs and top up old ones.

In the absence of any other forces affecting spending, and assuming continued economic growth and hence increased government surpluses, we might expect a return to the spending instrument, though couched more carefully in terms of investments. There has been another important change in public attitudes and public policy discourse, however, that might upset this equation—the popularity of tax cuts. It should be remembered that a good part of the success in erasing deficits and achieving balanced budgets was through increased tax rates and increased tax revenues. This was combined with a growing sense that Canadian taxes were too high in comparison to the United States, and thus a key factor in a putative "brain drain" and persistently lower levels of economic productivity. Alberta led the way in first reducing taxes after it had achieved balanced budgets, and then announced in its 1999 budget that it would move to a single-rate, flat tax uncoupled from the federal income tax system. The February 2000 Alberta budget announced that this new system, with an 11 percent single rate on taxable income and substantially increased personal exemptions, would go into effect in January 2001. The Ontario Conservatives slashed income taxes in the two fiscal years before they achieved balance. Tax cuts were a major feature of federal budgets between 2000 and 2003, and again all three national parties offered some degree of tax relief in the June 2004 election (the Liberals with only minor reductions for seniors and those with disabilities; the Tories with major personal and corporate cuts; the NDP with increases for the wealthy combined with reductions for middle- and lower-income groups). But it is clear that tax-cutting as a strategy is more comfortable for the right, whereas the left will emphasize "fairness" in taxation with targeted and relatively minor reductions.

If the pressure to reduce taxes keeps up, it may reduce the scope to spend profligately on new programs. To this might be added a growing sense that government grants and contributions are often badly managed, and that money is wasted in hundreds of small and large ways in Ottawa and provincial capitals. Occasional stories like the one in Box 4.3 serve to sharpen public skepticism, and officials and policymakers will have to show how their spending programs and management of public money are beneficial, efficacious, and prudent. This is primarily a question of evaluation, which we take up in Chapter 7.

Box 4.3   THE PRIVACY COMMISSIONER'S
TRAVEL EXPENSES

Below are excerpts from the auditor general's report on the travel and hospitality expenses of former Privacy Commissioner Radwanski:

126. The former Commissioner and the Senior Director General flew business class wherever possible, even on short domestic flights. Both almost always stayed at expensive hotels and ate at costly restaurants.

127. Hotel costs of the former Commissioner and his Senior Director General usually exceeded the published guideline rates allowed to government employees. Our audit determined that in about 80 percent of their domestic travel, they exceeded the Treasury Board guidelines for accommodations by 70 percent on average. In 60 percent of their international travel they also exceeded Treasury Board accommodation guidelines, and by 50 percent on average. On three nights in London, England, for example, the former Commissioner and the Senior Director General each spent more than $500 per night on hotel accommodations. None of their travel claims included documentation to justify exceeding the guideline limits, even though Treasury Board policies require such justification.

128. We also found that two hotel rooms at $330 each per night had been booked in Washington, DC for two nights. Although the hotel rooms had been paid for, they were not used on the first night; on the second day they were used, according to the former Commissioner, only as a place to "freshen up" and make telephone calls after a two-hour flight.

129. The cost of meals claimed during travel usually exceeded Treasury Board guidelines. Our review of domestic and international travel found that spending on meals exceeded the guidelines over 60 percent of the time. Examples of unreasonable meal expenditures include over $300 in London on lunch for two and over $100 in Hawaii and $100 in London on breakfast for two. On three occasions, in Hawaii, Brussels, and London, the former Commissioner and the Senior Director General spent over $550 per day on meals for two.

130. Travel meal expenditures are not to include alcohol. We calculated that during all the international trips of the former Commissioner, over $31,000 was paid for meals and refreshments. Taking into account that Treasury Board meal allowances for international travel vary by city to reflect the cost of living, we estimated that government employees with similar itineraries would have been entitled to claim about $14,000. Using his "discretion," therefore, the former Commissioner incurred about $17,000 more than that for meals and refreshments abroad—more than twice the amount set out in the guidelines. . . . In our opinion, this was an abuse of the discretion accorded to a deputy head.

SOURCE: Auditor General of Canada. (2003). *Report on the Office of the Privacy Commissioner of Canada*. Retrieved August 12, 2004, from http://www.oag-bvg.gc .ca/domino/reports.nsf/html/20030930ce.html

TAXATION

Canadian governments tackled their deficits in the 1990s by cutting some expenditures, but they also benefited from increased tax revenues. As Purchase and Hirshhorn (1994) show, total tax revenues in Canada "increased from 31.3 percent in 1983 to 37 percent in 1992" (p. 36). Moreover, while corporate taxes actually declined in this period, "taxes on individuals have increased sharply" (p. 37). Federal government revenues were $116 billion in 1993–94; in 2000–01 they were $162 billion; and in 2002-03 they were $177 billion. Projections to 2006 show a steady increase in revenues, half of which come from personal taxes (Department of Finance, 2004, p. 64). While most Canadians welcomed the eradication of government deficits in the 1990s, they were not entirely pleased with the high taxes they had to pay to achieve it. By 2000, the debate over taxes had become sharpened, with many commentators arguing that tax rates were too high, and moreover that they were stifling economic growth. The Canadian tax burden was already high compared to trading partners and the G-7, and increases would reduce competitiveness. Ralph Klein took this notion to its extreme in promoting what he called the "Alberta advantage" of low taxes compared to other Canadian provinces. As we noted above, all three major national parties favour tax reductions of some sort, with the key difference being their magnitude and incidence. The outrage at the 2004 Ontario budget's reimposition of a health care premium seems to suggest that the public may be able to live with current tax rates but is unlikely to support increases.

A countertrend to reduced income taxes is an increase in user charges and service fees. The deepest reasons for this are also the murkiest, and perhaps the most controversial: as citizens become more resistant to redistributive government, they become more resistant to redistributive (i.e., general) taxation. Fees and charges seem to link services more directly to beneficiaries. Through user charges and service fees, special benefits enjoyed by only a minority of citizens are paid for in whole or in part by that minority. One study estimated that user fees accounted for 17 percent of total government revenues in 1990 and that reliance on them, by at least Ontario municipal governments, was increasing (Sproule-Jones, 1994, p. 7). In a related development, governments also seem more willing to "earmark" certain tax revenues to cover specific expenses, another trend that started in the mid-1990s (Thirsk and Bird, 1994, p. 130). A June 2000 report of the federal Standing Committee on Finance noted that while user charges contributed a negligible amount to Ottawa's revenues (about 2.4 percent), there were some 391 of them spread over 47 departments and agencies (Standing Committee on Finance, 2000). The government had encouraged departments to rely more on user charges and cost recovery in its 1997 Cost Recovery and Charging Policy.

REGULATION

Just as the character of expenditures and taxes as policy instruments has changed, so has regulation. The pressures on regulatory instruments have been somewhat contradictory. On the one hand, all other things being equal, governments that have less money to spend will shift to less expensive regulatory instruments to achieve the same ends. But as we argued in Chapter 2, the very nature of governance has changed, and spending cuts are usually accompanied by a sense that government as a whole should pull back. That makes regulatory instruments less feasible, since they rely on the direct use of authority, which has less legitimacy among modern publics. On the other hand, both international agreements and economic and technological forces constrain the use of regulatory instruments in many traditional areas such as telecommunications and broadcasting, utilities, foreign investment, and marketing boards. We will try to make sense of these contradictory pressures by addressing constraints on regulation, demands for regulation, and shifts in regulatory venues.

The constraints on the use of regulatory instruments come principally from four sources: international trade agreements, technology, economics, and cost. A large subset of economic regulatory instruments have been devoted in one fashion or another to the protection of domestic industries from excessive internal or foreign competition. Classic examples include regulations that prevented foreign banks from operating in Canada, regulations that gave domestic Canadian oil companies advantages over foreign-owned competitors, foreign investment guidelines, broadcasting rules that protected Canadian advertisers and cable companies, and agricultural marketing boards for everything from milk to potatoes. The 1989 Free Trade Agreement, and its successor, the North American Free Trade Agreement (NAFTA), with Canada, the United States, and Mexico, expressly forbids some forms of regulation that would advantage domestic industries over competitors from the partner countries. Agricultural marketing boards, for example, are facing intense pressures under the NAFTA provisions on agriculture and food products. While environmental, health, and cultural regulations are in principle shielded from NAFTA, the larger free-trade logic of the agreement increasingly puts these provisions under some pressure. The World Trade Organization (WTO), the successor to the GATT, was explicitly designed to establish clearer and more efficient institutional mechanisms to deal with a wider variety of trade issues (e.g., services, farming, and manufactured goods). On standards, for example, the Uruguay Round Agreement on Technical Barriers to Trade

> seeks to ensure that technical regulations and standards, as well as testing and certification procedures, do not create unnecessary obstacles to trade. The agreement recognizes the rights of countries to adopt such measures, to the extent they consider appropriate—for example, for human, animal or plant life or health, for the protection of the environment or to meet other consumer interests. Moreover, members are not prevented from taking measures necessary to ensure their standards of protection are met. The agreement encourages countries to use international standards where these are appropriate, but it does not require them to change their levels of protection as a result of standardization. The agreement sets out a code of good practice for the preparation, adoption and application of standards by central government bodies as well as provisions under which local government and nongovernmental bodies should frame and use technical regulations. It requires that procedures for determining the conformity of products with national standards be fair and equitable, particularly between domestically produced goods and the equivalent imported goods. In addition, it encourages the mutual recognition of conformity assessments— in other words if the authorities of the exporting country determine a product to be in conformity with a technical standard, the authorities of the importing country should normally accept that determination. (World Trade Organization 1996)

As we note below, however, internationalization has also provided a fresh context for "**re-regulation**" that brings domestic policy targets into a wider, international regime. This can actually strengthen domestic regulation, not constrain it. Doern and colleagues point out that in fact there has been an increase in some business framework and environmental regulation, and that in contrast to the conventional view that the last two decades have been primarily an era of **deregulation**, "it is evident that, overall, the density and extent of rule making by, or on behalf of, the state has increased" (Doern et al., 1999a, p. 5). This is in part due to pressures in health and safety regulation, often driven by technology. Food products, clean air standards, water quality, and the impact of biotechnology across a host of areas drive a demand for more, not less, regulation. Another important change to regulation as a governing instrument and as part of policy design has been the internationalization of regulatory regimes. If we think of regulation in its broadest sense—rules and standards about conduct, backed by sanctions of some sort—then many of our domestic regulatory regimes are becoming linked with international ones. This reflects one side of the process of globalization discussed in Chapter 2. As the forces and factors important to policy shift to the international level, governments increasingly will have to cooperate at that level in order to continue to have some influence on their domestic practices: "Not only are fundamental trade rules crossing borders and affecting practices in various 'domestic' regulatory realms, but newer 'crosswalks' institutions are being negotiated between heretofore separate international realms, such as competition, the environment, intellectual property, and investment" (Doern et al., 1999a, p. 21).

These organizational constraints on regulatory instruments mirror the constraints that some of these instruments face as a result of technological and economic changes. The key to conventional regulatory instruments is the government's ability to first forbid some activity or outcome and then permit it under certain conditions. This assumes that the activity or outcome in question can indeed be controlled and monitored. When regulatory authorities can be bypassed, then the regime collapses or becomes irrelevant. Substantial changes in technology and competitive markets were the foundation for the massive deregulation movement in trucking, airlines, and energy in the 1980s (Schultz, 1994). Before the advent of satellite dishes, for example, what Canadians watched on TV could be controlled by the regulator. It is less clear what the Canadian Radio-Television and Telecommunications Commission (CRTC) can do about what Canadians watch in a 500-channel universe where most of those channels are being broadcast by entities beyond the CRTC's control. This does not even include the impact of broadcasting over the Internet.

These forces help us understand the constraints and limits on regulatory instruments, forces that lie behind much of what has been labelled "deregulation" in the past decade. However, there are countervailing pressures that make regulatory instruments attractive, and that in fact mean that what has been going on is better described as "re-regulation" in some areas and even an intensification of the state's regulatory role in others. Ironically, the argument that government should be reduced and restructured can work to the advantage of regulatory instruments. The downsizing comes principally in expenditures and direct service provision, leaving a stronger role for governments in the establishment of framework legislation or regulation: "Deregulation in Canada has resulted in a more focused and likely more robust regulatory role by government. Case studies of deregulation in various sectors show that major deregulatory actions have been accompanied by refinements and creations of new regulatory instruments" (Doern et al. 1999b, 394). Governments, so the argument runs, should steer not row, and this draws them toward regulatory instruments that focus more on frameworks and outcomes than minute rules. As well, some areas of regulation remain quite popular with the public, whatever the apparent rising antipathy to government as a whole. Mad Cow and SARS were simply the most visible instances where people expected governments to act forcefully, but there have also been scares of potable water and genetically modified foods. Indeed, even as major areas of economic regulation were being cut back in the 1980s, social regulations were, in some cases, actually increasing. Human rights legislation, regulations against discrimination, and efforts to control violence and pornography have enjoyed continuing support. Moreover, the forms of regulation may adapt. Prince (1999) reminds us of the importance of what he calls civic regulation: rule-making "with respect to numerous social aspects of human behaviour and needs, moral conduct and standards, intergovernmental relations, and human rights and civil liberties" (p. 204). He agrees that this arena of state regulation is probably expanding due to pressures for "intervention and protection from citizens, interest groups, social movements, and governments" (p. 221). Certainly, the shift to postmaterial values and rights discourse discussed in Chapter 2 is part of the reason for this, along with an increasing insistence by more "business-minded" governments on standards of conduct by recipients of social assistance and other forms of public aid.

The trends in regulation are therefore complicated. First, it is undeniable that there has been a combination of pressures in the last two decades to re-examine the effects and the management of economic regulations. This has been driven in part by technological changes (e.g., in communications and in financial services) and partly by deliberate decisions to deregulate taken by conservative governments around the world. The Canadian variant was several reviews of regulation undertaken in the 1970s, which eventually yielded the Regulatory Impact Assessment Statement regime of the mid-1980s (Mihlar, 1999) and more recently, a revised Government of Canada Regulatory Policy (1999a). Second, while some regulatory agencies and their oversight have been weakened, for instance in transportation, resources, and utilities, they have also become in some instances more focused and strategic. Third, new areas of civic and environmental and even economic regulation have arisen that are being managed by all three levels of government, sometimes alone but often in concert. Fourth, domestic regulation is increasingly affected by international factors, institutions, and decisions, and in many cases "bridges" between domestic and international regulatory agencies are being constructed in order to facilitate harmonization of standards. Fifth, the rhythms of regulation and deregulation vary considerably by country. The United States—which often seems to set the tone in policy discussions—has accepted deregulation and minimal state intrusion as a matter of rhetorical faith, whereas Canada and many European countries are considerably more cautious (Peters, 1998; Wilks and Doern, 1998).

A perfect illustration of these developments can be seen in the federal government's most recent attempt to rethink regulation, the External Advisory Committee on Smart Regulation. First announced in the 2002 Speech from the Throne, the Committee was asked to develop a regulatory strategy for the twenty-first century, based on a sense that the context for regulation is changing in fundamental ways:

> Regulators in the 21st century must take into account a new set of realities, such as the multiplication of governance sites and actors (e.g., international organizations, business or industry groups), increased occurrence of litigation, the limitations of government-centered regulatory action, the pressures from industry to have more flexibility to meet regulatory objectives, the demands of citizens to better protect health and safety and the demands of the public and industry groups to have more say in what governments do and how they do it. Over the years, these emerging realities have exerted greater pressure on traditional regulatory action. (External Advisory Committee on Smart Regulation, 2004)

The concept of "smart regulation" has several components. Possibly the most important driver is a sense of rising competitive pressures, particularly international ones, a more rapid cycle of innovation and technological development, coupled with public concerns about health, safety, and consumer choice. The basic saw-off is between providing companies with light, flexible, and responsive regulatory regimes that allow them to bring products to market quickly and capitalize on a clear, consistent, but not overbearing regulatory system, and making sure that that regulatory system continues to protect consumers while not patronizing them.

NEW EMPHASES: INFORMATION, PARTNERSHIPS, INTERNATIONALISM, AND INSTITUTIONAL DESIGN

The mark of the inventive policy designer is the ability to come up with new ways of doing things, and there have been some fresh techniques or devices both discussed and implemented in some countries in recent years (e.g., tradable pollution permits). This section will focus, however, on four categories of policy instruments and how emphasis has shifted to make them comparatively more important than ever before.

As we noted above, information is typically considered to be a weak and relatively unobtrusive instrument in the government toolkit. We also noted, however, somewhat less benign uses of information through "regulation by shaming" and the robust use of advertising, exhortation, and public awareness campaigns. In fact, information as a technique in delivering policy outcomes may be gaining importance for at least four reasons. The first is that spending, regulatory, and taxation instruments have been constrained in the new governance environment. By comparison, information is often less expensive as an instrument and gives the impression of being less invasive.

The second reason is somewhat more complex, but reflects the new approaches to public management discussed in Chapter 2, and which we will take up again in Chapter 5 in greater detail. Two major emphases in this new thinking are **"citizen engagement"** and better accountability mechanisms from government to the public. While these are clearly related, the first refers to bringing citizens and groups into the decision-making process, while the second refers more to techniques of providing **transparency** in public decisionmaking. Canada's Access to Information Act, first passed in 1983, is a good example of this approach in that it established the principle that government information should be kept from the public only under specific circumstances; in all other cases the emphasis should be on openness. More recent versions of the use of information and transparency for public policy purposes involve better accountability through performance or outcome measures. It is now widely assumed that engagement, transparency, and accountability may in themselves become factors in policy development. In short, if governments promise to do certain things, and their promises and their performance are a matter of public record, sooner or later that information will be used to hold them accountable. The Social Union Framework Agreement (SUFA) for example, was signed by Ottawa and nine provinces and the territories in 1999 (Quebec did not sign) to provide a new framework for the development of social policy in Canada. Section 3 of the agreement states,

> "Canada's Social Union can be strengthened by enhancing each government's transparency and accountability to its constituents. Each government therefore agrees to . . . Share information and best practices to support the development of outcome measures, and work with other governments to develop, over time, comparable indicators to measure progress on agreed objectives (Privy Council Office, 1999).

The Romanow Commission in its 2002 report on the Canadian health care system made a similar suggestion on information and reporting: it recommended the establishment of a Health Council, which would begin the work of developing common indicators that could then pave the way for a national performance review system. The Health Accord signed a year later also called for annual reporting by governments to citizens about how their health dollars are being spent.

The third reason that information is becoming a more important resource and instrument for governments is due to the rise of the "information society" and the "knowledge-based economy" or KBE. While a good deal of what defines these phenomena are still unclear, it seems undeniable today that information technology is driving a revolution in the way that citizens and consumers get goods and services from government and the private sector. Every level of government across the country is experimenting with ways of using information in new ways to manage program delivery and handle policy problems. It is simply a given now that information technology is a major economic driver, and that knowledge and innovation are the key comparative advantages now for firms as well as national economies. The federal government's vision of "e-government" or "government on-line" is also emblematic of a focus on information as a main conduit of interaction between governments and citizens. One fascinating example that has not made its way to Canada yet but may in the future is toll pricing of inner-city roads (*The Economist*, 2004). Toll pricing of highways, bridges, or tunnels is nothing new, but toll pricing city centres or entire national road networks is (Switzerland, Austria, and Germany currently charge trucks, and Britain will follow in 2008). Traffic congestion in city cores can be seen as a supply and demand problem; "too many cars" is a function of either not enough or inefficient roadways, or too many cars for the existing system. Typically, the policy response to increasing congestion has been to expand supply through building more roads or bypasses, but for reasons of expense and the environment, that is becoming too expensive. The alternative is to control or reduce demand. This can be done in various ways, such as high parking fees or even physical controls through licensing schemes that allow only certain cars in on certain days, for example. In 2003, London joined Singapore as the second major city to implement a system that makes drivers pay to enter the centre of the city. The entire scheme depends on information technology that allows precise pricing of the sort that would have been impossible or too costly in the past. In London's case, drivers pay a charge of £5 per day (this can be paid at corner stores, by phone, or on the Internet). The nearly 700 cameras within the city centre monitor license plates, and send the data via fibre optics to a data centre that matches those plate numbers to a database of licensed users for that day or period. Violators receive fines by mail. The result? Congestion in the charging zone fell by 30 percent, significantly higher than expected, though revenues were below expectations. The Swiss system charges trucks throughout the entire national road system, and uses GPS (global positioning system) technology. The combination of GPS, cameras, fibre optics, databases, cell phones, smart cards, wireless transmission of data, and small computers has the potential to revolutionize program delivery, especially to the extent that programs are themselves largely information based. The key aspects of this revolution are twofold. First, there is a new and growing ability to price public goods in unobtrusive and inexpensive ways. That is the secret of London's toll system. What at one time would have seemed impossible in terms of monitoring and implementation costs, now occurs almost automatically. This effect will make itself most evident in transportation. Second, there is increasing capacity to individualize program delivery, since it is now possible to deal with individual clients (data capacity is much higher) and not simply categories of clients. This will probably have its greatest effect in social services, health, and education. Finally, the other side of these developments is the potential of increasing surveillance and threats to privacy.

Information has become more important for a fourth reason as well. As governments have become more active in the realm of civic regulation such as antidiscrimination, they inevitably get into the persuasion game, since the policy problems here are primarily attitudinal. Policy concerns about health and lifestyle in this period also contributed to the importance of changing hearts and minds on key issues such as exercise and eating habits. Contemporary concerns about violence, stereotyping, and abuse ensure that policy instruments that both convey information and try to exhort certain behaviours will remain important. In addition, however, governments increasingly find themselves with less money, and greater reliance on partners for the delivery of programs, as will be explained in Chapter 5. This interdependency depends on the exchange of information and the building up of relationships. Lindquist (1992) has even urged policymakers to conceptualize their role as "stewards" of policy communities. Stewardship depends on information exchange. The more that government finds itself operating in networks, relying on partners, and enhancing and facilitating the capacities of societal actors to do things, the more its primary role is to provide critical information, help circulate it, and encourage policy learning. This can go beyond simple distribution of information to calling attention to new policy problems—providing leadership, in short.

A new emphasis on partnerships is another development in policy targets and hence policy instruments. Partnerships will be discussed in greater detail in Chapter 5, but the basic logic is that government can either get out of some of the things that it has traditionally done and leave them to the private or nonprofit sectors, or it can continue to do those things in direct partnerships with those sectors. An example is care for the elderly, which is provided primarily by for-profit and nonprofit organizations that receive the bulk of their funding from provincial governments. The first mode suggests an oversight capacity for government once the service has been devolved. The second implies a direct partnership with a community association, industry group, or NGO. If partnerships are conceived of as a policy instrument, then they will not simply appear; they have to be created. This requires some skill, as well as a grasp of the different types of partnering that can be undertaken (e.g., one of consultation versus a roundtable format or working together to implement programs).

The third new emphasis in policy is the international system itself. The traditional organization of the foreign policy dossier called for a single foreign affairs department that would channel issues from domestic departments into the international system. With the internationalization of so many policy fields, and with the substantive policy expertise in fact lodged in "domestic" departments, more and more of these departments are engaged in international negotiations. The Department of Foreign Affairs tries to coordinate this at the national level, but the sheer scope of international representations by every government body, from local municipalities to federal departments, makes it a difficult task. Yet, international agreements and international negotiations are becoming a routine instrument in the pursuit of domestic policy. Moreover, it is not simply a matter of single policy fields being projected upward to the international level but linkages across policy fields being developed by international agencies. A good example is environmental issues being entwined with economic and development questions, not to mention technology transfer and agriculture. Under these circumstances, just about everyone can get into the game.

A final, unconventional category that seems to be attracting increasing attention is **procedural** (Howlett, 2000) or institutional instruments (Kirschen, 1964). Governments "increasingly come to rely on the use of a different set of 'procedural' tools designed to indirectly affect outcomes through the manipulation of policy processes" (Howlett, 2000, p. 413). Many of these instruments are aimed less at delivery of policy and programs than at the restructuring of relationships either within the state or between the state and social partners. Collaborative partnerships, for example, "require some fundamental changes in the organizational and traditional values of the public sector. . . . [They] require a new willingness to share authority and the development of a learning culture" (Armstrong and Lenihan, 1999, p. 12).

Another way to see this category of instruments is as focusing on organization or network-type targets. Organizational instruments take the state itself—its structure and management—as a target of public policy. As Osborne and Gaebler (1993) famously argued, there is a continuing role for government but not in its bureaucratic guise. It is necessary to restructure government so that incentives to perform efficiently and well are clear and pervasive. **Performance indicators** and pay linked to performance help do that. Other mechanisms are designed to introduce market forces into the provision of public services, from contracting out to full privatization. As Kettl (1995) points out, these organizational instruments assume that "key relationships in government can be viewed as a series of contract-like connections" (p. 35). If so, then contracts should be as specific and transparent as possible.

Network targets are primarily groups and individuals in civil society, outside the state. The role of government is to facilitate and empower rather than to deliver and direct. Adjustment programs, capacity building, the dissemination of information, participation and partnerships, rights enforcement, funding interest groups and developing stakeholder networks—all of these make sense only if organizations and individuals are granted high levels of autonomy and legitimacy as policy actors in their own right, not merely as recipients of government programs. As McDonnell and Elmore (1987) argue, policy instruments in this category have the character of "inducements" rather than mandates and hinge on "how much variation policymakers are willing to tolerate in the production of things of value" (p. 15). If individuals, organizations, and communities are to have choice and autonomy, then the tolerance for variation has to increase substantially. Framework policy, decentralization, and information policy instruments clearly presume that policy outcomes will depend on a degree of "**co-production**" with other actors. Of course, "co-production" also means a greater degree of mutual interdependence—governments cannot control all processes and outcomes. Therefore, this approach also requires a greater tolerance for potential failure and the possibility that partners will both make mistakes and have to learn from them. It puts the policy designer less in the position of being an "engineer" than an "animateur," relying primarily on process values and politics (Linder and Peters, 1995). We will return to these types of instruments in the next chapter.

CONCLUSION

We should address two questions in closing this chapter. First, is there a uniform tilt to the new toolbox of policy instruments? Second, has the toolbox become so small and empty that governments are virtually powerless to do anything worthwhile?

Readers will have noticed that there does appear to be a tilt to the way in which instruments and policy design have been going. The history of deficits and the current pressures of globalization, combined with citizen disaffection, generally propel governments not simply to do more with less but to do less with less. If possible, policy should depend on market mechanisms and individual choice, and minimize spending and regulation. In practice, of course, this is precisely the prescription adopted by Canadian governments in the last few years, whatever their political stripe. Conservative governments have had more bloodlust on this question, slashing with greater determination and less regret than NDP or Liberal governments, but the latter have adopted much of the same rhetoric and policy approaches. Small, leaner government and less obtrusive instruments seem to be the order of the day.

The picture is more complicated than this, however. First, as we noted in Chapter 2, postmaterialist values are not uniformly pro-market, for example, when it comes to the environment. Second, there is substantial angst about some major social policy questions such as youth crime, violent pornography, decaying family structures, racism, school behaviour, and educational performance, not to mention a host of health and safety concerns. It is far from clear that governments or citizens in these areas are prepared to accept nostrums of minimal government and market mechanisms. Third, the same market forces that drive globalization and competitiveness generate anxieties about jobs, communities, and lifestyle. Some more extreme scenarios draw a grim portrait of highly polarized societies, with a small elite of global citizens jetting off to their next conference or business meeting while the majority drifts in a world of intermittent employment, corroded infrastructure, and the commercialization of virtually every aspect of life. Finally, it is important not to overestimate the ease with which global pressures penetrate national social, economic, and political systems. The institutional configuration of these systems can make it more or less easy for global pressures to be channelled through to governments (Neville, 2002). For example, despite globalization and two free trade agreements with the United States, Canadian and American health and social policy systems are in some instances vastly different.

The policy literature is coming to recognize this, principally by urging the importance of values in public policy. Though this is a larger issue than instrument choice, the discussion in this chapter has shown that the tilt of the toolbox is to maximize individual choice and minimize government intervention. But public policy is not purely instrumental; it sends signals to citizens about who they are and how they should behave. For better or worse, it gives them a picture of appropriate social and political relations. Policy implementation that depends increasingly on market mechanisms and individual choice will encourage citizens to see their relations to government and to each other as primarily ones of exchange—a set of quasi-economic transactions for individual benefit. As Aaron, Mann, and Taylor (1994) point out: "In the jargon of the social scientists, analysts have begun to recognize that values and norms are not 'exogenous,' or independent of public policy. And the idea that values can change, combined with the recognition that responses to policies depend on people's preferences—that is, their values—leads to thinking about how public policy might change values directly or indirectly and thereby change the responses of public policies themselves" (p. 3). Their point is twofold: (1) effective public policies depend on a certain temperament of cooperation and support from citizens, and to neglect the nurturing of that temperament would be a huge mistake, and (2) governments have a legitimate, though carefully balanced, role in supporting and developing some key social values, such as trust, community, and empathy.

These are ultimately questions of policy design for democracy, an issue that the literature on policy instruments often avoids and that practising policymakers usually sidestep. But it is worth asking these questions. What effect will downsized government have on citizenship? How far should we go in encouraging individual self-reliance before eroding common bonds and a public space? Marc Landy (1993), for example, defines citizenship as "a station that lies between self-absorption and absorption with abstractions. . . . It involves an ongoing effort to synthesize questions of 'what is best for the world' with 'what is best for me'" (p. 20). This is a vision that stresses duty, responsibility, and democratic deliberation. March and Olsen (1995) define the civic temperament this way: "democratic civility achieves its primary claims by stimulating empathetic feelings in citizens, attitudes that allow for sympathetic consideration of the plights and possibilities of others, capacities for feeling sorrow and joy in concert with others. Civility in conflict is encouraged by encounters of understanding, generosity, and restraint" (p. 61). Schneider and Ingram (1997) are concerned about "degenerative policy designs" that, in their view, "send different messages to different target populations, but these messages encourage most of the target groups to take only their own interests into account in their expectations of government thereby leading to irresponsible citizenship and the demise of community" (p. 197).

These phrases sound soft when compared to the tough talk usually associated with developing economic competitiveness. That tough talk has served to justify smaller government. Some recent economic thinking about what truly makes economies competitive, however, suggests that these softer policy targets may be vitally important. Recent work on **social capital,** for example, seeks to explain both efficient government and competitive economies in terms of social bonds of association and trust. The phenomenal success of Robert Putnam's *Making Democracy Work* (1993) and *Bowling Alone* (2000) suggests that concerns about social capital cut across ideological lines. Francis Fukuyama (1995) has argued that economic performance depends on social capital and is a function of trust, which he defines as the "expectation that arises within a community of regular, honest, and cooperative behaviour, based on commonly shared norms, on the part of other members of that community" (p. 26). Both economic and political "performance" can be seen as forms of "collective action" problems, where what is rational from a collective point of view (say, a clean environment) runs up against incentives for individuals to free-ride and maximize their self-interest (say, the profits that can be made when all your competitors install antipollution equipment but you do not). If people cooperate, they are all better off. Community and social cohesion have become watchwords for government policy throughout North America.

The above should help provide the answer to our second question of whether the toolkit has shrunk or been emptied. As has been mentioned many times in this book, modern governments have had their hands tied by fiscal pressures, internationalization, and shifts in ideology that demand less intervention. There seems to be little tolerance for deficit spending, and there is pressure to at least hold the line on taxes, if not reduce them. Internationalization means that the domestic economy is much more exposed to global competition, and investors sit ready to judge government policy by pulling out of currency and bond markets if they see something they dislike.

This is not the whole story, however. As we noted earlier in this chapter, the same forces of globalization that constrain governments create powerful pressures for them to act on behalf of their domestic constituencies. Governments remain massively involved in health, education, and social security, and by 2005 most governments in Canada could count on healthy revenues and even surpluses. New issues such as youth unemployment, Aboriginal self-government, information technologies, and building social capital also demand attention. Information resources and technologies of power (e.g., surveillance) have also improved considerably. What is different is that policymakers have to be a bit more clever than they once were. Without the easy option of throwing money at a problem, policy suddenly demands more imaginative use of other instruments. If internationalization threatens an important domestic industry, the trick is to find a way, within the rules, to help. If government cannot do something on its own, it needs to create the conditions to work with others to achieve the objectives. Both of these are tricks about converting policy tools into implementation, the subject of the next chapter.

KEY TERMS

alternative service delivery—the use of nontraditional means to deliver public services, e.g., commercialized firms, partnerships, single-window service centres

binding rules—rules or regulations that have the coercive power of law behind them

cash transfer—money provided by the government for broad support rather than in connection with a specific project or endeavour

citizen engagement—bringing citizens and groups directly into the decisionmaking and policy implementation process

contract—a binding agreement between two or more parties

contributions—cash transfer subject to performance conditions that are specified in a contribution agreement

co-production—production of goods or services jointly by various partners

decision (legal)—rendered by an adjudicative body; the application of law

deregulation—the process of reducing the number, incidence, and cost of regulations

exhortation—the use of information resources to make direct appeals

expenditure—disbursement of monies

grants—cash transfers with few if any performance conditions attached, though other requirements may be built into the grant

guidelines—codes or frameworks to guide action, without coercive support

incorporation by reference—when legislation refers to other legislation or codes, particularly those developed by private parties, and thereby gives them the force of law

instrument design—the generic term for the selection and calibration of different policy instruments through programming to achieve policy objectives

investment—a cash payment that implies a return of some sort, a benefit, or a profit

legislation—laws formally passed by an elected legislature and ratified by the executive

legitimate coercion—the application of force backed by law

licence—permits to engage in activities that may involve a mix of prohibition, permission, and conditions

loan—cash transfer that requires eventual repayment

moral suasion—the ability to persuade others based on one's institutional prominence or authority

nodality—the generic category of information resources at the disposal of governments

partnership—working jointly and cooperatively with others, in some formal arrangement, for the production and delivery of goods and services

performance indicator—some measure of how well a service or activity is doing, either through financial or output measures, or client satisfaction

permission—regulatory device that permits a certain activity under specific conditions

policy design—the process of choosing the most appropriate instrument to deal with the policy problem as it has been defined in order to achieve a given policy goal

procedural policy instrument—instruments that alter institutional rules and arrangements to try to induce behaviour

prohibitions—regulatory device that forbids certain activities under certain conditions

quasi-legislation—regulations and legal decisions that have the force of law but that have not been duly passed by the legislature

recognition—regulatory device that uses the government's capacity to recognize certain qualities or achievements as a "sign of approval"

regulation—the generic category of policy instruments that rely on the government's capacity to command and prohibit

re-regulation—a process of developing new regulatory regimes for arenas that had been previously regulated in more traditional formats

secondary legislation—regulations announced under the regulatory powers of a statute and that therefore have the force of law without necessarily being passed by the legislature

self-regulation—the delegation of the state regulatory power to a nongovernmental organization or private association

service fee—fee attached to the provision of some service, such as issuing a passport

shaming—publication of unwelcome information in order to force targets to change their behaviour in order to protect their reputations

sin tax—traditionally, taxes levied on cigarettes and alcohol

social capital—the degree to which members of a community trust each other and engage in reciprocal relations based on that trust

static response—a deliberate choice not to intervene, made after an analysis of the problem

statute—a duly passed act of the legislature

subsidy—cash transfers that are closely calibrated to the costs of engaging in an activity that the government regards favourably

tax—a compulsory levy that is not generally connected to any specific service and is intended to provide general purpose revenues to the government

tax expenditure—the technique of foregoing certain owed taxes (and hence losing or "spending" tax dollars) in order to subsidize an activity

transparency—clear accountability, reporting, and publication provisions for the provision of services as well as the decisionmaking process

user charge—the charge levied on a category of person or user of a service, not the service itself

voluntary code—standards or codes developed by private sector organizations themselves; sometimes known as codes of conduct, codes of practice, voluntary initiatives, guidelines, and non-regulatory agreements

voucher—"coupons" for stipulated amounts of public financial support attached to a service that may be redeemed under certain conditions

Weblinks

Auditor General of Canada
http://www.oag-bvg.gc.ca/domino/oag-bvg.nsf/html/menue.html

Cabinet Directive on Law-Making (2003)
http://www.pco-bcp.gc.ca/default.asp?Page=Publications&Language=
E&doc=legislation/lmgcabinetdirective_e.htm

Expert Advisory Committee on Smart Regulation
http://www.smartregulation.gc.ca/en/index.asp

Standing Committee on Finance
http://www.parl.gc.ca/InfoComDoc/36/2/FINA/Studies/Reports/fina01/
07%2Dtoc%2De.html

The Tools of Government Workbooks
http://www.jhu.edu/~ccss/toolsworkbooks/

Further Readings

Bardach, E. (2000). *A practical guide for policy analysis: The eightfold path to more effective problem solving.* New York: Chatham House Publishers.

Bemelmans-Videc, M.-L., Rist, R. C., and Vedung, E. (Eds.) (1998). *Carrots, sticks and sermons: Policy instruments and their evaluation* (pp. 59–76). New Brunswick, NJ: Transaction Publishers.

Hood, C. (1984). *The tools of government.* London: Macmillan.

Salamon, L. M. (Ed.) (2002). *The tools of government: A guide to the new governance.* New York: Oxford University Press.

Schneider, A. L., and Ingram, H. (1997). *Policy design for democracy.* Lawrence: University Press of Kansas.

REFERENCES

Aaron, H. J., Mann, T. E., and Taylor, T. (Eds.). (1994). *Values and public policy.* Washington, DC: The Brookings Institution.

Accor Services. (2004). About us. Retrieved August 12, 2004, from http://www.accorservices.com

Armstrong, J., and Lenihan, D. G. (1999). *From controlling to collaborating: When governments want to be partners.* Toronto: Institute of Public Administration of Canada, New Directions—Number 3.

Auditor General of Canada. (1998). *Annual report 1998. Grants and contributions: Selected programs in Industry Canada and Department of Canadian Heritage.* Retrieved August 12, 2004, from www.oag-bvg.gc.ca/domino/reports.nsf/html/9827ce.html

Auditor General of Canada. (2002). *Report to the Minister of Public Works and Government Services on three contracts awarded to Groupaction.* Retrieved August 12, 2004, from http://www.oag-bvg.gc.ca/domino/reports.nsf/html/02sprepe.html

Baldwin, R. (1995). *Rules and government.* Oxford: Clarendon Press.

Campbell, R. M. (1999). The fourth fiscal era: Can there be a "post-neo-conservative" fiscal policy? In L. A. Pal (Ed.), *How Ottawa spends 1999–2000: Shape shifting: Canada governance toward the 21st century* (pp. 113–49). Toronto: Oxford University Press.

CRTC. (1999). Press release. Retrieved September 2000 from http://www.crtc.gc.ca/eng/news/releases/1999/R990517e.htm

Department of Finance (Canada). (2004). *The budget plan 2004.* Retrieved August 12, 2004, from http://www.fin.gc.ca/budget04/pdf/bp2004e.pdf

Doern, G. B., and Phidd, R. W. (1992). *Canadian public policy: Ideas, structure, process* (2nd ed.). Toronto: Nelson.

Doern, G. B., and Wilson, V. S. (Eds.). (1974). *Issues in Canadian public policy.* Toronto: Methuen.

Doern, G. B., et al. (1999a). Canadian regulatory institutions: Converging and colliding regimes. In G. B. Doern et al. (Eds.), *Changing the rules: Canadian regulatory regimes and institutions* (pp. 3–26). Toronto: University of Toronto Press.

Doern, G. B., et al. (1999b). Conclusions. In G. B. Doern et al. (Eds.), *Changing the rules: Canadian regulatory regimes and institutions* (pp. 389–406). Toronto: University of Toronto Press.

The Economist. (2004, June 12–18). The road tolls for thee, pp. 30–32.

External Advisory Committee on Smart Regulation. (2004). *Instruments for government action*. Retrieved August 12, 2004, from http://www.smartregulation.gc.ca/en/05/01/i5-01.asp

Fukuyama, F. (1995). *Trust: The social virtues and the creation of prosperity*. New York: Free Press.

Ganz, G. (1987). *Quasi-legislation: Recent developments in secondary legislation*. London: Sweet and Maxwell.

Good, D. A. (2003) *The politics of public management: The HRDC audit of grants and contributions*. Toronto: University of Toronto Press.

Government of Canada. (1999a). *Regulatory policy*. Retrieved September 2000 from http://www.pco-bcp.gc.ca/raoics-srdc/reg-pol/ reg-pol_e.htm

Government of Canada. (1996b, September 30). *Building the information society: Moving Canada into the 21st century*. Retrieved September 2000 from http://info.ic.gc.ca/info-highway/society/toc_e.html

Graham, M. (2002). *Democracy by disclosure: The rise of technopopulism*. Washington, DC: Brookings Institution.

Hood, C. (1984). *The tools of government*. London: Macmillan.

Howlett, M., and Ramesh, M. (2003). *Studying public policy: Policy cycles and policy subsystems*. 2nd ed. Toronto: Oxford University Press.

Howlett, M. (2000, Winter). Managing the 'hollow state': Procedural policy instruments and modern governance. *Canadian Public Administration*, 43, 412–31.

Industry Canada. (1998). *Voluntary codes: A guide for their development and use*. Retrieved August 12, 2004, from http://strategis.ic.gc.ca/ volcodes

Kettl, D. F. (1995). Building lasting reform: Enduring questions, missing answers. In D. F. Kettl and J. J. DiIulio Jr. (Eds.), *Inside the reinvention machine: Appraising governmental reform* (pp. 9–83). Washington, DC: The Brookings Institution.

Keyes, J. M. (1996). Power tools: The form and function of legal instruments for government action. *Canadian Journal of Administrative Law and Practice*, 10, 133–74.

Kirschen, E. S., et al. (1964). *Economic policy in our time* (3 vols.). Amsterdam: North-Holland.

Landy, M. (1993). Policy shapes and citizenship. In H. Ingram and S. Rathgeb Smith (Eds.), *Public policy for democracy* (pp. 19–44). Washington, DC: The Brookings Institution.

Lemaire, D. (1998). The stick: Regulation as a tool of government. In M.-L. Bemelmans-Videc, R. C. Rist, and E. Vedung (Eds.), *Carrots, sticks and sermons: Policy instruments and their evaluation* (pp. 59–76). New Brunswick, NJ: Transaction Publishers.

Linder, S. H., and Peters, B. G. (1989). Instruments of government: Perceptions and contexts. *Journal of Public Policy, 9*, 35–58.

Linder, S. H., and Peters, B. G. (1995). The two traditions of institutional designing: Dialogue versus decision? In D. L. Weimer (Ed.), *Institutional design* (pp. 133–60). Dordrecht, Netherlands: Kluwer.

Lindquist, E. (1992, Summer). Public managers and policy communities: Learning to meet new challenges. *Canadian Public Administration, 35*, 127–59.

March, J. G., and Olsen, J. P. (1995). *Democratic governance.* New York: Free Press.

McDonnell, L. M., and Elmore, R. F. (1987). *Alternative policy instruments.* Santa Monica, CA: Center for Policy Research in Education.

Mihlar, F. (1999). The federal government and the "RIAS" process: Origins, need and non-compliance. In G. B. Doern et al. (Eds.), *Changing the rules: Canadian regulatory regimes and institutions* (pp. 275–92). Toronto: University of Toronto Press.

Neville, A. (Ed.) (2002). *Policy choices in a globalized world.* New York: Nova Science Publishers.

Orsini, M. (2002, September). The politics of naming, blaming and claiming: HIV, Hepatitis C and the emergence of blood activism in Canada. *Canadian Journal of Political Science, 35*, 475–98.

Osborne, D., and Gaebler, T. (1993). *Reinventing government: How the entrepreneurial spirit is transforming the public sector.* New York: Penguin.

Perry, G. (2004). Naming and shaming: States fight tax delinquency online. *Accounting Today* (March). Retrieved August 12, 2004, from http://www.webcpa.com/AccountingToday/index.cfm/txtFuse/dspShellContent/fuseAction/DISPLAY/numContentID/51373/numSiteID/7/numTaxonomyTypeID/10/numTaxonomyID/196.htm

Peters, B. G. (1998). Institutionalization and deinstitutionalization: Regulatory institutions in American government. In G. B. Doern and S. Wilks (Eds.), *Changing regulatory institutions in Britain and North America* (pp. 51–79). Toronto: University of Toronto Press.

Prince, M. J. (1999). Civic regulation: Regulating citizenship, morality, social order, and the welfare state. In G. B. Doern et al. (Eds.), *Changing the rules: Canadian regulatory regimes and institutions* (pp. 201–27). Toronto: University of Toronto Press.

Privy Council Office (Canada). (1999). *A framework to improve the social union for Canadians.* Retrieved September 4, 2004, from http://www.tbs-sct.gc.ca/asd-dmps/db/isuc_s_e.asp

Privy Council Office (Canada). (2003). *Cabinet directive on law-making.* Retrieved September 4, 2004, from http://www.pco-bcp.gc.ca/default.asp?Page=Publications&Language=E&doc=legislation/lmgcabinetdirective_e.htm

Purchase, B., and Hirshhorn, R. (1994). *Searching for good governance.* Kingston, ON: Queen's School of Policy Studies.

Putnam, R. (1993). *Making democracy work: Civic traditions in modern Italy.* Princeton, NJ: Princeton University Press.

Putnam, R. (2000). *Bowling alone: The collapse and revival of American community.* New York: Simon and Schuster.

Salamon, L. M. (Ed.) (2002). *The tools of government: A guide to the new governance.* New York: Oxford University Press.

Schneider, A., and Ingram, H. (1990). Behavioral assumptions of policy tools. *Journal of Politics, 52,* 510–29.

Schneider, A. L., and Ingram, H. (1997). *Policy design for democracy.* Lawrence: University Press of Kansas.

Schultz, R. (1994). Deregulation Canadian-style: State reduction of recasting? In I. Gow and L. Bernier (Eds.), *A downsized state? Canada and Québec compared* (pp. 129–47). Montreal: Presses de l'Université du Québec.

Sproule-Jones, M. (1994). User fees. In A. M. Maslove (Ed.), *Taxes as instruments of public policy* (pp. 3–38). Toronto: University of Toronto Press.

Standing Committee on Finance (Canada). (2000). *Challenge for change: A study of cost-recovery.* Retrieved August 12, 2004, from http://www.parl.gc.ca/InfoComDoc/36/2/FINA/Studies/Reports/fina01/07%2Dtoc%2De.html

Statistics Canada. (2003). *Consolidated provincial government, revenue and expenditures, provinces and territories.* Retrieved August 12, 2004, from http://www.statcan.ca/english/Pgdb/govt56a.htm

Steuerle, C. E., and Twombly, E. C. (2002). Vouchers. In L. M. Salamon (Ed.), *The tools of government: A guide to the new governance* (pp. 445–65). New York: Oxford University Press.

Thirsk, W. R., and Bird, R. M. (1994). Earmarked taxes in Ontario: Solution or problem? In A. M. Maslove (Ed.), *Taxing and spending: Issues of process* (pp. 129–84). Toronto: University of Toronto Press.

Vedung, E. (1998). Policy instruments: Typologies and theories. In M.-L. Bemelmans-Videc, R. C. Rist, and E. Vedung (Eds.), *Carrots, sticks and sermons: Policy instruments and their evaluation* (pp. 21–58). New Brunswick, NJ: Transaction Publishers.

Vedung, E., and van der Doelen, F. C. J. (1998). The sermon: Information programs in the public policy process—Choice, effects, and evaluation. In M.-L. Bemelmans-Videc, R. C. Rist, and E. Vedung (Eds.), *Carrots, sticks and sermons: Policy instruments and their evaluation* (pp. 103–28). New Brunswick, NJ: Transaction Publishers.

Wilks, S., and Doern, G. B. (1998). Conclusions. In G. B. Doern and S. Wilks (Eds.), *Changing regulatory institutions in Britain and North America* (pp. 376–95). Toronto: University of Toronto Press.

World Trade Organization. (1996, September 30). *Technical regulations and standards.* Retrieved September 2000 from gatekeeper.unicc.org/wto/comp_ leg_wpf. html#Technical

Chapter 5

Policy Implementation

Say "implementation" and you say "organization." Whereas Chapter 4 dealt with policy instruments—the means or techniques of getting things done—this chapter addresses the challenges of organizing and delivering outcomes through those instruments. The policy literature often states that no one paid much attention to implementation until the 1970s, but this is wrong. Policy analysts themselves did not pay much attention to it, but the field of public administration has concentrated on implementation for most of its history, since a good deal of administrative science, or management, as it is now called, deals with harnessing personnel and other resources in order to get things done. The subject of implementation brings public administration and public policy analysis about as close as they ever come. Even then, the policy literature has paid less attention to organizational details than the political and intellectual constraints in implementation. This chapter will pick up the discussion from Chapter 4 and look at design questions (how we achieve our objectives) from the point of view of organizing services and programs. Implementation studies have the reputation of being the dismal science of policy studies, since much of the work here tends to emphasize how tough it is to get anything accomplished. However, in contrast to theory, the practice of public administration and policy implementation has been undergoing a revolution in recent years. With decentralization, partnerships, client focus, quality service standards, subsidiarity, special operating agencies, privatization, and commercialization, the list of new management practices is long. As one would expect, there is considerable debate whether these new forms of policy implementation represent improvements or decline.

Implementation and policy design are conceptually distinct, though they overlap in practice. Think of design as the blueprint for the policy and implementation as its execution. Looked at in this way, the relationship between the two aspects of the policy process raises an interesting question: is it possible for badly designed policies to be well implemented, and good policy designs to be badly implemented? Box 5.1 (page 192) illustrates a rough set of relationships that can exist between implementation

Box 5.1	DESIGN AND IMPLEMENTATION	
DESIGN	**IMPLEMENTATION**	
	Effective	*Ineffective*
Strong	Success	Implementation Failure
Weak	Design Failure	Total Failure

and design. A well-designed policy that has good implementation is almost a definition of success: a good idea well executed. There is another degree of success however, which might be thought of as implementation failure—a good idea that suffers from inadequate execution. It must be said that this explanation of failure is the refuge of many a policy designer. The idea was fine, but the follow-through was responsible for less than spectacular results. More on this in a moment. One point to keep in mind is that there is still hope—since the design is sound, failure is a matter of organization, personnel, or resources. It is also possible to have design failure—the policy is badly designed in terms of problem definition or instruments or goals, but is executed reasonably well. Total failure—and total misery—occur when both design and implementation are seriously flawed. To be realistic, most policies will have shortcomings in design and in implementation; what we are considering here is very weak design combined unhappily with very weak implementation.

We can see from these crude categories that implementation makes a distinct contribution to the success or failure of a policy.

> The study of policy implementation is crucial for the study of public administration and public policy. Policy implementation is the stage of policymaking between the establishment of a policy, such as the passage of a legislative act, the issuing of an executive order, the handing down of a judicial decision, or the promulgation of a regulatory rule, and the consequences of the policy for the people whom it affects. If the policy is inappropriate, if it cannot alleviate the problem for which it was designed, it will probably be a failure no matter how well implemented. But even a brilliant policy poorly implemented may fail to achieve the goals of its designers. (Edwards, 1984, ix)

The design phase is about determining the problem, the goals, and the most appropriate instruments for a solution. Even if all of that goes well, and the conceptualization of the policy problem is broadly correct, the follow-through can fail. Knowing this, of course, the smart designer builds considerations about implementation into the policy design from the beginning, though this too can raise problems if we presume that there should be both some degree of flexibility in the way policies are implemented as well as input from below. In this chapter we will assume that the policies are well designed and concentrate on principles and mechanisms of implementation. The first section quickly reviews some of the conventional wisdom of the policy literature, while the second reviews the exploding world of new forms of public management and service delivery.

IMPLEMENTATION THEORY

Recall the discussion of instruments and policy design in the last chapter. In elaborating a set of programs that combine various instruments in order to put the policy into effect, what would one want in order to ensure success?

Box 5.2 (page 194) draws on Hogwood and Gunn's (1984) classic list of requirements (chap. 11). The image of the successful implementor that arises from this list of requirements is someone or some organization that has brains, strong planning capacity, resources, authority to act, and complete understanding of the goals. It is, in short, a world without friction, without scarcity, without confusion, miscommunication, conflict, or misunderstanding. It is also a world of hierarchy and power, where the implementor decides and those decisions cascade down to the final point of delivery without obstruction or misinterpretation. Little wonder, then, that perfect implementation never happens, and, as Hogwood and Gunn (1984) conclude, some degree of failure "is almost inevitable" (p. 198).

The Hogwood and Gunn list of requirements is developed from the administrator's or implementor's point of view. Another approach that picks up many of the same variables, but also incorporates some system-level considerations, was offered by Sabatier and Mazmanian (1981). Box 5.3 summarizes the framework. It hinges on three broad categories of variables. First, the tractability of the problem: some issues, like traffic congestion, are easier to deal with than others, like disposal of nuclear wastes. A good causal theory, a relatively narrow range of targeted behaviour, a small population target group, and a small desired change in behaviour as a result of policy make implementation more successful, all other things being equal. Second, Sabatier and Mazmanian also incorporate legislative and institutional variables. The statute should be clear, and the implementing agency well resourced. Linkages to cooperating agencies should be designed with a minimum of veto points and strong lines of accountability. The statute should be implemented by agencies or individuals sympathetic to its goals, and

Box 5.2	ELEMENTS FOR SUCCESSFUL IMPLEMENTATION
No insurmountable external constraints	• Usually organizations and individuals that will not cooperate, but can include acts of nature
Adequate time and sufficient resources	• Time, money, and people
Required combinations	• Time, money, and people in the right order and mix
Valid theory	• Good design, especially cause-and-effect relationships
Causal connections are reasonable, clear, and direct	• Focus on causal variables that can realistically be addressed by public policy, rather than, for example, large systemic ones that are resistant to intervention
Dependency relationships are minimal	• Authority is not fragmented or dispersed
Agreed objectives	• Everyone sings from the same song sheet; no dispute about ends
Correct sequence of tasks	• Doing first things first, and so on
Communication	• Clear communication and understanding
Compliance	• No sabotage, recalcitrance, or rebellion

SOURCE: Hogwood, B.W., and Gunn, L.A. (1984). *Policy analysis for the real world*, Oxford: Oxford University Press, chap. 11.

outside access to the decisionmaking process should be skewed toward supporters rather than critics.

A third category is broad socioeconomic and political variables that determine the fate of implementation. These overlap in part with forces

Box 5.3 **A CONCEPTUAL FRAMEWORK OF THE IMPLEMENTATION PROCESS**

TRACTABILITY OF THE PROBLEM
1. Availability of valid technical theory and technology
2. Diversity of target-group behaviour
3. Target group as percentage of the population
4. Extent of behavioral change required

ABILITY OF STATUTE TO STRUCTURE IMPLEMENTATION
1. Clear and consistent objectives
2. Incorporation of adequate causal theory
3. Financial resources
4. Hierarchical integration with and among implementing institutions
5. Decision-rules of implementing agencies
6. Recruitment of implementing official
7. Formal access by outsiders

NONSTATUTORY VARIABLES AFFECTING IMPLEMENTATION
1. Socioeconomic conditions and technology
2. Media attention to the problem
3. Public support
4. Attitudes and resources of constituency groups
5. Support from sovereigns
6. Commitment and leadership skills of implementing officials

SOURCE: Sabatier and Mazmanian. (1981). The implementation of public policy: A framework of analysis. In D. A. Mazmanian and P. A. Sabatier (Eds.), *Effective policy implementation* (p. 7). Lexington, MA: Lexington Books.

discussed in Chapter 3, maintaining the sense in the public and the political system that the problem to which the policy is being directed is important and requires attention. In sum, the chances of successful implementation, which Sabatier and Mazmanian define as "the translation of statutory objectives into the policy decisions of implementing agencies" are maximized if

the statute stipulates unambiguous objectives; assigns implementation to sympathetic agencies who will give it high priority;

minimizes the number of veto points and provides sufficient incentives to overcome resistance among recalcitrant officials; provides sufficient financial resources to conduct the technical analyses and process individual cases; and biases the decision-rules and access points in favor of statutory objectives. Conformity of policy decisions with statutory objectives is also very dependent on the ability of supportive constituency groups and legislative/executive sovereigns to intervene actively in the process to supplement the agency's resources and to counter resistance from target groups. (pp. 21–22)

Even this is a daunting list—it highlights clear objectives, sympathetic agencies, authority, resources, fidelity to statute and rules, leadership, and public support—showing why the study of implementation appears to be the dismal science of policy analysis. The book that arguably kicked off interest in implementation by policy analysts was by Jeffrey L. Pressman and Aaron Wildavsky (1984), with the appropriately pessimistic title: *Implementation: How Great Expectations in Washington Are Dashed in Oakland: Or, Why It's Amazing that Federal Programs Work at All, This Being a Saga of the Economic Development Administration as Told by Two Sympathetic Observers Who Seek to Build Morals on a Foundation of Ruined Hopes*. The book examines an urban employment scheme called the Oakland Project, announced in 1966. At the time, Oakland had an unemployment rate of 8.4 percent, concentrated among inner-city Blacks. The program was to spend $23 million on a variety of public works projects and would be administered by the Economic Development Administration (EDA). Some 3000 jobs were to be created through an innovative scheme whereby employers seeking EDA loans or support would have to submit an employment plan showing how they would recruit target group members. As Pressman and Wildavsky pointed out, the Oakland Project enjoyed wide political support, and was well funded, with monies in place. Yet three years later, only $3 million had been spent, most of that for a freeway overpass and architects' fees. Why did the Oakland Project fail?

From the beginning, "the success of the EDA program depended on agreement among a diverse group of participants with differing organizational objectives" (p. 30). The project had, at minimum, fifteen different sets of actors, some within the same agency. They included, among others, five different sets from within the EDA itself; the Department of Health, Education, and Welfare; the Department of Labor; the U.S. Navy; the City of Oakland; and Black leaders. Beyond this there were all the private sector actors who were supposed to create jobs with the help of EDA funds. Levels of commitment, perceptions of urgency, and capacity varied enormously among these actors. Moreover, the implementation process was marked by a sequence of tasks that had to be completed or agreements struck before the process could move on. Pressman and Wildavsky called these "**decision points**" that required "clearance" by multiple sets of actors in order for implementation to go forward. They hypothesized that 30 decision points required a cumulative total of 70 **clearances**. Assuming an 80 percent probability of agreement on each clearance point, the chances of completion were one in a million. Even if one assumed an unrealistically high probability of 99 percent for each clearance, the odds for successful implementation were only about one in two. "However you look at it, the ultimate probability of success is very low" (p. 107).

One might argue that the Oakland Project succumbed to the fragmentation that characterizes the American political system. It is true that parliamentary systems like Canada's have a higher degree of executive dominance and institutional capacity to implement from the top down (Atkinson, 1993; Pal and Weaver, 2003). But Canada's is also a federal system, which reduces the executive dominance to some degree at the centre. The other notable feature of the Oakland Project was the high consensus around it. In cases where principles differ; where problem definitions are widely divergent; or where actors have incentives to impede, delay, or frustrate, it could be expected that policies will face even greater odds against implementation.

Fortunately, things are not so grim. Subsequent work has shown that the probability of successful implementation increases if one adopts assumptions that are plausible, but only slightly different from those held by Pressman and Wildavsky in their study. After all, things do get accomplished, however imperfectly. The Pressman–Wildavsky implementation model consists of a chain of statistically independent nodes or clearance points with an attached probability. Relax the model in five ways and the probability for clearance increases substantially (Alexander, 1989). First, it is unrealistic to assume that actors will make only one attempt at clearance. They may persist in multiple tries. Second, clearance points are not always independent; they might be packaged or bundled in ways so that one clearance ripples through several others. Third, there is a bandwagon effect at times where previous clearances actually increase the probability of future clearances. This usually happens in threshold decisions where a certain number of agreements are necessary before a large payoff can be received. This puts pressure on holdouts. A good example is labour negotiations, where both sides try to "build momentum" on a series of minor issues before they tackle the larger ones. Fourth, program-reduction strategies may be used to shorten the "**decision chain.**" If the proposed program is being held hostage at one clearance point because of some feature that requires agreement from reluctant supporters, it is possible to cut out that component and proceed to the next decision point. Finally, one can assume higher probabilities of clearance than 99 percent in some instances, and this has a marked effect on overall clearance probabilities.

All of these techniques, in one way or another, involve trying to make the implementation process more controlled. But what if, as Eugene Bardach (1977) wrote years ago, "the character and degree of many implementation problems are inherently unpredictable" (p. 5)? Bardach took the dynamic conceptualization of implementation first developed by Pressman and Wildavsky—dynamic in the sense that it occurs over time—and arrived at the notion of "games" as a way of understanding the essentially defensive nature of implementation:

> The idea of "games," therefore . . . directs us to look at the players, what they regard as the stakes, their strategies and tactics, their resources for playing, the rules of play (which stipulate the conditions for winning), the rules of "fair" play (which stipulate the boundaries beyond which lie fraud or illegitimacy), the nature of the communications (or lack of them) among players, the degree of uncertainty surrounding the possible outcomes. The game metaphor also directs our attention to who is not willing to play and for what reasons, and to who insists on changes in some of the game's parameters as a condition of playing. (p. 56)

In reflecting on what makes the implementation game successful, what enables implementors to deal with its inevitably unpredictable character, Bardach offered several strategies. First, avoid implementation designs that rely on complex management systems, large organizations, and lots of clearances. Implement through the market, if possible; deliver cash directly to people rather than services that require elaborate bureaucracies, and aim at small and feasible targets. Second, engage in scenario-writing to work out different possible consequences of a string of actions and interactions. Third, and most importantly, fix the game in the sense of "repairing" it when it goes off the rails and in the sense of "adjusting certain elements of the system of games . . . so as to lead to a more preferred outcome" (Bardach, 1977, p. 274). This amounts to paying attention to the policy-formation process (Winter, 1990, pp. 25–26).

If the prospects for implementation were as bleak as some of the earlier literature suggested, then policymaking would seem a hopeless enterprise. It may be that we have unrealistically high notions of what constitutes policy success. Ironically, because perceptions of government became more negative over the 1970s and 1980s, the public sector may be presumed to be doing worse than it actually is: "by adopting new ways of looking at and evaluating public policymaking, we have ourselves constructed a significant number of the fiascoes we subsequently 'observed'" (Bovens and t'Hart, 1996, p. 146). However, the lessons of implementation cannot be ignored. It is difficult to make things happen, and it becomes increasingly difficult the further removed the situation is from the preconditions identified by Hogwood and Gunn. It can also be more difficult than it need be, if we expect perfect implementation through control. If top-down control is our standard, if we see implementation as the formal elaboration of some unitary design, then almost by definition that is unlikely to happen, given what we know about the limits of organizations and the impact of politics on decisionmaking. Majone and Wildavsky (1984) urge an image of implementation as evolution, not as control:

> Implementation is evolution. Since it takes place in a world we never made, we are usually right in the middle of the process, with events having occurred before and (we hope) continuing afterward. . . . When we act to implement a policy, we change it. When we vary the amount or type of resource inputs we also intend to alter outputs, even if only to put them back on the track where they were once supposed to be. In this way, the policy theory is transformed to produce different results. As we learn from experience what is feasible or preferable, we correct errors. To the degree that these corrections make a difference at all, they change our policy ideas as well as the policy outcomes, because the idea is embedded in the action. (p. 177)

Implementation is therefore an execution process, an elaboration, a realization of schemes and conceptions, the building of links in often long chains of decision and agreement. It can also be seen as a process of communications, an "implementation subsystem full of messages, messengers, channels, and targets" (Goggin et al., 1990, p. 33). It takes place in a world of multiple powers and authorities, organizations, and personalities, and therefore is inevitably a struggle. Even this fails to capture the reality, since it still implies an evolution from the design or blueprint, when in fact what may be happening is closer to the loop or cycle mentioned in the preceding quote, where implementation is a function of combined "top-down" and "bottom-up" processes. Indeed, some students of implementation have been so impressed by the degree to which the fortunes of policies are determined at the final point of delivery that they have urged a **"backward mapping"** technique to work out what the policy should actually be, as opposed to more conventional **"forward mapping."**

> Forward mapping . . . begins at the top of the process, with as clear a statement as possible of the policymaker's intent, and proceeds through a sequence of increasingly more specific steps to define what is expected of implementers at each level. At the bottom of the process, one states, again with as much precision as possible, what a satisfactory outcome would be, measured in terms of the original statement of intent. . . . [Backward mapping] begins, not with a statement of intent, but with a statement of the specific behavior at the lowest level of the implementation process that generates the need for a policy. Only after that behavior is described does the analysis presume to state an objective; the objective is first stated as a set of organizational operations and then as a set of effects, or outcomes, that will result from these operations. Having established a relatively precise target at the lowest level of the system, the analysis backs up through the structure of implementing agencies, asking at each level two questions: What is the ability of this unit to affect the behavior that is the target of the policy? And what resources does this unit require in order to have that effect? In the final stage of analysis the analyst or policymaker describes a policy that directs resources at the organizational units likely to have the greatest effect. (Elmore, 1982, pp. 19, 21)

In sum, the conventional work on implementation has tended to highlight its multidimensionality, difficulty, ambiguity, and a growing realization of its importance. The multidimensionality arises from the understanding that implementation can be viewed as an organizational process, something internal to bureaucracies and focused on the challenge of balancing discretion with accountability. Implementation can also be viewed primarily as a political process of bargaining among actors who, while not necessarily equal in resources, can each affect outcomes. It can also be seen from the perspective of individuals, personalities, and leadership capacities, either in organizations or political structures. The difficulty of implementation lies in the high demands for success. As Hogwood and Gunn (1984), as well as Sabatier and Mazmanian (1981) illustrate, it is a lot easier to outline the requirements for successful implementation than to actually fulfill them. The ambiguity of implementation reflects the complex symbiosis between theory and practice: policy is initially nothing more than ideas or conceptualizations, while implementation is the specific means of execution and elaboration in practice. Theory guides practice, but practice must, of necessity, add details that were never contemplated in the origins of the policy. Finally, the importance of implementation comes through precisely this contribution of practice—it is, in effect, the test of the policy theory (assuming it goes well). By testing, we learn. So a properly designed implementation process should provide a mechanism for **policy feedback**, learning, and improvement.

Implementation, however, is not a matter of merely empirically deciding what works and then developing checklists of factors to consider as one plugs along. As Linder and Peters (1990) note, looking at policy from the top down, the "implementation solution" criterion seems to be clarity, so that compliance can be ensured down the line. From the bottom up, however, the main criterion appears to be flexibility and discretion, and hence policy design should emphasize simplicity (pp. 64–65). Bardach (1977) made the same point: "even when we know what ought to be done, and can get political leaders to agree to mandate it, government is probably ill-suited to do the job. At the very least, it is likely that the bureaucratic and regulatory strategies government has traditionally relied upon are ineffective if not mischievous" (p. 4). The factors that we consider to be important in implementation, in other words, depend on the way in which we perceive governance. To take an extreme example, if the scope of government were to be reduced to its nineteenth-century proportions of maintaining public safety and infrastructure such as roads and sewers, it is unlikely that any student of public policy would dream of implementation as a major issue. Implementation is a concern only when there are lots of complex policies to implement. Moreover, the nature of the issues and challenges we confront in implementation also depend on the modes of implementation that we characteristically use. When governments deliver services like education directly themselves, accountability and compliance are more or less presumed to flow from the line relationships that extend down from the ministry to the local schools. Imagine a situation where all educational services were delivered by third parties, and the ministry's role was to develop curricula and distribute support to parents in the form of vouchers. Key implementation issues would suddenly become related to compliance with curricular guidelines and fraud in the use of the vouchers.

Like everything else in policymaking, the world of implementation has changed drastically in recent years. The main trends have been toward **decentralization**, devolution of responsibilities to other government jurisdictions or third parties, and restructuring accountability relationships within government departments. There is extensive public administration literature on these developments. Not all of it is complimentary, but it recognizes that something fundamental has been going on across the industrialized world as more and more countries join the bandwagon of the new public management (NPM).

THE NEW PUBLIC MANAGEMENT IN CANADA

The broad outlines of the philosophical premises of the new public management were sketched in Chapter 2. These premises imply a different form of governance and different types of agencies and accountability relationships. Not surprisingly, to the degree that the NPM took root in Canada, it had an influence on mechanisms of implementation.

The sources of the NPM are various. Politically, the first wave of radical governmental reform came with the Thatcher regime in Britain in the late 1970s and early 1980s. According to Savoie (1994), these initiatives became one of the key inspirations for the Mulroney-era changes to the public service (p. 231). The massive changes undertaken by the New Zealand government in the mid-1980s were another harbinger of things to come. Intellectually, the management revolution has been led by gurus such as Peters and Waterman (1982) and Osborne and Gaebler (1993). While the political roots of the NPM were initially in the conservative end of the political spectrum, over the last decade governments of every political stripe have accepted at least part of the message and have started to reform their internal structures and connections with social partners. In New Zealand, change was initiated by a Labour government. In Canada, the Saskatchewan NDP government was the first to balance its budget, ahead of Conservative Alberta. Currently, in the United Kingdom, it is Tony Blair's "New Labour" government that is pushing ahead substantial public sector reforms focusing on performance.

The broad appeal of NPM ideas (despite the variable uptake among different countries) suggests that deeper forces are at work: the bundle of factors described in Chapter 2 that links globalization, technology, and shifts in postwar paradigms to the nature of the nation-state. As the Clerk of the Privy Council put it in a speech in May 2000,

> So what does globalization mean for public servants—for executives as leaders in the Public Service of Canada? More specifically, what does globalization mean for how we do our work in policy, service delivery and management. On *policy:* it means putting public involvement at the centre of a policy development process that has a solid evidence basis. It means undertaking forward-looking research to fill knowledge gaps. It means aggressively seeking good practices from around the world as well as the expertise resident in academia, think tanks, nongovernmental organizations (NGOs) and international organizations. Both policy developers and researchers must be able to work inter-departmentally and to take the time necessary to

consider the big picture, so as to craft policy that is integrated and attuned to a global environment. On *service delivery:* it means using electronic technology to modernize service delivery, and bringing citizens closer to government. (Privy Council Office, 2000)

It is important to note the conflicting pressures behind these forces since they help explain some of the confusing characteristics of the NPM. On the one hand, the NPM is all about reorganization and restructuring and relies heavily on market terminology such as **quality management** and **client satisfaction**. On the other hand, the larger debate of which the NPM is a part—redesigning our governance systems to incorporate more participation, citizen control, democracy, and responsiveness—is considerably broader in scope than the narrow maxims of the NPM would imply. We will come back to this question of the tensions that underlie the new thinking about implementation in the conclusion to this chapter.

What are the key principles of the NPM? First, as we noted in chapters 1 and 2, it is critical of traditional bureaucracies. Bureaucracy in this perspective is inflexible, slow, rule bound, and clumsy. Second, a basic question is posed as to whether government should be involved in the policy area in the first place. This seems like much more than a management issue, and it is. But it represents a sea change in thinking that presumes that the lines between state and civil society are drawn in different ways, ways that return substantial responsibilities to nongovernmental actors. Third, if it is determined that a government policy response is appropriate to the problem, the mode of delivery or broad implementation strategy stresses a strong focus on nongovernmental actors (communities, private corporations, citizens) as primary partners in delivery. Fourth, there is greater attention to outcomes and **performance** than ever before, with a special emphasis on clear standards of service to which agencies can be held accountable as much as possible. Agencies are encouraged to think of service recipients as customers or clients. Fifth, organizationally, the NPM looks to new hybrid forms of delivery that may have greater flexibility and also to a sharper distinction between policymaking functions in the executive and service functions that can be delivered on a contractual basis by some entity, either at arm's length or in the department.

These principles permit a fairly wide variation in practice, and governments that have moved in this direction have done so to different degrees and in different configurations, though it is fair to say that the NPM has indeed been a global movement. Moreover, there are important ideological differences that still surface, whatever the similarities in approach. In Canada, for example, while both provincial NDP and Conservative governments have been interested in decentralization and partnerships, the NDP governments have leaned more in the direction of the nonprofit NGO sector than the private, for-profit sector. It must also be remembered that the NPM itself requires implementation, and government organizations may adopt the rhetoric but not the reality of the approach. However, despite these caveats, governments of all political stripes in Canada have come to think about their role and their capacities quite differently, thereby calling into being new forms of policy implementation.

At the federal level, the inauguration of new ways of thinking about management and program delivery came with the 1989 initiative entitled **PS2000**. According to Paul Tellier (1990), who was then the Clerk of the Privy Council and responsible for launching PS2000, the program had three core objectives: better service, improved personnel management, and flexibility. The federal bureaucracy was to become a supple, responsive organization that could quickly adapt to external changes and demands. Together, these objectives would shift public sector thinking away from a philosophy of control to a philosophy of **empowerment**. The process was undertaken through the establishment of ten task forces consisting of deputy and assistant deputy ministers addressing the following issues: classification; the structure of the management category in the public sector classification system; salaries and benefits; staffing; staff relations; staff training; adaptation of the work force to external changes; resource management; administrative policies and services common to departments; and service to the public.

The Task Force on Service to the Public (PS2000) reviewed "best practices" in the public service with an eye to developing a "template for the model of the ideal service organization" (Rawson, 1991, p. 491). Though it found that individual public servants were keen to provide good service, the system as a whole did not encourage it. Improved service to the public would come only from strong leadership and a commitment to empowering front-line public servants, those who deal directly with clients. Along with empowerment, there was a need to decentralize wherever possible, and to ensure that the bureaucracy actually valued high service achievement by recognizing and rewarding it. Despite this NPM rhetoric, however, PS2000 focused on management rather than structure, certainly when compared with the radical structural changes introduced in Britain under the Next Steps program. Whereas Next Steps called for a radical restructuring of government departments and agencies on the assumption that organizational change would lead to new behaviour, the PS2000 approach, even in an area like service to the public, avoided structure in favour of recommendations about management and culture.

The ten PS2000 Task Force reports submitted over 300 recommendations, many of which dealt with minor administrative changes. Some of the others were on the pattern of the recommendations coming from the Service to the Public Task Force: broad statements of principle that called primarily for changes in the way that people think. By 1992 the entire process had bogged down. Paul Tellier had left his post as Clerk of the Privy Council, and the government became preoccupied with constitutional and other policy issues, as well as the impending election. The 1992 progress report on PS2000 showed very thin results across the federal public service. In 1993, however, a major federal government reorganization was launched. Once more, the issue was efficiency and effectiveness, but this time it was to be achieved through a radical reduction and recombination of federal government departments from thirty-two to twenty-five. Despite resistance and a bumpy implementation, the reorganization went ahead and was accepted in all but a few details (for example, immigration was moved out of Public Security) by the newly elected Chrétien government in October 1993.

The 1994 federal budget announced the successor to PS2000, the Program Review (though PS2000 was never formally abandoned). Linked to a deficit-reduction strategy, Program Review's "main objective was to review all federal programs in order to bring about the most effective and cost-efficient way of delivering programs and services that are appropriate to the federal government's role in the Canadian federation" (Ministry of Finance, 1995, p. 33). As described in Chapter 2, ministers were asked to review all their programs in light of the six tests or questions: serving the public, necessity of government involvement, the federal role, scope for partnerships, efficiency, and affordability. Note that the first four of these speak directly to the issue of implementation or how government programs are delivered to the public. Coupled with large budget cuts, the effect of the Program Review was a major downsizing of the federal civil service. In its first sixteen months in office, the Liberal government cut 15 000 full-time-equivalent positions. In the February 27, 1995, budget, the finance minister announced further cuts of 45 000 positions over the next three years (Lee and Hobbs, 1996, pp. 355–56). In terms of program cuts, the average decline in departmental spending between 1994 and 1999 was 20 percent, and while a few programs were increased (elderly benefits and Indian Affairs), a large number saw cuts in the order of 30 percent to 40 percent. Transport saw its budget reduced by almost 70 percent.

Just as important as the financial impact of Program Review, however, was its impact on and reflection of a new way of thinking about government services. The most extensive presentation of the new vision came in the government's blueprint entitled *Getting Government Right:*

A Progress Report (Treasury Board of Canada, 1996a). Its strategy had four objectives: (1) clarification of federal roles and responsibilities, (2) better targeting of resources on high priority social and economic issues, (3) better and more accessible government "involving clients more in decision making and using modern and practical service delivery tools," and (4) more affordable government. Overarching these goals was a fundamental rethinking of services and the best ways of delivering them:

> A central thrust of the renewal agenda has been to determine where the federal government is best placed to deliver programs or services and where these programs and services are more appropriately delivered by others. The net result is significant changes both in the services the federal government provides and in how it delivers them. The federal government is increasing its use of partnerships with other levels of government, the private sector and citizens to better manage collective and particular interests within Canada's economic and social union. In addition, by paying greater attention to how well it delivers services, the federal government is finding better ways to manage its operations efficiently and provide quality service to Canadians. (Treasury Board of Canada, 1996a, p. 7)

Program Review officially ended in March 1999, but the management approach outlined in *Getting Government Right* continued, with the result that "the shape, size, and operating practices of the federal public service . . . had been altered dramatically and even irrevocably. . . . From a single focus on deficit reduction, attention has turned to implementing a new type of governance, one that will respond efficaciously to a multiplicity of challenges" such as globalization, demographic shifts, the information society, and eroding citizen trust (Potter, 2000, p. 95). A prime example of fundamental change was Transport Canada: in November 1996 it transferred the Air Navigation System to NAV Canada, a private, not-for-profit corporation that would depend on user charges for its revenues; it transferred 104 of 149 airports to local communities, while it would retain responsibility for national safety and security standards; and it transferred (to port authorities and provincial and local governments) or closed 311 of over 500 harbours and ports (Treasury Board of Canada, 1998). Other departments experienced major changes in focus—Agriculture and Agri-Food Canada and Natural Resources Canada, for example, shifted away from providing grants and contributions to their respective constituencies to being research- and service-based departments. In horizontal terms, the government also launched an Alternative Service Delivery (ASD) initiative in 1996, which was then supplemented by a **Quality Services Initiative** and finally an approach that stressed citizen-centred **service delivery** (Treasury Board of Canada, 2000a).

These changes demonstrated an unusually firm commitment not only to deal with the deficit and spending, but also to move more fundamentally and deeply on a public sector reform agenda. *Getting Government Right* was replete with urges to move away from direct delivery to frameworks, to a greater use of partnerships, and to more market mechanisms to ensure quality and responsiveness. The emphasis on partnerships was particularly strong, with some variant of the word being used thirty-seven times in a thirty-page document. As well, there was a strong focus on outcomes of service and on treating the recipient as a client or customer—a focus that was maintained over the ensuing years. While momentum flagged in the last years of the Chrétien government, the early days of the Martin government were once again rededicated to public sector reform (see below).

At the same time, it is important to gauge the limits of this revolution in governance and place it in a comparative context. To begin with, the strategies discussed in *Getting Government Right* are only part of what can be a major restructuring of government itself. In all places where the NPM has been implemented, there have been moves to change the nature of executive agencies and their relations to service or delivery agencies. The logic behind this is that mixing policy development functions with delivery of services in a traditional, hierarchical, civil service bureaucracy is not conducive to efficiency and flexibility. If the objective is the highest standards of service to the public, then these functions should be clarified and distinguished in some way so that service delivery need not be hobbled by considerations that are more appropriate to policy development and advising the executive. Simply put, many of the things that enhance the neutrality and capacity of the civil service as a support for government reduce its capacity to serve the public.

The clearest and earliest example of this approach to the organization of government functions was the United Kingdom's Next Steps initiative, formally launched in 1988 with the release of the report entitled *Improving Management in Government: The Next Steps* from the Prime Minister's Efficiency Unit. Greer (1994) asserts that the ideas presented in this document were not in themselves radical, addressing age-old questions of how to improve the delivery of public services and what to do about accountability, but that what distinguished Next Steps was that it actually succeeded in implementing these changes (p. 23). The key change was to devolve "the delivery of most public services to *executive,* or *Next Steps agencies,* while policy roles that have traditionally been the role of the senior public service, and related administrative functions, remain the responsibility of departments" (Canadian Centre for Management Development, 1996, p. 33). As we noted in Chapter 2, by 1998 over 377 000 civil servants worked in 138 Next Steps agencies and four departments.

Also as noted in Chapter 2, the Blair government continued its efforts on public sector reform, especially in its second term. The Service First program was replaced in 2002 with the Office of Public Services Reform, guided by the *Principles into Practice* document. In January 2004 Prime Minister Blair, after a bruising national debate on reforming university financing, left no doubt about his continued commitment to management and governance reform. This excerpt from his speech is reproduced at length because it provides a flavour both for the logic and the fervour of the NPM (a particular version of NPM, with an emphasis on consumers of services and on performance):

> Since the creation of the modern welfare state politicians and managers have tended to see their job as damping down public expectation, minimising the scope for complaint or redress, suppressing dissatisfaction. We are starting to change this culture, to understand that service users with high expectations and the power to choose and to be heard are the best drivers of further improvement. By arming the public with greater choice and by strengthening their individual and collective voice we are making them partners in service improvement.
>
> This might seem like common sense but we need to understand the legacy of professional domination of service provision. The sixties and seventies were a period of unprecedented expansion in public services. Government provided the funds for services but allowed the professionals and their managers at the local level—whether housing managers, consultants or teachers—to define not just the way services were delivered but also the standards to which they were delivered. And this too often meant services where standards were too low, an unacceptable variability in delivery, which entrenched inequality and service users—parents, patients and tenants—who were disempowered and demoralised.
>
> In recent decades governments across the developed world have sought to address underperformance. Separating the role of purchaser of public services from that of provider has been possible to break up some of the old monolithic public service bureaucracies. The use of explicit contracts has raised standards of performance. And regulation and inspection, together with the publication of an increasingly wide range of performance indicators,

have increased the accountability of public service professionals. These new approaches have significantly raised standards.

But change driven from the centre has its limits. It is vital that service reform is to be driven from the bottom, as well as enabled by the centre. That is why the priority for reform—the principle tying together the different elements of change—is to put the public at the heart of public services, making 'Power to the people' the guiding principle of public sector improvement and reform. (Guardian Unlimited, 2004)

The United Kingdom model has restructured government through a division between policy advice (or development) and delivery. The agencies are retained in the departments, even though they function according to their own framework agreements. The New Zealand model, launched in the mid-1980s, is similar in principle but quite different in design. Launched by Labour governments, the reforms were remarkable for their boldness, rigour, and scope. New Zealand became the poster boy for the NPM around the world, and indeed in 1993 was ranked first by the World Competitiveness Survey for the quality of its government. The objectives and principles behind the reforms were also enunciated with admirable clarity. The objectives were to improve effectiveness, efficiency, and accountability; to reduce expenditures and the size of the public sector; to improve transparency and quality of services. Three key principles in achieving these objectives were that ministers be responsible for selecting outcomes while department executives be responsible for determining inputs (with minimum interference) for achieving those outcomes; that, wherever possible, publicly funded services be open to tender and competition; and that decisionmaking powers be as decentralized and as close to the consumer as possible (Boston et al., 1996, pp. 4–5).

New Zealand, at the time of its reforms, had retained many more commercial and quasi-commercial functions within departmental structures than was characteristic of other Commonwealth countries, and so the first step in the government reorganization was the establishment of "state-owned enterprises" to act as commercially viable providers of government services. A group of these were later privatized in the sale of government assets in 1989 (Seidle, 1995, p. 55). The next stage was the application of a similar model to the provision of operational services within the government itself. This in itself was not unknown in some European countries—Sweden is an example of the "**functional model**" in "which the tasks of policy advice and implementation are generally carried out by separate agencies" (Boston et al., 1996, p. 69). The alternative, which still characterizes most OECD countries, including Canada, is a "**sectoral model**" that vertically integrates advice and delivery within a ministry or department. In all the cases, the philosophical preference in the New Zealand reforms was to buy these services from commercialized entities, state-owned enterprises, or the public sector. Where that was not possible, however, there was an attempt to divide groups of services and operations into distinct entities. By 1995, fewer than half of government departments had any significant service delivery functions (Boston et al., 1996, p. 78). This model of governance has been retained, despite modest changes, and New Zealand remains committed as of 2005 to the continued pursuit of public sector efficiency and effectiveness, principally through a "managing for results" framework (State Services Commission, 2004).

These United Kingdom and New Zealand examples are only part of a larger international trend that in one form or another has taken up restructuring the public sector to more sharply define services, agencies that provide them, and accountability relationships both to government and to clients. We addressed this international "policy movement" in Chapter 1. The OECD Programme on Public Governance and Management provides a good sense of the current priorities: budgeting in the public sector, connecting government and citizens, ethics and corruption, human resources management, public sector statistics, regulatory reform, and strategic policymaking. Whereas the emphasis in the mid-1990s seemed to be more on structural reform of governments, there has recently been a shift in attention toward strategic management, particularly of **horizontal issues** that cut across various policy areas, public sector culture (i.e., ethics), human resource management, and continued focus on regulation in the broadest sense of both law and rule-making by other agencies. In a 2004 review of public spending trends among its member states, the OECD noted that the reform movement has not abated:

> The traditional model of public administration, which focuses on controlling inputs and on the conformity of spending appropriations to legal and procedural rules, has been viewed as having two main drawbacks. First, by failing to specify clearly either the core policy objectives or the money allocated to reach them, it may not stimulate debate about overall policy priorities. . . . Second, it may hinder cost-effectiveness by not allowing room for managerial autonomy and flexibility, while making it difficult to respond to the users' needs. To address these problems, many countries have adopted a more result-focused management approach.
>
> . . . In clarifying results based objectives for public bodies, the emphasis on client needs and satisfaction has been strengthened

in a number of countries, for example by elaborating "Citizen's Charters" (Canada, Ireland, Italy, Norway and United Kingdom) or by making "service declarations" (Norway). In the United Kingdom, Italy and Norway, most public agencies have made such commitments. In Ireland, improvements in the quality of customer service have been encouraged through the articulation of customer service principles and the publication of Customer Action Plans. In Canada, the Treasury Board's Service Improvement Initiatives commit departments to achieving a target of a minimum 10 per cent increase in measured client satisfaction with their services by 2005. If this target were achieved, client satisfaction would exceed current levels in the private sector and in local governments. Other measures include the promotion of e-government (as in Denmark, Finland, Luxembourg and Italy) to take advantage of ICT technology as a means of strengthening administrative efficiency and increasing client satisfaction, particularly via the effective extension of opening hours. (OECD, 2004, pp. 25–26)

Figure 5.1 (page 212) illustrates the rich range of reforms undertaken by OECD members. The data are self-reported, and do not give a sense of magnitude or depth, but they do demonstrate that public sector reform is a global phenomenon.

How does Canada fare in terms of these larger organizational and process reform trends? Clearly, there has been a wide-ranging acceptance of many of the finer principles of the NPM, but it should be clear in examining the United Kingdom, New Zealand, and other international cases that the Canadian variant has been somewhat tepid on several fronts, that the "style of these reforms was generally moderate, as was the substance" (Gow, 2004, p. 11; also see Cheung, 1997). In the earlier phases of both PS2000 and the subsequent reforms of the cabinet system, for example, there was never the same level of public political commitment and leadership to management change in Canada as there was in the other three countries. The PS2000 exercise was driven primarily by the mandarinate, with little interest from the executive. Aucoin (1995) cites the auditor general of Canada's 1993 study to the effect that "Canadian reforms under the Conservatives had met with less than the desired success precisely because the required political and public service leadership had been lacking" (p. 13). In the other Westminster democracies, leadership on management change had come directly from the top, from prime ministers and senior cabinet ministers. Even with the change in government in 1993, Aucoin argued that there still appeared "to be no interest in mounting a comprehensive program of public management

Figure 5.1   Management Reform in the OECD

Summary of country recommendations[a]

	Canada	Czech Republic	Denmark	Finland	France	Germany	Greece	Hungary	Iceland	Ireland	Italy	Japan	Korea	Mexico	New Zealand	Norway	Poland	Portugal	Sweden	Switzerland	United Kingdom	Total[b]
Adopting a results-focused budgeting and management approach																						
Move towards results objectives																						
• Improve the quality and encourage the use of performance indicators...	X				X		X	X							X	X	X				X	9
... putting more emphasis on outcomes (as opposed to outputs)														X	X						X	3
• Increase commitment to service improvements and client satisfaction	X		X								X											3
• Improve consistency across objectives and co-ordination between agencies															X				X		X	3
• Move to performance-based budgeting...	X							X	X	X						X						5
... extending it to sub-national governments			X	X								X								X		4
Increase managerial autonomy																						
• By giving managers enhanced discretion as to how they reach objectives	X												X	X		X						4
• By increasing the ability of public agencies to carry over unused appropriations												X				X						2
Strengthen accountability frameworks																						
• Develop appropriate instruments to evaluate outcomes								X								X					X	3
• Strengthen performance evaluation and auditing	X				X	X		X		X	X	X	X	X	X		X				X X	13
• Rely more on activity-based funding systems for public entities[c]...																X		X	X			3
... while safeguarding against cost overruns																X						1
Reforming human resource management																						
Modernize staffing policies																						
• Streamline recruitment procedures...	X														X							2
and use more open recruitment									X							X						2
• Encourage mobility of staff within public service							X				X			X					X			4
• Rely more on fixed-term contracts					X														X			2
Allow wages to reflect market conditions...	X				X						X					X	X					5
... and allow for more functional and regional flexibility in public sector pay schemes					X																	1
Rely more on performance-related approaches to personnel management...	X	X	X	X		X	X		X	X	X			X		X	X	X			X	14
... while taking measures to limit wage overruns	X										X											2

a) These policy recommendations are derived from the public spending chapter for individual OECD country reviews published in 2000 for Japan and Mexico; 2001 for Canada and Czech Republic; 2002 for Denmark, Germany, Greece, Hungary, Italy, New Zealand, Norway, Poland, Sweden, Switzerland, and the United Kingdom; 2003 for Finland, France, Iceland, Ireland, Korea, and Portugal.

b) Number of countries for which these recommendations were spelled out among the 21 countries for which in-depth public expenditure chapters in final form are available.

c) In the case of Portugal and Switzerland, this recommendation applies to the hospital sector.

Source: Individual country in-depth chapters on public expenditure.

reform" (p. 16). The fundamentals of the NPM as experienced in New Zealand and the United Kingdom require a combination of rather radical restructuring around the separation of policy from operations, with a determined focus on service that in turn demands the development and application of performance standards. In Canada, at both federal and provincial levels, restructuring has not gone very far, with the main organizational vehicle remaining the department or ministry.

A good example of federal government hesitancy on the re-organizational front comes from the establishment of **Special Operating Agencies** (SOAs), the closest Canadian equivalent to Next Steps agencies. Whereas in the United Kingdom special agencies were central to the government's policy on management because that policy was focused on a single overarching strategy of structural reform, the Canadian approach to SOAs was "part of a larger management improvement complex of strategies" (Armstrong, 1991, p. 6). Remember as well that New Zealand radically separated advice and delivery agencies from ministries. In Canada, five SOAs were created by the end of 1990, and by early 1991 there were fifteen. No new ones were created for another two years, at which point a "stock-taking" exercise was launched that took a year (Seidle, 1995, p. 85). In 1995 the federal Translation Bureau became an SOA, and three others were announced, leading Borins (1995) to note that the "British government, following Sweden, has concluded that over 60 per cent of its activities can be given over to executive agencies while a much more hesitant Canadian federal government has given over to special operating agencies less than 5 per cent of its activities" (p. 125).

As of 2004 there were only seventeen federal SOAs (Treasury Board of Canada, 2004a). Six, or less than half, serve the "public": the Passport Office, the Canadian Intellectual Property Office, Measurement Canada, the Superintendent of Bankruptcy, Technology Partnerships Canada, and Canadian Investment and Savings. Clearly, only the Passport Office and perhaps the Canadian Intellectual Property Office are truly visible and known to the public; the others provide services to segments of industry or business. The remaining SOAs largely provide services to other government departments (e.g., Consulting and Audit Canada and the Translation Bureau). The overall profile of Canadian efforts in this area, therefore, is unimpressive compared to the pace set by some other OECD countries. An additional factor is that the flexibilities for these Canadian SOAs are more limited than counterparts in other countries—they have to seek more approvals, even within their framework agreements, and their employees remain public servants under public service union contracts.

However, the appetite for reform is not completely sated. For example, in December 2003, the new Martin government announced some important changes in cabinet machinery and public management in the federal public sector. New ministries were created (Public Safety and Emergency Preparedness); Foreign Affairs and International Trade was split into two departments; Human Resources Development Canada was split into a new department of Human Resources and Skills Development and a new department of Social Development (focusing on income security issues and programs); the Treasury Board Secretariat (TBS) was refocused on comptrollership; and a minister was given responsibility for democratic reform. Under Prime Minister Chrétien, the Cabinet organization chart looked deceptively simple. The full Cabinet was supported by four committees: Economic Union, Social Union, Treasury Board, and Special Committee of Cabinet. This was replaced with nine committees: Priorities and Planning; Operations; Treasury Board; Domestic Affairs; Global Affairs; Canada–U.S.; Security, Public Health and Emergencies; Expenditure Review; and Aboriginal Affairs.

The most interesting innovations were on the public management front. The Expenditure Review Committee, for example, was designed to lead a program review exercise (to report in the fall of 2004) that was intended to instill a new culture of "continuous reallocation" in the federal government. This is complemented by a refocused TBS and stronger comptrollership functions, projected directly into departments but reporting to the comptroller general. Within the TBS, the Office of the Comptroller General was strengthened, and each department was to have departmental comptrollers reporting on and approving departmental expenditure plans (no doubt as a response to the criticisms of government spending control). In a move reminiscent of the mid-1990s Program Review, the Expenditure Review process would examine all government programs in terms of seven tests: public interest, role of government, federalism, partnership, value for money, efficiency, and affordability (Treasury Board of Canada, 2004b). The exercise was to focus on departmental reviews of the thirty largest departments, reviews of key horizontal policy areas, and government operation reviews. The goal was to identify $3 billion in savings over four years. There was also to be a review of Crown corporations, and enhancements to public service training. As the President of the Treasury Board put it: "Like all democratically elected governments throughout the industrialized world, we face an urgent need to fundamentally transform the way public sector management works. I want Canada to be at the forefront of change, not playing catch-up." Of course, the federal minority government that was elected in June 2004 may slow the pace of management reform. The Liberals ran a left-wing campaign, and found themselves requiring the support of the NDP to survive in government. This meant that in order to survive, the Liberals would have to pander to NDP preferences, which usually imply large spending on social programs. As well, public sector reform is normally not a vote-getter.

The NPM and its implications for implementation, of course, affect the entire public sector, not just the federal government. In fact, while Ottawa traditionally has "been the leader in the field of administrative reform in Canada" (Gow, 1994, p. 75), it is probable that the momentum of innovation in management practices has shifted to the provinces and municipalities, or that they are at least as committed to innovation, if not more so, as the federal government. The 2003 Institute for Public Administration of Canada Innovative Management Awards, for example, received a total of ninety submissions, of which twenty were from the federal sector, forty-six from the provincial sector, and twenty-four from the municipal sector (IPAC, 2004). Nonetheless, there is no evidence that any of the provinces or municipalities have made major organizational departures on the scale of a New Zealand reform effort. The Canadian approach does appear to cling to a sectoral organization that for the most part puts policy advice and service delivery under the same umbrella. There has been some evolution in this in the past five years, but the changes have not been radical. On the other hand, innovations on service delivery and reporting within those organizational structures have been developing rapidly.

THE NPM AND IMPLEMENTATION

We can conclude from the previous section that something indeed has changed about the organization and delivery of public services at every level of government in Canada. Moreover, these changes echo structural reforms that have been under way for at least a decade in the other major Westminster democracies as well as the United States. The Canadian experience until the 1990s was, in comparative terms, less far reaching, radical, or publicly debated than was true of the United Kingdom or New Zealand. In the first half of the 1990s, management reform, while defended in terms of higher standards of service to the public, was driven largely by fiscal constraints at both the federal and provincial levels of government. But the fiscal constraints should be given their due: as we noted in Chapter 4, without those constraints it would have been easy to continue doing business as usual.

Things have changed, and "alternative service delivery," "quality service," "citizen-centred service," "results," and "performance" are the order of the day. Box 5.4 (page 216) shows examples of cutting-edge

Box 5.4   ## 2003 IPAC INNOVATIVE MANAGEMENT AWARD WINNERS

GOLD AWARD: STATISTICS CANADA'S EDUCATION OUTREACH PROGRAM

Statistics Canada is helping Canadian students and their teachers gain more knowledge about Canada, and learn how to find and analyze Canadian facts. The program has had widespread success since its introduction in 1999. Teachers and students access the agency's online Learning Resources site (www. statcan.ca) at a rate of more than 4,000 visits a day. More than 10,000 teachers have been introduced to hundreds of lesson plans and other practical products that promote the use of data in student learning.

SILVER AWARD: YUKON DEVELOPMENT CORPORATION—YUKON ENERGY SOLUTIONS: INTEGRATED, EFFECTIVE, AFFORDABLE, SUSTAINABLE

Yukon Development Corporation has implemented an innovative strategy that has crossed jurisdictional boundaries to capture and integrate the knowledge of many organizations in generating and conserving energy. The result has been energy savings for consumers, reduced greenhouse gas emissions and the acquisition of new knowledge about renewable energy resources. The strategy is led by Yukon Development, a Crown corporation, and its subsidiaries, a regulated electrical utility called Yukon Energy Corporation and a technical services company called the Energy Solutions Centre Inc.

BRONZE AWARD: NEWFOUNDLAND AND LABRADOR STATISTICS AGENCY— COMMUNITY ACCOUNTS

People in Newfoundland and Labrador have something that no other province has: a way to see for themselves how their communities are faring economically and socially, and to measure how well their governments are doing in promoting their well-being. Community Accounts is an Internet-based system, accessible at http://www.communityaccounts.ca, that provides inter-related social and economic information for Newfoundland and Labrador and overcomes geographical, functional, and organizational barriers to people's knowledge.

BRONZE AWARD: ALBERTA AGRICULTURE, FOOD AND RURAL DEVELOPMENT—ROPIN' KNOWLEDGE AND HERDIN' CATS

Knowledge is the competitive edge for Alberta's agriculture and food industry. Alberta Agriculture, Food and Rural Development manages that knowledge and ensures that people can find it quickly. Since 1999, its Ropin' Knowledge and Herdin' Cats project has developed management practices and Web-based tools to improve knowledge transfer among staff, partners and customers, resulting in better services at lower cost. The department's Web site, called Ropin' the Web (www.agric.gov.ab.ca), is a major knowledge delivery channel with more than 40 million annual page visits.

SOURCE: IPAC. 2003 *Winners and Finalists.* Retrieved August 12, 2004, from http://www.ipac.ca/awards/innovation/past_winners/2003_winners_and_finalists/index.html

Canadian public management projects. They were four finalists for the Institute of Public Administration of Canada's 2003 Innovative Management Awards. The theme for that year was knowledge management. All four used innovative web-based tools to maximize information and knowledge for learning as well as community development.

The examples in Box 5.4 are Canadian, but the **innovation networks** that now appear to bind together public administrators, managers, consultants, and academics have ensured that examples of public sector innovation in program delivery are as widely available as possible. The John F. Kennedy School at Harvard University, for example, sponsors *Innovations in American Government* (John F. Kennedy School, 2004). The program has awarded innovations in public management since 1986. In 2002 there were five winners from the federal, state, and local level that exemplified new models for working effectively and producing results. Summaries are provided in Box 5.5 (page 218).

These are simply the tip of the NPM iceberg. As part of *Getting Government Right,* Ottawa early on committed itself to new frameworks for alternative service delivery and quality services, which have now evolved into a focus on client or citizen satisfaction. The *Framework for Alternative Service Delivery* (Treasury Board of Canada, 1996b), for

Box 5.5   INNOVATIONS IN AMERICAN
                                       GOVERNMENT WINNERS, 2003

LA BODEGA DE LA FAMILIA

STATE OF NEW YORK

Every day, La Bodega de la Familia proves that engaged and supported families can be an effective supplement to traditional criminal justice responses to drug addiction. Housed in a store-front on Manhattan's Lower East Side, La Bodega employs its signature service, Family Case Management, to tap the natural strengths and resources of families to help their loved ones succeed under parole and probation supervision.

FIRSTGOV.GOV

GENERAL SERVICES ADMINISTRATION

To help citizens connect with government, the U.S. Government created an official web portal, FirstGov.gov, connected to 22,000 federal websites and 180 million pages of information from federal, state and local governments. FirstGov, organized around citizens' needs, provides direct, easy access to transactions, services, and information: everything from paying taxes to buying stamps, applying for college loans to ascertaining benefits, getting a passport application to finding a government job.

ENERGY EFFICIENCY UTILITY

STATE OF VERMONT

Vermont electric power companies faced the dilemma of maintaining sales while implementing laws encouraging customers who use less power. The result: a patchwork of efficiency programs. Vermont's solution: the nation's first energy efficiency utility, an independent ratepayer-funded entity, with no interest in energy sales, that delivers efficiency services to 43,000 customers. The program has saved 58,000-megawatt hours—as much as Vermont's second largest city consumed in 2001.

THE OHIO APPALACHIAN CENTER FOR HIGHER EDUCATION (OACHE)

STATE OF OHIO

A stereotyped view of "college material" can be a barrier to higher education. To remedy that for young Ohioans, the Center works with colleges, universities, K-12 schools, and the private sector to help school districts and campuses with career planning, financial aid, field visits, and guest speakers. As a result, students and parents can make informed decisions about higher education starting as early as fifth grade.

311 SYSTEM

CITY OF CHICAGO, IL

Like people everywhere, Chicagoans need non-emergency services and information about city events and programs. The City met the challenge by setting up a 311 facility, a 24/7 shopping center for non-emergency services. Callers use one easy-to-remember number and get highly trained, multilingual operators using software that channels service requests to the correct departments. It's a model system that helps city government respond more efficiently to the needs of its people.

SOURCE: Retrieved September 4, 2004, from http://www.ashinstitute.harvard .edu/Ash/pr_20032.htm

example, explained the approach, which has been widely adopted by all levels of government in Canada:

Governments implementing alternative program delivery try to select the best way to deliver programs, activities, services and functions to achieve government objectives, while creating a more client-oriented, affordable and innovative program delivery environment. They can do this in numerous ways, including: establishing more service-oriented and businesslike special operating agencies (SOAs) and other flexible service delivery arrangements; establishing new forms of cooperation among departments such as sharing the provision of administration services at the local level; setting up Crown corporations; negotiating partnering arrangements with other levels of government and the private and voluntary sectors; devolving programs and services to the provinces; commercializing government services to improve efficiency while protecting the public interest; and privatizing government programs and services that no longer serve a public policy purpose. (Treasury Board of Canada, 1996b)

There is a strong emphasis in this, as there is in the examples of the IPAC and Kennedy School innovation winners, on client or **citizen-centred service.** If the mid-1990s was a period of structural reform (however modest in the Canadian case), more recently the focus has shifted to service, satisfaction, and quality. This does not necessarily mean that in the pursuit of these objectives public managers will not reform their organizations, but it probably means that the reforms will take place more at the street level in terms of combinations of human and other resources to achieve better outcomes. At the same time, the commitment to service and quality that seems to be seeping into every nook and cranny of the public sector is forcing decisionmakers to ask radical questions about how services should be delivered and whether they should be delivered at all through the public sector. Market mechanisms, nonprofit agencies, commercial ventures, and other hybrid forms of organization are definitely on the table and are now part of the policy design/implementation tool kit.

Quality service emerged as a reform priority in the late 1990s. A wide network of Canadian public servants and policymakers became concerned about the "service gap" or the distance between what citizens expect from their governments and the level of satisfaction that they have with what they actually get. By focusing on citizens first, and assessing their needs and their levels of satisfaction, public service managers could then ensure that clients get what they want (instead of what managers think they want) and allocate resources accordingly. The 1998 *Citizens First* survey showed that Canadians in fact rated many public services quite highly:

Almost every Canadian survey that has compared public and private sector services has found that citizens rate the performance of government services significantly below that of private sector services. Coupled with "bad-news stories" in the media, a common belief has emerged that private sector service is better than public sector service. *Citizens First* sets the record straight about citizens' ratings of public sector service. It reports that Canadians *do not* rate the quality of private sector services higher than that of public sector service. Canadians gave seven private sector services an average rating of 62 out of 100, and similar ratings to public sector services used in the past year.

More specifically, federal services received an average rating of 60 out of 100, provincial services an average rating of 62, and municipal services an average rating of 64. The fact is, some public sector services rate higher than some private sector services, just as the converse is true. . . . (Canadian Centre for Management Development, 1999, p. 8)

These findings were largely supported in the following two biennial surveys undertaken in 2000 and 2002. The 2002 survey also asked citizens about their priorities for improvement. The findings provide an interesting snapshot of what matters most to people in terms of government services (see Boxes 5.6 and 5.7, pp. 222, 224). The seriousness with which this dimension of implementation is being taken is illustrated by the Service Improvement Initiative that was launched in 2000 and then regalvanized in 2004. A total of forty-seven departments and agencies were required to participate in the initiative, whose target was a minimum 10 percent increase in client satisfaction by 2005. This would require measurements of current client satisfaction, benchmarks, annual improvement plans, and public progress reports. In describing the initiative, the policy document stated:

The essence of the *Service Improvement Initiative* is that the continuous and measurable improvement of client satisfaction is the most reliable indicator of improvement in service quality and service performance: it is what quality and continuous improvement should now mean, and how they should be primarily, though not exclusively, measured. Leading-edge service organizations in the public sector, like their counterparts in the private sector, now use a results-based approach to the continuous improvement of client satisfaction, integrated with the annual business planning cycle. (Treasury Board of Canada, 2000b)

This emphasis on quality and service would be largely empty if there were no way of assessing the success of achieving quality and service goals, and finding out what clients and citizens actually think about the services that they receive. Hence, the emphasis on service is almost inevitably linked to an emphasis on performance assessment, measurement, and results. We will take up the question of performance measurement in Chapter 7, but it can be noted here that there are many ways of assessing outcomes and performance, from actual program impacts on specific targets to levels of satisfaction with services. As we will see in Chapter 7, there is a wide variety of approaches to measuring and reporting on performance; the important thing is that it is being done, and that in comparison with the older tradition of public administration, it is new. In the past, the reporting function focused primarily on the appropriate administration of resources, while policy evaluation took care of cost-benefit analyses of impact analyses. Performance and satisfaction matter now because citizens matter more.

Another clear characteristic of the federal government's approach to public sector reform and alternative service delivery is the centrality of

Box 5.6	MUNICIPAL, PROVINCIAL, AND TERRITORIAL SERVICES— PRIORITIES FOR IMPROVEMENT

Service	Percent choosing the service as a priority
Hospitals	57
Road maintenance & snow removal	40
Health care outside hospitals	31
Drinking water treatment	23
Publicly funded schools	22
Public transit	19
Public housing	16
Colleges and universities	15
Recycling	14
Family services, counselling, children's aid	14
Emergency shelters and hostels	12
Municipal police force	12
Public health care	12
Social assistance, welfare	11
Sewage & waste water treatment	11
Public or subsidized day care	10
Garbage collection	10
Job training	9
Workers' compensation	8
Motor vehicle registration	8
Mental health services	7
Student loans, bursaries	7
Ambulance services	7

Service	Percent choosing the service as a priority
Municipal parks	7
Public libraries	7
Automobile insurance	6
Provincial parks	5
Fire department	4
Provincial courts	4
Small business startup services	4
Provincial jails	3
Property tax collection	3
Health card applications	3
Birth, marriage, death registration	3
Provincial police	3
Planning and land development	2
Agricultural services	2
Building permits	2
Provincial museums	1
Hunting & fishing licences	1

SOURCE: *Citizens First 3*. (2003). Ottawa: The Institute for Citizen-Centred Service and the Institute of Public Administration of Canada, p. 85.

partnerships. We will discuss this in Chapter 6 in the context of policy communities and networks, and provided the broader context for this shift in Chapter 2 in terms of shifting governance regimes. Today, implementation is neither primarily about doing it alone nor shifting public responsibilities completely to the private sector. It is about doing it in concert with partners from the voluntary sector, from interest groups and NGOs, from the private and not-for-profit sectors. As Figure 5.2 (page 224) outlines, the range of available modes and partners in alternative service delivery is virtually limitless, with various permutations and combinations of commercialized, voluntary, and purely public services, and every hybrid in between. The main dimensions are commercialization, private/public, and independence from government. Combined with initiatives to improve the quality of services, enhance performance, and publicize results, it is clear that the world of implementation and policy instruments has changed significantly.

Figure 5.2   Opportunities for Program Delivery Alternatives

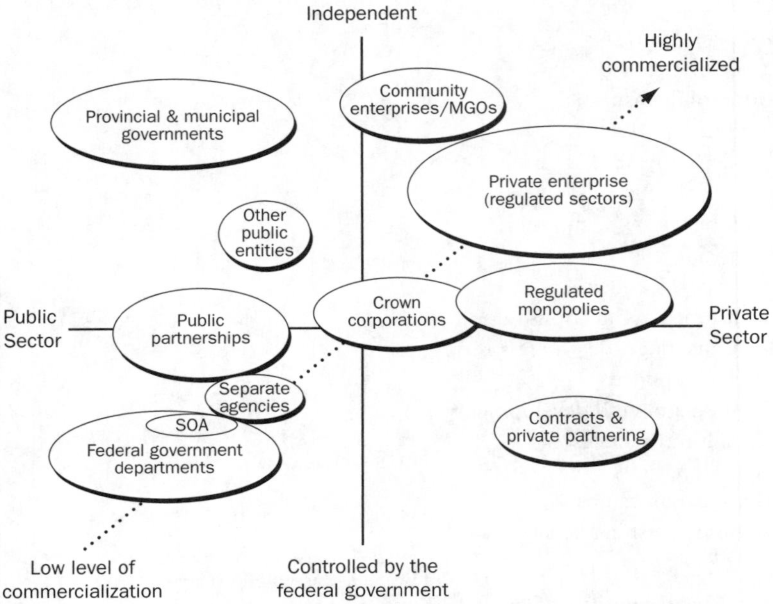

SOURCE: Treasury Board of Canada. (1996). *A framework for alternative service delivery.* Retrieved August 12, 2004, from http://www.tbs-sct.gc.ca/tb/pubs/promgt/apd/fr/fr2-1e.gif

Box 5.7	FEDERAL SERVICES—PRIORITIES FOR IMPROVEMENT	
	Percent choosing the service as a priority	
Service	*2002*	*2000*
Employment Insurance	29	27
Customs & Immigration border services	26	16
Canada Post	25	28
Health Canada: Information on health issues	24	26
Canada Customs & Revenue Agency (formerly Revenue Canada)	24	29
CPP/OAS	23	26
Human Resource Centre Canada (HRCC)	16	29

Service	Percent choosing the service as a priority	
	2002	2000
RCMP	14	17
National parole/prisons	14	12
Federal courts	12	12
Access to information	12	–
National parks	11	12
Passports	10	7
Citizenship services	7	6
Information services	6	7
Financial services: CMHC, farm credit	5	6
Coast Guard	4	5
NFB, museums, art galleries	3	5

SOURCE: *Citizens First 3*. (2003). Ottawa: The Institute for Citizen-Centred Service and the Institute of Public Administration of Canada, p. 86.

CONCLUSION

It is easy enough to see what is different about implementation—new organizational forms, clearer standards, use of information technology, partnerships, a service orientation, and public exposure of plans and performance. It is clear from Figure 5.2 that partnering in some format is becoming a critical aspect of governance and service delivery. This poses fresh challenges for public managers and policy analysts, since our traditional paradigms of service delivery have relied on a top-down, centralized control model. When governments act as partners, providing support and frameworks rather than services directly, it changes the nature of the implementation game quite dramatically, for example, through highlighting accountability issues, monitoring, and learning loops. In terms of the theory discussed in the first part of this chapter, modern implementation practices seem to combine strategies of autonomy to reduce blockages in decisionmaking (e.g., SOAs) and strategies of interdependency that will actually demand greater attention to communication and cooperation (e.g., partnerships; Savoie, 2004, p. 7).

It should also be clear from this chapter that while the world of policy implementation has changed, the tableaux of those changes is confusing and difficult to trace. The broad principles are straightforward, and any self-respecting acolyte of the NPM can read them off the rosaries of reinvention and reengineering. In practice, however, we saw that the range of experiments is quite broad (for the NPM, happily so, since from a thousand management flowers will the sweet seeds of inspiration grow), as well as varied in intensity. Currently, Ottawa seems to be undergoing a culture shift/shock that appears to be genuinely, if slowly, inducing managers and policymakers to think differently. The Service Improvement Initiative is a case in point.

We have argued that many of these changes are being driven by deep forces that are difficult, if not impossible, to avoid, and that these changes in governance cut across ideological lines. The NPM is not so benign, however, that it lacks severe critics. For one thing, the NPM and the new implementation strategies it calls up were associated with a pre-occupation with the deficit, and principally with its expenditure side. There are those who argue that this is merely a business agenda, not some new science of management. As well, the reason for innovation, of course, is reduced resources, and especially reduced personnel. The human cost was in public sector jobs, with literally thousands of people let go (though in the case of Ottawa, employment increased steadily after 1999 to bring levels back to where they had been in 1995; Statistics Canada, 2004). Those who remained standing in the rubble of public sector institutions had little choice but to seek partners and support. A big part of the equation had thus been determined: a smaller public sector, doing fewer things with fewer resources. It was only a matter of time before circumstances demanded innovation, though the rhetoric of NPM also places a premium on innovation and service directly. We saw this in the public sector reform philosophy of Tony Blair, which places a great emphasis on responsive public services and performance.

Of all the critiques of the NPM, the most common is that it takes business and the marketplace as the standard for public services, when in fact the public sector has specific characteristics of its own:

> The public policy dimension is unique to public management as governance. Citizen-centred service requires attention to critical issues of law, rights, and due process not present in the marketplace of private service delivery. And managing the public service entails managing in a context of constraints and motivations that are distinct to the public sector. To the degree that privatization and contracting out cannot be extended to all functions of government, public administration, even in a highly devolved management regime, remains subject to political and administrative dynamics that require their own distinctive modes of reform and renewal. (Aucoin, 2002, 50)

An equally fundamental critique is that at the end of the day, the NPM transforms much less than it promises, and indeed there may be perverse effects that lead to the opposite of what was intended (Gregory, 2002). For example, the NPM promises to reduce bureaucracy, but since it is a managerial initiative, it actually seeks new mechanisms of control that can sometimes increase practical bureaucracy—reporting requirements as an example. While the power of central agencies is supposed to be attenuated in favour of contracts and more flexibility for agency heads, the centre never recedes completely, and in the Canadian case, did not diminish noticeably at all. In countries where the NPM went further, such as New Zealand, there continue to be tensions around political account-ability. A full-blooded NPM promises a sharper distinction between policymaking (political direction) and implementation (execution), but when things go wrong, the public still holds politicians accountable. Another problem is the NPM promise of great responsiveness and flexi-bility to get things done, which can lead to cutting procedural corners.

So, are all the initiatives associated with the NPM just whistling in the dark? Or worse, are they smokescreens for what is, in fact, an outright attack on the virtues of the public sector? On balance, this book accepts these changes as being broadly beneficial to the citizenry insofar as ser-vice, efficiency, effectiveness, performance, and results are enhanced. It also supports the idea of decentralization and devolution as much as is feasible to community groups and local entities, and as much choice and individualization of public programs as possible. However, we should also be aware of the potential shortcomings and challenges of doing implementation in a different key.

First, we need to be wary of the interests that are served, and those that are not, by catchphrases like "citizen-centred service delivery," "ASD," and "partnerships." There is always the danger, for example, that sur-veys that seem to be searching for citizens' views on services might in the end be used more as legitimizing instruments to support what govern-ments are doing anyway. The same can be said of performance and results reporting. What should be honest attempts at transparency can easily become weapons of government propaganda, skewing the num-bers in such a way as to declare perfection. As well, it cannot be lost on many observers that the craze for quality and service has exploded just at the time when many services were either being reduced or eliminated. The energy and resources flowing into measurements, benchmarks, surveys, reports, and indicators may serve to persuade the citizenry that governments actually care about what they are doing, when in fact much of government may steam along as usual. Most analyses of quality ser-vice initiatives and performance measurement are well aware of these human and political dynamics, and so consequently stress leadership, organizational commitment, and culture change as key ingredients in achieving genuinely different outcomes.

Second, we should acknowledge that the NPM does actually mean "new" public management in the sense that it entails different values and practices (Hood, 1998). We noted earlier that traditional public administration relies on hierarchical models, whereas the NPM celebrates administrative entrepreneurship, networks, collaboration, innovation, and responsiveness. It is more than a matter of style, however; management style means changes to management practice and institutions and procedures, and that can mean changes in outcomes. A perfect illustration is the grants and contributions scandal that occurred in Human Resources Development Canada (HRDC) in 1999–2000 (Good, 2003). At the time, HRDC was a huge department, accounting for over half of total federal government expenditures. Out of a total budget of over $57 billion, some $3.3 billion went to grants and contributions. Initial media reports claimed that an internal audit of grants and contributions had uncovered $1 billion in misspent funds; more careful analysis in the ensuing months showed the real sum to be about $85 000. The internal audit done in 2000, which was released to a media and opposition party frenzy, in fact highlighted missing documentation and sloppy information management practices. Part of the reason was the sheer size of the programs and of the department, but part was due to the impact of budget cuts and the NPM in the previous years. During Program Review, for example, HRDC was required to cut 20 percent of its staff. At the same time it was expected to maintain program quality. Like other federal departments and the government as a whole (Borins, 2002), HRDC did not embark on radical NPM changes. But it did alter its management style: "When it came to public management reform, HRDC took an approach that stressed quality service, flexibility in program delivery at the local level, partnership arrangements, elimination of unnecessary administrative barriers, accountability for program results, and a supported and empowered workforce" (Good, 2003, p. 56). The combination of staff cuts, decentralization, partnerships, and flexibility formed the backdrop for what turned out to be management failure. In short, there were real—and in this instance, negative— consequences to the implementation of a new management paradigm in HRDC.

Third, we need to recognize the challenges and problems involved in partnerships, since partnerships (and horizontal coordination) form such a prominent part of the NPM. We raise some of these in Chapter 6, but it is worth addressing them briefly here. The current enthusiasm for partnerships assumes that civil society organizations—these are typically the entities involved in a partnership—have the capacity to take on new responsibilities. Hall and Reed (1998) caution

> As our governments attempt to untie and re-weave the social
> safety net, it is an easy temptation to presume that there is a
> second safety net underneath—the non-profit sector—with the
> capacity to hold a good part of what the first cannot. Looked at
> carefully, the second safety net is simply too small and too vul-
> nerable to be counted on to hold an additional load of help,
> caring and supporting services. (p. 18)

It is not merely a matter of weakness or inadequate resources; Hall
and Reed point out that nonprofit organizations operate in different
ways from government departments, on a different scale, with different values and procedures. The easy assumption that they can step into
the breach and immediately partner with government is flawed. We
need as well to be cautious about our assumptions about contracting
out social services. Most attempts to do so rely on outcome or performance measures, as government departments develop agreements with
third parties to provide certain services and give them the flexibility to
achieve them as they see fit. However, those same government departments lack a comprehensive assessment of the impacts of their interventions and so have quite imperfect knowledge about how to assess
the performance of commercial firms (Panet and Trebilcock, 1998,
p. 28). Other types of public-private sector partnerships to deliver different types of goods and services (e.g., infrastructure), have run up
against problems in that the private sector actors, as befits commercial
entities, often demand confidentiality about key aspects of their agreement or activities, thus short-circuiting important public policy values
(Boase, 2000).

The issue is one that has been touched on repeatedly in this chapter—
accountability. The traditional governance model under a parliamentary
regime like Canada's assumes that monies are spent by government
departments and agencies that are accountable to their ministers, and
through them to the government as a whole, and ultimately to the
legislature and the people. Alternative service delivery "implies a separation of policy and implementation that is practical only if there is ongoing communication between policymakers and service providers"
(Armstrong, 1998, p. 2). It is that separation that threatens conventional
practices of democratic accountability. In late 1999, for example, the
auditor general released a report on new governance arrangements that
had been developed in the mid-1990s in response to budget cuts and new
management thinking. He found seventy-seven such new arrangements
that collectively spend $5 billion of taxpayers' money annually. "Under
these arrangements, the federal government involves external partners in

the planning, design and achievement of federal objectives, replacing delivery by federal employees, contractors or agents. These partners are not accountable to ministers and Parliament" (Auditor General, 1999).

In many respects, these are broad questions of governance and not merely technical ones of implementation. We will address these larger issues in our conclusions in Chapter 9. Chapter 7 will take up the difficult question of asking how we might measure whether all this innovation, alternative service delivery, and quality actually results in efficiencies and positive impact. The next chapter, however, considers the question of the participants in the policy process.

KEY TERMS

backward mapping—a technique to work out what the policy will look like in terms of delivery of programs at the final point of service, and hence what the implementation needs are at that point

clearances—the number of agreements required by multiple sets of actors in order for implementation to go forward

client satisfaction—degree to which customers or clients of a service are happy with that service

citizen-centred service delivery—ensuring that clients get what they want and that resources are allocated accordingly by focusing on citizens first and assessing their needs and their levels of satisfaction

decentralization—devolution of responsibilities to other government jurisdictions or third parties, and restructuring accountability relationships within government departments

decision chain—the sequence of agreements, decisions, or clearances that have to be surmounted in order for the implementation process to move forward

decision points—a single stage in a decision chain requiring clearances and agreements before movement to the next point is possible

empowerment—the provision of real powers and authorities to the government's other partners in the policy process

forward mapping—the conventional technique of implementation analysis that starts with as clear a statement as possible of the policy-maker's intent and proceeds through a sequence of increasingly specific steps to define what is expected of implementers at each level

functional model—the model in which the tasks of policy advice and implementation are generally carried out by separate agencies

horizontal issues—issues that cut across various policy areas

innovation networks—networks that bind together public administrators, managers, consultants, and academics to ensure that examples of public sector innovation in program delivery are as widely available as possible

performance—empirical indicator of how well a program or organization is operating with respect to clearly articulated goals

policy feedback—information about the consequences or impacts of a policy that goes back into its improvement and redesign

PS2000—a 1989–1993 federal public sector reform initiative inaugurated in 1989, which had three core objectives: better service, improved personnel management, and flexibility

quality management—managing programs and services with a high priority placed on quality, performance measures, and reporting

Quality Services Initiative—the late 1990s federal initiative that stresses citizen-centered service delivery

sectoral model—a model that vertically integrates advice and delivery within a ministry or department

service delivery—procedures and organizational resources devoted to getting services to clients

Special Operating Agency (SOA)—agency that continues to work in the public sector but with special, more relaxed rules that give it more scope to be flexible and service oriented

Weblinks

Innovations in American Government
http://www.innovations.harvard.edu

Institute for Citizen-Centred Service
http://www.iccs-isac.org/eng/about.htm

Institute of Public Administration of Canada Innovation Award
http://www.ipac.ca/news/Innovation_award_2004.html

OECD
http://www.olis.oecd.org

Treasury Board of Canada
http://www.tbs-sct.gc.ca/index_e.asp

Further Readings

Aucoin, P. (1995). *The new public management: Canada in a comparative perspective.* Montreal: Institute for Research on Public Policy.

Bardach, E. (1977). *The implementation game: What happens after a bill becomes a law.* Cambridge, MA: MIT Press.

Good, D. A. (2003). *The politics of public management: The HRDC audit of grants and contributions.* Toronto: University of Toronto Press.

Hupe, P. L., and Hill, M. (2002). *Implementing public policy: Governance in theory and in practice.* Thousand Oaks, CA: Sage.

Pressman, J. L., and Wildavsky, A. (1984). *Implementation: How great expectations in Washington are dashed in Oakland: Or, why it's amazing that federal programs work at all, this being a saga of the economic development administration as told by two sympathetic observers who seek to build morals on a foundation of ruined hopes* (3rd ed.). Berkeley: University of California Press.

REFERENCES

Alexander, E. R. (1989). Improbable implementation: The Pressman-Wildavsky paradox revisited. *Journal of Public Policy, 9,* 451–65.

Armstrong, J. (1991). Special operating agencies: Evolution or revolution? *Optimum, 22*(2), 5–12.

Armstrong, J. (1998). Some thoughts on alternative service delivery. *Optimum, 28*(1), 1–10.

Atkinson, M. (1993). Public policy and the new institutionalism. In M. Atkinson (Ed.), *Governing Canada: Institutions and public policy* (pp. 17–45). Toronto: Harcourt Brace Jovanovich.

Aucoin, P. (1995). *The new public management: Canada in a comparative perspective.* Montreal: Institute for Research on Public Policy.

Aucoin, P. (2002). Beyond the "new" in public management reform in Canada: Catching the next wave. In C. Dunn (Ed.), *The handbook of Canadian public administration* (pp. 36–52). Toronto: Oxford University Press.

Auditor General of Canada. (1999, November). *Report of the auditor general of Canada.* Chapter 23: Involving others in governing: Accountability at risk. Retrieved August 12, 2004, from http://www.oag-bvg.gc.ca/domino/reports.nsf/html/9923ce.html

Bardach, E. (1977). *The implementation game: What happens after a bill becomes a law.* Cambridge, MA: MIT Press.

Boase, J. P. (2000). Beyond government? The appeal of public-private partnerships. *Canadian Public Administration,* 43(1), 75–92.

Borins, S. (1995, Spring). The new public management is here to stay. *Canadian Public Administration,* 38, 122–32.

Borins, S. (2002). Transformation of the public sector: Canada in comparative perspective. In C. Dunn (Ed.), *The handbook of Canadian public administration* (pp. 3–17). Toronto: Oxford University Press.

Boston, J., et al. (1996). *Public management: The New Zealand model.* Auckland: Oxford University Press.

Bovens, M., and t'Hart, P. (1996). *Understanding policy fiascoes.* New Brunswick, NJ: Transaction Publishers.

Canadian Centre for Management Development. (1996). *Key characteristics of departments and executive agencies in the Westminster democracies.* Ottawa: Canadian Centre for Management Development.

Canadian Centre for Management Development. (1999). *Citizen-centred service: Responding to the needs of Canadians.* Retrieved September 4, 2004, from http://www.iccs-isac.org/eng/pubs/ CCHandbook.pdf

Cheung, A. (1997, September). Understanding public sector reforms: Global trends and diverse agendas. *International Review of Administrative Science,* 63 (4), 435–57.

Edwards III, G. C. (1984). Introduction. In G. C. Edwards III (Ed.), *Public policy implementation* (pp. ix–xv). Greenwich, CT: JAI Press.

Elmore, R. F. (1982). Backward mapping: Implementation research and policy decisions. In W. Williams (Ed.), *Studying implementation: Methodological and administrative issues* (pp. 18–35). Chatham, NJ: Chatham House.

Goggin, M. L., et al. (1990). *Implementation theory and practice: Toward a third generation.* Glenview, IL: Scott, Foresman/Little, Brown Higher Education.

Good, D. A. (2003). *The politics of public management: The HRDC audit of grants and contributions.* Toronto: University of Toronto Press.

Gow, J. I. (1994). *Learning from others: Administrative innovations among Canadian governments.* Toronto: Institute of Public Administration of Canada.

Gow, J. I. (2004). *A Canadian model of public administration?* Ottawa: Canada School of Public Service.

Greer, P. (1994). *Transforming central government: The Next Steps initiative.* Buckingham, UK: Open University Press.

Gregory, R. (2002). Transforming governmental culture: A sceptical view of new public management. In T. Christensen and Per Laegried (Eds.), *New public management: The transformation of ideas and practice* (pp. 231–58). Aldershot: Ashgate.

Guardian Unlimited. (2004). *Full text of Tony Blair's speech.* Retrieved August 12, 2004, from http://society.guardian.co.uk/ futureforpublicservices/comment/0,8146,1134531,00.html

Hall, M. H., and Reed, P. B. (1998). Shifting the burden: How much can government download to the non-profit sector? *Canadian Public Administration,* 41(1), 1–20.

Hogwood, B. W., and Gunn, L. A. (1984). *Policy analysis for the real world.* Oxford: Oxford University Press.

Hood, C. (1998). *The art of the state: Culture, rhetoric, and public management.* Oxford: Clarendon Press.

IPAC. (2004). *Innovation award.* Retrieved August 12, 2004, from http://www.ipac.ca/news/Innovation_award_2004.html

John F. Kennedy School of Government. (2004). *Innovations in American government.* Retrieved August 12, 2004, from http://www .innovations.harvard.edu

Lee, I., and Hobbs, C. (1996). Pink slips and running shoes: The Liberal government's downsizing of the public service. In G. Swimmer (Ed.), *How Ottawa spends, 1996–97: Life under the knife* (pp. 337–78). Ottawa: Carleton University Press.

Linder, S. H., and Peters, B. G. (1990). Research perspectives on the design of public policy: Implementation, formulation, and design. In D. J. Palumbo and D. J. Calista (Eds.), *Implementation and the policy process: Opening up the black box* (pp. 51–66). New York: Greenwood Press.

Majone, G., and Wildavsky, A. (1984). Implementation as evolution. In J. L. Pressman and A. Wildavsky (Eds.), *Implementation: How great expectations in Washington are dashed in Oakland: Or, why it's amazing that federal programs work at all, this being a saga of the economic development administration as told by two sympathetic observers who seek to build morals on a foundation of ruined hopes* (3rd ed.) (pp. 163–80). Berkeley: University of California Press.

Ministry of Finance (Canada). (1995). *Budget speech.* Ottawa: Ministry of Finance.

Osborne, D., and Gaebler, T. (1993). *Reinventing government: How the entrepreneurial spirit is transforming the public sector.* New York: Penguin.

OECD. (2004). *Enhancing the effectiveness of public spending: Experience in OECD countries.* Retrieved August 12, 2004, from http://www.olis.oecd.org/olis/2004doc.nsf/43bb6130e5e86e5fc12569fa005d004c/2459ff79232247fdc1256e3f0021af66/$FILE/JT00158260.PDF

Pal, L. A., and Weaver, K. W. (Eds.) (2003). *The government taketh away: The politics of pain in the United States and Canada.* Washington, DC: Georgetown University Press.

Panet, P. de L., and Trebilcock, M. J. (1998). Contracting-out social services. *Canadian Public Administration,* 41(1), 21–50.

Peters, T., and Waterman, R. H. (1982). *In search of excellence.* New York: Harper.

Potter, E. H. (2000). Treasury Board as a management board: The re-invention of a central agency. In L. A. Pal (Ed.), *How Ottawa spends 2000–2001: Past imperfect, future tense* (pp. 95–129). Toronto: Oxford University Press.

Pressman, J. L., and Wildavsky, A. (1984). *Implementation: How great expectations in Washington are dashed in Oakland: Or, why it's amazing that federal programs work at all, this being a saga of the economic development administration as told by two sympathetic observers who seek to build morals on a foundation of ruined hopes* (3rd ed.). Berkeley: University of California Press.

Privy Council Office. (2000). Fonctionnaires sans frontières: Operating at the speed of the public interest, Notes for an Address by Mel Cappe. Retrieved September 4, 2004, from http://www.pco-bcp.gc.ca/default.asp?Language=E&Page=clerkspeechesmessages&Sub=Clerks Speeches&Doc=2000_may31_e.htm

Rawson, B. (1991, Autumn). Public Service 2000 service to the public task force: Findings and implications. *Canadian Public Administration,* 34, 490–500.

Sabatier, P. A., and Mazmanian, D. A. (1981). The implementation of public policy: A framework of analysis. In D. A. Mazmanian and P. A. Sabatier (Eds.), *Effective policy implementation* (pp. 3–35). Lexington, MA: Lexington Books.

Savoie, D. J. (1994). *Thatcher, Reagan, Mulroney: In search of a new bureaucracy.* Toronto: University of Toronto Press.

Savoie, D. J. (2004, Spring). Searching for accountability in a government without boundaries. *Canadian Public Administration*, 47, 1–26.

Seidle, F. L. (1995). *Rethinking the delivery of public services to citizens*. Montreal: The Institute for Research on Public Policy.

State Services Commission. (2004). Retrieved August 12, 2004, from http://www.ssc.govt.nz/display/home.asp

Statistics Canada. (2004). *Employment and average weekly earnings (including overtime), public administration and all industries*. Retrieved August 12, 2004, from http://www.statcan.ca/english/Pgdb/govt18.htm

Tellier, P. M. (1990, Summer). Public Service 2000: The renewal of the public service. *Canadian Public Administration*, 33, 123–32.

Treasury Board of Canada. (1996a, September 30). *Getting government right: A progress report*. Retrieved September 4, 2004, from http://www.tbs-sct.gc.ca/report/govrev/Gfce.asp

Treasury Board of Canada. (1996b). *A framework for alternative service delivery*. Ottawa: Minister of Supply and Services.

Treasury Board of Canada. (1998). *Estimates: 1998–1999 program expenditure detail: A profile of departmental spending*. Retrieved August 12, 2004, from http://www.tbs-sct.gc.ca/tb/estimate/19981999/e98ped.pdf

Treasury Board of Canada. (2000a). *Business plan: 1999–2000 to 2001–2002*. Retrieved September 2000 from http://www.tbs-sct.gc.ca/report/businessplan/1999-2002/bp982_e.html#ret

Treasury Board of Canada. (2000b). *A policy framework for service improvement in the Government of Canada*. Retrieved August 12, 2004, from http://www.tbs-sct.gc.ca/pubs_pol/sipubs/si_as/pfsi1_e.asp#summ

Treasury Board of Canada. (2004a). *Population affiliation report*. Retrieved August 12, 2004, from http://www.tbs-sct.gc.ca/pubs_pol/hrpubs/popaffrep/sect6_e.asp

Treasury Board of Canada. (2004b). *Strengthening public sector management: An overview of the government action plan and key initiatives*. Retrieved August 12, 2004, from http://www.tbs-sct.gc.ca/spsm-rgsp/spsm-rgsp4_e.asp#Expenditure

Winter, S. (1990). Integrating implementation research. In D. J. Palumbo and D. J. Calista (Eds.), *Implementation and the policy process: Opening up the black box* (pp. 19–38). New York: Greenwood Press.

Chapter 6

*Policy
Communities
and Networks*

Chapter 1 outlined the foundations of traditional policy analysis, and the major critiques of those foundations. It pointed out that nonetheless, there is a resurgence of interest in making good policy but with a sensitivity to the limitations of the traditional approach and the challenges of contemporary governance. Chapter 2 explored those challenges and their broad consequences for how governments today, in Canada and throughout the world, are changing the way in which they organize their policy thinking, their policy processes, their organizations, and their partners. We developed a detailed understanding of these changes in chapters 3 to 5. What kind of conceptual lens can we use to understand the more complicated range of players and institutions involved in making policy, and how those players and institutions might change depending on circumstances and the policy issue at hand? In recent years the policy literature has placed great emphasis on policy communities and **policy networks,** two concepts that try to capture the degree to which any policy field or sector is populated by a host of government agencies, interest groups, associations, social movements, and so on. It has been argued that the nature of these policy communities is crucial both to policy development and to implementation. On the development side, governments need information that nongovernmental actors possess. On the implementation side, the more coherent the interests and organizations in a sector, the easier it is to implement a decision. This chapter reviews the literature on networks, and then shows how contemporary policymaking is coming to grips with issues of consultation, citizen engagement, and partnerships.

Politics without interests is an oxymoron, but for many years key strands of the policy literature were prepared to think about policymaking as a rational and largely technical enterprise consisting of priority-setting, options analysis, and careful consideration of costs and benefits. Interests did not enter the picture or, if they did, it was more as a complicating and confusing factor than a constituent component of the process (Nagel, 1988). As we noted in Chapter 1, the origins of policy analysis in the "policy sciences" were steeped in a sense that policy and politics would be immeasurably improved if the messy interplay of political interests could be tamed (if not completely supplanted) by the rational application of technical and expert knowledge:

> Insofar as possible, science and factual information should replace the politics of bargaining and negotiating that characterize pluralist democracy. Decision theorists documented the shortcomings of human judgement and argued that scientific studies could produce decisionmaking models or guidelines that would remove much of the error found in discretionary decisions by bureaucrats, program specialists, and even highly trained professionals such as judges or engineers. Many evaluators, declaring which programs worked and which ones did not, expected public officials to allocate funds accordingly. (Schneider and Ingram, 1997, pp. 30–31)

Chapter 2 described a different world in the making, one where the state is a central but not dominant player in policy processes, where citizens and **interest groups** demand more access to policy development and implementation, and consequently where there is a broader tableau of players and actors. The contemporary study and practice of public policymaking acknowledges this changed reality, and "policy networks" and "policy communities" have emerged as master concepts for conceptualizing new patterns of players and institutions. These are by no means the only frameworks, but they, and a small subset of others, will be examined here in some detail. A sampling of the larger universe of ideas about interests in the policy process is provided in Box 6.1.

Twenty years ago, the idea of policy networks was considered a "new key term" (Marin and Mayntz, 1991, p. 11), one that when joined to policy communities constituted "two of the most important conceptual innovations to emerge" in recent studies of the policy process (Atkinson and Coleman, 1992, p. 158; see Thatcher, 1998 for a detailed intellectual history). Even now policy network theory is "a major approach to the study of public policy making in Canada and elsewhere" (Howlett, 2002, p. 235). For some the concepts are at best "metaphors" (Dowding, 1995), and for others the overlap and confusion of the complementary network concepts (see Box 6.1) leads to little more than a "debate over terminology" (Lindquist, 1996, p. 219; for additional debates over the utility of the concept, see Marsh and Smith, 2000; Dowding, 2001; Marsh and Smith, 2001; Raab, 2001). While "**policy community**" and "policy network" are often used interchangeably, the former refers to a wider set of actors who understand the ideas and terminology that define

Box 6.1   CONCEPTUALIZING INTERESTS IN POLICYMAKING: A GLOSSARY

Concept	Definition	Key Source
Advocacy conditions	• A wide range of actors, including government from all levels, officials, interest organizations, research groups, journalists, and even other countries, who share a belief system about a policy area and over time demonstrate some degree of coordinated activity • An important feature is the idea that policy fields are marked by competing advocacy coalitions	• Sabatier and Jenkins-Smith, 1993
Discourse coalitions	• A range of policy actors united by broad ideas about the policy field, ideas that include assumptions, images, rhetoric, linguistic turns • Appears similar to advocacy coalitions but has a stronger emphasis on language and meaning	• Fischer and Forester, 1993
Epistemic community	• Originally developed in the field of international relations, this concept tries to capture the influence of international groups of scientific experts on policy-making, for example, in the environmental field • Emphasis on the power of ideas and expertise, as expressed through professional organizations or individuals	• Haas, 1992

(continued)

Box 6.1 (continued)

Concept	Definition	Key Source
Iron triangle	• The stable and cozy relationships among congressional committees, executive agencies (primarily regulatory), and economic interest groups • Implies long-term, stable interactions among a few actors, insulated from the rest of the policy process	• Carter, 1964 • Ripley and Franklin, 1984
Issue network	• Offered as a critique of the "iron triangle" concept in that most policy subsystems were actually quite fluid and changing, with actors coalescing as necessary around issues, not policy sectors	• Heclo and Wildavsky, 1974
Policy community	• The wide set of actors interested and informed about a policy issue, who share at least some common language, but who may be opponents on the issue • Differs from the advocacy coalition approach in that policy communities are presumed to include everyone active in a field	• Wright, 1988 • Coleman and Skogstad, 1990
Policy network	• A subset of actors in the policy community who have a consistently higher level of interest in the policy issue, and interact regularly • The most important feature is the discerning of patterns of relations that have consequences for the development and delivery of policy	• Atkinson and Coleman, 1992 • Van Waarden, 1992

Public interest groups	• Interest groups that advocate on behalf of the public good rather than the direct self-interest of their members • Emphasis is on advocacy for "causes" and the public interest rather than economic lobbying	• Berry, 1977 • Pal, 1993 • Stanbury, 1993 • Phillips, 1993
Social movement organizations	• Interest groups rooted in social transformations of the 1960s that led to new values, new class structures, and new social coalitions (e.g., environmentalism, feminism) • Key feature is the link between organizations and their social foundations, as well as the new dynamics of participation that arise with these organizations	• Offe, 1987 • Zald, 1987 • Klandermans and Tarrow, 1988 • Melucci, 1989
Subgovernment	• A generic concept that expresses the idea that policy does not get made in a single "system" but in subsystems that consist of microcosms of all the relevant political and institutional actors • This concept was developed in the 1950s as part of pluralist analyses of policymaking	• Truman, 1951 • Jordan, 1990 • Pross, 1992

a policy area and have some level of interest in that area, while the latter refers to a subset of those actors whose level of interest is consistently higher and who actually interact with each other. The concerns we will raise in this chapter tap into another issue as well: the degree to which the network concept goes far enough in capturing the realities and contradictions of contemporary policymaking. On the one hand, there has been tremendous pressure in Canada and elsewhere to broaden the policy development process to include more actors such as interest associations, experts, and citizens. Governments today favour alternative modes of program delivery, many of which stress partnerships. Consultation and partnering are the order of the day. On the other hand, as Lindquist points out (1996), despite the policy literature's emphasis on networks and communities, it still has had relatively little to offer in the way of tools to foster, develop, and manage relationships between governments and their policy communities (p. 220). More troubling still, it may be that even the existing literature is inadequate to the new, emerging dynamics of networks and policy communities. One small example is that the policy network concept was developed largely in the context of domestic politics. What happens when policy networks are global in scope, when movements mobilize around issues of planetary governance?

The next section provides background on the communities and networks literature, emphasizing (with Lindquist) the tension between the theoretical importance of the ideas and the poverty of practical insights for policymaking. The chapter then proceeds to analyze the ways in which the realities of policy communities and networks are intruding on the consciousness of policymakers themselves and being addressed through consultation, engagement schemes, and partnership models of implementing public programs. The conclusion returns to the tensions implied by these new pressures. Are our traditional forms of governance up to the challenge?

COMMUNITIES AND NETWORKS: CONCEPTUAL FRAMEWORKS

APPROACHES AND CONCEPTS

While there has been a harmonic convergence around the ideas of policy networks and communities, that convergence has come from several different directions. It is of more than mere antiquarian interest to explore the various sources of the network idea, since each of the origins suggests a different aspect of the policy process that was inadequately grasped by the older theoretical apparatuses. This will help us later in the chapter when we examine the contemporary changes in the policy process that are forcing even more radical conceptualizations of networks and webs of interest, cooperation, and conflict.

The broad backdrop to the various origins of network analyses is a concern with understanding the relationship between state and society and, in particular, the organization of interests in society. As banal and obvious as that sounds, the early postwar history of political science and public policy wrestled with the best way of theorizing the connections. While the Marxist literature addressed itself to various ways of thinking about the importance of class, the non-Marxist literature eventually settled on the notion of "**interest group pluralism**" as its master concept (for a broad survey of the literature, see Baumgartner and Leech, 1998). The pioneering postwar book on the subject was David Truman's *The Governmental Process* (1951). Truman, and others in that tradition, conceptualized society as consisting of an almost limitless array of interests that could mobilize around an almost equally limitless range of issues. If people shared interests, they would likely form groups. If issues arose that affected those interests in a policy sense, then the groups would politicize and lobby government. The pluralist tradition as a whole tended to de-emphasize the state or policymaking institutions and stressed the influence of lobbies and interest groups politics (Nordlinger, 1981, chap. 1; but see Almond, 1990, chap. 8). While pluralism did not use the contemporary terms of "**interest intermediation**" or "**associational system**," it drew a distinctive portrait of each. Interest intermediation, or the way in which societal interests interact with state institutions, was sketched as a highly variable, unpredictable, unstable process that depended on the organization of interests and government institutions in each policy sector or **subgovernment**. The associational system—the patterns of groups and organizations— was also depicted as a rather confusing constellation of small, medium, and large groups, competing and cooperating as they felt necessary.

We can identify at least four major sources of inspiration for the broad concept of networks as it has been applied in a variety of different forms. One of the first breaks with pluralism was over its portrait of the associational system and patterns of policymaking. Empirical case studies in the period showed that patterns were much more stable, and relationships far more closed, than pluralists had suggested. Policymaking took place not in the legislature or the executive but in "**iron triangles**" that truly were subgovernments in the sense that they might all be operating according to different principles, with different rhythms and often conflicting outcomes. By the mid-1970s the notion of iron triangles seemed like a caricature too, and Hugh Heclo (1978) crystallized the growing unease by identifying what he called "**issue networks**."

Heclo was not arguing for a new master concept but pointing out that the nature of the (American) policy system had changed. For one thing, the technical complexity of policy issues had increased, demanding the participation of policy experts and researchers rather than just narrow interests. There was a greater fluidity in issue generation as well, as the policy system constantly churned and produced new agenda items. Rather than the stable patterns of control that characterize iron triangles, Heclo saw issue networks as being quite permeable, with a kaleidoscope of changing faces as interest in (not a stake in) the policy issues waxed and waned.

A second important source of work on networks came from comparative research on industrial performance and economic policy. One of the earliest uses of the term "policy network" was in a book edited by Peter Katzenstein (1978a), *Between Power and Plenty*. Katzenstein and his colleagues were interested in the ways in which domestic political structures affected foreign economic policy. Since "the domestic structures in the advanced industrial states differ in important ways, so do the strategies of foreign economic policy which these states pursue" (Katzenstein, 1978b, p. 4). A key conditioning factor of foreign policy was the character of domestic interests and institutions, which could be termed the "policy network." Policy instruments were conditioned by the "character of the *policy network* spanning both the public and the private sector," and the key factors were the "differentiation of state from society and the centralization within each" (Katzenstein, 1978c, p. 308).

This branch of research had offshoots that remain highly relevant to the work on policy networks today. Work on "state structures" argued that each state had a characteristic pattern of associational and state institutions. This was a search for a single pattern at the broadest or deepest level of a given society that would affect policymaking across all sectors. For example, the work on **corporatism** urged that some countries were characterized by corporatist structures—centralized state agencies and highly centralized associational systems, working in tandem to develop and implement policy—and that, despite variances, corporatist dynamics would be discerned in most policy fields in that polity (Schmitter and Lembruch, 1979). This literature also suggested that corporatist political structures were more effective in the development of economic policy. This helped feed a debate about the nature of the state and its autonomy from social interests (Nordlinger, 1981; Skocpol, 1986), as well as a subsequent interest in political institutions (Weaver and Rockman, 1993). This style of analysis has stressed the structuring effect of state institutions on associational systems (e.g., Baumgartner, 1996; Coleman, 1994). Other work looked more at the relation between state and society in specific (usually economic) sectors and led directly to some of the most important contributions to network analysis.

A third source of inspiration for network analysis was the growing work on "new **social movements**" and "**public interest groups.**" Phillips (1999) defines a social movement as "(a) an informal network of organizations and individuals who, (b) on the basis of a collective identity and shared values, (c) engage in political and/or cultural struggle intended to break or expand the boundaries of the existing system, and (d) undertake collective action designed to affect both state and society" (p. 373; see also Carroll, 1992). She points out that social movement organizations rarely act alone (they are, after all, part of a social movement) and connect through various types of networks. The distinction between the movement and the organizations built upon it is important and gives a clue as to why the network idea spontaneously arose in this field of research. Any movement (e.g., environmental, consumers', women's) is bound to spawn a variety of organizations that address different aspects of its agenda, but those organizations will have a common cause and will seek to cooperate in order to maximize their policy impact.

Public interest groups have been defined as "an organizational entity that purports to represent very broad, diffuse, non-commercial interests which traditionally have received little explicit or direct representation in the processes by which agencies, courts, and legislatures make public policy" (Schuck, 1977, p. 133). Broadly speaking, these are citizens' organizations and typically are either very similar, or identical, to social movement organizations such as consumers' groups and environmental organizations. Both public interest groups and social movement organizations have a penchant for "expressive politics" or a political agenda that does not focus exclusively on material issues, and certainly not on direct political gain. While some skepticism is warranted regarding their altruism, it remains true that in structure and strategy, public interest groups differ markedly from traditional types of organizations. But as champions of what Chapter 2 called "**postmaterialist values**" these interest groups have been remarkably successful in promoting their policy agendas and mobilizing their resources. Berry's (1999) empirical analysis of the impact of these groups in the American congressional system in 205 cases between 1963 and 1991 concludes that "citizens groups have become prolific and enduring participants in legislative policymaking" (p. 32). Somewhat surprisingly, he also concludes that the most numerous and effective groups have been "liberal" ones (or postmaterialist in the pursuit of lifestyle, environmental, consumer, and moral issues) and that they have been able to "get Congress to consider policies that are obnoxious to business and energetically fought by corporations and trade groups" (p. 83). No equivalent studies have been done in Canada, but evidence from citizens' organizations around the Free Trade Agreement and the North American Free Trade Agreement suggests that the Canadian political system became more impervious to citizen lobbying in the 1990s, even while the networks of groups expanded considerably in the face of policies designed to support globalization (Ayres, 1998, p. 144).

A final source of inspiration for the network concept has been the changing nature of political reality, some elements of which are reflected in the sources described above and some of which were addressed in Chapter 2. Kenis and Schneider (1991, pp. 34–36) summarize these changes as follows:

1. *Emergence of organized society:* more and more of our social and political life is controlled by "organized collectivities," and as their importance and number increase, so will their interdependencies.

2. *Sectoralization:* the functional differentiation of policies, programs, and agencies.

3. *Crowded policy domains:* more organized collectivities and corporate actors means more intervention and participation within a given policy space.

4. *Scope of policy-making:* growth both in the number of policy domains and degree of intervention in them.

5. *Decentralization and fragmentation of the state:* the state increasingly consists of a host of discrete and loosely coordinated institutional entities.

6. *Blurring of boundaries between the public and private:* governments are increasingly involved at the interstices of civil society in implementing informal relationships (e.g., speech codes).

7. *Rise of private governments:* many political tasks can no longer be accomplished without the help of private organizations.

8. *Transnationalization of domestic politics:* policy issues are affected by factors at the international level and governments increasingly pursue policy objectives through international forums.

9. *The importance of information:* increased complexity demands better information and scientific expertise.

The result?

Increasingly unable to mobilize all necessary policy resources within their own realm, governments consequently become dependent upon the cooperation and joint resource mobilization of policy actors outside their hierarchical control. Policy networks should therefore be understood as those webs of relatively stable and ongoing relationships which mobilize dispersed resources so that collective (or parallel) action can be orchestrated toward the solution of a common policy problem. (Kenis and Schneider, 1991, p. 36)

Peters and Barker (1993) emphasize information requirements of the modern polity as well as the new demands for openness and participation as key ingredients forcing governments to engage in networks and communities.

But the multiplication of interest groups produces multiple sources of information that have become increasingly difficult to exclude from policy-making. Any official attempt to exclude unwanted information runs up against the increasing (sometimes legally mandated) openness of governments, as well as the increasing information needs of governments when making policy about complex topics. So governments experience political and perhaps legal trouble if they are exclusionary while also denying themselves potentially important information. The 'cozy little triangles' that once dominated policy-making now have become 'big sloppy hexagons.' (p. 9)

We will return to the question of how these new realities affect the policy process and generate network dynamics. At this point, it should be clear why the network/community concept is as important as it is: it has filtered through both policy studies and the broader study of government and politics because it reflects some important shifts in our forms of governance. The increasing complexity of both society and government; the importance of information and expert knowledge; the reliance of government on nongovernmental actors to both formulate and implement policy; shifts in class structure, values, and social groups: these are some of the forces that underpin an interest in networks and communities. All of these changes continue to exercise an important influence on modern policymaking, but they have been supplemented and reinforced by the broader factors described in Chapter 2.

In all the variants of network analysis, the central questions are, first, how to conceptualize the relationships between civil society and the state, and second, what difference certain patterns of relations make to policy outcomes. A third question of more relevance to the practitioner is rarely raised in this scholarly work but will be the focus for the second half of this chapter: how to manage and nurture relations between government agencies and their policy constituencies. But first, we will briefly examine the state of the art in conceptualizing policy networks.

POLICY NETWORK/COMMUNITY ANALYSIS

It is one thing to say that policy networks and communities are important; it is another thing to conceptualize those networks. Paul Pross (1995) offered an early definition as well as a diagrammatic portrait of policy communities. Policy communities are "groupings of government agencies, pressure groups, media people, and individuals, including academics, who, for various reasons, have an interest in a particular policy field and attempt to influence it" (p. 265). Figure 6.1 displays what Pross calls his "bubble diagram" of policy communities. Note that it divides the policy community in any given policy field into the "subgovernment" and the "**attentive public.**" Actual decisionmaking takes place in the subgovernment, which is dominated by large institutions, groups, and core government agencies. Players in the subgovernment, Pross argues, work to limit participation from outsiders. The attentive public are the outsiders whose main influence on the process is to generate ideas and discussion through conferences, publications, and occasional lobbying. In Pross's view, the policy community is actually an insulating device to keep a grip on the process; indeed, he argues that most of the inside players in a policy community try to keep debate within the realm of the technical and routine. Figure 6.1 shows a policy community in which the federal government is dominant, but the basic structure of core agencies in the subgovernment surrounded by other groups and agencies is generic.

There are several limitations to this way of thinking about policy communities. For one thing, it is largely static (though Pross is careful to argue that, in fact, policy communities are constantly in flux). For another, it does not travel well across policy fields. Some areas are indeed dominated by government agencies, and largely insulated from outside pressures—fiscal policy comes to mind. But many others are increasingly open to pressures from the attentive public, and that public is not prepared to be polite and keep policymaking at the level of routine. In social and educational policy, and increasingly in municipal policy, for example, fundamental assumptions about the role of governments are constantly being posed. Another problem is that in this model, foreign governments and foreign pressure groups are relegated to the margins. This metaphor is increasingly obsolete in a globalized and post-9/11

Figure 6.1 Policy Community "Bubble Diagram"

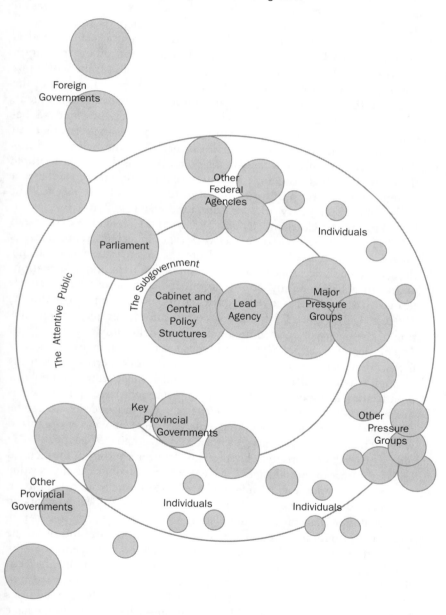

SOURCE: Pross, A.P. (1995). Pressure groups: Talking chameleons. In M.S. Whittington and G. Williams (Eds.), *Canadian politics in the 1990s* (p. 267). Toronto: Nelson Canada.

world. Finally, the model does not capture varying relations among the actors. The bubbles are large or small, but the figure as a whole gives no idea of the connections (or lack thereof) among the players.

Some of these limitations have been addressed in more refined models of policy networks (to which Pross's work is an important contribution). In a tradition that descends directly from Katzenstein's framework, this approach focuses on two variables: the nature of centralization in the state and the centralization or organization of the associational system. This is often termed a "structural approach" to network analysis because it focuses on patterns of relations among actors, patterns that can be mapped and are to some degree distinct from the beliefs or ideas that the actors themselves carry in the policy process. If we take a simple dichotomy of high organization/low organization, then we have a straightforward group of four categories to start with. In his excellent survey of the policy network literature, Lindquist (1992) draws on work by Atkinson and Coleman (1989a; 1989b) and Coleman and Skogstad (1990) to neatly summarize the network types in a chart, reproduced as Figure 6.2 (with five types). The degree of organization here means things like analytic capacity, access to important data and information, ability to act unilaterally, coordination, focus on long-term or short-term issues, and a reactive or anticipatory policy stance (Lindquist, 1992, p. 134). Figure 6.3 (page 252) offers another graphic representation of these networks, accompanied by brief definitions.

This depiction of policy network types has the advantage of variety. It is clear that there will be variation in policy networks across policy fields (though why that is, and if there are any underlying patterns to network organization in a specific political system, is a tougher question). Governments, or more precisely, the core agencies in the subgovernment, can be either well organized, strong, and policy capable or weakly organized without much policy capacity. Atkinson and Coleman (1989a, pp. 80–81) identify four conditions for what they call "state autonomy at the sectoral level": the bureau should have (1) a clear conception of its role and a value system that supports its mandate, as well as support from the minister, (2) a professional ethos distinct from that of its clients, (3) a body of law and regulation that it firmly administers, and (4) the capacity to generate its own information related to its mandate. In addition, the authors argue that state agencies are distinguished by their degree of concentration, by which they mean strong, informal alliances between the political executive and officials. By the same token, associational systems can be weak or strong. Atkinson and Coleman (1989a, pp. 82–83) identify six conditions for a "highly mobilized sector." Business groups (their focus) should have (1) separate associations representing different products and producers, without overlap or competition, (2) only one association that speaks

Figure 6.2 Policy Network Categories

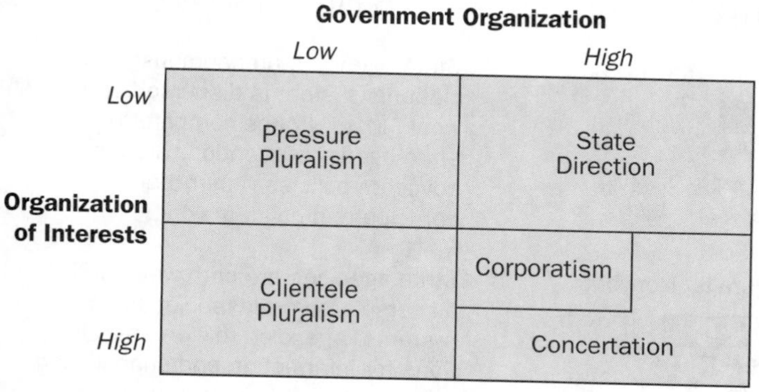

Government Organization

	Low	High
Low	Pressure Pluralism	State Direction
High	Clientele Pluralism	Corporatism / Concertation

Organization of Interests

SOURCE: Lindquist, E.A. (1992). Public managers and policy communities: Learning to meet new challenges. *Canadian Public Administration, 35*, 135.

for the sector as a whole, (3) a high proportion of firms represented in the sector's associations, (4) large firms that demonstrate leadership in the sector, (5) in-house capacity to generate information among firms and associations, and (6) associations that can strike deals with government and make them stick with members.

The Atkinson and Coleman schema actually yields eight categories of networks. The more criteria one adds, of course, the more types of networks one can generate. Van Waarden (1992), for example, argues that the major dimensions of policy networks are "(1) actors, (2) function, (3) structure, (4) institutionalization, (5) rules of conduct, (6) power relations, and (7) actor strategies" (p. 32). He further subdivides each of these dimensions to arrive at a list of thirty-eight criteria defining thirteen different types of policy networks! Recognizing that this is unmanageable, Van Waarden recommends concentrating on three criteria: the number and type of societal actors involved, the major functions of networks (e.g., negotiation, consultation, coordination, cooperation in policy formation, or implementation), and the balance of power between state and societal interests.

Apart from pretty diagrams, what do policy networks tell us about policymaking? Most of the network literature has been applied to economic policy fields and assumes that concentration plus organization equals policy-capable systems. While this makes some intuitive sense, it needs to be treated cautiously. For one thing, it has a vaguely undemocratic flavour. The more hierarchical, coordinated, and tidy the policy sector, the fewer opportunities there will be for the "attentive public" to get

Figure 6.3   Definitions of Policy Networks

TYPE	CHARACTERISTICS
Pressure Pluralist Network 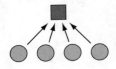	State agency is autonomous; associational system is dispersed and weak. Many groups compete for state agency's attention. Groups advocate policies rather than participate in policy-making.
Clientele Pluralist Network 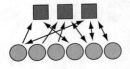	State agencies are both weak and dispersed, as are associational systems. Agencies rely on associations for information and support and allow them to participate in policy-making.
Corporatist Network	State agency is strong and autonomous; associational system comprises a few large and powerful groups, usually representing consumer and producer interests. Groups and agency both participate in policy formulation and implementation.
Concertation Network	State agency is strong and autonomous; associational system is dominated by one organization that represents it. Agency and organization are equal partners in long-term planning and policy-making.
State-Directed Network 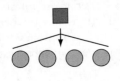	State agency is strong and autonomous; associational system is weak and dispersed. State dominates policy sector and associational system.

■ = State Agencies   ⬤ = Organizations

SOURCE: Pal, L. (1992). *Public policy analysis: An introduction*, 2nd ed. Toronto: Nelson, p. 112.

into the act. Current policy thinking is that the wider the networks and the more competition among players, the better policy outcomes will be. For another, as policy sectors get more complex and more globalized, the demands for information from all sectors and connections among the players rise exponentially. The tightly coordinated policy networks recommended in this literature may not be adequate to the new dynamics of modern policy process. Howlett (2002) zeroes in on this issue by attempting to correlate the nature of policy change with the nature of the policy networks associated with the policy field. He hypothesized that the more closed the subsystem of actors to new ideas and to new actors, the more difficult it would be to make radical changes in policy. His empirical findings demonstrated that

> [S]ubsystem structure is important because when the same core sets of policy actors are involved in defining policy options, the common understanding of a policy problem and the solutions they develop from shared experiences, combined with the durability of subsystem members' interests, promotes "incremental" change. Paradigmatic policy changes representing a significant, though not necessarily total, break from the past policy goals and programme specifications, on the other hand, was [sic] found to have occurred only when new ideas and interests could penetrate policy subsystems. (pp. 259–60)

In addition to the structure of networks, some approaches argue that the tactics and skills of actors in those networks are an important factor in explaining outcomes (Marsh and Smith, 2000). This is essentially an attempt to make the concept more dynamic, and to understand policy networks as both structures and processes. At any given point, a network can be mapped or visualized in terms of its characteristics (Raab, 2002) or the actual processes over time that give rise to those characteristics, and that have feedback loops from outcomes that in turn affect the network and its behaviour. For example, it's one thing to know that a soccer team is "structurally" weak because of the quality of its players and how they interact on the field. It's quite another thing to observe the same team in action, watching the flow of play, how they react to each other and their opponents. This latter, more dynamic way of viewing networks allows us to bring in both communication/interaction and learning or reacting to the results of that interaction (Pemberton, 2000).

ADVOCACY COALITIONS

A relatively new entry in the network literature is sufficiently well articulated to deserve separate treatment. The **advocacy coalition** framework (ACF) shares many of the insights of the policy community/ subgovernment literature but approaches networks completely differently from the work discussed above. As Paul Sabatier (1993) describes it,

> The advocacy coalition framework (ACF) has at least four basic premises: (1) that understanding the process of policy change— and the role of policy-oriented learning therein—requires a time perspective of a decade or more; (2) that the most useful way to think about policy change over such a time span is through a focus on "policy subsystems," that is, the interaction of actors from different institutions who follow and seek to influence governmental decisions in a policy area; (3) that those subsystems must include an intergovernmental dimension, that is, they must involve all levels of government (at least for domestic policy); and, (4) that public policies (or programs) can be conceptualized in the same manner as belief systems, that is, as sets of value priorities and causal assumptions about how to realize them. (p. 16)

A distinctive feature of the ACF is its emphasis on the role of ideas and values in the policy process. The ACF assumes that both policy actors and policies themselves can be understood in terms of the structure of their belief systems. These systems have three key elements. The first is the deep or normative core, which consists of fundamental axioms about human nature, justice, and priorities among values such as security, health, and life. These ideas are very difficult to change through policy arguments. The second set of ideas is the near (policy) core, and it comprises notions about the proper scope of government activity, distributions of power and authority, orientations on substantive policy conflicts, and basic choices about policy instruments. These are difficult to change but can be altered if experience seriously differs from theory. The final set contains secondary aspects and consists of instrumental decisions needed to implement the policy core such as decisions about administrative rules, budgetary allocations, and statutory interpretation. These are comparatively easy to shift or change and constitute the bulk of technical policy argumentation.

Figure 6.4 illustrates the main elements of the ACF. Note that it has both a strong dynamic quality as well as a contextual dimension that places policy subsystems into the larger socioeconomic and political situation of the polity. The relatively stable parameters are system variables that change only slowly over time but set the stage in terms of institutions as well as resources for policy actors. The external events embrace both unpredictable shocks to the subsystem as well as the interaction effects with other subsystems. Together, these provide constraints, resources, and opportunities for the policy subsystem, which, in the ACF,

Figure 6.4   The Advocacy Coalition Framework

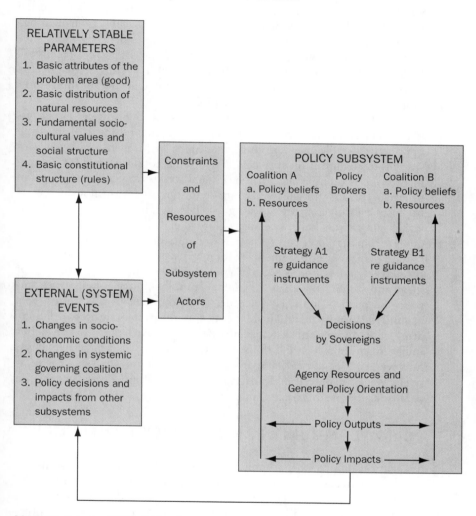

SOURCE: Sabatier (1993). Policy change over a decade or more. In P. A. Sabatier and H. Jenkins-Smith (Eds.). *Policy change and learning: An advocacy coalition approach.* Boulder, CO: Westview, p. 18. See also Sabatier and Jenkins-Smith (1999).

is dominated by a number of advocacy coalitions, "composed of people from various governmental and private organizations who share a set of normative and causal beliefs and who often act in concert" (Sabatier, 1993, p. 18). These coalitions pursue competing strategies to achieve their policy objectives, a conflict that is usually mediated by policy brokers interested in compromise. At any given time, the policy sector will be dominated by a winning coalition. The framework is interested in what it calls "policy-oriented learning" or "relatively enduring alterations of thought or behavioral intentions that result from experience and are concerned with the attainment (or revision) of policy objectives" (Sabatier, 1993, p. 19). Most change in policy subsystems occurs because of external shocks, but instrumental learning is important, especially if the goal is better public policy.

The ACF also has several distinct hypotheses about how policy subsystems operate. Among them are (1) in any subsystem, the lineup of allies and opponents is stable over periods of a decade or so, (2) there is more consensus within coalitions on core beliefs than on secondary ones, (3) government policies rarely change if the original sponsoring coalition is still in power, (4) policies for which there are quantitative data are more amenable to policy learning than areas distinguished by qualitative data, and (5) policy learning across belief systems is more likely when there exists a prestigious forum that forces professionals from all sides to participate.

The ACF is a useful framework for mapping out, in a dynamic fashion, the players, issues, and debates in a policy subsystem. Its incorporation of ideas and values, as well as the impact (usually limited) of expertise and scientific professionals, is welcome. Also, the idea of a coalition gets around the more rigid and insular conceptualization in the network literature that divides subsystems into decisionmakers and attentive, but impotent, publics. Unlike the structural approach to policy networks, however, it does not provide any *a priori* typologies. Indeed, it is relatively weak in describing patterns of relationships either among the coalitions themselves or among brokers.

POLICY COMMUNITIES AND POLICY MANAGEMENT

The various approaches to policy networks discussed above give us the ability to map actors, understand their relationships, and possibly make some predictions about policy processes characterized by different types of networks or coalitions. But do these theories go far enough in capturing the contemporary complexities of the policy process? As we argued, the network idea itself can be seen as a response to changing political realities. If the realities continue to change, should the concept of networks be refined as well?

THE CONTEMPORARY IMPORTANCE OF POLICY NETWORKS

It is no coincidence that the concepts related to policy communities and networks began to multiply and develop just around the time that associational systems were becoming more complex. We saw earlier that Heclo's idea of "issue networks" was explicitly designed to capture the idea of a more fluid, information-based policy system in which government departments and industry players (what Pross calls the subgovernment) were no longer entirely dominant. Both Canada and the United States saw a surge in the growth of various social movements and public interest groups in the 1970s (Paltiel, 1982; Walker, 1991). While there are no reliable data on broad trends in the last decade, there is no doubt that groups continue to multiply across most sectors, though not likely at the same pace that marked the 1970s and early 1980s. The complexity, intensity, and importance of the associational system and policy networks/communities for policymaking continues to be affected by the various factors outlined in Chapter 2, along with several other factors that define the new mode of governance that is emerging in Canada and elsewhere.

For one thing, the rights revolution in Canada, the United States, and, to a lesser extent, in Europe continues to multiply the types of claims made against the state. In the American case, for example, Melnick (1994) traces the development of what he calls "programmatic rights" that the American judiciary has over the past twenty years discovered in federal statutes, such as the right of disabled children to free, appropriate public education. "The new understanding of rights, in contrast, has led the judiciary to enlarge public responsibilities and to increase the power of the national government" (p. 17). In the Canadian case, Cairns (1993) has remarked on the increasing diversity of interests and identities in Canada and the difficulty for politicians of "representing, accommodating, and transcending the diversities of Canadian society" (p. 201). He also succeeds in tying this increasing diversity to the problem of representation. Groups and associations today, at least those founded on an identity as opposed to an interest, demand to represent themselves in order to have an authentic voice speaking on their behalf. This limits the capacity of the associational system to aggregate interests and streamline the consultative process. As Ignatieff (2000) remarks, "The minute groups start claiming rights, self-righteousness begins and conflicts become irreconcilable" (p. 78).

Globalization and increasingly sophisticated forms of communications also continue to change the nature of policy networks. With the exception of the notion of **epistemic communities** (see Box 6.1)—which draws explicitly on international connections among experts—most of the communities/networks and associational literature still presume a national or domestic framework. As policy issues increasingly get driven upward to the international level, and as NGOs increasingly respond by connecting to counterparts everywhere around the globe, the idea that policy networks are primarily domestic needs rethinking. Domestic human rights groups, for example, now are routinely connected to international networks (Keck and Sikkink, 1998), as are groups organized around population issues, economic development, and the environment. Chapter 1 pointed to the emergence of a "global civil society," something that has been anticipated as an aspect of a new world order for some time (Falk, 1987; Walker, 1988; for a recent snapshot see Messner, 2002; Glasius, Kaldor and Anheier, 2003; Scholte, 2004). One recent report calculates that there are over 175 000 nonprofit, voluntary organizations in Canada, and that half of all Canadians—about 12 million people—are involved in at least one nongovernmental organization. Leading domestic organizations have complex and wide-ranging contacts with counterparts around the world, particularly if they have mandates that encourage cross-border collaboration, such as in the environment, trade, or human rights (*Canadian Development Report,* 1999). As we noted in Chapter 2, this emergence, while not entirely new (think of the global Anti-Slavery Society of the 1800s), has benefited greatly from modern information and communications technologies (Deibert, 1997, pp. 157–76). Technology makes it easier for both domestic and international networks "to raise funds, to acquire information, monitor issues, communicate views, and mobilize constituents to a threat or opportunity for group action" (Stanbury and Vertinsky, 1994, p. 91). It is not just technology, however, or globalization in terms of transnational corporations. International agencies such as the UN, for example, particularly in the 1990s, "accelerated the global associational revolution by affirming the right of nongovernmental actors to participate in shaping national and global policies on the environment, population, human rights, economic development, and women" (Batliwala, 2002, p. 394). International UN conferences on the environment (Rio in 1992), human rights (Vienna in 1993), population (Cairo in 1994), social policy (Copenhagen in 1995), women (Beijing in 1995), and housing and cities (Istanbul in 1996) became platforms for the development of international networks of activists.

Some illustrations will show how the ground has shifted in NGO organization and global connections. A first, early one is the 1997 Land Mines Convention, which hinged on a massive international campaign to ban the use, production, and stockpiling of antipersonnel (AP) mines throughout the world. The specific problem with AP mines is that they remain in place well after military conflicts between belligerents are over and thereby become a threat to innocent civilians traversing the area. It was estimated that there were 26 000 casualties per year due to AP mines, casualties that leave their victims—if they live—with shattered or severed limbs. The movement to ban production and use of AP mines, and eventually to put existing ones out of commission, was led by the International Campaign to Ban Landmines (ICBL). The ICBL consisted of over 1000 NGOs from over 60 countries. "It is a loosely organized and unstructured network—with only a handful of key full-time and paid activists—that draws on the resources, both financial and human, of a broad spectrum of member organizations interconnected by fax machines, the Internet, periodic conferences, and a common goal" (Cameron, Lawson, and Tomlin, 1998, p. 5). The Canadian government played a major role in 1996 in sponsoring two key conferences of states, international agencies, and NGOs to accelerate the progress toward a global ban, and eventually to negotiate a treaty. However, it was the ICBL (along with the International Red Cross) that really propelled the issue forward and provided the broad support and prodding governments needed. The ICBL was formed in 1992 from a cluster of six NGOs active in the AP mines issue and in human rights. One of the most interesting aspects of the ICBL was its lack of conventional organization and coordination. It operated without a secretariat, a central office, bureaucracy, or an overarching media strategy, and individual NGO members were free to pursue their own means of lobbying and campaigning as they saw fit within their local circumstances (Williams and Goose, 1998, pp. 22–23). Coordination was achieved largely through frequent exchanges of information and face-to-face contacts, in which fax, e-mail, and telephone played an important, but not determining role. It was all the more remarkable, therefore, that by the October 1996 Ottawa conference, the ICBL was given a seat at the table of governments and was actively engaged in drafting language that would feed into the December 1997 conference that produced the treaty. Significantly, the United States was opposed to the ban but in the end could not pressure governments to abandon it, and so remained a nonsignatory. The ICBL and Jody Williams, its co-ordinator, received the 1997 Nobel Peace Prize for their work.

Another case was the still-born Multilateral Agreement on Trade (MAI). The MAI reveals another dimension of NGO organizing in a globalized world. It showed the capacity of local or national communities of NGOs to organize collectively in the face of what they considered a global threat. The MAI was a goal of the Organisation for Economic Co-operation and Development (OECD), a treaty that would have relaxed investment rules and prohibited some government measures to control and even ban foreign investments in industries like health care and culture/entertainment. The Canadian NGO community became aware of the MAI negotiations in 1997 and immediately mobilized a national campaign under the leadership of the Council of Canadians to persuade the Canadian government to pull out. The Council of Canadians formed the umbrella for some forty NGOs from a wide variety of sectors, appearing before parliamentary committees, publishing materials attacking the MAI as an assault on Canadian culture and health care, and organizing with groups around the world to lobby their governments and the OECD. In October 1998, the pressure was finally too much, and a week before OECD meetings on the MAI were to commence, the government of France pulled out, citing the different nature of opposition surrounding the treaty. That opposition was global and coordinated, largely relying on new tools such as the Internet to instantly distribute information and strategies. As Deibert notes, "it certainly is clear now that no international negotiation process of significance will take place without dozens, perhaps hundreds, even thousands of non-governmental organizations and activists orbiting alongside. With the Internet as their information infrastructure, these activists have carved out an ethereal, non-territorial space, circulating in and around the traditional political spaces inhabited by states" (Deibert, 2002, p. 103). This shift to transnational campaigns was a distinctive strategy of citizens' organizations in the post-NAFTA period (Ayres, 1998, p. 141), and was specifically evident in the mobilization against the negotiation of the Free Trade of the Americas Agreement (Ayres, 2003). As we noted with landmines, however, this transnationalization of NGO activity is not always a matter of protest. It can sometimes mean global cooperation with a network of states to deal with international problems. NGOs, for example, met with states and corporations to hammer out a system of regulations to prevent the trade of conflict diamonds. They are increasingly involved in supporting UN peacekeeping missions such as the one in Iraq (Grant, MacLean, and Shaw, 2003).

Along with rights, identities, and globalization, science and science-related issues are increasingly important in policymaking. The greater the scientific dimension of a policy issue, the greater the importance of scientific or specialized information and those who possess it. The concept of epistemic communities captures both the new prominence of scientific specializations and their international connections. Scientific expertise in this context means more than the physical sciences; it embraces the growing importance of such social science disciplines as economics, psychology, criminology, social welfare, and management. The burgeoning field of environmental policy depends on scientific assessments, many of which are not much more than "guesstimates" but that are crucial nonetheless for coming to terms with problems such as ozone depletion and the impact of toxic substances. A case in point is the current debate over the effect of pesticides on humans and the environment. In May 2000 the House of Commons Standing Committee on

Environment and Sustainable Development released its report entitled *Pesticides: Making the Right Choice for the Protection of Health and the Environment*. It noted that there were some 7000 registered pesticides in Canada with over 500 active ingredients but that many of these substances had not been re-evaluated for years. While recommending a "precautionary principle" that would call for an absolute priority for the protection of human health and the environment, the Committee also acknowledged the need for large amounts of new scientific research to clear up many ambiguities and uncertainties about the actual and potential impact of pesticides.

A knowledge-dependent policy process poses several challenges for policymakers. One is the need to somehow balance expertise with democracy. Scientists and experts make claims and recommendations based on notions of truth, not majority wishes. The fear is that an overly rational policy process will be driven more by small cliques of experts than by the democratic desires and participation of the public. The problem is even more acute when an issue is highly contentious and disputed. A case in point is genetically modified (GM) foods. The Canadian Biotechnology Advisory Committee submitted a report in 2002 recommending an improved regulatory regime, and its first two recommendations concerned governance and transparency, and public involvement (Canadian Biotechnology Advisory Committee, 2002).

Another challenge for public managers is how to connect with communities of scholars and researchers who possess the specific expertise required in a policy field. As government departments are downsized, some of them may lose crucial analytical capacities and as a consequence become more dependent on outside knowledge producers. In short, policy networks are not merely about interests but about information and expertise that should be a foundation for policy development and implementation.

Another aspect of communities and networks that is changing in the current policy climate is their alignment with levels of government. This involves two interesting dynamics. The first is the more obvious one of the last few years: as governments devolve more of their policy responsibilities to jurisdictions that are closer to the people or closer to the policy problem (even as they shift some responsibilities upward), policy communities change to reflect the new "core" in the subgovernment. Municipal restructuring in Ontario, for example, compelled amalgamation in cities like Toronto and Ottawa. Services that were once dispersed are now part of single regional or consolidated governments in both cases, and local policy communities that previously would have been fragmented in terms of different communities now have to re-organize and focus their efforts on a new "core" government. The other dynamic reflects some of the forces cited in Chapter 2, wherein the lines between policy fields get increasingly blurred, thereby encouraging governments to "migrate" into new areas to meet their policy objectives. A good example is the Government of Canada–Voluntary Sector Initiative announced in June 2000 (Phillips, 2003). Ottawa has belatedly recognized the importance of the "third sector" for the quality of life for Canadians and for the quality of service delivery in many areas and will pour over $90 million in five years to support this sector. The voluntary sector/charitable policy community will change fundamentally.

Finally, governments are increasingly attracted to the ideas of partnerships and **framework policies** (setting parameters but letting others deliver programs). Partly this is due to lack of money, and shifting responsibilities onto third parties is a way of offloading expenses. However, the broad consensus that appears to be emerging about the limitations of governments, and the virtues of setting frameworks within which private actors can pursue their interests, places greater emphasis on partnerships between the public and private/nonprofit sectors. Policy communities and networks are important today not only because they represent interests that have to be integrated into the policy process, or information that is crucial to analysis, but because they are relatively untried sinews for implementation and delivery. The concept of working partnerships for the development and delivery of services implies a very different set of relationships than is typically envisaged in the communities/networks literature. That literature focuses more on the political dynamics of interest representation, whereas the challenges of partnerships focus more on the logistics of joint action to achieve common goals.

The preceding suggests a somewhat confusing array of forces that serve to make policy communities and networks even more important than they have been in the past, but also perhaps more challenging to integrate into the policy process. The associational system shows no signs of shrinking, and some elements of it, such as those involved in the delivery of public services, may face considerable pressures to expand. The rights revolution and salience of identity politics encourage people to expand the number of communities and networks to which they belong. Information technologies make possible even wider, global connections of interests and communities. Movements like human rights, environment, and women's issues are truly global in scope. At the same time, some policy issues get driven further down, and so some networks that would have had their centre of gravity at the national level now become truly local or regional. Finally, the information and organizational capacities of policy communities are being viewed in a different light by policymakers; these are resources they need, and they have to think of new ways to develop linkages.

We can conclude then that contemporary importance of policy networks and communities has not diminished; indeed, it has grown. However, the realities of the policy process continue to change the nature and dynamic of those communities, posing substantial challenges for policymakers. Lindquist (1992; 1996) offers the concept of "stewardship" to capture what these challenges entail. Assuming that policy communities and networks are crucial components in the development and implementation of public policy, a core responsibility for any public manager is the improvement of learning and adaptive capacities, leading to higher levels of policy debate and relevant policy expertise. What this entails in practice depends on the type of policy community in question and its specific needs. Capacity-building for intellectual communities may mean enhancing informational resources and communication abilities. For communities involved in policy delivery, it may mean development of organizational capacity through training. Whatever it means, thinking about the policy networks and communities relevant to one's policy responsibilities is a key responsibility for the public manager in 2005 and beyond.

CONSULTING, ENGAGING, AND PARTNERING

The two big trends in policy community relations or management have been public consultations/citizen engagement and partnerships. Both of these can be viewed cynically. Consultations and citizen engagement can be seen as empty theatrics where interest groups rant predictably while decisionmakers watch the clock, waiting for it all to be over so that they can then go and make the decisions they were going to make anyway. Both also keep everyone busy in a ritualistic way, ultimately validating what decisionmakers wanted to do in the first place (Cooke and Kothari, 2001). Partnerships can be viewed as an attempt to get out of key areas of government responsibility by shifting delivery (but not adequate financial or logistical support) over to the private/nonprofit sector. There is a strong element of truth in both of these critiques, but they capture, at best, only half of the reality. Policymakers realize the limitations of these strategies (and sometimes manipulate those limitations to their own ends), but they also genuinely believe that consultation in policy design and partnership in policy delivery are important aspects of their jobs. They may not always like it, but they will undertake it, often willingly but also because some form of consultation with the public is increasingly mandated as an aspect of public policy development. There are real puzzles in this engagement, however—challenges that have to be recognized and addressed if governance is to evolve into the next decade. With consultations, the challenge is balancing public demands with the realities of hard decisions. With partnerships, the challenge is balancing accountability with autonomy.

CONSULTATION AND ENGAGEMENT

The dictionary definition of consultation is simply to ask for advice or opinion, or a type of communication between two or more parties. Any government that purports to be democratic, one would think, is intrinsically a government that consults. The recent emphasis on consultation therefore seems a bit puzzling from this perspective. If governments have not been consulting when making and implementing policy, then what have they been doing? In fact, there is a more specific meaning to consultation in the current context, one that reflects the forces described in Chapter 2. Almost any form of communication can be seen as a consultation, if by that term we mean only the exchange of information or views. Government polling, for example, might be seen as a form of consultation since it probes for the views of citizens on a wide variety of subjects. The same might be true of task forces, royal commissions, parliamentary committees, referenda, and even elections, all of which are often described as consultations with the public. Using the term this broadly, however, wrings out almost any of its usefulness.

Consultation is different. First, it is usually focused on the operational and programmatic level, as opposed to broad values or directions for policy development. One can still consult about broad values, but these should be clearly connected to specific issues and programs. The interlocutors, therefore, are the agencies responsible for program design and delivery, and direct clients or stakeholders in the relevant policy community or network. This distinguishes consultation as a policy management activity from broader forms of political representation, such as parliamentary committee hearings on a piece of legislation, for example. The objective is ongoing development and management of the policy or program in question, not the establishment of parameters for political discussion and debate.

The emphasis on consultation with stakeholders at the federal level goes back to the early 1990s, for example, with the report of the PS2000 Task Force on Service to the Public, which argued that consultation should become a routine aspect of public policymaking (Privy Council Office, 1993). As a result, Canada has had long experience with consultations and engagement (Wyman, Shulman and Ham, 1999). Consultation practices vary quite widely across departments, depending on the issues and the preferences of ministers and senior officials. Ever since 1992, federal departments and agencies have been formally urged to consider public consultation a key part of the development of policy.

The 2003 federal Guide to Making Federal Acts and Regulations notes that consultation in instrument choice is "essential" to making good choices, and includes public consultation under the rubric of "good governance guidelines" (Privy Council Office, 2003). The 2004 federal guide to drafting a **Memorandum to Cabinet,** the policy document outlining the rationale for any proposed bill, requires the statement of a consultation strategy (Privy Council Office, 2004). The rules of strict confidentiality of draft legislation have also been relaxed somewhat, so that consultations can now be undertaken around proposed laws. The only federal policy area in which consultations are mandated is in the creation of new regulations. The 1999 Government of Canada Regulatory Policy says that all regulatory authorities must ensure that "Canadians are consulted, and that they have an opportunity to participate in developing or modifying regulations and regulatory programs" (Privy Council Office, 1999). The guidelines go on to say

> Regulatory authorities must clearly set out the processes they use to allow interested parties to express their opinions and provide input. In particular, authorities must be able to identify and contact interested stakeholders, including, where appropriate, representatives from public interest, labour and consumer groups. If stakeholder groups indicate a preference for a particular consultation mechanism, they should be accommodated, time and resources permitting. Consultation efforts should be coordinated between authorities to reduce duplication and burden on stakeholders. (Privy Council Office, 1999)

As we noted above, and as these guidelines make clear, the focus of consultations is largely programmatic and practical—it is intended to improve policy development, design, and implementation processes. It is not usually understood to entail a broad discussion and exchange of values that underpin policy proposals. The term for this sort of communication—one that seems to have become increasingly popular in the late 1990s—is "citizen engagement."

The shift to "engagement" from "consultation" seems to have occurred, in part, because of the continued lack of trust that citizens have toward government and dissatisfaction with the connotations of consultation—a process that suggests a fairly passive communication of views from "stakeholders" to government officials who will ultimately make the key decisions. With a decline in trust has come a decline in citizen participation in politics and public deliberation. The February 2004 Speech from the Throne explicitly acknowledged, for example, that Canadians lack trust in government and that the renewal of trust would require engagement. One can trace the earliest emergence of the idea of public participation in Canada at the level of local government in the 1970s, linked in part to trying to get citizens involved in increasingly complex land-use planning issues (Graham and Phillips, 1998, p. 5) but also because of civil activism and municipal reform movements (Thomas, 1995). But the concern is now part of the wider "policy movement" discussed in Chapter 1. The OECD, for example, in 1999 launched a survey on "Strengthening Government-Citizen Connections" with the participation of twenty-one member countries and the European Commission:

> OECD countries clearly view the issue of government-citizen relations with growing concern. Several countries cited low or declining confidence in public institutions as one motivation for recent initiatives to strengthen government-citizen connections. A related trend cited by many of these countries was declining participation in political parties. Many others cited pressures created by increased citizen demands for information and expectations that government provide more responsive and better quality service. There is a growing perception in the OECD countries that representative democracy is not working as well as it has in the past. Thus, governments are looking to new or improved models and approaches for better informing and involving citizens in the policy-making process. (OECD, 2000, p. 1; also see OECD, 2001)

The concern to engage citizens is therefore also in part a reflection of a deeper concern about the eroding democratic foundation of contemporary politics and policymaking. Citizen engagement thus has both an instrumental dimension—trying to tap into the knowledge and perspectives of citizens themselves, unfiltered by media or interest groups—and a legitimating dimension—to try to shore up the public's support for policy initiatives by bringing the public more actively into the process.

Of course, the real challenge in citizen engagement is developing techniques to actually engage citizens. Consultations, as we described them above, can naturally be assumed to attract stakeholders and interest groups, but even in that context it is a challenge to go beyond simple tabling of inflexible views and to move to a more deliberative process. Seasoned policymakers wince at the idea of consultation that simply collects together "the usual suspects" who have a particular axe to grind. Citizen engagement is exactly what it says—somehow getting ordinary citizens to come forward and thoughtfully engage on a policy question. Various innovative techniques have been suggested to genuinely bring citizens into an informed dialogue and exchange with government. Some, like **study circles,** are designed to facilitate decisionmaking at the community level. Study circles are championed by the Study Circles Resource Center in Pomfret, Connecticut (http://www.studycircles.org), and the model entails bringing people from all over a neighbourhood, town, or city together in small groups of eight to twelve who work through the same issue for a period of time and then all come together to share ideas and develop plans. The technique has been used in over 100 communities in the United States to address citizens' concerns about schools, youth, violence, and other issues.

Another technique is **citizens' juries,** developed by the Jefferson Center in Minneapolis, Minnesota (http://www.jefferson-center.org). A randomly selected jury of about eighteen individuals hears from a variety of expert witnesses and deliberates together on a given issue. The jury then presents its recommendations to the public. The technique has been used in the United States to address issues such as national health care reform, budget priorities, environmental issues, and local school needs, as well as by organizations in Great Britain, Germany, Denmark, Spain, Australia, and other countries. This small-scale consultation stands in contrast to **deliberative polling,** a technique pioneered by the American social scientist James Fishkin (1991). It involves between 250 and 600 people who form a representative sample of the community, and who are polled for their preliminary views on an issue. They then engage in small group discussions and pose questions to experts and politicians, and are once again polled at the end of the process once they have had the opportunity to reflect and deliberate. Similar techniques include standing panels, community issue groups, and consensus conferences. An innovative Canadian variant is citizens' dialogue, pioneered by the Canadian Policy Research Networks. The technique involves a carefully selected representative panel of citizens (usually several hundred) across Canada, or if it is a provincial issue, in that province, who meet and have a structured dialogue on important issues. The dialogue usually lasts for a day and is steered by a professional facilitator. A sounding is taken at the beginning of the dialogue, and then again at the end, to see where and how opinions have changed. The technique was used, for example, in the Commission on the Future of Health Care in Canada (the Romanow Commission; see Box 6.2).

It is easier to list principles and techniques than to put them into practice, particularly by governments; most of the techniques cited above were pioneered and are used by nonprofit organizations. Whereas consultation and engagement at all levels of government has become a sort of policy mantra, the realities and challenges are more complex. For one thing, consultations are only one stream of information and advice into the policy process, but those who are consulted naturally want to see their efforts reflected in policy outputs. As well, the

Box 6.2   CITIZENS' DIALOGUE ON HEALTH CARE

The Commission partnered with the Canadian Policy Research Networks, a not-for-profit policy think-tank, to organize 12 regional one-day "deliberative dialogue" sessions across the country. Each session brought together some 40 randomly selected Canadians. At the outset of the process, participants completed a questionnaire probing their perceptions of the challenges confronting Canada's health care system and their preferred solutions for addressing them. They were subsequently provided with a workbook outlining four scenarios for revitalizing the health care system that included arguments for and against each scenario. (An analysis of historical public opinion research data indicated that each of the scenarios enjoyed a relatively high level of public support—despite the seemingly irreconcilable values-base implicit among them. The purpose of the "deliberative dialogue" sessions was to oblige Canadians to make difficult choices between the competing scenarios.)

Working with professional facilitators, participants spent the balance of the day discussing the four scenarios and their likely consequences. At the end of the day, participants were asked to complete a second questionnaire to assess whether their initial perceptions had changed and if so, why. The results of the 12 sessions were analyzed and common themes and directions noted. A national public opinion survey was then undertaken to assess whether the results of the "deliberative dialogue" process would be validated. The four scenarios were:

- More public investment—The first scenario was to add more resources (such as doctors, nurses, and equipment) to deal with medicare's current problems by increasing public spending, either through a tax increase or by re-allocating funds from other government programs.

- Share the costs and responsibilities—The second scenario was to add more resources to deal with current problems not by increasing public spending but through a system of user co-payments for health care services that would provide an incentive for people not to over-use the system as well as needed funds.

- Increase private choice—The third scenario was to give Canadians increased choice in accessing private providers for health care services. Side-by-side with the public system, Canadians also could access health care services from a private sector provider (either for-profit or not-for profit) and pay for it from their own resources or private insurance.

- Reorganize service delivery—The fourth scenario was to reorganize service delivery in order to provide more integrated care, realize efficiencies and expand coverage. Under this scenario, each Canadian would sign up with a health care provider network that would work as a team to provide more co-ordinated, cost-effective services and improved access to care.

SOURCE: Commission on the Future of Health Care in Canada. (2002). *Building on values: The future of health care in Canada*, pp. 271–72.

openness demanded by consultation can run against the organizational grain of government, which sometimes requires a high degree of confidentiality (e.g., sensitive information about third parties) or strong executive action (e.g., responding to an emergency).

PARTNERSHIPS AND HORIZONTAL MANAGEMENT

There is some overlap between the concept of consultation and of partnership. Indeed, Kernaghan's (1993) classification of partnerships has consultation as one end of a continuum of power sharing over decisions and implementation: (1) consultative partnerships: exchanging advice and information, (2) contributory partnerships: money or other forms of support for projects managed by a third party, (3) operational partnerships: sharing work in achieving goals, but the main decisions are still made by one partner, usually government, and (4) collaborative partnerships: sharing both work and decisionmaking (pp. 62–65). While it seems puzzling that public officials would willingly relinquish some of their autonomy, there has been a rising interest in collaborative partnerships, both with private sector entities and nonprofit, noncommercial organizations such as those in the social services sector. And partnerships can also involve different government departments, either at the same level or across jurisdictions. The reasons for partnering reflect our earlier arguments in this chapter. Government wants to save money, and partnerships with firms or nonprofit organizations can be a way of offloading services. But governments also recognize some of their own limitations in directly delivering services, and so partnerships can be a means of improving service delivery, getting better feedback, and encouraging civic engagement.

There is a great variety of partnership forms (Rosenau, 2000), but as a general mode of implementation (and of policymaking), it is seen as a major departure as well as a major challenge. This is because traditional governance is hierarchical, and sees government authorities as having the core responsibility for delivering services. True partnerships imply a degree of equality and shared responsibility. From a management perspective, that means that new skills of collaboration and coordination will be required as partnerships become more pervasive. This type of management is called "horizontal" management and has attracted a great deal of attention recently:

> Horizontal management can be defined as the coordination and management of a set of activities between two or more organizational units, where the units in question do not have hierarchical control over each other and where the aim is to generate outcomes that cannot be achieved by units working in isolation. (Bakvis and Juillet, 2004, 9)

Governments around the world are increasingly concerned with policy coherence and developing "horizontality." In a sense, any government is itself an example of horizontal management; cabinets are, for example, mechanisms to develop collective decisionmaking across portfolios. Central agencies like the Privy Council Office or the Treasury Board are also mechanisms of coordination. What is new is that this interest in horizontality is extending to all levels of government bureaucracy, with the growing expectation that government departments will work more closely and collaboratively with each other to solve problems that cut across bureaucratic jurisdictions, that they will work more closely and collaboratively with other departments in other jurisdictions, and that they will increasingly partner with nongovernmental actors. While horizontal management is not necessarily the best way to approach every policy issue, at the federal level there is a sense that it is a reality that is here to stay.

It is best to think of horizontal management as a continuum running from a minimalist to a maximalist level of coordination (Peters, 1998). The minimal level entails nothing more than mutual recognition of activities and an effort not to duplicate or interfere. At the maximalist end of the continuum, one will find partnerships based on formal agreements about objectives, resource sharing, and coordinating procedures. Partnering arrangements can be of various types: consultative (sharing information), operational (sharing work), or truly collaborative (sharing decisionmaking).

There is sufficient experience and interest in horizontal management to have developed a set of best practices. According to the Auditor

General of Canada (2000), the key success factors are

- Identifying an effective co-ordination structure (establishing roles and responsibilities and promoting coordination through levers and incentives);
- Agreeing on common objectives, results, and strategies (this includes defining performance expectations and how departments will contribute);
- Measuring results to track performance;
- Using information to improve performance; and
- Effectively reporting performance.

According to Canadian Centre for Management Development (CCMD)—now the Canada School of Public Service—Roundtable discussions and research on horizontality, the key themes were

- Leadership that marshals the powers of influence and persuasion is the key driver. It is best exercised through dialogue, with an emphasis on active listening.
- A culture that values collaboration and trust among partners is essential.
- Horizontal initiatives have a life cycle that makes timing crucial.
- Continual reflection and adjustment are required to maintain momentum.
- Managers of horizontal initiatives need to maintain contact with vertical structures for the sake of securing accountability, authority, and resources.
- Support systems (knowledge bases, resource allocations, and the like) too often work against horizontal management and need to be adapted. (Fitzpatrick, 2000)

CCMD argued that the key dimensions of horizontal management were mobilizing teams and networks, developing shared frameworks, building supportive structures, and maintaining momentum (Hopkins, Couture and Moore, 2001). As with the best practices above, these call for different skill sets from public managers. They also pose important organizational challenges. Perhaps the pre-eminent one is accountability. When governments enter into partnerships, by necessity they relinquish power and control. In cases of substantial loss of control, however, the government agency is still in some measure responsible for the expenditure of public funds and for outcomes, yet those expenditures and outcomes may be determined more by the partner than by the government agency. Government organizations are used to operating in a hierarchical, top-down fashion, but partnering implies spheres of autonomy as well as coordination for the different partners. How to combine that autonomy, the prime contribution of the partnership agreement, with accountability for performance and results? As Langford puts it: "As part of this move, contemporary managers must develop the relationship-building, negotiating, contract management, risk assessment, and performance measurement skills required to work effectively in a partnership world" (Langford, 1999, p. 108).

CONCLUSION

This chapter has examined the two sides of policy communities and networks: (1) the academic side with its emphasis on the explanation and description of patterns of associational-state linkages in policy domains, and (2) the public management approach to consultation and partnerships. The two overlap in important ways but are also distinct. They share the insight that contemporary governance entails a substantial degree of private/nonprofit/public cooperation and interaction at every phase of the policy process, and that the quality of policy outcomes often depends on the nature of these interactions. However, the emphasis in the policy communities and networks literature has been on describing the actors and evaluating the implications of the broad character of their relationships in terms of associational and organizational cohesion. The work on consultation/engagement and partnerships has had a more microscopic and management orientation: how do we get these things to work at the level of a specific program or policy issue?

In keeping with the theme of this book, both streams converge on the same idea: modern policymaking cannot be directed by government and simply supplemented by representations from the public or interest groups. That model died years ago, as analysts and practitioners realized the importance of new social movements, public interest groups, more complex associational systems, and the strategic value of information. As we argued in this chapter, networks are, if anything, more important now than before, even as their fundamental characteristics have changed in light of globalization and other forces. Government has a more sober assessment of its own capacities. It cannot monopolize information anymore, and, in many policy areas, is heavily dependent on the specialized expertise or experience of its partners. The image of a towering Leviathan has to be replaced with that of a prone Gulliver, tied with myriad strings to interests and policy sectors. The key point about networks is that they are systems of mutual interdependence where no one actor—including government—can dominate the rest.

The government's policy role remains crucial, but it shifts its focus to network management strategies. "Network management provides a way for actors to cooperate without solutions being forcibly imposed or cooperation becoming redundant as a result of decentralization or privatization" (Kickert and Koppenjan, 1997, p. 43).

Does that mean that government is necessarily weaker? In some ways, yes. In other ways, however, network management actually suggests a broadening and deepening of government influence through its leverage in policy networks and partnerships. The crucial question is the degree to which government remains a leader in these networks and partnerships. Also, we sometimes forget the other powers and instruments that governments have at their disposal to encourage private/public partnerships. This is what some analysts have referred to as "strategic governance" (de Bruijn and ten Heuvelhof, 1995). Policy networks, for example, are characterized by the interdependency of actors, the complexity of coalitions and organizational players, the reluctance to cooperate because of uncertainties about real interests and ultimate outcomes, and instability in that players shift constantly. Government can facilitate the effectiveness of networks by addressing these characteristics; for example, by distributing information, by helping organizations and interests coalesce and participate, and by developing novel proposals for exchange and cooperation.

If policy communities and networks are as important to the policy process as we suspect, then policy analysis and policy management have to change considerably. Analysis has to come to terms with the fact that policy outcomes depend crucially on the actors in the community and the nature of the network. Policy management has to shift its attention to new organizational forms of public sector and private sector cooperation and interaction.

KEY TERMS

advocacy coalition—a wide range of actors, including government from all levels, officials, interest organizations, research groups, journalists, and even other countries, who share a belief system about a policy area and over time demonstrate some degree of coordinated activities

associational system—constellation of small, medium, and large groups, competing and cooperating as they feel necessary

attentive public—the outsiders whose main influence on the process is to generate ideas and discussion through conferences, publications, and occasional lobbying

citizens' juries—a randomly selected jury of about eighteen individuals that hears from a variety of expert witnesses and deliberates together on a given issue

consultation—process whereby government gauges the views and opinions of nongovernmental organizations, citizen groups, and associations

corporatism—a system wherein centralized state agencies and centralized associational systems work closely to develop and implement policy

deliberative polling—a technique that usually involves between 250 and 600 people who form a representative sample of the community and who are first polled on their views on an issue, informed in some depth on that issue, and then polled again

epistemic community—originally developed in the field of international relations, this concept tries to capture the influence of international groups of scientific experts on policymaking; for example, in the environmental field

framework policies—a technique whereby government sets the broad parameters for policy outcomes but lets others deliver programs

interest group—an voluntary, membership-based organization that lobbies governments on issues of concern to its members

interest group pluralism—a system in which a wide variety of interests succeed in getting themselves heard throughout government

interest intermediation—the process whereby societal interests interact with state institutions

iron triangle—the stable and cozy relationships among congressional committees, executive agencies (primarily regulatory), and economic interest groups

issue network—offered as a critique of the "iron triangle" concept in that most policy subsystems were actually quite fluid and changing, with actors coalescing as necessary around issues, not policy sectors

Memorandum to Cabinet—the policy document outlining the rationale for any proposed bill, which now must state what consultations the Minister has undertaken or plans to undertake

policy community—the actors in a policy network, presumably those who share at least some common language and conceptual reference points but who may be opponents on the issue

policy network—the patterns of relations among members of the policy community

postmaterialist values—term used to describe the amalgam of conditions consisting of the rise of postmaterialism, the increased salience of rights, and the new emphasis on "difference"

public interest group—interest groups whose emphasis is on advocacy for "causes" and the public interest rather than economic lobbying

social movement—an informal network of organizations and individuals who, on the basis of a collective identity and shared values, engage in political and/or cultural struggle intended to break or expand the boundaries of the existing system, and undertake collective action designed to affect both state and society

social movement organization—interest groups rooted in social transformations of the 1960s that led to new values, new class structures, and new social coalitions (e.g., environmentalism, feminism)

strategic governance—the use of the powers and instruments that governments have at their disposal to encourage private/public partnerships, networks, framework agreements, and broad direction for the policy system as a whole

study circles—a consultation technique designed to facilitate broadly based, grassroots decisionmaking at the community level

subgovernment—a generic concept that expresses the idea that policy does not get made in a single "system" but in subsystems that consist of microcosms of all the relevant political and institutional actors

Weblinks

Canadian Policy Research Networks
http://www.cprn.org/en

Global Policy Forum (United Nations)
http://www.globalpolicy.org/ngos

The Center for Deliberative Democracy
http://cdd.stanford.edu

The Canadian Council for Public-Private Partnerships
http://www.pppcouncil.ca

Further Readings

Cameron, D. R., and Stein, J. G. (Eds.). (2002). *Street protests and fantasy parks: Globalization, culture, and the state.* Vancouver: UBC Press.

Keck, M. E., and Sikkink, K. (1998). *Activists beyond borders: Advocacy networks in international politics.* Ithaca: Cornell University Press.

Kickert, W. J. M., Klijn, E.-H., and Koppenjan, J. F. M. (Eds.) (1997). *Managing complex networks: Strategies for the public sector.* London: Sage.

Sabatier, P. A., and Jenkins-Smith, H. (Eds.). (1993). *Policy change and learning: An advocacy coalition approach.* Boulder, CO: Westview.

Treasury Board of Canada. *The partnership handbook.* Retrieved August 13, 2004, from http://www.hrsdc.gc.ca/en/epb/sid/cia/partnership/handbook.shtml

REFERENCES

Almond, G. (1990). *A discipline divided: Schools and sects in political science.* Newbury Park, CA: Sage.

Atkinson, M. M., and Coleman, W. D. (1989a). *The state, business, and industrial change in Canada.* Toronto: University of Toronto Press.

Atkinson, M. M., and Coleman, W. D. (1989b). Strong states and weak states: Sectoral policy networks in advanced capitalist economies. *British Journal of Political Science, 19*, 47–67.

Atkinson, M. M., and Coleman, W. D. (1992, April). Policy networks, policy communities and the problems of governance. *Governance, 5*, 154–80.

Auditor General of Canada. (2000). *Managing departments for results and managing horizontal issues for results.* Retrieved August 13, 2004, from www.oag-bvg.gc.ca/domino/reports/nsf/html/0020ce.html

Ayres, J. M. (1998). *Defying conventional wisdom: Political movements and popular contention against North American free trade.* Toronto: University of Toronto Press.

Ayres, J. M. (2003). Contesting neoliberalism: The political economy of transnational protest. In M. G. Cohen and S. McBride (Eds.), *Global turbulence: Social activists' and state responses to globalization* (pp. 89–104). Aldershot: Ashgate.

Bakvis, H., and Juillet, L. (2004) *The horizontal challenge: Line departments, central agencies, and leadership.* Ottawa: Canadian School of Public Service.

Batliwala, S. (2002, December). Grassroots movements as transnational actors: Implications for global civil society. *Voluntas: International Journal of Voluntary and Nonprofit Organizations, 13*, 393–408.

Baumgartner, F. R. (1996, January). Public interest groups in France and the United States. *Governance, 9*, 1–22.

Baumgartner, F. R., and Leech, B. L. (1998). *Basic interests: The importance of groups in politics and in political science.* Princeton: Princeton University Press.

Berry, J. M. (1977). *Lobbying for the people: The political behavior of public interest groups.* Princeton: Princeton University Press.

Berry, J. M. (1999). *The new Liberalism: The rising power of citizen groups.* Washington, DC: Brookings Institution Press.

Cairns, A. C. (1993). The fragmentation of Canadian citizenship. In W. Kaplan (Ed.), *Belonging: The meaning and future of Canadian citizenship* (pp. 181–220). Montreal: McGill-Queen's University Press.

Cameron, M., Lawson, R. J., and Tomlin, B. W. (1998). To walk without fear. In M. A. Cameron, R. J. Lawson, and B. W. Tomlin (Eds.), *To walk without fear: The global movement to ban landmines* (pp. 1–17). Toronto: Oxford University Press.

Canadian Centre for Philanthropy. (2000). *Federal/voluntary sector initiative.* Retrieved September 4, 2004, from http://www.ccp.ca

Canadian Development Report 1999. (2000). Ottawa: North-South Institute.

Carroll, W. K. (Ed.). (1992). *Organizing dissent.* Toronto: Garamond.

Carter, D. (1964). *Power in Washington: A critical look at today's struggle in the nation's capital.* New York: Random House.

Coleman, W. D. (1994, July). Banking, interest intermediation and political power. *European Journal of Political Research, 26,* 31–58.

Coleman, W. D., and Skogstad, G. (1990). Policy communities and policy networks: A structural approach. In W. D. Coleman and G. Skogstad (Eds.), *Organized interests and public policy* (pp. 14–33). Toronto: Copp-Clark.

Cooke, B., and Kothari, U. (Eds.). (2001). *Participation: The new tyranny.* London: Zed Books.

Deibert, R. J. (1997). *Parchment, printing, and hypermedia: Communication in world order transformation.* New York: Columbia University Press.

Deibert, R. J. (2002). Civil society activism on the World Wide Web: The case of the anti-MAI lobby. In D. R. Cameron and J. G. Stein (Eds.), *Street protests and fantasy parks: Globalization, culture, and the state* (pp. 88–108). Vancouver: UBC Press.

de Bruijn, J. A., and ven Heuvelhof, E. F. (1995). Policy networks and governance. In D. Weimer (Ed.), *Institutional design* (pp. 161–79). Boston: Kluwer Academic Publishers.

Dowding, K. (1995). Model or metaphor? A critical review of the policy network approach. *Political Studies, 43,* 136–58.

Dowding, K. (2001, March). There must be end to confusion: Policy networks, intellectual fatigue, and the need for political science methods courses in British universities. *Political Studies, 49,* 89–105.

Falk, R. (1987). The global promise of social movements: Explorations at the edge of time. *Alternatives, 7,* 173–96.

Fischer, F., and Forester, J. (Eds.). (1993). *The argumentative turn in policy analysis and planning.* Durham, NC: Duke University Press.

Fishkin, J. S. (1991). *Democracy and deliberation: New directions for democratic reform.* New Haven, CT: Yale University Press.

Fitzpatrick, T. (2000). *Horizontal management: Trends in governance and accountability.* Action-Research Roundtable on the Management of Horizontal Issues. Ottawa: Canadian Centre for Management Development. Retrieved September 4, 2004, from http://dsp-psd .pwgsc.gc.ca/Collection/SC94-112-2000E.pdf

Glasius, M., Kaldor, M., and Anheier, H. (2003). *Global civil society 2002.* Oxford: Oxford University Press.

Graham, K. A., and Phillips, S. D. (1998). Making public participation more effective: Issues for local government. In K. A. Graham and S. D. Phillips (Eds.), *Citizen engagement: Lessons in participation from local government* (pp. 1–24). Toronto: Institute of Public Administration of Canada.

Grant, J. A., MacLean, S. J., and Shaw, T. M. (2003). Emergent transnational coalitions around diamonds and oil in civil conflicts in Africa. In M. G. Cohen and S. McBride (Eds.), *Global turbulence: Social activists' and state responses to globalization* (pp. 124–39). Aldershot: Ashgate.

Haas, P. M. (1992, Winter). Introduction: Epistemic communities and international policy coordination. *International Organization, 46,* 1–35.

Heclo, H. (1978). Issue networks and the executive establishment. In A. King (Ed.), *The new American political system* (pp. 87–124). Washington, DC: American Enterprise Institute for Public Policy Research.

Heclo, H., and Wildavsky, A. (1974). *The private government of public money.* London: Macmillan.

Hopkins, M., Couture, C., and Moore, E. (2001). *Moving from the heroic to the everyday: Lessons learned from leading horizontal projects.* Roundtable on the Management of Horizontal Initiatives.

Ottawa: Canadian Centre for Management Development. Retrieved September 4, 2004, from http://www.myschool-monecole.gc.ca/research/publications/html/horinz_rt/e.pdf

Howlett, M. (2002, June). Do networks matter? Linking policy network structure to policy outcomes: Evidence from four Canadian policy sectors 1990–2000. *Canadian Journal of Political Science, 35,* 235–67.

Ignatieff, M. (2000). *The rights revolution.* Toronto: House of Anansi.

Jordan, G. (1990). Subgovernments, policy communities and networks: Refilling the old bottles? *Journal of Theoretical Politics, 2,* 319–38.

Katzenstein, P. J. (1978a). *Between power and plenty: Foreign economic policies of advanced industrial states.* Madison: University of Wisconsin Press.

Katzenstein, P. J. (1978b). Introduction: Domestic and international forces and strategies of foreign economic policy. In P. J. Katzenstein (Ed.), *Between power and plenty: Foreign economic policies of advanced industrial states* (pp. 3–22). Madison: University of Wisconsin Press.

Katzenstein, P. J. (1978c). Conclusion: Domestic structures and strategies of foreign economic policy. In P. J. Katzenstein (Ed.), *Between power and plenty: Foreign economic policies of advanced industrial states* (pp. 295–336). Madison: University of Wisconsin Press.

Keck, M. E., and Sikkink, K. (1998). *Activists beyond borders: Advocacy networks in international politics.* Ithaca: Cornell University Press.

Kenis, P., and Schneider, V. (1991). Policy networks and policy analysis: Scrutinizing a new analytical toolbox. In B. Marin and R. Mayntz (Eds.), *Policy networks: Empirical evidence and theoretical considerations* (pp. 25–59). Boulder, CO: Westview Press.

Kernaghan, K. (1993, Spring). Partnership and public administration: Conceptual and practical considerations. *Canadian Public Administration, 36,* 57–76.

Kickert, W. J. M., and Koppenjan, J. F. M. (1997). Public management and network management: An overview. In W. J. M. Kickert, E.-H. Klijn, and J. F. M. Koppenjan (Eds.), *Managing complex networks: Strategies for the public sector* (pp. 35–61). London: Sage.

Klandermans, B., and Tarrow, S. (1988). Mobilization into social movements: Synthesizing European and American approaches. *International Social Movement Research, 1,* 1–38.

Langford, J. (1999). Governance challenges of public-private partnerships. In S. Delacourt and D. G. Lenihan (Eds.), *Collaborative government: Is there a Canadian way?* (pp. 105–11). Toronto: Institute of Public Administration of Canada.

Lindquist, E. A. (1992, Summer). Public managers and policy communities: Learning to meet new challenges. *Canadian Public Administration, 35,* 127–59.

Lindquist, E. A. (1996). New agendas for research on policy communities: Policy analysis, administration, and governance. In L. Dobuzinskis, M. Howlett, and D. Laycock (Eds.), *Policy studies in Canada: The state of the art* (pp. 219–41). Toronto: University of Toronto Press.

Marin, B., and Mayntz, R. (1991). Introduction: Studying policy networks. In B. Marin and R. Mayntz (Eds.), *Policy networks: Empirical evidence and theoretical considerations* (pp. 11–23). Boulder, CO: Westview Press.

Marsh, D., and Smith, M. (2000, March). Understanding policy networks: Towards a dialectical approach. *Political Studies, 48,* 4–21.

Marsh, D., and Smith, M. J. (2001, August). There is more than one way to do political science: On different ways to study policy networks. *Political Studies, 49,* 528–41.

Melnick, R. S. (1994). *Between the lines: Interpreting welfare rights.* Washington, DC: The Brookings Institution.

Melucci, A. (1989). *Nomads of the present: Social movements and individual needs in contemporary society.* Philadelphia: Temple University Press.

Messner, D. (2002). World society—structures and trends. In P. Kennedy, D. Messner, and F. Nuscheler (Eds.), *Global trends and global governance* (pp. 22–64). London: Pluto Press.

Nagel, S. (1988). *Policy studies: Integration and evaluation.* New York: Praeger.

Nordlinger, E. A. (1981). *On the autonomy of the democratic state.* Cambridge, MA: Harvard University Press.

OECD. (2000, December–February). *Focus: Public Management Newsletter,* no. 15.

OECD (2001). *Engaging citizens in policy-making: Information, consultation and public participation.* PUMA Policy Brief No. 10. Retrieved August 13, 2004, from http://www.oecd.org/dataoecd/24/34/2384040.pdf

Offe, C. (1987). Challenging the boundaries of institutional politics. In C. S. Maier (Ed.), *Changing boundaries of the political: Essays on the evolving balance between the state and society, public and private in Europe* (pp. 63–105). Cambridge, UK: Cambridge University Press.

Pal, L. A. (1992). *Public policy analysis: An introduction*, 2nd ed. Toronto: Nelson.

Pal, L. A. (1993). *Interests of state: The politics of language, multiculturalism and feminism in Canada.* Montreal: McGill-Queen's University Press.

Paltiel, K. Z. (1982). The changing environment and role of special interest groups. *Canadian Public Administration, 25,* 198–210.

Pemberton, H. (2000, December). Policy networks and policy learning: UK economic policy in the 1960s and 1970s. *Public Administration,* 78, 771–92.

Peters, B. G. (1998). *Managing horizontal government: The politics of coordination.* Ottawa: Canadian Centre for Management Development. Research Paper No. 21, 1998.

Peters, B. G., and Barker, A. (Eds.). (1993). *Advising West European governments: Inquiries, expertise and public policy.* Pittsburgh: University of Pittsburgh Press.

Phillips, S. D. (1993, Winter). Of public interest groups and sceptics: A realist's reply to Professor Stanbury. *Canadian Public Administration,* 36, 606–16.

Phillips, S. D. (1999). New social movements in Canadian politics: Past their apex? In J. P. Bickerton and A. G. Gagnon (Eds.), *Canadian politics* (3rd ed.) (pp. 371–91). Peterborough, ON: Broadview Press.

Phillips, S. D. (2003). In accordance: Canada's voluntary sector accord from idea to implementation. In K. L. Brock (Ed.), *Delicate dances: Public policy and the nonprofit sector* (pp. 17–62). Montreal and Kingston: McGill-Queen's University Press.

Privy Council Office (Canada). (1993). *Task force report: Service to the public.* Ottawa: Minister of Supply and Services.

Privy Council Office (Canada). (1999). *Government of Canada regulatory policy.* Retrieved September 4, 2004, from http://www .pco-bcp.gc.ca/raoics-srdc/default.asp?Language=E&Page= Publications&Sub=GovernmentofCanadaRegula

Privy Council Office (Canada). (2003). *Guide to making federal acts and regulations.* 2nd ed. Retrieved August 13, 2004, from http://www .pco-bcp.gc.ca/default .asp?Language=E&Page=Publications&doc=legislation/lmgtoc_e.htm

Privy Council Office (Canada). (2004). *Memorandum to Cabinet.* Retrieved August 13, 2004, from http://www.pco-bcp.gc.ca/default .asp?Language=E&Page=publications&Sub=mc&Doc=mc_e.htm

Pross, A. P. (1992). *Group politics and public policy* (2nd ed.). Toronto: Oxford University Press.

Pross, A. P. (1995). Pressure groups: Talking chameleons. In M. S. Whittington and G. Williams (Eds.), *Canadian politics in the 1990s* (pp. 252–75). Toronto: Nelson Canada.

Raab, C. (2001, August). Understanding policy networks: A comment on Marsh and Smith. *Political Studies, 49,* 551–56.

Raab, C. (2002, October). Where do policy networks come from? *Journal of Public Administration Research and Theory, 12,* 581–622.

Ripley, R. B., and Franklin, G. A. (1984). *Congress, the bureaucracy and public policy* (2nd ed.). Homewood, IL: Dorsey.

Rosenau, P. V. (Ed.). (2000). *Public-private policy partnerships.* Cambridge: MIT Press.

Sabatier, P. A. (1993). Policy change over a decade or more. In P. A. Sabatier and H. Jenkins-Smith (Eds.), *Policy change and learning: An advocacy coalition approach* (pp. 13–39). Boulder, CO: Westview.

Sabatier, P. A., and Jenkins-Smith, H. (Eds.). (1993). *Policy change and learning: An advocacy coalition approach.* Boulder, CO: Westview.

Sabatier, P. A., and Jenkins-Smith, H. (1999). The advocacy coalition framework: An assessment. In P. A. Sabatier (Ed.), *Theories of the policy process* (pp. 117–66). Boulder, CO: Westview.

Schmitter, P. C., and Lembruch, G. (Eds.). (1979). *Trends towards corporatist intermediation.* Beverly Hills, CA: Sage.

Schneider, A. L., and Ingram, H. (1997). *Policy design for democracy.* Lawrence: University Press of Kansas.

Scholte, J. A. (2004). Civil society and democratically accountable global governance. *Government and Opposition, 39,* 211–33.

Schuck, P. H. (1977, March/April). Public interest groups and the policy process. *Public Administration Review, 37,* 132–40.

Skocpol, T. (1986). Rediscovering the state: Strategies of analysis in current research. In P. B. Evans, D. Reuschemeyer, and T. Skocpol (Eds.), *Bringing the state back in* (pp. 3–37). Cambridge, UK: Cambridge University Press.

Stanbury, W. T. (1993, Winter). A sceptic's guide to the claims of so-called public interest groups. *Canadian Public Administration, 36,* 580–605.

Stanbury, W. T., and Vertinsky, I. B. (1994, Winter). Information technologies and transnational interest groups: The challenge for diplomacy. *Canadian Foreign Policy,* 2, 87–99.

Thatcher, M. (1998, October). The development of policy network analyses: From modest origins to overarching frameworks. *Journal of Theoretical Politics,* 10, 389–416.

Thomas, T. (1995). When "they" is "we": Movements, municipal parties, and participatory politics. In J. Lightbody (Ed.), *Canadian metropolitics: Governing our cities* (pp. 115–36). Toronto: Copp Clark.

Truman, D. (1951). *The governmental process: Political interests and public opinion.* New York: Alfred A. Knopf.

Van Waarden, F. (1992). Dimensions and types of policy networks. *European Journal of Political Research,* 21, 29–52.

Walker, J. (1991). *Mobilizing interest groups in America: Patrons, professions and social movements.* Ann Arbor: University of Michigan Press.

Walker, R. B. J. (1988). *One world, many worlds: Struggles for a just world peace.* Boulder, CO: Lynne Rienner Publishers.

Weaver, R. K., and Rockman, B. A. (1993). Assessing the effects of institutions. In R. K. Weaver and B. A. Rockman (Eds.), *Do institutions matter? Government capabilities in the United States and abroad* (pp. 1–41). Washington, DC: The Brookings Institution.

Williams, J., and Goose, S. (1998). The international campaign to ban landmines. In M. A. Cameron, R. J. Lawson, and B. W. Tomlin (Eds.), *To walk without fear: The global movement to ban landmines* (pp. 20–47). Toronto: Oxford University Press.

Wright, M. (1988). Policy community, policy network, and comparative industrial policies. *Political Studies,* 36, 593–614.

Wyman, M., Shulman, D., and Ham, L. (1999). *Learning to engage: Experiences with civic engagement in Canada.* Ottawa: Canadian Policy Research Networks. Retrieved August 13, 2004, from http://www.cprn.org/en/doc.cfm?doc=86

Zald, M. N. (1987). *Social movements in an organizational society: Collected essays.* New Brunswick, NJ: Transaction.

Chapter 7   *Evaluation*

Consult any text on policy analysis and you will find passages extolling the indispensability of program evaluation. It could hardly be otherwise, given that program evaluation is primarily about trying to figure out how successful a policy has been, whether it met its objectives, how far it fell short, and what might be done to improve its impact. The same passages that extol evaluation, however, are usually complemented by ones that say that it is expensive, difficult, rarely conclusive, and politically unpopular. Precisely because evaluation is so potentially crucial to the fortunes of a policy or program, opponents and supporters work hard to get the evaluation results they need to strengthen their case. That is, if evaluation takes place at all. Not only is it politically sensitive (who wants to hear bad news?), it can seem secondary to the really important job of designing and implementing solutions to public problems. Policy evaluation therefore has enjoyed more theoretical than practical popularity, and in Canada at least, has not been enthusiastically supported either as a government or a third-party (i.e., foundation or think-tank) activity. This is changing. The new emphasis on results, coupled with a gradual shift to special operating agencies, contracted-out services, and partnerships, increases the need for evaluation because it places new pressures on governments to be accountable. Not only does evaluation have a higher profile, but also different forms of evaluation (such as client satisfaction and overall program performance) are becoming increasingly important. Thus, what is happening in this field directly reflects developments described in chapters 3 to 6.

Policy analysis, defined as the disciplined application of intellect to public problems, encompasses everything from reading a newspaper to careful scientific research. In practice, much of what passes for professional policy analysis is called policy evaluation. It is conducted by governments as well as private firms, assumes a mastery of certain quantitative and qualitative techniques, and is aimed at the improvement or betterment of public policies and programs. Its central questions are: Does this program do what it is supposed to be doing? If not, why not? What should be done? Policy analysis is openly prescriptive, and serves to monitor government activities. Policies attempt to solve or manage public problems; at some point governments (and citizens) need to know whether interventions are making a difference and are worthwhile. Since most government services are on a not-for-profit basis, there are no clear market signals (i.e., profit, loss, increase or decrease in demand) to measure performance.

The improvement of programs is the core function or purpose of evaluation as it is conducted in governments, but there are other purposes as well. Rossi, Freeman, and Lipsey (1999) highlight four (pp. 40–43). The first is the one we have already mentioned and will develop further below—program improvement. Typically this means working with program managers as the program is being implemented, or what is called **formative evaluation**. Another purpose is for **accountability**—in this instance, the objective is oversight once the program is close to completion, or what is called **summative evaluation**. Evaluations can also be done to generate more general knowledge that may or may not be directly relevant to the program but that might cast light on a social issue or casual questions. Finally, evaluations can be done as a political ruse or for public relations—either to produce data to support a program or justify a decision that has already been made. In this chapter, we will concentrate on evaluation with the first objective.

Policy evaluation seems deceptively simple, but determining whether a program has its intended effect, in a world in which every effect has multiple causes, and every cause a vast stream of effects, is always difficult, and sometimes impossible. Information is sometimes faulty or nonexistent, people uncooperative, policies objectives vague, or measuring instruments weak. As well, evaluation is by its nature unpopular. Who wants to be told their program is a failure? Evaluation often delivers unpleasant truths, creating great temptations to shoot, or at least ignore, the messenger. However, despite these built-in limitations and liabilities, as well as a history of, at best, tepid support from most policy managers, evaluation experienced a renewed popularity in the mid-1990s. The 1995 OECD update on public management developments in twenty-five countries, for example, noted: "A wide range of performance-oriented initiatives has been reported in 1994 as the shift of management focus from processes to results gains momentum. Those mentioned here cover two main aspects: a drive for better reporting of performance; and increased emphasis on setting targets for service quality levels and measuring results against them" (p. 10).

There are several reasons for this resurgence. First, evaluation is typically championed by the management consulting industry, since that is where a great deal of its claims to expertise lie (Saint-Martin, 2000). As governments in recent years have tried to borrow more management practices from the private sector, they have also tended to import a greater profile for evaluation. Second, fiscal pressures in recent years have made it necessary to use old money for new projects, forcing evaluations of areas where policy results are relatively weak and monies can be reallocated. A third, related reason is that many of the new techniques of governance discussed in chapters 3 to 6 on design, implementation, and policy communities demand better accountability mechanisms. That, therefore, means evaluation or assessment. When public agencies used to be largely responsible for the delivery of public programs, public managers assumed that accountability for performance was built into the organization of delivery. Once delivery and design are severed, or once policies and programs are coproduced with the private and nonprofit sectors, government is primarily either writing cheques or setting frameworks. If government is not to do this blindly, it needs to clarify what it wants out of a relationship, and how the results will be monitored and measured. A fourth reason is entangled with the sense that citizens have declining levels of trust in public authorities and public policies. Rigorous evaluation of the performance of public agencies, and the communication of that evaluation to the wider public, is one means for re-establishing support for public institutions. "Today, global and domestic forces demand more effective management and higher levels of organizational performance. Leaders and managers in public and nonprofit organizations face demanding constituencies, higher public expectations, and aggressive media scrutiny" (Wholey, 2003, p. 44).

This chapter has two primary objectives. The first is to introduce some of the main techniques used in evaluation research, as well as some of the benchmarks and rules of thumb for successful evaluations. This section is merely an overview of the logic of the techniques, and does not pretend to be comprehensive. The second objective is to review the history of federal government evaluation efforts in the last twenty years, and provide a sense of context about the state of evaluation in this country and the potential for its new and enhanced status. To date, Canadian practice has restricted evaluation to more of a management tool than a real challenge to government programs. The chapter closes with a discussion of the place of evaluation both in policy analysis and in democratic governance.

TYPES OF EVALUATION

Michael Patton (1997) argues that "**program evaluation** is the systematic collection of information about the activities, characteristics, and outcomes of programs to make judgments about the program, improve program effectiveness, and/or inform decisions about future programming"

(p. 23). Weiss defines evaluation as "the *systematic assessment* of the *operations* and/or the *outcomes* of a program or policy, compared to a set of *explicit* or *implicit standards,* as a means of contributing to the *improvement* of the program or policy" (1998, p. 4; emphasis in original). Rossi, Freeman, and Lipsey (1999) define program evaluation as "the use of social research procedures to systematically investigate the effectiveness of social intervention programs that is adapted to their political and organizational environments and designed to inform social action in ways that improve social conditions" (p. 20).

Several features of these definitions should be noted. First, they refer to "practice" and "application" of techniques. Second, they identify "improvement" of public policy decisionmaking processes as the ultimate goal of evaluation. Third, they highlight the "systematic" character of evaluation research. Evaluation presents itself, in short, as a scientific, systematic, empirically oriented, applied discipline or set of disciplines that analyzes current programs in order to generate intelligent information that can be used to improve those programs or the decision processes that produced them. The creative and intuitive aspect of evaluation should not be understated: Patton (1987) lists 100 different types of evaluation and argues persuasively that each one demands creativity (pp. 98–205). As we mentioned in Chapter 1, one of the most deceptively simple things about a policy is stating its goals. Before a program can be evaluated, its underlying problem definition and its goals must be understood, and so evaluators spend a good deal of time in what is usually termed the pre-evaluation phase, talking to program administrators and piecing together what people think they are doing. This is closer to cultural anthropology than regression analysis. Nonetheless, it is fair to say that of all the subfields within policy analysis, evaluation has remained closest to the traditional empiricist model. Evaluators are the accountants of the policy profession and, like balance sheets, their reports on effectiveness and impact can sometimes be received with glum resignation. Indeed, because the traditional empirical techniques used in most conventional evaluations are fairly standardized (even though they vary in their application case by case), and because evaluation results are supposed to be neutral and unbiased, there has been a greater momentum behind the professionalization of evaluation than other fields of policy analysis. The American Evaluation Association (formed in 1986), for example, adopted in 1994 its guiding principles for evaluators (their order does not imply priority, which will vary according to context):

1. *Systematic inquiry:* Evaluators conduct systematic, data-based inquiries about whatever is being evaluated.

2. *Competence:* Evaluators provide competent performance to stakeholders.

3. *Integrity/honesty:* Evaluators ensure the honesty and integrity of the entire evaluation process.

4. *Respect for people:* Evaluators respect the security, dignity and self-worth of the respondents, program participants, clients, and other stakeholders with whom they interact.

5. *Responsibilities for general and public welfare:* Evaluators articulate and take into account the diversity of interests and values that may be related to the general and public welfare. (American Evaluation Association, 2000)

The Canadian Evaluation Society has similar guidelines that emphasize competence, integrity, and accountability (Canadian Evaluation Society, 2000). Evaluators must be aware that while they are engaged in providing information to improve programs, ultimately those programs are delivered by people and for people, and moreover their assessments inevitably will be coloured to some degree by choices and values.

While our definitions of evaluation appear to give evaluation a wide scope of application in policymaking, indeed to the point that it seems synonymous with policy analysis itself, it is worth keeping some fundamental distinctions in mind between policy analysis and evaluation (Geva-May and Pal, 1999). A careful reading shows that evaluation is almost always linked to existing programs, either through the analysis of those programs themselves or of information relevant to them. Because of their expertise, evaluators are also often involved in generating and analyzing data that are relevant to problem definition, trend forecasting, and program design aspects such as target populations. Rossi, Freeman, and Lipsey (1999) term these **"diagnostic procedures"** that entail, for example, the use of census data, existing **social indicators** such as literacy or crime rates, and surveys to determine the nature and scope of a problem (pp. 120–25). **Needs assessment** can be even more specific, for example, the health needs of a small rural community, and would depend on specially designed surveys and reviews of existing data. This is certainly a respectable and important component of evaluation (but, as we shall see below, a fairly small part of what evaluators and policy analysts actually do) but is not its core. The core of program evaluation "includes the measurement of program performance—resource expenditures, program activities, and program outcomes—and the testing of causal assumptions linking these three elements" (Wholey, 1994, p. 15). Figure 7.1 (page 290) illustrates these three categories with some illustrative questions.

Figure 7.1   Core Categories of Program Evaluation

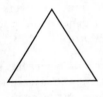

Process Evaluation (Program Activities)

What are the components of the program?
How is the program delivered?

Impact Evaluation (Outcomes)

Did the program have the intended effects?
If not, why not?

Efficiency Evaluation (Costs/Benefits)

What was the ratio of benefit to costs in this program?
Given what we spent, did we get the most out of it?

Before program evaluation can be conducted, therefore, we normally have programs in place—evaluation typically is *ex post* analysis, or after the launch of a program. As obvious as this seems, it reminds us that the very first step in any policy evaluation is trying to understand the policy and its programs, primarily in terms described in Chapter 1— what is the problem, what are the goals, and how are programs designed to address that problem? As Weiss points out, there are many cases where programs are quite unambiguous—changing highway speeds, increasing benefits in some income support program, or introducing a new medical testing program such as mammograms for a target population. However, many other programs, and often the most interesting or controversial ones, combine resources, people, and practices in complex ways. "In most social programs, it takes effort to understand the content of the program, what actually goes on. Operations often differ markedly from day to day and from staff member to staff member" (1998, p. 49). Regional development programs, sweeping changes in curriculum, or new gun control regulations are not easy to describe, nor is it self-evident what the program "really is." This is because the program on the ground may be different—in the way that its administrators understand it and implement it—from what the program is on paper. An evaluator who measured the "paper program" might be evaluating something that in fact does not exist. By the same token, not knowing the "real" program means that the evaluator may not be asking the right questions or gathering the right data.

Before conducting an evaluation, therefore, evaluators should learn about the program as it really is as well as what it was designed to be. They can review previous evaluations, published literature, and program materials, and conduct both formal and information interviews with a variety of program and policy personnel as well as clients to put the puzzle together. They can then develop two related models to help them map out what the program is and how it tries to accomplish its objectives. The first guide is **program theory,** or hypotheses and explanations about the "causal links that tie program inputs to expected program outputs" (Weiss, 1998, p. 55). We discuss this in detail below in connection with **impact evaluation,** but it is a theory about how the program will exercise its ultimate effect or outcome. For example, a training program for unemployed youth has a target of increasing the numbers of youth who get jobs. The program theory might also be that the reason the youth are unemployed is because of lack of skills, and so by providing training, the program provides the skills and makes the youth more attractive to employers. However, it might be that the program offers young people the opportunity to widen their circle of contacts, and thereby learn about more job opportunities. In both instances, the program and the outcomes are the same, but the "mechanisms" (what Weiss terms not the activities themselves but the responses to these activities) are different.

The second guide or map that is useful for evaluators (especially when they conduct **process evaluations**) is the **implementation theory** that lies behind the program. These are the specific activities and resources that are mobilized in connection with each of the links in the program's **causal chain** or **logic model.** To use the youth training program once again as an example, the implementation theory would detail steps such as publicizing the program among targeted youth groups and arranging the counselling and the content of the training, the rooms, and other forms of support. For program administrators, the assumption— since their job is to implement the program as it was designed in the belief that it is supposed to work—is that if all the steps in the implementation theory are fulfilled, the program will achieve its results.

Evaluation is enhanced considerably if evaluators have a grasp of both program theory and implementation theory and the relationship between the two. (See Figure 7.2 on page 292 for an example of the relationship between the two.)

IMPACT EVALUATION

A central evaluative question is whether a policy or program has an impact. Evaluating outcomes is critical to determining whether a program is successful or not in terms of its intended effects. Impact evaluation

Figure 7.2   Program Theory and Implementation Theory (Example)

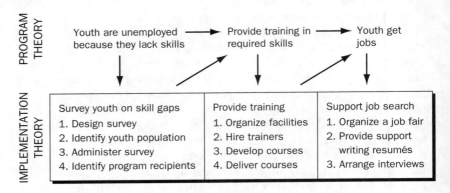

takes the program as the independent or causal variable and tries to isolate its effect from other influences in the environment. This assumes that goals are clear, but sometimes they are not. As we noted above, in addition to trying to understand the goals, the evaluator should also develop a map of the causal theory that underpins the program, along with mechanisms of change. This not only helps in determining what data to gather and which indicators to highlight but also provides alternative path explanations that might be examined if the evaluation turns up ambiguous results. In the training example, if the employment rate for youth who complete the program is lower than expected, this might be because the skill enhancement occurred only for those youth who had certain background characteristics (e.g., finished secondary school, had had at least one other training program, etc.).

Having determined a program theory, impact evaluation goes on to look at actual causal chains by examining the program's effects. Impact evaluation tries to isolate causes and effects, but this is no easy task since any single cause or effect is (or may be seen to be) intimately bound to numerous other causes and effects. A single effect may conceivably have several causes, and the policy intervention is only one of them. Figure 7.3 provides a schematic diagram of the assumption and the problem. It helps to begin with a simple model of policy impact: here, some policy P is intended to affect some casual variable C, which will then have a desired effect on some outcome O. Note that a policy or program never has a direct influence on behaviour; it is always targeted on some factor that is assumed to influence behaviour, and by influencing that factor yields desired outcomes. Speed limits, for example, assume that accidents are in part caused by driving too quickly. Accident rates are the O or outcome, while speeding is C. A program to either set

Figure 7.3 Causal Model of Program Impact

A. Simple Model of Program Impact

B. Complex Model of Program Impact

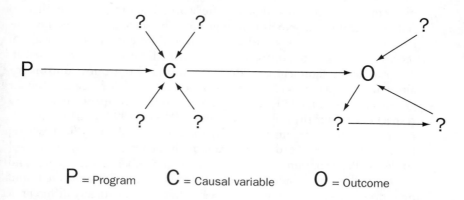

P = Program C = Causal variable O = Outcome

lower limits or enforce them more rigorously could be two examples of interventions. But now consider the more complex model in Figure 7.3. It adds variables to the C and the O categories. Speeding itself can be regarded as a **dependent variable,** something caused by other factors. Speeding is affected by such things as weather conditions, road congestion, safety quality of cars, and so on. If an antispeeding campaign were found to be associated with lower accident rates, would that mean that the program was successful? Not at all, since it may be that there were fewer speeders about, or that other conditions were responsible for the diminution of accident rates.

Various strategies have been developed to deal with this problem. They all rely on statistical techniques to a greater or lesser degree, and all strive to control or neutralize the extraneous causal variables that might have produced the effect. In cases where these preferred strategies are unavailable, too expensive, or time consuming, a technique called "meta-analysis" is sometimes used. Instead of gathering new data, evaluators review the existing literature on a specific program, treating each evaluation study as a single case. This "pooling" of evaluations requires a fairly large set, however, sometimes in the hundreds, in order to be valid. One advantage of meta-analysis, on the other hand, is that this pooling increases the number of "observations" of the effects of a particular intervention in a variety of settings and thereby can increase the confidence level of any assertions about its effects. Weiss points out, for example, that meta-analysis has in some instances shown that many kinds of social programs that were once thought to have little effect in fact have statistically significant cumulative outcomes (1998, p. 242).

The ideal method to try to empirically isolate cause and effect is the classic **experimental design**. In this design, people are randomly assigned to one of two groups; measures are taken of target variables before the program is introduced and again afterward. The program is applied to only one group, the **experimental group**. The second group is the **control group**. If there is a sufficiently large difference in post-program scores, then the program or intervention is deemed to have caused it. The **random assignment** of individuals to the two groups controls for alternative explanations or causes, since the odds of being in either group are the same. In aggregate, the groups are identical in every respect except for the policy intervention (Weiss, 1998, p. 215). Experimental designs are frequently used in the educational policy field, where, for example, a new reading program might be tested on two groups of students. Pre-program reading scores for the experimental group and the control group would be gathered, the program administered, and post-program scores compared to see if they are statistically different.

Despite their statistical superiority as a measure of impact, experimental designs are rarely used in policy evaluation. They are costly and usually time consuming; decisionmakers frequently want quick answers. There are also political and ethical problems with separating people into experimental and control groups. Many public programs deliver benefits to the populace, and from a political perspective it might be imprudent to deliberately withhold a benefit from some group simply to meet testing requirements. As Rossi, Freeman, and Lipsey (1999) point out, randomized experiments can be used only with what they call "**partial-coverage programs**" (p. 259). Yet ethical dilemmas also arise with these, as in the controversy over withholding potentially beneficial AIDS drugs. In the medical field, for example, there are periodic debates about the efficacy of new, expensive drugs until they have been thoroughly tested. They appear to assist some patients, but do they have an appreciable impact on national health? Finally, some important policy variables cannot be disaggregated to observe differential effects on separate groups. Interest rates, the value of the dollar, and budget deficits are examples of policy variables that apply nationally or not at all. Classic experimental designs are useless in trying to determine their impact.

Nonetheless, while rare in comparison with other techniques, program evaluation based on experimental design does take place. In Canada the leading exponent is the nonprofit Social Research and Development Corporation (SRDC)—itself modelled after the Manpower Demonstration Research Corporation started over twenty years ago in the United States. SRDC brings together researchers around the analysis and evaluation of social programs in multiple locales and over extended time periods to see what actually works and what does not. As the SRDC puts it,

What makes SRDC unique in Canada is its experience in designing, implementing, and evaluating large-scale demonstration projects using random assignment evaluation designs. This pioneering work involves combining rigorous quantitative analysis with innovative qualitative research techniques in order to be able to tell what works, for whom it works, and why it works. . . . SRDC's core research activities are focused on rigorous impact and benefit-cost evaluations of new program models. However, we also conduct implementation research and formative evaluations designed to study the process by which new programs are introduced, and to identify obstacles to implementation and bottlenecks in service delivery. (SRDC, 2004)

The SRDC's four main projects are the Self-Sufficiency Project (SSP), the Earnings Supplement Project (ESP), the Community Employment Innovation Program (CEIP), and *learn*$ave. All four are test programs supported and funded by Human Resources Development Canada (HRDC), now split into two departments. SSP was started in 1992 by New Brunswick and British Columbia and is an earnings supplement to poor, single parents on welfare that tries to increase household income and encourage work. Almost 10 000 people voluntarily participated in the project. The ESP provided a supplement to recipients of Employment Insurance (EI) to help them choose work, even at lower than their previous wages, rather than long-term attachment to EI. It had over 11 000 participants. CEIP is targeted at individuals who are eligible for EI or on social assistance and gives them the opportunity to volunteer for community service employment. Those who take up the offer will stop receiving EI or social assistance benefits and receive a weekly $300 stipend instead. Finally, *learn*$ave is a program that revolves around a matched savings program entitled Individual Development Accounts. Low-income Canadians receive $3 for each dollar they deposit in the account, for a total of up to $6000 over three years. The accounts can be used only for training, education, and small-business start-ups. Once the experiment is concluded, SRDC will conduct an evaluation of whether the scheme actually induced participants to save and invest more in education.

In all four cases, the fundamental question is whether people, if given the proper incentives, would prefer work over income support, whether once they get jobs they keep them or find other employment, and whether they are prepared to invest in themselves. Income assistance like welfare or EI is considered by many to be "passive" in that it does not encourage people back into the labour force, and worse, induces dependency after long periods of time. But EI and social assistance are both designed in ways that impose penalties on people when they find jobs—their benefits are cut or reduced significantly—and it is difficult to know what the effect of earnings supplement programs might be. In both the SSP and ESP, the SRDC conducted long-term evaluations based on experimental design—they divided the participants into control and program groups and tried to compare the impact of the two programs over time. Box 7.1 provides some details on the methodology behind evaluating the ESP.

Box 7.1	SOCIAL RESEARCH AND DEMONSTRATION CORPORATION

EVALUATING THE EARNINGS SUPPLEMENT PROJECT [EXCERPTS]

The primary goal of the supplement for displaced workers was to shorten their often long and painful re-employment process and to provide them with a source of income in a form that promoted employment. It was hoped that doing so would help to compensate displaced workers for the losses they incurred due to economic change. In addition, it was hoped that, by encouraging re-employment, the supplement would reduce the cost of unemployment benefits.

The goal of the supplement for repeat users of unemployment benefits was to stimulate off-season employment and promote a shift toward year-round jobs. It was hoped that doing so would reduce their long-term dependence on unemployment benefits.

A randomized experiment, the best way known to measure program impacts, was used to measure the effects of ESP on full-time employment, earnings, and unemployment benefit payments. Eligible sample members were randomly assigned either to a supplement group that was offered the supplement program, or to a control group that was not. Both groups could receive all unemployment benefits to which they were entitled normally.

Choosing the groups in this way helped to ensure that the supplement offer was their only initial systematic difference. Thus, comparisons of their future experiences provided varied estimates of the impacts of ESP on these experiences. . . .

ESP was conducted as part of the unemployment benefit claims process for displaced workers in five cities: Granby, Oshawa, Toronto, Winnipeg, and Saskatoon. When individuals applied for regular unemployment benefits, local HRCC [Human Resource Centre of Canada] staff used a brief screening form to determine whether they met the criteria established for identifying displaced workers. Claimants who met these criteria were encouraged to apply for ESP. When the research team received notice that an ESP applicant's first unemployment benefit cheque had been issued, the applicant was then randomly assigned by computer to the supplement program or the control group.

If supplement group members found a new full-time job (with 30 or more hours of work per week) within 26 weeks, and if that job paid less than their previous weekly insurable earnings, they could receive supplement payments equal to 75 percent of the difference for up to two years after random assignment, up to a maximum of $250 per week. In addition, supplement group members who found full-time employment within 26 weeks that paid as much or more than they used to make could initiate a supplement that would protect them for up to two years against a future re-employment earnings loss. It was hoped that this offer of supplement payments for some plus "earnings insurance" for others would provide a strong inducement to return quickly to full-time work.

Sample members' attitudes, behaviour, and experiences were documented through multiple data sources. In addition, a field study was conducted to examine how the program was implemented. . . .

Two main data sources were used for the analysis. A 15-month follow-up survey provided information on job-search behaviour, employment, earnings, and wage rates; unemployment benefit administrative records provided information on the duration and amount of unemployment benefit payments. Additional information from focus groups, in-depth telephone interviews, and records of calls to the ESP toll-free information line was used to help interpret the impact findings.

SOURCE: Bloom, Howard, et al. (1999). *Testing a re-employment incentive for displaced workers: The Earnings Supplement Project.* Ottawa: Social Research and Demonstration Corporation, pp. ES1–2, 45.

Experimental designs of the type engineered by the SRDC are time consuming and expensive, as well as technically challenging. In the face of these difficulties, rigorous experimental design often gives way to other, **quasi-experimental** forms of impact evaluation. One technique is to use time series data to establish **pre-program and post-program** comparisons. Another, weaker form of impact evaluation is the **single observation** or pre-experimental design. In this method, a program or policy is implemented and then measurements are taken of outcomes. Assume, for example, that a government job creation program allocates $300 million for employment in depressed regions. Within a year it is found that 80 percent of program participants are regularly employed. This actually says little about the real program impact, however, because the participants might have been self-selecting (i.e., only motivated individuals participated) or because the economy might have improved generally. A variation of the single observation technique is the pre-program/post-program scheme, which does try to compare scores before and after an intervention, but only for a single group. Without a control group, it is impossible to tell whether any differences in the scores are due to the program intervention or some other cause. A final, widely used, but not very powerful, design for determining impact is **contrasted groups**. In this design, program recipients are compared to nonrecipients, and the differences are ascribed to the program.

PROCESS EVALUATION

Process evaluation monitors an existing program to assess the effort put into it (Posvac and Carey, 1980, p. 12). This is not the same as measuring success. As Patton (2002) puts it, process evaluation involves looking at "*how* something happens rather than or in addition to examining outputs and outcomes" (p. 159). Typically, reporting systems are developed to provide agencies with information about target populations, extent of coverage, and delivery mechanisms. Process evaluation can review program guidelines, the organization of field offices, staff training, communications systems, and even staff morale to improve organizational performance. It takes the program for granted and aims at improving the process whereby goals are met. This may sound a tad pedestrian, but is both conceptually important and, in practical terms, accounts for a great deal of what actually passes for program evaluation:

> Process evaluations aim at elucidating and understanding the internal dynamics of how a program, organization, or relationship operates. Process studies focus on the following kinds of

questions: What are the things people experience that makes this program what it is? How are clients brought into the program, and how do they move through the program once they are participants? How is what people do related to what they're trying to (or actually do) accomplish? What are the strengths and weaknesses of the program from the perspective of participants and staff? What is the nature of staff-client interactions? . . . Process data permit judgments about the extent to which the program or organization is operating the way it is supposed to be operating, revealing areas in which relationships can be improved as well as highlighting strengths of the program that should be preserved. (Patton, 2002, pp. 159–60)

Process evaluation is clearly linked to implementation and can be thought of as the evaluation of implementation procedures. This helps clarify the importance of process evaluation to program evaluation as a whole, as well as its link to impact analysis. In Chapter 5 we pointed out that the quality of implementation is quite distinct from the quality of a program—bad programs can be well implemented, and vice versa. Process evaluation is a natural complement to impact evaluation, since we need to know whether observed outcomes are the result of the program intervention as it was planned or are due to quirks in the delivery. In other words, program theory and design (the causal links and interventions sketched in Figure 7.3) may be fine, but the execution is flawed. If we can assure ourselves that execution is as planned, then any failures will be due to program design. This, of course, makes it sound as though implementation and impact can be neatly severed, and they cannot. But they do represent different orientations in evaluative work.

Scheirer (1994, p. 45) points out that the full description of "**program components**" is the foundation of process analysis, though the concept of "**program logic**" is sometimes used to sketch out the causal links for impact evaluation (Framst, 1995). Scheirer defines program components as "strategies, activities, behaviors, media products, and technologies needed to deliver the program, along with a specification of the intended recipients and delivery situations" (p. 45). This is tougher than it sounds and requires extended interviews with both program administrators and clients to see what the components are and how well they are being implemented. The next trick is to determine what good or effective implementation entails. It is not directly linked to desired outcomes, which is the realm of impact evaluation. Rather, it tries to determine what the desired outcome is, and then asks what steps or mechanisms the program itself envisions in delivering the intervention to achieve that outcome. A training program for middle-aged unemployed workers, for example, assumes that better training will lead to jobs. This is questionable in many cases, but the process evaluator takes it as given. She then asks what program components go into the delivery of that training: classrooms, syllabus, materials, staff, and equipment. It should be possible to develop criteria that let us measure whether a training program is being delivered well or badly (e.g., rundown facilities, disorganization, unqualified instructors, broken equipment). If delivery quality varies, then assuming that the program is properly designed, the path to improvement is to work on better implementation. If the quality of implementation is generally high across a range of sites, but outcomes are still poor, then the problem would seem to be in program design.

As we will see in the next section of this chapter, the general field of process evaluation has grown dramatically in the last twenty years. Evaluation as a whole has become more important as governments are under pressure to be more results oriented. Impact evaluation, the analysis of results, is not easy or cheap, and there is a natural inclination to assume the design is fine, and that disappointing outcomes must be due to inadequate effort. At the same time, governments are looking more to consumer or client satisfaction as a key program outcome, and this often has more to do with delivery parameters than with the causal modelling underlying program design. Delivery parameters are more commonly referred to as "benchmarks," and typically focus on performance rather than process, though the two are related. Performance measures or benchmarks for concrete services are usually based on measures of workload, efficiency, effectiveness, or productivity. There is a particularly rich mine of such measures at the municipal level (Ammons, 1996). Finally, as more and more programs are delivered by nongovernmental organizations, and as more of their financial and organizational support comes from groups of partners (firms, government, foundations), these partners want to monitor how well things are proceeding. Monitoring tends to be more casual and less systematic than process evaluation, but they are "similar kinds of inquiry" (Weiss, 1998, p. 181). These, and other forces, have conspired in recent years to raise the profile of process analysis quite significantly.

A species of process evaluation known as performance reporting or managing for results, has become quite important in Canada, the United States, and many other OECD countries. In fact, in the United States, as a result of the 1993 Government Performance and Results Act, all federal government agencies must submit to the Director of the Office of Management and Budget and to Congress strategic plans on performance goals and evaluation plans to measure that performance.

Performance reporting and management depends on the distinction between inputs, outputs, outcomes, and indicators (Schacter, 1999).

Inputs are the resources allocated to programs and organizations. Outputs are the activities government agencies undertake, such as the provision of services. Outcomes are the eventual results of those activities in terms of the public good. Indicators are the empirical measures of inputs, outputs, and outcomes. The thrust of performance measurement is to train attention on outcomes—what ultimately matters the most— and link them to a logical model that connects inputs (resources) with activities, outputs, and outcomes. Looked at in this way, performance measurement is about much more than simply measuring things—it entails a management regime that requires a public organization to have a clear idea of what its objectives are, and a regular means of reporting on its success in achieving those objectives. Performance reporting is thus different from policy or program evaluation, which typically takes place near the end of a program's life and is more of a one-time analysis of program impacts. Performance measurement should be viewed as part of a larger management regime, which should try to link results with strategic planning and budgeting and resource allocation.

It is important to get several key factors right in order to do performance measurement properly and successfully (*The Performance Based Management Handbook,* 2001).

- *Clarity about the program:* Since performance measurement is about measuring the success of a program, it is vital to know what that program is about and what its intended objectives are. This is more difficult than it seems, since different people in an organization may have different ideas about what their program is actually about. "Profile—a concise description of the policy, program or initiative, including a discussion of the background, need, target population, delivery approach, resources, governance structure and planned results" (Treasury Board of Canada, 2001a)

- *Logic model:* At the heart of any process of performance reporting is a "logic model" that ties inputs to activities, to short-term, intermediate, and final or ultimate outcomes. Part of the challenge of performance measurement is coming up with indicators for these different levels of outcomes, and coming to judgments about the specific contribution of an agency and its activities to eventual outcomes. A logic model is an illustration of the results chain or how the activities of a policy, program, or initiative are expected to lead to the achievement of the final outcomes. (Treasury Board of Canada, 2001a)

- *Judgment:* The paradox of performance measurement is that while it is driven by a desire for precision and a clear assessment of the contribution of government programs to specific outcomes, the literature acknowledges that there are huge technical problems associated with disentangling the specific effect of those programs from all of the other factors that might contribute to those outcomes. This means that successful performance measurement has to acknowledge that there is always an element of judgment. That judgment can be disciplined and careful, but it still is judgment. It is important to acknowledge the limits of both the indicators one chooses and the evidence for those indicators. This in turn has consequences for the presentation of the performance report. Rather than try to come up with hard, conclusive links between inputs, activities, and outcomes, evaluators are encouraged to tell a **"performance story"** that provides a credible portrait in narrative form of results and expectations, mentioning both anticipated as well as unanticipated outcomes (Mayne, 2003, pp. 13–14).

- *Attribution:* A key challenge in performance measurement is attribution, or determining what a program's contribution has been to a specific outcome. The more difficult question is usually determining just what contribution the specific program in question made to the outcome. How much of the success (or failure) can we attribute to the program? What has been the contribution made by the program? Despite the measurement difficulty, attribution is a problem that cannot be ignored when trying to assess the performance of government programs. Without an answer to this question, little can be said about the worth of the program, nor can advice be provided about future directions (Mayne, 2001).

- *Credible indicators:* Performance can be measured only if there are indicators of both outputs and outcomes. Selecting indicators is not automatic, even if a program is explicit about what its intended outcomes are supposed to be. Successful performance measurement depends in part on finding credible indicators that tell you something important about a program, and that can be successfully measured.

- *Linking resources to results:* Performance measurement is not an end in itself. It should contribute to the wider process of governmental resource allocation. In principle, if programs are found to be underperforming, resources should be moved out of them to other programs that are achieving deeper public benefits. Moreover, linking resources to results is a mechanism for supporting transparency in government decisions as well as stronger accountability to citizens.

- *Sustainability—part of a strategy:* Performance measurement needs to be part of a broader, ongoing strategy of performance assessment. It cannot be episodic or occasional. This feature touches quite closely on the issue of organizational culture, since it highlights the fact that proponents of performance measurement are not simply looking for a new tool of governance, but at changing the way in which governance operates. The ultimate goal is government that continually tries to do better, to be more responsive, and to assess its activities against standards and benchmarks. This is a strategic focus, not simply a technical one.

Getting these factors right is a critical ingredient in the successful establishment of a performance measurement regime. At one level, most of these factors reflect technical considerations and methodological issues—this is clear, for example, for the design of a logic model that links inputs to ultimate outcomes, the selection of indicators, and dealing with the attribution problem. But at another level, performance measurement requires organizational change—this is clear, for example, for linking resources to results, and sustainability. But it is also implied in the more technical success factors. "Know the program" means development of consensus on program objectives. The same is true for designing a logic model. The exercise of judgment and allocation of attribution requires reflection on an organization's environment—the organization has to be outward looking.

What then does performance measurement demand of organizations and the people who work in them? The literature highlights four organizational implications of performance measurement. The first is that if a true performance measurement regime is established, it means a focus on performance and outcomes rather than on process or outputs. The latter are clearly easier and safer to deal with. The second is a willingness to be evaluated at both an organizational and a personal level (at minimum through the performance of programs for which one is responsible). The third is a focus on continuous improvement; if performance measurement is to mean anything, it needs to be linked both to the development and adjustment of new programs and to resource allocation. The fourth is greater transparency and accountability; performance measurement means reporting both to the public and to senior managers and political managers.

Combined, these implications can make life in public organizations quite uncomfortable. Assuming that there are sufficient resources in place to establish an effective performance measurement regime, the critical success factor boils down to people thinking and behaving differently in their organizations.

EFFICIENCY EVALUATION

Even if a policy achieves all its objectives and impacts, this might be at an exorbitant cost. Having the desired impact means a policy is effective, but if it is achieved only at great cost, it may not be efficient. Two major techniques are typically used to address this sort of concern: cost-benefit and **cost-effectiveness analysis** (for a detailed overview, see Rossi, Freeman and Lipsey, 1999, chap. 11). Both techniques focus on the problem of resource allocation, since the issue of efficiency in public programs is really the issue of alternative and superior allocations of scarce resources.

Cost-Benefit Analysis

The logic of **cost-benefit analysis** is quite simple. The question is not only whether a policy or program has an impact but also at what cost. Policymakers want to relate costs and benefits in some way. Private businesses do this by measuring profits, though they also monitor other indicators such as productivity. Profit equals income minus expenses, both of which are calculated in monetary terms. As well, business firms measure income (or benefits) from their own perspective, not from the perspective of the consumer using a given product. Government services rarely yield revenue, and since they are services to the community, what counts as "income" is the benefit from the point of view of the community. The translation of these **social benefits** into purely monetary terms is sometimes difficult compared to a private firm, which simply bases its calculations on a market price. The challenge for government is to go beyond the bottom line (which is either impossible or inappropriate for public programs), and calculate the net social benefit by calculating the difference between total benefits and total costs associated with a program. Thus the basic steps in cost-benefit analysis are logically quite clear (these are explained in more detail below): decide on the accounting unit (whose costs and benefits are to be calculated); catalogue all costs and all benefits over time; monetize (attach a monetary value) to those costs and benefits; discount those costs and benefits over the period of time that the project or program will be operating; and determine the net social benefit.

Table 7.1 gives a simplified example of three policy choices for which costs and benefits have been calculated. Both choices A and B have higher net benefits than choice C, but each of them is less efficient in terms of the ratio of benefits to costs. In other words, each dollar of expenditure in choice C purchases $2 of benefits while choices A and B purchase only $1.50 of benefits. The table also illustrates some of the problems of program choice. Alternative C is clearly the most efficient and would be chosen on that basis. But it also delivers the least net benefit, $1 million compared to $3 million and $2 million for alternatives A and B respectively. One technique is to try to combine net benefit and ratio measures in some way, for example, by comparing the gain in net benefits to the loss in efficiency. The proportional loss in efficiency by

Table 7.1
NET BENEFIT AND COST-BENEFIT CALCULATIONS

Alternative	Benefits	Costs	Benefits – Costs	Benefit/Cost Ratio
A	$9 000 000	$6 000 000	$3 000 000	1.50
B	$6 000 000	$4 000 000	$2 000 000	1.50
C	$2 000 000	$1 000 000	$1 000 000	2.00

moving from C to A (25 percent) is outweighed by the gain in net benefits (200 percent) so that from this perspective, A might be the preferred alternative. A is also preferred over B since, while the ratios of benefits to costs are the same, the net benefits of A are greater than those of B. These examples show that the selection of alternatives is not a mechanical process that follows easily once costs and benefits have been determined. While in the abstract it may seem easy to choose efficiency over net benefits, in the real world, decision criteria are less sharp.

It may appear that a cost-benefit ratio greater than one is self-evidently good, since there is some net gain for an investment of resources. But benefits and costs affect different categories of people, and thus may involve equity considerations or the proportional distribution of benefits and losses equally to similar groups. Cost-benefit analysis, however, is not concerned with distributional or equity issues; it relies on a social welfare criterion known as **Pareto optimality**. This criterion states that a change is worthwhile if at least one person is made better off while no one else is worse off. It is not the same as an increase in total benefits, if that increase depends on someone else's loss. For example, consider a string of ten rural homes, nine of which have barely adequate road access and the tenth none at all. A tax levy on all ten homes to build a new road connecting them could possibly be Pareto optimal, as long as the benefits of improved access for the nine homes equalled the levy. The tenth home would of course be much better off. In this example, everyone is at least as well off as before, and one person may be much better off. Few policy decisions are this clear. The limitations of the Pareto criterion led economists to develop another, more flexible one: the **Kaldor-Hicks criterion**, which identifies potential Pareto improvements as those that, assuming that net gainers could compensate losers, would leave at least one person better off without anyone else worse off. The redistribution is hypothetical, and so in effect the Kaldor-Hicks version of Pareto optimality is a criterion of net benefits. Potential Pareto improvements, it is argued, will increase total societal benefits (for both winners and losers) over time.

Practising evaluators normally leave these arcane matters of social welfare functions to academic economists. From a practical perspective, the tough issues in cost-benefit analysis are the determination and quantification of costs and benefits. Two such general problems are the selection of the **accounting unit** and the issue of **intangibles.** The accounting unit problem is about whose costs and benefits are to be measured. Three basic choices are the individual, the government, and society. Consider an employment agency decision on whether to provide counselling services to its clients. One way of assessing costs and benefits is to focus on the individual program participants: costs might include less time for leisure or job search, while benefits might be increased job skills. From the governmental or agency perspective, costs would be the budgetary ones of mounting the program, while benefits might be increased hiring rates and tax revenues as former clients get jobs. The societal perspective is the most comprehensive, weighing costs and benefits for total national income. Benefits, for instance, might include the value to the national economy of the jobs that clients get. The estimates of benefits and costs will differ depending on the accounting unit chosen.

The problem of intangibles concerns the difficulty of placing monetary values on some costs and benefits. Aesthetic considerations in town planning, the value people place on leisure, the sense of security provided by universal health care: all are presumably important in determining costs and benefits but are difficult to quantify. It is arguable that cost-benefit analyses of public programs tend to estimate costs (program or budget costs) more accurately than benefits, many of which are intangible. Educational policy evaluation, for example, has trouble measuring such benefits as civility and cultural breadth and tends by default to concentrate on job-related benefits. Cost-benefit calculations usually avoid quantifying intangibles, preferring instead to simply mention them as considerations. A related issue is that even if costs and benefits can be monetized, not all of them have an equal chance of occurring. Evaluations thus sometimes attach probabilities to costs and benefits.

The careful classification and treatment of different types of costs is the first step in competent cost-benefit analysis. One important category is **opportunity cost** or the foregone benefits of doing one thing and not another. Assuming scarce resources, doing one thing always means foregoing something else. Cost-benefit analysis, insofar as it tries to facilitate comparisons across alternatives, tries to address the issue of opportunity cost. Other common distinctions are made in determining costs.

External versus internal costs and benefits refer to indirect or unintended spillovers from a program. For example, polluting industries sometimes create jobs at home (internal benefit) while generating environmental costs elsewhere (external costs). Incremental versus **sunk costs** is another important distinction. Sunk costs are those incurred in the past; incremental costs are additional or future costs expended to mount or continue a program. A final distinction is between total and **marginal costs.** The total costs of a new counselling program for unwed mothers, for example, would include the proportion of total costs of the agency (e.g., clerical services, furniture, building, heat, light, etc.) accounted for by the program. But since these costs would occur anyway, the marginal cost of the program would be the additional resources devoted to it.

Costs and benefits usually do not occur immediately, and each may flow in different streams. In the case of capital projects or pensions, it may take many years before benefits are realized. This raises a problem of measurement, since most people prefer their benefits to come now and their costs to come later. The element of time therefore has to be assessed in estimates of future costs and benefits. The usual procedure is to apply a **discount rate** to the present value of costs and benefits incurred in a project, to arrive at a measure of net present value (Boardman et al., 2001, chaps. 6, 10). The trick is in selecting an appropriate rate. The predominant method assesses the opportunity costs of capital, meaning the rate of return if program sums were invested in the private sector. If the economy were uncluttered by monopolies or by taxation regimes that alter pretax rates of return and restrictive foreign trade, then market rate of interest could be taken as the discount rate. Because rates of return are affected by these institutional features, economists make numerous and contentious adjustments to arrive at estimates of the real discount rate.

Cost-Effectiveness Analysis

Cost-effectiveness analysis is closely related to cost-benefit analysis and shares many of its concepts. It is a somewhat simpler and more limited technique, but one that acknowledges the shortcomings of cost-benefit approaches. Cost-effectiveness analysis restricts itself to comparing different program alternatives for achieving a given set of goals. It thus differs from cost-benefit analysis, which purports to compare programs with different goals in terms of a common denominator of benefits. Cost-effectiveness analysis refrains from efforts to monetize benefits. It simply takes program goals or outcomes as given, and then assesses different cost strategies for achieving those goals. It assumes that the least-cost strategy is the preferred alternative. Cost-effectiveness techniques can also be applied in reverse by assuming a fixed budget and choosing alternatives that provide the highest rate of goal achievement—the "biggest bang for the buck." So, "cost-effectiveness analysis is most appropriately used where there is already general agreement on the nature of the program outcomes and where the outcomes of the alternatives being compared are the same or very similar" (Guess and Farnham, 2000, p. 251).

Typical cost-effectiveness analysis relates the monetized costs of a program to a nonmonetized measure of effects. A fisheries department, for example, may want to increase the fish stock in a lake by 30 percent over five years, or by 100 000 fish. It can choose between restricting fishing licences and stocking the lake. Restricting licences would require greater surveillance expenditures in the amount of $30 000 per year, while restocking the lake might incur a one-time expenditure of $100 000. Over five years, the first alternative yields a cost-effectiveness ratio of $1.50 per fish, while the second costs $1.00 per fish. It would appear that the second alternative would be more efficient or cost-effective.

Cost-effectiveness analysis poses the same problems as cost-benefit analysis. Which costs to consider? In the fisheries case, only departmental costs were counted, but the first alternative should also include foregone fishing by those excluded from licences. Defining the different types of costs and their relationship would also be necessary as would discounting for the project over the implementation period. But cost-effectiveness analysis makes no judgments of relative benefits; it passes these considerations on to decisionmakers, who apply other criteria. A cost-effectiveness analysis may help determine the cheapest way to build a fighter jet but is incapable of showing whether other uses of those funds would be of greater benefit to society.

POLICY EVALUATION IN CANADA

The tone of the first part of this chapter certainly conveys the impression that program evaluation is an essential part of any reasonable approach to policymaking: how could we presume to make policies and programs, trying to solve policy problems, if we had no idea of impact or efficacy? As odd as it may sound, however, evaluation as it is currently understood and practised is a relatively recent development in governance. Its first golden age was in the 1970s, after which it went into slight decline, though another golden (or at least, silver) age may be dawning. This relatively late start, however, coincides with the rise of the policy analysis movement itself. Both, as Chapter 1 showed, were postwar phenomena associated with the rise of more activist government, particularly in the

1960s. Program evaluation, for example, depends on the application of social science tools that themselves were developed only in this period. More subtly, program evaluation depends on viewing what government does in program terms. We do that now, because after a quarter century of public policy development and the assumption that governments have a wide horizon of responsibilities to deal with social problems, we simply take it for granted that government activity can be understood in terms of numerous clusters of programs, which, after all, are interventions to solve social issues. There was a time when the scope of government was considerably narrower, and its activities could be understood more simply in terms of activities like building roads or bridges, or providing relatively uncomplicated services like education. If everyone gets the same basic education, and the presumption is that the content of that education should adhere to well-established guidelines (e.g., the three Rs, the literary canon), then there is not much point in talking about programs. The type of policy evaluation that goes on within this framework is typically a financial audit, to ensure that monies are spent appropriately. When, however, the different needs of different students (e.g., recent immigrants, people with disabilities, gifted children, girls, boys, adults, illiterate people) have to be addressed, and when different educational goals are targeted (e.g., occupational, academic, life skills), then suddenly what once passed as simply education now needs to be understood in terms of a range of specialized education programs. The type of evaluation that goes on in this context shifts from financial audits to program evaluation of outcomes and efficiency.

As Sutherland (1990) points out, the term "program" first came into formal use in the Canadian federal government's estimates of expenditure only after 1971" (p. 140). Previously, a program "could be anything from the whole effort and apparatus of unemployment insurance to a regrouping of activities to realize a short-term special project" (p. 140). The change was due to the introduction and implementation of the **planning-programming-budgeting system** (PPBS), pioneered in the United States (and ironically, abandoned the same year that the Canadian federal government succeeded in applying it across all departments and in the expenditure budget process). PPBS was foreshadowed in 1969 with the Treasury Board's release of its PPBS Guide (Government of Canada, 1969). The idea was that PPBS would be gradually introduced into the Canadian budgetary process, eventually encouraging all departments to state their activities in programmatic terms, that is, in terms of goals and objectives, specific costs associated with programs designed to achieve those goals, and resources devoted to each program. Ideally, this would permit comparisons across all government agencies of related goals and their related programs. Moreover, the 1969 Guide presumed that once goals and associated programs and resources were identified, then the work of evaluation (principally cost-benefit) could go forward almost automatically. Again, to quote Sutherland (1990): "It was thought that both alternative ways of delivering the same program and different programs could be compared with one another in productivity terms—output per input unit. Analysts would be able to compare strategies for reaching given goals within a given program, but also to compare programs/goals with one another in terms of their expensiveness" (p. 143).

As Savoie (1990) notes, at the time, PPBS was thought by most practitioners and observers to hold "great promise, and few dissident voices were heard" (p. 57). Some provincial governments swiftly followed suit, most notably New Brunswick, which introduced PPBS in 1970. However, by the mid-1970s, the bloom was off the PPBS rose. Some of the wilting had to do with the failure of PPBS to help manage expenditures. In the Canadian context, PPBS had been introduced as part of the budget system, on the assumption that rigorous analysis and comparison of objectives and programs would automatically generate information that would clarify planning as well as facilitate reallocations of resources to more efficient and effective programs. That did not happen, in part because the logic of PPBS was entangled with another agenda at the time to reduce central agency control over departments. Given that PPBS did not produce a lot of good analysis, the result was less overview and more spending (Savoie, 1990, pp. 60–61). The second problem was that, even with substantially new resources being devoted to analysis, evaluation, and consulting, the results of cost-benefit and performance analysis "could generate only a drop in the ocean of analysis that would be required if every identified purpose-oriented spending entity was to be tracked" (Sutherland, 1990, p. 144).

There were two responses to this. The first was from the Treasury Board and consisted of an odd blend of both extending and limiting the scope of program evaluation. In 1977 it issued Treasury Board Policy Circular 1977–47, which for the first time formally stated the requirement that all federal government programs periodically undergo an evaluation (Leclerc, 1992, p. 51). The 1977 circular was followed in 1981 with a formal guide to evaluation that remained in place for a decade (Treasury Board of Canada, Office of the Comptroller General, 1981). However, whereas the earlier PPBS framework had implicitly assumed that evaluations would take place automatically, rely principally on cost-benefit analysis, and generate comparative information across programs, the new policy left the evaluation cycle (three to five years) and the selection of programs to be reviewed up to administrators; it did not recommend any specific form of evaluation, and eschewed comparison (Sutherland, 1990, pp. 144–45). Thus, with a kind of logic that would delight Lewis Carroll, program evaluation became both universally mandated for all federal government programs over time and yet was left up to the discretion of departmental managers as to targets and techniques of evaluation. We will come to some assessments of the scope and impact of program evaluation in the federal government as a result of these policies, but it should be clear that the context had been set for *ad hoc,* politically inspired, and relatively insipid evaluation. Evaluation as it came to be understood and institutionalized in Canada evolved into a "strategic management tool for departments and agencies" (Segsworth, 1992, p. 305). Program evaluation sank into the soft folds of the bureaucratic underbelly and became an information source for managers to improve programs rather than a real tool of accountability and comparison. In itself, there is nothing objectionable in the use of program evaluation for management purposes, but its almost exclusive dedication to this end falls far short of its potential.

The second response to the failure of PPBS came from the auditor general of Canada. J. J. Macdonnell was appointed auditor general in 1973 and began to press for the establishment of a comptroller general for the government of Canada. (A position by that name had existed previously but had been abolished in the mid-1960s.) Macdonnell was a private sector accountant and wanted to establish private sector accounting practices in the government. He tried to persuade senior cabinet ministers of the idea, but they balked at the duplication of existing Treasury Board functions. Macdonnell then dropped a verbal bomb in his 1976 report when he stated that "I am deeply concerned that Parliament—and indeed the Government—has lost, or is close to losing, effective control of the public purse" (Auditor General of Canada, 1976, p. 9). The media seized on this, and the government was forced to announce a Royal Commission on Financial Management and Accountability as well as negotiate with Macdonnell on the establishment of the Office of Comptroller General. The office was indeed established, with "full responsibility for the coordination of evaluation planning, for policy guidance, and for assessing the quality of evaluation findings in studies carried out by departments" (Savoie, 1990, p. 114). However, it was more a political sop than an indication of commitment to evaluation. Nonetheless, it happened that "program evaluation did indeed develop into a growth industry and that it grew around the Office of the Comptroller General" (Savoie, 1990, p. 114). The special link through program evaluation was thus established between the comptroller general, the auditor general, and departments. The comptroller general provides guidelines and advice on evaluation, but evaluations themselves are conducted by departments. The auditor general cannot independently conduct evaluations but reports on the success or failure of evaluation across the government. Nonetheless, as a result of these changes, "the scope of the 'audit' of government spending in federal Canada has undergone a more significant transformation than in any other Westminster system . . . from reporting on the ledgers of expenditure to contesting . . . the legitimacy of policy conceived by election Governments" (Sutherland, 1999, p. 112).

The 1981 evaluation guide was updated and altered in 1991 as a result of a policy shift to reflect the logic of PS2000. This change, and the 1994 amendment discussed below, both illustrate the degree to which evaluation is a reflection of the institutional and policy environment and not simply a bundle of techniques that can be generically applied. The key change was a new emphasis on evaluations that would focus on quality of service to the public. In a document entitled *Into the 90s: Government Program Evaluation Perspectives*, the comptroller general explained the new approach:

> PS2000 is about reorienting the Public Service. One of the reforms it calls for is the restoration of the preeminence of service to the public when carrying out the functions of government. Establishing a consultative, client-centred corporate culture requires research, and program evaluation offers a unique range of skills and experience to improve the delivery and cost-effectiveness of programs. A sample of recent evaluations shows that a variety of service issues were addressed and that some of them led to better quality of service to the public.

> But, program evaluation offers more than just balanced, analytic methods and a digest of lessons learned. Many evaluators employ client-based consultations to carry out and market their studies. With a little broadening and some deepening of the stakeholder base, this approach could become an effective conduit for program managers not only to assess the quality of their service to the public but also to create a receptive environment for change. (Treasury Board of Canada, Office of the Comptroller General, 1991, pp. 1–2)

What did this new evaluation industry achieve between 1977 and the early 1990s? First, the quantity of evaluations began to rise dramatically. In 1980 there were only seven program evaluations in the government of Canada that met the definition in the guidelines. By 1984–85, thirty-seven federal departments were conducting them and there were over 100 studies (Savoie, 1990, p. 114). The annual number of evaluations has settled around that level. The auditor general reported that in 1991–92 there were eighty evaluations conducted across the federal government, compared with ninety-nine in 1987–88 (Auditor General of Canada, 1993, p. 247). The auditor general conducted wide-ranging reviews of the evaluation function in the federal government in his annual reports in 1983 and 1986 and was generally critical of their quality. The 1993 report, based on data from forty-two program evaluation units, noted that both the annual number of evaluations and the resources devoted to them were in decline (pp. 244–45). Examining a sample of these, the report noted that "in only about half of the programs did evaluation deal with program relevance and cost-effectiveness" (p. 230):

> Evaluation managers attached the greatest importance to helping management resolve operational issues and improve programs. They placed a much lower priority on the role of evaluation in challenging existing programs to support resource allocation decisions, and on evaluating large program units to support accountability to Parliament. (p. 245)

The 1996 annual report of the auditor general, while noting that the context for evaluation in the federal government had changed quite dramatically in three years since its last review of evaluation, still found the government's efforts wanting (Auditor General of Canada, 1996, chap. 3). In examining four departments in detail, the auditor general found that evaluations still focused on smaller operational details of greater interest to administrators than to Parliament or the public. On balance, there had been some improvements, but the auditor general's conclusions were still mixed: "We still see weaknesses in planning, in monitoring action in response to the findings of evaluation studies, and in implementing systematic approaches to assessing the performance of evaluation units" (Auditor General of Canada, 1996, chap. 3).

What of the impact of evaluation studies? The evidence is mixed. Certainly, the auditor general has consistently crabbed about the low quality and general ineffectiveness of program evaluation. However, some other studies suggest that evaluations do have an impact. In a study of 200 evaluations conducted between 1983 and 1989, it was found that almost half (45 percent) led to operational improvements in programs, with the next largest category (26 percent) used to "improve understanding of program cost-effectiveness and to improve monitoring" (cited in Leclerc, 1992, p. 52). While many studies (16 percent) influenced program redesign or implementation, only about 4 percent had no impact. Segsworth (1992) concurs that there was an impact in this early period but that it was limited more to program operations rather than live-or-die decisions about program continuity:

> Evaluation research is utilized in Canada. The policy suggests that the primary users would be senior managers in departments and the Executive Branch. This has happened. It is also true that Parliament has not used evaluation studies to any great extent over the past 15 years since the policy on program evaluation was introduced. (p. 308)

Savoie (1990), on the other hand, noted for the same period that there were "few supporters in Ottawa of program evaluations" (p. 114) and that "one would be hard pressed to point to even a handful of programs that have been reduced or eliminated as a result of an evaluation study" (p. 115).

If this indeed were the end of the story, then we might conclude that evaluation in the government of Canada plays a relatively minor role in operations and review, with periodic harping from the auditor general to maximize the potential of program evaluation for policy decisionmaking. However, events over the last five years suggest that evaluation, or at least policy reflection of a more fundamental sort, is enjoying greater prominence. It began, as we outlined earlier, with the 1995 budget and the Program Review. In that phase, in the late 1990s, the focus was on spending cuts, and so evaluation was driven by fiscal considerations. After achieving surplus in 1998, the gears shifted to a focus on prudent financial management and a focus on results.

By 1994, PS2000 had been submerged in a broader agenda of Program Review, and the new guidelines aimed to integrate the evaluation function with this new agenda. One of the most important features of the new framework was that it was indeed a framework. It brought together guidelines for program review, internal audit, and evaluation under one roof. Program Review goals set the parameters for the other functions, all of which were harnessed to "support the principles of managing by results" (Treasury Board of Canada, 1994, p. 1-1-2). Another key feature was the attempt to integrate the evaluative function more closely with management. In characteristic Canadian fashion, evaluation still remained a management tool, and the 1994 policy urged a "productive alliance between managers and review professionals that will link review more visibly to management decision-making and innovation, as well as accountability" (Treasury Board of Canada, 1994, p. 1-1-2).

The 1994 policy was superseded by a new one in 2001. The focus remained on linking evaluation to management:

> Managing for results is the prime responsibility of public service managers. As outlined in the management framework for

the federal government, Results for Canadians, public service managers are expected to define anticipated results, continually focus attention towards results achievement, measure performance regularly and objectively, and learn and adjust to improve efficiency and effectiveness.

Managers must be accountable for their performance to higher management, to ministers, to Parliament and to Canadians.

Evaluation—like internal audit, risk management capacity and other management tools—helps managers to operate effectively in this environment. Evaluation can support managers' efforts to track and report on actual performance and help decision-makers objectively assess program or policy results. This distinguishes evaluation from internal audit—a function that provides assurances on a department or agency's risk management strategy, management control framework and information, both financial and non-financial, used for decision-making and reporting. (Treasury Board of Canada, 2001b)

Supporting the new *Results for Canadians* management framework and the new evaluation policy was the development of a template for a Results-based Management and Accountability Framework (RMAF). Departments were required, in addition to the normal reporting functions, to develop RMAFs for all policies and programs. The key components of an RMAF are

1. *Profile*—a concise description of the policy, program or initiative, including a discussion of the background, need, target population, delivery approach, resources, governance structure and planned results.

2. *Logic model*—an illustration of the results chain or how the activities of a policy, program or initiative are expected to lead to the achievement of the final . . . outcomes.

3. *Ongoing performance measurement strategy*—a plan for the ongoing measurement of performance, including the identification of indicators for the outputs and outcomes in the logic model and a measurement strategy describing how these indicators will be collected, how often and at what cost.

4. *Evaluation strategy*—a plan for the evaluation of the policy, program or initiative, including the identification of formative and summative evaluation issues and questions, the identification of associated data requirements, and a data collection strategy which will serve as the foundation for subsequent evaluation activities.

5. *Reporting strategy*—a plan to ensure the systematic reporting on the results of ongoing performance measurement as well as evaluation, to ensure that all reporting requirements are met. (Treasury Board of Canada, 2001a)

In 2003, the Treasury Board conducted an interim evaluation of its evaluation policy (Treasury Board of Canada, 2003). The policy had been in existence for only eighteen months, but continued funding for initiatives under the policy was contingent on an evaluation. The results were mixed. Implementation of the policy varied significantly among departments, and smaller agencies reported limited or nonexistent evaluation functions. While departments were making improvements, there was still a "capacity gap" of roughly one-third in terms of personnel needs to staff evaluation positions. More worryingly, the report noted that "Projected workloads are forecast to increase at a rate of approximately 200% over the upcoming two years while the number of evaluation staff is expected to increase by only 20–30% over the same time period." The general evaluation capacity in both large and small (but especially small) departments was considered "minimal," and it was not clear whether RMAFs were being effectively implemented.

These were, to say the least, somewhat sobering conclusions, particularly in an environment where the federal government had from 2000 to 2004 made results and performance and reporting the cornerstones of its public sector management policy. For example, the 2000 Treasury Board president's annual report, *Results for Canadians,* listed four key management commitments: citizen focus, values, responsible spending, and results.

> A modern management agenda requires managers to look beyond activities and outputs to focus on actual results—the impacts and effects of their programs. Managing for results requires attention from the beginning of an initiative to its end. It means clearly defining the results to be achieved, delivering the program or service, measuring and evaluating performance and making adjustments to improve both efficiency and effectiveness. It also means reporting on performance in ways that make sense to Canadians.
>
> A results-based management approach allows departments to serve Canadians better by distinguishing program strengths and weaknesses and providing guidance on what does and does not work.
>
> The challenge for the future is to apply results-based management to all major activities, functions, services and programs

of the Government of Canada, whether they are delivered directly to Canadians or are part of internal administration. This will continue to advance sound management practice and strengthen accountability throughout departments and agencies. (Treasury Board of Canada, 2000)

This was accompanied by a reporting regime developed in the late 1990s, consisting of annual **departmental performance reports (DPRs)**, and **reports on plans and priorities (RPP)**. So, in terms of formal policies, there could be no doubt that by 2004 there was a strong emphasis on evaluation, reporting, and results. But the interim evaluation conducted by Treasury Board indicated that on the ground, the evaluation function was much weaker than it might appear, and quite uneven across departments. Once again we see the influence of new public management (NPM) thinking on the organization and process of government—particularly toward a new **results orientation**—but in this instance with a particularly Canadian twist. In Britain, for example, the same efforts to de-bureaucratize the public sector have not relied on what is essentially "self-reporting" by departments and agencies. There, the shift to "performance accountability" from "compliance accountability" was accompanied by some reduction in internal regulation but also by a "shift towards more oversight regulation in government, involving more formal procedures and in places increased confrontation between regulator and regulatee" (Hood et al., 1999, p. 194). The Canadian approach hinges on the concept of "modern comptrollership," which, while not devoid of oversight controls, tends to rely less on detailed monitoring and rather more on "advice and guidance" from the Treasury Board (Potter, 2000, p. 98) and concordats between departments and the Board. Thus, in the Canadian context, performance reporting and the commitment to results must be seen as part of a larger shift in the organizational framework of government and policymaking.

The irony in all this is that after years of efforts and high-sounding principle, the federal government's reputation for fiscal probity and for results by 2004 was no better—and possibly worse—than in 1995. A series of sensational "scandals" seemed to fix in the public mind (with the help of opposition parties and the media) that Ottawa was about as circumspect in its spending as a sailor on shore leave. The HRDC affair, discussed earlier, was the first. The gun registry—which ballooned to over $1 billion after officials promised it would cost $2 million after cost recovery—became emblematic of wildly costly policies that had dubious results. The Groupaction scandal in early 2004 was the last nail in the coffin, as far as public opinion went. The reality was surely different, as we noted with the HRDC affair—a so-called billion-dollar boondoggle ended up actually being a matter of $85 000. But there can be no avoiding the conclusion that performance evaluation and reporting has not made as much headway in the federal government as one would think studying the policy documents. There are several possible reasons for this. First, as we noted, the Canadian approach has been to avoid strong external evaluation functions, and integrate evaluation with management. There is nothing wrong with this, but it does leave the fox guarding the chicken coop. Second, it has to be recognized that performance evaluation takes place in specific institutional contexts. De Bruijn (2002) talks about the "perverse effects" of performance measurement: among other things, it can stimulate strategic behaviour where organizations focus on performance indicators only (in order to score points); it can stifle innovation if organizations decide that innovation is too risky (and hence will lose performance points); and good performance may even sometimes lead to punishment (for example, when a well-performing organization gets its budget cut because "it's doing so well it can probably do as well with less"). Introducing a performance regime without addressing these perversities mean that it might become more a charade than a viable management tool.

CONCLUSION

Program evaluation has always enjoyed support, in principle, from policymakers. The logic of policy analysis, as described in Chapter 1, emphasizes careful definition of policy problems, consideration of options, and interventions that lead to amelioration or improvement. Policy as intervention depends on some idea of causal connections. In this sense, every policy or program is a guess, a hypothesis about social problems. Evaluation serves the vital function of providing empirical feedback on those hypotheses in action: did they work, what impact did the intervention have, at what cost? It is for this reason that public policy theory urges the integration of policy evaluation into every stage of the policy process; since evaluation in a sense is the collective memory of what worked and what did not, integration of that information can save errors and effort.

But just as evaluation has been granted this pivotal role in theory, in practice it has been viewed skeptically and often marginalized in the policy process. The reasons are not hard to understand. Even the strongest partisans of evaluation acknowledge the often severe methodological limitations of answering impact and efficiency questions. More art than science, it is always possible to find reasons why positive or negative evaluation results are flawed. These very limitations, as well as the sheer expense of doing thorough evaluations, have usually limited evaluation to routine monitoring or process studies. Also, as we noted, there is the paradox that while evaluation seems essential in theory, in practice it can appear to be a frill when compared to direct program responsibilities and delivery. Thus, evaluation has been the poor cousin of the policy process, often relegated to small policy analysis units divorced from direct policy management responsibilities. "By the early 1980s analytical units were reported to be in decline. Few new units were being established and existing units had declined in organizational influence and importance" (Hollander and Prince, 1993, p. 196). Insofar as evaluation tends to be the dismal science of policy analysis—showing that impacts are weak or dubious, and often much more expensive than first anticipated—nobody really appreciates the bad news.

To these generic reasons for the limited impact of evaluation should be added some specific Canadian twists. First, as we noted in the brief history of the Office of Comptroller General, the establishment of evaluation guidelines and institutions in the Canadian federal government in the early 1980s was done partly to placate the auditor general and was implemented without much enthusiasm. Second, the Canadian practice, and this is true of the provincial level of government as well, has been to use evaluation as a management tool. Evaluation units have been embedded in departments, and departmental managers have been responsible for the evaluation function, governed by loose central agency guidelines. This contrasts with the United States, where congressional committees aggressively sponsor evaluation of programs within their policy fields as a challenge to the executive and where independent **think-tanks** and policy groups abound. The parliamentary system tends to be more closed to outside influences than the U.S. congressional system, and so the "evaluation climate" created by vibrant and vocal think-tanks is not as rich in Canada as it is in the United States. To this must be added cultural (Canada seems to encourage less policy entrepreneurship) and economic (Canada's philanthropists have not channelled as much money into think-tanks and foundations) influences (Abelson and Carberry, 1998; Abelson and Lindquist, 2000; Abelson, 2002). The best estimate is that there are only about 100 think-tanks in Canada and, among them, fewer than ten major nongovernmental, noncommercial policy institutes (e.g., C. D. Howe Research Institute, Canada West Foundation, Conference Board of Canada, Canadian Tax Foundation, Fraser Institute, Institute for Research on Public Policy, Canadian Institute for Economic Policy, and Canadian Energy Research Institute). Despite the high visibility of some think-tanks and policy institutes in the media and at specific points in the policy cycle (Abelson, 1999), and the occasionally headline-grabbing report (e.g., the Fraser

Institute's 2004 report on legalizing and taxing marijuana), most think-tanks generate relatively bland publications.

Canadian parliamentary committees have shown scant interest in evaluation studies. Evaluation reports are usually kept within departments as part of their policy development process, and public inquiries about particular studies are usually discouraged by claiming that these studies are sensitive or secret. Public debate about evaluation results of policies or programs is rarely stimulated by the media, and Canada lacks serious, wide-circulation media, such as *The Atlantic Monthly*, which act as vehicles for debating and evaluating public policy issues.

Despite this gloomy assessment of evaluation and its potential to influence policymaking, this chapter has shown that evaluation may be enjoying a fitful renaissance of sorts. Evaluation may not only be getting marginally more important in government, but also the nature of evaluation itself may be changing. For example, the new emphasis on results of performance management means that the goals or outcomes of policy and programs are defined more broadly than ever before, and evaluation is supposed to find indicators and measures, something that practising evaluators are not always sure is possible. A focus on results will encourage more impact-oriented evaluations. However, current policy paradigms stress client satisfaction and a service orientation as outcomes. This means that the old division between process and impact analysis might be blurring, and increasingly the key impacts sought by policymakers are satisfaction and support of the process and program itself. This is abetted by the new information resources available to policymakers.

When one thinks like a client or a customer, one is thinking in terms not only of concrete results of a program intervention but also of how one was treated in the process that led to that intervention. Critics of the NPM described in Chapter 5 are rightly cautious about the shift from citizen to customer in contemporary policy talk. At one level it may indeed represent a diminished sense of the public purpose and public role of citizens in policymaking. But that shift also has some empowering aspects—a "program recipient" is a potentially more passive category than "customer." As evaluation stresses customer satisfaction, we can expect more resources to flow to client polling, focus groups, and other feedback mechanisms to guide policy and program development. The federal government has noted that continuous "improvement in client service depends on the capacity of departments and agencies to measure levels of satisfaction, to set improvement targets, to develop plans to meet those targets, to monitor implementation and to report back on progress" (Treasury Board of Canada, 2000).

There is a great deal to be skeptical about in policy and program evaluation, in performance measurement and results, but we prefer to end on an optimistic and uplifting note. Yes, in practice, evaluation studies can seem so insipid, qualified, and immersed in murky politics as to appear useless. Some critics dismiss evaluation as a policy sideshow, a carnival of dubious methodological handsprings and somersaults that rarely yields serious results. For other critics, insofar as evaluation is dominated by expert discourse, it threatens democracy by drawing debate away from ordinary citizens and entrapping it in a closed universe of language only a few can speak. This fear is surely overdrawn, particularly given the limited role that evaluation has played in Canadian policymaking and the new emphasis on making performance and results measurement accessible to citizens. We are tempted to make the opposite argument, though well aware that it holds certain dangers as well. The basic questions that form the foundations of program evaluation are vital to any democratic discussion of public policy—what works and at what cost? These are not the only questions that one can pose about policy, but they are important ones, which if seriously addressed can only benefit policy discussion. Canadian efforts should continue to emphasize the importance of broad evaluation of policy, as well as the wider exposure and dissemination of evaluation results.

KEY TERMS

accountability—the quality of being accountable to another for one's actions; entailing an obligation to respond to questions and regularly report

accounting unit—in doing cost-benefit analysis, the unit or jurisdiction in which costs and benefits will be ascribed

causal chain—the link of various causes and effects in producing outcomes in the implementation process

contrasted group design—an experimental evaluation design where recipients are compared to nonrecipients, and the differences are ascribed to the program

control group—in experimental designs, the randomly assigned group that will not be the recipient of the intervention or program and that will form the basis of comparison with the experimental group

cost-benefit analysis—evaluation of a program in terms of its total costs compared to its total benefits, expressed in monetary terms

cost-effectiveness analysis—compares different program alternatives for achieving a given set of goals; it is also applied by considering a fixed budget and choosing alternatives that provide the highest rate of goal achievement

departmental performance report (DPR)—annual report on performance of each federal department for the previous fiscal year

dependent variable—the variable that is being explained

diagnostic procedures—procedures in which the evaluators are often involved in generating and analyzing data that are relevant to problem definition, trend forecasting, and program design aspects

discount rate—the rate chosen to discount future benefits, usually assessed as the opportunity costs of capital, meaning the rate of return if program sums were invested in the private sector

experimental design—the evaluation of impact based on randomly assigned experimental and control groups

experimental group—the randomly assigned group to which the program or intervention is applied in an experimental design

formative evaluation—evaluation designed to support development and improvement of a program as it is being implemented

impact evaluation—analysis of the actual effect or impact of a program on its intended target, along with unintended consequences

implementation theory—the specific activities and resources that need to be mobilized in connection with each of the links in the program's causal chain to achieve the desired outcome

intangibles—the costs and benefits of a program for which it is difficult to place monetary values

Kaldor-Hicks criterion—identifies potential Pareto improvements as those that, assuming that net gainers could compensate losers, would leave at least one person better off without anyone else worse off

logic model—usually a graphical representation of the links between program inputs, activities, outputs, immediate outcomes, and long-term results

marginal cost—the additional unit of cost of doing something

meta-analysis—a technique where evaluators review the existing literature on a specific program, treating each evaluation study as a single case and building statistical conclusions based on these observations

modern comptrollership—tends to rely less on detailed monitoring and rather more on "advice and guidance" from the Treasury Board and concordats between departments and the Board

needs assessment—a review of the service and support needs of a particular agency or group

opportunity cost—the foregone benefits of doing one thing and not another

Pareto optimality—the criterion of optimization that states that a change is worthwhile if at least one person is made better off while no one else is worse off

partial-coverage program—program that is not available for the entire population that might need it, either because of resource constraints or other reasons

performance story—reporting of program results in such a way as to highlight both successes and shortcomings, the challenges faced by the organization, and what it might do in the future to improve results

planning-programming-budgeting system (PPBS)—encourages departments to state their activities in programmatic terms, that is, in terms of goals and objectives, specific costs associated with programs designed to achieve those goals, and resources devoted to each program

pre-program/post-program design—an evaluation technique that uses time-series data for the period before program implementation and after to draw conclusions about the likely impact of the intervention

process evaluation—monitors an existing program to assess the effort and organizational resources put into it

program components—typically, the strategies, activities, behaviours, media products, and technologies needed to deliver the program, along with a specification of the intended recipients and delivery situations

program evaluation—an essential part of any reasonable approach to policymaking that assesses, in some sense, how well programs are doing in terms of their stated objectives

program logic—sketches out the assumed causal links that will yield specified outcomes in order to conduct impact evaluation

program theory—the hypotheses and explanations about the causal links that tie program inputs to expected program outputs

RPPs (reports on plans and priorities)—annual report required from each federal government department and agency about their plans and priorities for the coming fiscal year

quasi-experimental design—all contrasted or comparing group designs that fall short of the demand for completely random assignment of the groups

random assignment of groups—a method used in experimental design where the odds of being in either the experimental or control group are the same

results orientation—a management focus on new forms of review, audit, and evaluation based on results

single observation design—a method of evaluation that relies on a measure of impact only after the program is introduced

social benefits—the benefits obtained from the point of view of the community of the services provided by government

social indicators—data that represent important characteristics of society such as crime, literacy, health; contrasted to the usual economic indicators such as inflation and unemployment

summative evaluation—an evaluation undertaken at the end of a program to gauge its success

sunk cost—costs that have incurred in the past and that are not recoverable

think-tanks—nongovernmental, sometimes for-profit and sometimes nonprofit, organizations dedicated to research and discussion of policy issues with the wider public and decisionmakers

Weblinks

American Evaluation Association
http://www.eval.org

Canadian Evaluation Society
http://www.evaluationcanada.ca

International Society for Performance Improvement
http://www.ispi.org

Manpower Research Demonstration Corporation
http://www.mdrc.org

Social Research and Development Corporation
http://www.srdc.org

Further Readings

Boardman, A. E., Greenberg, D. H., Vining, A., and Weimer, D. L. (2001). *Cost-benefit analysis: Concepts and practice*. Upper Saddle River, NJ: Prentice-Hall.

de Bruijn, H. (2002). *Managing performance in the public sector.* London: Routledge.

Mayne, J. (2003). *Reporting on outcomes: Setting performance expectations and telling performance stories.* Ottawa: Office of the Auditor General of Canada. Retrieved September 4, 2004, from http://www.oag-bvg.gc.ca/domino/other.nsf/html/200305dpl_e.html/$file/200305dpl_e.pdf

Patton, M. Q. (2002). *Qualitative research and evaluation methods* (3rd ed.). Thousand Oaks, CA: Sage.

Rossi, P. H., Freeman, H. E., and Lipsey, M. W. (1999). *Evaluation: A systematic approach* (6th ed.). Thousand Oaks, CA: Sage Publications.

REFERENCES

Abelson, D. E., and Carberry, C. M. (1998). Following suit of falling behind?: A comparative analysis of think tanks in Canada and the United States. *Canadian Journal of Political Science, 31*(3), 525–56.

Abelson, D. E. (1999). Public visibility and policy relevance: Assessing the impact and influence of Canadian policy institutes. *Canadian Public Administration, 42*(2), 240–70.

Abelson, D. E., and Lindquist, E. A. (2000). Think tanks in North America. In J. G. McGann and R. K. Weaver (Eds.), *Think tanks and civil society: Catalysts for ideas and action* (pp. 37–66). New Brunswick, NJ: Transaction Publishers.

Abelson, D. E. (2002). *Do think tanks matter?: Assessing the impact of public policy institutes.* Montreal: McGill-Queen's University Press.

American Evaluation Society. (2000). *Guiding principles for evaluators.* Retrieved August 16, 2004, from http://www.eval.org/evaluationdocuments/aeaprin6.html

Ammons, D. N. (1996). *Municipal benchmarks: Assessing local performance and establishing community standards.* Thousand Oaks, CA: Sage.

Auditor General of Canada. (1976). *Annual report 1976.* Ottawa: Information Canada.

Auditor General of Canada. (1993). *Annual report 1993.* Ottawa: Minister of Supply and Services.

Auditor General of Canada. (1996). *Annual report 1996.* Retrieved September 14, 2004, from http://www.og-bvg.gc.ca/domino/reports.nsf/html/96menu_e.html

Boardman, A. E., Greenberg, D. H., Vining, A., and Weimer, D. L. (2001). *Cost-benefit analysis: Concepts and practice.* Upper Saddle River, NJ: Prentice-Hall.

Canadian Evaluation Society. (2000). *CES Guidelines for Ethical Conduct.* Retrieved August 16, 2004, from http://www.evaluationcanada .ca/site.cgi?section=5&ssection=4&_lang=an

de Bruijn, H. (2002). *Managing performance in the public sector.* London: Routledge.

Framst, G. (1995, October/November). Application of program logic model to agricultural technology transfer programs. *Canadian Journal of Program Evaluation, 10,* 123–32.

Geva-May, I., and Pal, L. A. (1999). Good fences make good neighbours: Policy evaluation and policy analysis—exploring the differences. *Evaluation, 5*(3), 259–77.

Government of Canada. (1969). *Planning, programming and budgeting guide.* Ottawa: Information Canada.

Guess, G. M., and Farnham, P. G. (2000). *Cases in public policy analysis.* Washington: Georgetown University Press.

Hollander, M. J., and Prince, M. J. (1993, Summer). Analytical units in federal and provincial governments: Origins, functions and suggestions for effectiveness. *Canadian Public Administration, 36,* 190–224.

Hood, C., et al. (1999). *Regulation inside government: Waste-watchers, quality police, and sleaze-busters.* Oxford: Oxford University Press.

Leclerc, G. (1992). Institutionalizing evaluation in Canada. In J. Mayne, J. Hudson, M. L. Bemelmans-Videc, and R. Conner (Eds.), *Advancing public policy evaluation: Learning from international experiences* (pp. 49–58). Amsterdam: North Holland.

Mayne, J. (2001, Spring). Addressing attribution through contribution analysis: Using performance measures sensibly. *The Canadian Journal of Program Evaluation, 16,* 1–24.

Mayne, J. (2003). *Reporting on outcomes: Setting performance expectations and telling performance stories.* Ottawa: Office of the Auditor General of Canada. Retrieved September 4, 2004, from http:// www.oag-bvg.gc.ca/domino/other.nsf/html/200305dp._e.html/$file/ 200305dpl_e.pdf

Organisation for Economic Co-operation and Development. (1995). *Public management developments: Update 1995.* Paris: OECD.

Patton, M. Q. (1987). *Creative evaluation* (2nd ed.). Newbury Park, CA: Sage.

Patton, M. Q. (1997). *Utilization-focused evaluation: The new century text* (3rd ed.). Thousand Oaks, CA: Sage Publications.

Patton, M. Q. (2002). *Qualitative research and evaluation methods* (3rd ed.). Thousand Oaks, CA: Sage.

The performance-based management handbook: A six-volume compilation of techniques and tools for implementing the Government Performance and Results Act of 1993. (2001). Washington: Training Resources and Data Exchange, Performance-Based Management Special Interest Group for the Office of Strategic Planning and Program Evaluation, 2001. Retrieved August 16, 2004, from http://www.orau.gov/pbm/pbmhandbook/pbmhandbook.html

Posvac, E. J., and Carey, R. G. (1980). *Program evaluation: Methods and case studies.* Englewood Cliffs, NJ: Prentice-Hall.

Potter, E. H. (2000). Treasury board as a management board: The reinvention of a central agency. In L. A. Pal (Ed.), *How Ottawa spends 2000–2001: Past imperfect, future tense,* (pp. 95–129). Toronto: Oxford University Press.

Rossi, P. H., Freeman, H. E., and Lipsey, M. W. (1999). *Evaluation: A systematic approach* (6th ed.). Thousand Oaks, CA: Sage Publications.

Saint-Martin, D. (2000). *Building the new managerialist state: Consultants and the politics of public sector reform in comparative perspective.* Oxford: Oxford University Press.

Savoie, D. J. (1990). *The politics of public spending in Canada.* Toronto: University of Toronto Press.

Schacter, M. (1999). *Means . . . ends . . . indicators: Performance measurement in the public sector.* Ottawa: Institute on Governance.

Scheirer, M. A. (1994). Designing and using process evaluation. In J. S. Wholey, H. P. Hatry, and K. E. Newcomer (Eds.), *Handbook of practical program evaluation* (pp. 40–68). San Francisco: Jossey-Bass.

Segsworth, R. V. (1992). Public access to evaluation in Canada. In J. Mayne, J. Hudson, M. L. Bemelmans-Videc, and R. Conner (Eds.), *Advancing public policy evaluation: Learning from international experiences* (pp. 301–12). Amsterdam: North Holland.

SRDC. (2004). *About SRDC.* Retrieved August 16, 2004, from http://www.srdc.org/english/about/about.htm

Sutherland, S. L. (1990, Summer). The evolution of program budget ideas in Canada: Does parliament benefit from estimates reform? *Canadian Public Administration, 33,* 133–64.

Sutherland, S. L. (1999). Bossing democracy: The value-for-money audit and the electorate's loss of political power to the auditor general. In

R. M. Bird, M. J. Trebilcock, and T. A. Wilson (Eds.), *Rationality in public policy: Retrospect and prospect, a tribute to Douglas Hartle* (pp. 109–40). Toronto: Canadian Tax Foundation, Canadian Tax Paper No. 104.

Treasury Board of Canada. (1981). *Guide on the program evaluation function.* Ottawa: Minister of Supply and Services.

Treasury Board of Canada. (1991). *Into the 90s: Government program evaluation perspectives.* Ottawa: Office of the Comptroller General.

Treasury Board of Canada. (1994, July). *Treasury Board manual— Review, internal audit and evaluation* (Amendment RIE/94-1). Ottawa: Treasury Board of Canada.

Treasury Board of Canada. (2000). *Results for Canadians: A management framework for the government of Canada.* Retrieved August 16, 2004, from http://www.tbs-sct.gc.ca/res_can/rc_e.html

Treasury Board of Canada. (2001a). *Guide for the development of results-based management and accountability frameworks.* Retrieved August 16, 2004, from http://www.tbs-sct.gc.ca/eval/pubs/RMAF-CGRR/rmaf-cgrr-01-e.asp

Treasury Board of Canada. (2001b). *Evaluation policy.* Retrieved August 16, 2004, from http://www.tbs-sct.gc.ca/pubs_pol/dcgpubs/tbm_161/ep-pe1_e.asp

Treasury Board of Canada. (2003). *Interim evaluation of the Treasury Board's evaluation policy.* Retrieved August 16, 2004, from http://www.tbs-sct.gc.ca/eval/tools_outils/int-prov_e.asp#exsum

Weiss, C. H. (1998). *Evaluation* (2nd ed.). Upper Saddle River, NJ: Prentice Hall.

Wholey, J. S. (1994). Assessing the feasibility and likely usefulness of evaluation. In J. S. Wholey, H. P. Hatry, and K. E. Newcomer (Eds.), *Handbook of practical program evaluation* (pp. 15–39). San Francisco: Jossey-Bass.

Wholey, J. S. (2003). Improving performance and accountability: Responding to emerging management challenges. In S. I. Donaldson and Michael Scriven (Eds.), *Evaluating social programs and problems* (pp. 43–61). Mahwah, NJ: Lawrence Erlbaum Associates.

Chapter 8   *Policymaking under Pressure*

The last edition of this book was written before the 9/11 attack on the World Trade Towers, before SARS, before Mad Cow, before the HRDC scandal, before West Nile virus, before the most recent outbreak of avian flu in Asia, before the electrical blackout that plunged 50 million North Americans into darkness, before the foot-and-mouth crisis, before anthrax scares, before the MyDoom or Love Bug viruses, before hurricane Isabel, and before the Groupaction sponsorship scandal. This book is based on the idea that the context for policymaking has changed significantly in recent years, and that we consequently need to rethink our tools and the way that we do policy analysis. One major and relatively new change seems to be the degree to which policymaking increasingly takes place under pressure, in circumstances of adversity and uncertainty, dealing with crises, disasters, and emergencies. There are several reasons for this: the increasing interdependency of complex systems such as the Internet or pan-continental energy grids; the rapid transmission of disease because of global markets for food products and enhanced ability of individuals to travel around the world; the possibility that environmental changes are inducing new natural disasters (e.g., flooding, climate change, erosion); the ability of modern media to both instantly magnify events and broadcast them in real time; international terrorism; and conflict zones that drive refugees to seek safety. Whatever the reasons, the modern reality of policymaking is marked increasingly by dealing with crisis. The problem is that most of the models of decisionmaking used in the policy literature are models predicated on the normal, the everyday, the linear, and the expected. What happens when policymakers are confronted with the abnormal, the unusual, the uncertain, and the unexpected? This chapter provides an overview of some themes in an increasingly important area of policymaking and public management: handling crisis and emergency.

Conventional policy theory and practice is strongly influenced by the rational model described in Chapter 1. The model assumes a series of logical steps and processes to come to decisions about public policy. We mentioned some of the assumptions that underpin the model, and some of the challenges. But we can go a little deeper. The model tends to assume a relatively small number of decisionmakers, perhaps even only one. It assumes, if not complete information, at least reasonably high levels of information and data to inform decisions, a high degree of certainty in short. In order for the sequence to take place at all, the model assumes that there is sufficient time for that sequence to unfold. And finally, coupled to the assumption that there is sufficient information to make choices, is the notion that problems are reasonably well defined.

There are many instances of public policy in which these assumptions, or at least approximations to these assumptions, hold reasonably well. Routine or "normal" policy analysis therefore can be undertaken more or less within the broad framework of the rational model: problems are defined, models of causal variables developed, data gathered, options or alternatives generated, and choices made based on some set of criteria. But we also know that the real world of public policy is marked at times—and seems increasingly to be marked—by emergencies and crises. Policy decisions have to be made under pressure, and all the assumptions of the rational model are stretched if not broken. Most crises and emergencies involve multiple actors, with overlapping authorities. Instead of single decisionmakers there are many, and they have to be coordinated. Instead of reasonably high levels of information and data, crisis and emergency is marked by randomness and uncertainty. Time seems to be truncated, and major decisions have to be made quickly. Finally, as we noted with the SARS crisis and problem definition in Chapter 3, the policy problem is often ill defined or so complex that it defies easy categorization and analysis.

While we commonly think of crisis and emergency as the same thing, there is distinction between them that affects the way we think about them and the way we react to them. An **emergency** is an abnormal and unexpected threat event that requires immediate action. A **crisis** is a turning point or moment of danger that threatens the integrity and even survival of an entire system. A house fire, for example, would usually be considered an emergency rather than a family crisis. The latter would be some event or development that threatens the existence of the family as such (the death of a member). Something can be a crisis and an emergency at the same time, from different perspectives. A forest fire or a flood that threatens to destroy a community is evidently a crisis for that community since it threatens its very existence. From the government's perspective, it is an emergency since it does not threaten the government's existence. As well, emergencies can quickly evolve into crises. The September 11 attack on the World Trade Center was a massive emergency, but for a short time it looked as well as if it might be a crisis for all the United States (in case this was the first phase of an attack on the country) and the government (in case leading members of the administration were killed). There is somewhat less scope for interpretation in the cases of emergency, though naturally there can be differences in point of view. But most emergencies by definition are abnormalities with severe consequences occurring in a short space of time. We can mistake some unwanted events as emergencies (e.g., someone faints, but others think it is a heart attack), but generally emergencies are defined in terms of significant and immediate threat, usually to physical property or life. A crisis, since it is a threat event that affects the integrity of the system, is more debatable precisely because a judgment has to be made about what the system is, what its component elements are, how they work together to maintain that system, and why the threat event might undermine those elements. A "cabinet crisis" requires a judgment about whether a threat event (e.g., the resignation of a prominent minister) might bring down the government as a whole. What kind of threat event could undermine the integrity of the entire United Nations system, and thereby be a crisis?

There is obviously a relationship between emergency and crisis, but they call forth different types of responses and different forms of public management. These will be explored later in the chapter. For the moment, it is worth trying to discern the generic elements of a substantial threat event, whether it falls into one category or another. Substantial threat events seem to be determined by four factors: randomness, severity, uniqueness, and time compression. Figure 8.1 charts the variances as running from low to high, and carves out four quadrants with different configurations. Events that are highly random (not expected), severe in terms of consequences, unique or previously not encountered and hence

Figure 8.1 Categorizing Threat Events

	Low	**Severity**	High	
High / Random	New but not lethal flu virus		Terrorist attacks Pandemic Computer virus Ice storm	High / Unique
	Typical flu virus		Forest fires Floods	Low
Low				
	Low	**Time Compression**	High	

without an information base, and compressed in time (moving rapidly; requiring rapid response), pose the greatest type of threat. Events that are low on all four dimensions pose the least threat and are the easiest to manage. The other two categories are mixed. Events like some floods and forest fires are predictable to a degree, but still pose severe threats and need a quick response. Since they have happened before and have typical configurations, there are routines in place to deal with them. In the other category, at the top left quadrant, severity is low, but the event is unexpected or difficult to predict, and largely unknown. Types of events can migrate into different quadrants as more is known about them. A flu virus that is unknown in one year, even while it is predictable that it will move through the population in the fall and winter, is unique. Once the strain has been determined, a vaccine can be prepared the next year.

Severity is a key factor in every scenario, and can be defined in terms of scope and intensity of negative impact. The wider the scope of a threat event, and the greater its intensity or negative impact, the more pressure there will be for a rapid response. Time compression is to some extent, though not exclusively, a function of severity. SARS was a greater threat than Mad Cow disease because of its potential severity (an immediate life-threatening pandemic versus a threat of longer duration), and time compression was a function of that severity but also because how easily and quickly the disease spread.

The challenge for contemporary policymakers is that crisis and emergency, threat events that promise severe negative impacts with wide scope, seem to be increasingly common. While a good deal of policymaking is still "normal" in the sense that while difficult, threat events can be handled through normal political processes, more and more seem to fall into the category of emergency or crisis. By definition, crises and emergencies are events that strain a policymaking system and perhaps even cause it to collapse. Too many emergencies—indeed sometimes only one—that are not handled well can pose a crisis for the system. The question is what techniques of analysis and of management can be drawn upon to deal with these types of challenges. The rest of the chapter begins by reviewing some of the theoretical foundations of crisis management and policymaking under pressure, and then moves to risk assessment, emergency preparedness, and crisis management.

MODELLING CHAOS

Some of the ingredients of policymaking under pressure have been mentioned above, but are there more precise ways of conceptualizing those elements? One of the first attempts in the policy literature to come to grips with this problem was Ira Sharkansky's (1986) notion of "policy-making under adversity":

> Shifts and time-compressed turns in the nature of issues make traditional policy paradigms, policy assumptions, policy habits, policy "grammars," and grand policies increasingly doubtful. Recent, present, and foreseeable shifts and jumps in policy issues include transformations in expectations, aspirations, and beliefs; inflections of the internal dynamics of policies, which make their linear continuation with only incremental changes impossible or counterproductive; jumps in the material features of policy issues; and emergence of new and unprecedented problems. (Sharkansky, 1986, p. 23)

It is the discontinuities, the "jumps" that create challenges. As we noted above, if normal policymaking may be seen as incremental, with each step more or less predictably or controllably emanating from the last, then what is nonincremental, unpredictable to a certain degree, and not immediately controllable has the potential to create crisis. On August 14, 2003, for example, parts of the northeastern United States and Ontario experienced a power blackout. It lasted for four days in some parts of the United States, and Ontario saw rolling blackouts for more than a week before power was restored (U.S.–Canada Power System Outage Taskforce, 2004). The outage was estimated to have cost the United States upward of US$10 billion, and as much as $2.3 billion in lost manufacturing shipments from Ontario. This was a shift and jump with vengeance. The linear continuity of power at a flip of a switch is taken for granted by citizens, and while there are peaks and surges in demand, these can normally be managed. Ironically, that day was considered normal, without unusually heavy power demands in and around Ohio, where the first system collapse occurred. Due to a combination of human and software error, failures in that region's power grid were not noticed in time, and because of the integration of the North American power grid system, a failure in Ohio rippled through and hit Ontario and several other U.S. states. We will discuss the nature of causation in chaotic events in a moment, but the point here is the shift and jump that Sharkansky mentions. In terms of Figure 8.1, this was a high threat event or emergency, because it scored high on severity, unexpectedness, and uniqueness and time compression.

Shifts and jumps indicate a break from a linear routine. Every threat event contains a large element of surprise that makes it different from normal. People who live in earthquake zones, for example, know that there is likely to be an earthquake sometime, but not exactly when. In some instances, like SARS, the event is a total surprise since it literally has never happened before. Beyond the element of surprise, however, crises or emergencies as nonlinear *policy* problems are collective action problems. Comfort (1999), for example, looks at what she calls "shared risk" problems—crises or emergencies that affect large communities— as **nonlinear policy problems.** Her case study examples are of earthquakes and emergency response to them:

> Shared risk is nonlinear in that small differences in initial conditions, repeated in actions over time, lead to unpredictable outcomes. It is also dynamic, in that a change in the performance of one sub-unit of the affected system may directly influence that of other units in its immediate vicinity, creating a ripple effect of failure throughout the system. Problems of shared risk are not easily amenable to control strategies, particularly if the control is externally imposed. They appear to be more problems of collective learning, involving multiple groups at different levels of understanding, commitment, and skill, as well as requiring different types of knowledge, authority, and action for effective resolution. . . . Methods for addressing problems of shared risk differ from those used in traditional policy analysis. Since the problems are nonlinear and dynamic, the assumptions underlying this inquiry are those related to discovery rather than control. Traditional means of bounding the problem are ineffective, since the boundaries between the environment and the participants are open. The threat may affect different groups within the subsystem differently, and these differences, iterated over time, lead to different consequences for the whole system. (pp. 4–5)

The idea of nonlinearity in policy problems of situations poses more than an incidental challenge to policy analysis. As we noted in Chapter 1, the conventional discipline is based on a rational model, which in turn owes its core assumptions to deeply embedded assumptions in what constitutes knowledge and techniques to generate knowledge. There has been a long debate in the policy literature about the "positivist" orientation of conventional policy analysis—briefly described in Chapter 1—that has emphasized the importance of argument and interpretation rather than rigid scientific method in grappling with policy problems. This critique links conventional policy analysis to conventional epistemology in the sciences, and argues for a different approach. Another strand in this critique is to base the challenge on new scientific theories that break with Newtonian mechanics and deterministic science. The theories include quantum mechanics, complexity theory, chaos theory, and cognitive science (Morçöl, 2002). The difference is between seeing the world as a clock or as a cloud. A clock has deterministic mechanisms, the system works on the basis of clear causality and connections, and the clock as a whole is stably configured as a clock and nothing else. Imagine a cloud, either of vapour or of thousands of tiny insects. Its boundary is constantly shifting and changing, its shape elongates and contracts, and yet it is still recognizably a cloud. The mechanisms of interaction are much more challenging to explain—there are no pulleys or gears, only what appear to be random interactions of particles or insects that constantly ripple through the system.

As an example, Comfort (1999, pp. 8–9) has drawn eight key concepts from this scientific literature on complexity and chaos that portray dynamic, nonlinear systems that generate self-organization (for example, communities responding to an earthquake). First, the evolution and dynamics of these communities, like all complex systems, depend greatly on initial conditions and characteristics of the system. Even small differences among systems in these initial conditions can have far-reaching consequences. Second, random events occurring outside the system can have great effects on the system itself, and take it into unpredicted directions. Third, these random events are irreversible within the system in the sense that whatever impacts they have become part of the system itself. Comfort's example is how an unexpected earthquake led to revisions in building codes that significantly altered construction in seismic zones in California. Fourth, feedback loops of communication and coordination lead to adaptation by mutual adjustment (our cloud example above, or a school of fish). Fifth, because multiple actors create constraints for action through the need for coordination, centres of energy and influence crop up in these systems (leaders or "strange attractors") that move the system forward. Sixth, this forward motion in a complex system can involve a transition to a new equilibrium of a substantially changed system. Seventh, the behaviour of the system often yields unpredictable results, and, finally, these systems can develop recurring patterns of behaviour in different contexts to achieve similar system-wide goals. Later in this chapter we will examine the implications for policy and in particular for emergency preparedness and response from these ideas.

A final illustration of thinking differently about complex systems and change that casts light on shifts and jumps is the idea of the **tipping point**. Gladwell (2000) argues that the world is full of instances—from fashion to crime rates to drug use—of often abrupt, dramatic and inexplicable changes. Certain books and clothing styles appear out of nowhere and become social phenomena. Inner-city crime can suddenly leap up, or decline precipitously. These phenomena are equivalent to systems that undergo a sudden transition. Gladwell is focusing on social systems and rapid transitions, and argues that these tipping points are analogous to epidemics and function with similar mechanisms. "Epidemics are a function of the people who transmit infectious agents, the infectious agent itself, and the environment in which the infections agent is operating. When an epidemic tips, when it is jolted out of equilibrium, it tips because something has happened, some change has occurred in one (or two or three) of those areas" (pp. 18–19). He somewhat dramatically calls these three agents of change the Law of the Few, the Stickiness Factor, and the Power of Context.

The Law of the Few builds on the simple insight that epidemics typically are spread by just a tiny subset of everyone who gets infected. The most jarring example is of Gaetan Dugas, the French Canadian flight attendant who claimed to have had 2500 sexual partners all over North America and who was linked to 40 of the earliest AIDS cases in New York and California. In social dynamics, the idea is that a small number of unique individuals spread the word. Not just any individual, however. Gladwell identifies three types of individuals whose unique gifts make a huge difference in the social distribution of information: connectors, mavens (a Yiddish word that means collectors of knowledge), and salesmen. Connectors are that type of person with lots of social connections, and moreover, social connections to the right people—others who themselves are influential in their circle. Connectors are people who span various social worlds and who can effectively "market" an idea or a product. Mavens on the other hand are basically information brokers who know a great amount of detail about something, and pass that information along to connectors, who in turn distribute it more widely. Salesmen are another select group of people "with the skills to persuade us when we are unconvinced of what we are hearing" (Gladwell, 2000, p. 70).

If the social epidemics depend on the nature of the messenger, they also depend on the nature of the message, or what Gladwell calls the stickiness factor, or how memorable something is, which in turn depends on small cues and small aspects of the message that appeal to people. Finally, the power of context is analogous to the conditions in which a medical epidemic takes place—the same communicable disease in a context of poverty and crowding versus sanitation and space. Gladwell cites the well-known "broken windows" theory of crime contagion (Kelling and Coles, 1996). The idea is that broken windows in a community signal to passersby that no one cares about that community, and soon more windows get broken. All sorts of small disorders like this—graffiti, for example—encourage an epidemic of crime because criminals are encouraged to believe that no one cares enough to challenge their behaviour. The classic illustration of this was the condition of the New York subway system in the mid-1980s—inefficient and overrun by petty crime. A consultant at the time encouraged the city to focus on the lurid graffiti that graced almost every subway car, because it was a visible symbol of the system's decay. The city established cleaning stations and ensured that any car with graffiti was cleaned immediately. It took six years. At the same time, in the face of serious crimes on the subway, the authorities bore down on fare cheating, on the same principle that a small expression (it was estimated there were 170 000 people a day using the system without paying) of disorder sent a clear message that any other criminal act was fine.

In a striking similarity to complexity and chaos theory, the idea of a tipping point at which something changes dramatically and exponentially also argues that small changes in small aspects of initial conditions can have large effects:

> Merely by manipulating the size of the group, we can dramatically improve its receptivity to new ideas. By tinkering with the presentation of information, we can significantly improve its stickiness. Simply by finding and reaching those few special people who hold so much social power, we can shape the course of social epidemics. In the end, Tipping Points are a reaffirmation of the potential for change and the power of intelligent action. (Gladwell, 2000, p. 259)

Tipping points, chaos theory, complexity theory—all seem far removed from practical policymaking. But in fact, they are conceptual schemes and approaches that try in some measure to capture reality in ways superior to a more linear, rationalist, positivist model. What are some of the practical implications of these types of more dynamic models for the way we think about public policy? For one thing, initial conditions make a difference in how systems evolve. Coupled with this is an emphasis on a system of interactions, and not a single problem. Conventional policy analysis, as explained in Chapter 3, begins with problem structuring. Even though we alluded to the fact that problems are complex and that they come in clusters, it is still largely an analysis that focuses on one vector of issues or challenges. And it presumes that one can make an intervention along that vector and change causal relations and thus change outcomes. An example might be an inner-city community-based program to counsel teenagers on sexuality and drugs. A conventional approach would see the "problem" in terms of negative outcomes from unsafe sexual practices and dependency on drugs. Obviously, the analysis would highlight the role of schools and families, but it would target youth themselves as "clients" of the program and seek interventions—probably on a large scale in order to produce results on a large scale. A complex systems approach would look at teenagers within the community context, and at "systems" embedded in teenage groups (peer pressure, social bonding, what is considered "cool") and take that as a point of departure. It might also be sensitive to the fact that the same program might have very different results depending on what community and what groups of youths were being supported—the initial conditions of each system would make a big difference in outcomes. A real-world example is Canada's program on fetal alcohol syndrome and fetal alcohol effects for First Nations. As the program documentation notes, the earlier approaches to this problem tended to focus on individuals who came to be "isolated from their families and communities, and the communities' men, pregnant women, and mothers have been impacted by shame, guilt, and grief" (Health Canada, 2004). Now, people are "beginning to realize that FAS/FAE are community issues that need to be addressed on an individual, family, and community level, utilizing partnerships at the regional and national level."

A second implication is the importance and indeed the inevitability of random events that can shock a system and change its trajectory dramatically. "Planning for the unexpected" is of course difficult to do, but this mindset encourages a mentality of monitoring the environment as well as internal processes regularly. It might also encourage deliberate redundancy in systems that are fragile or whose failure will have far-reaching consequences. Redundant systems in the financial sector, for example, are routine in order to avoid the possibility of breakdown due to external events. A third implication is that large changes can come from small interventions. This is the insight embedded in the idea of tipping points, but it is a feature as well of other complex systems theories. From a policy point of view, it implies that significant change can be generated from small, focused interventions that take system characteristics seriously. Fourth, in line with the notion that complex systems have internal mechanisms of modest equilibrium, there is an emphasis on feedback loops of communication and information. When a school of fish is observed in motion, it seems almost like a single organism, even while it is made up of hundreds of actors mutually adjusting to the myriad of each other's actions. Complex social systems—from loose coalitions to formal organizations—also require inordinate amounts of communication and information exchange to work. This is a lesson from the implementation literature, of course, but it takes on a new angle in the context of complex systems theory. In traditional implementation thinking, the problem is communication from above down the line, to ensure that the original policy idea unfolds as planned and that everyone is more or less operating in the same framework. From a complex systems perspective, the communication has to be 360 degrees in three dimensions. It is about information moving up as well as sideways and from top to down. It is about information and communication as the loose glue that ties the system together, but also makes it possible to adapt and adjust. In the real world, of course, we increasingly see instances of this kind of complex system behaviour. The 2004 federal election was called the first Blackberry election, after the ubiquitous device that allows anywhere-anytime e-mail and telephone communications. In this case, political parties were able to behave like schools of piranhas, with each member mutually adjusting through immediate communication to everyone else in the school.

The final implication is about adaptation. The conventional approach to policy analysis and implementation sees it as a linear unfolding. But bring in randomness, unpredictability, and the influence of small events, and it is likely that at any given point the system (an organization, a political party) will need to respond to shocks and either regroup or transform itself in the light of that external shock. This means adaptation that maintains the integrity of the system in some fashion. This requires communication and, more importantly, system learning. There needs to be a capacity to build on experiences, incorporate them into practice, and embed them into some sort of collective memory. Conventional theory also presumes a fairly flat organization. Learning does not happen as well in systems that are grounded in command-and-control frameworks. Interestingly, Sharkansky assumed that policymaking under adversity would require "power concentration" (Sharkansky, 1986, p. 123). More contemporary complex systems theory argues that what is required in fact for resilience is distributed and shared responsibility so that lessons can be learned quickly and moved through the system. Well-functioning organizations do this all the time; they do not merely monitor, they absorb and try to learn from experiences. This is not as easy as it sounds, and an organization truly devoted to learning and adaptation requires a host of mechanisms to make it work.

Having looked through some theoretical lenses on the issues of emergency and crisis, we can now turn to real-world examples. The next sections address three important areas that fall under the rubric of policymaking under pressure: risk assessment, emergency management, and crisis management.

RISK ASSESSMENT

From a policy perspective, **risk** is increasingly an important component about thinking through policy issues and managing policy organizations. This is due in part to the events of 9/11, which sensitized all organizations, private and public, to threats and risks. In this sense, risk is associated with threats to government assets and personnel, and can arise from cataclysmic terrorist acts or simple accidents in the field. A second factor is the rise in insurance costs, which makes risk management more than a matter of taking out a policy; it becomes a matter of actively mitigating or avoiding risks. Finally, the public is less tolerant of even small errors made by private and public organizations, and is more ready to litigate in a climate where courts are prepared to hand out increasingly punitive damages.

The federal government has had a **risk management** policy in place since 2001. Box 8.1 provides a flavour of what is required by departments and agencies. The policy states

> The importance of risk management has been growing steadily during the last several years. There is increasing awareness and expectation in Canada and abroad of the need to manage risks, rather than leaving them solely to insurance.
>
> The risk environment has been evolving rapidly, as advancing technological and social developments bring forth new or hitherto dormant risks associated with such phenomena as hijacking, hazardous materials, pollution, electronic data, and exposure to legal and political liability. The government has an obligation to be fully aware of the state of the art in risk management, and to prevent losses and unnecessary expenditures. (Treasury Board of Canada, 2001a)

Box 8.1   GOVERNMENT OF CANADA RISK MANAGEMENT POLICY

POLICY REQUIREMENTS

IDENTIFICATION

1. Departments must identify the potential perils, factors and types of risk to which their assets, program activities and interests are exposed.

MINIMIZATION

2. Departments must analyze and assess the risks identified, and design and implement cost-effective risk prevention, reduction or avoidance control measures.

3. Departments must:
   (a) select underwriting options;

(b) self-underwrite the risks to which the government alone is exposed and over which it generally has control, and provide for and absorb, through their annual appropriations, any cost that may arise from self-underwriting;

(c) ensure that contractors do not procure insurance on risks that are clearly the responsibility of the government, and that contractors are not indemnified by the government against the risks to which only the contractors are exposed.

4. Departments must plan and budget for containment, compensation, restoration and disaster recovery.

CONTAINMENT

5. Departments must activate emergency organizations, systems, and contingency plans, and initiate recovery measures.

COMPENSATION, RESTORATION AND RECOVERY

6. Departments must:
   (a) investigate incidents to determine their causes;
   (b) assess the extent and value of damages and determine potential legal liability; and
   (c) make incident reports.

7. Departments must settle and pay claims by or against the Crown and against its servants in an adequate and timely manner, and generally refer cases involving legal proceedings, and claims associated with a contract, to the Department of Justice.

8. Departments must repair or replace damaged assets and operating systems to return operations to normal as soon as possible.

9. Departments must:
   (a) report each fiscal year in the Public Accounts: all payments of claims against the Crown; all ex gratia payments; court awards; and all losses of $1,000 or more including accidental destruction of, damage to, or theft of, assets that would normally be covered by insurance had insurance existed;
   (b) report to the appropriate law enforcement agencies losses over $1,000 which are due to suspected illegal activity; and
   (c) maintain their own data-base as part of the feedback system of management information.

10. Departments must establish new or improved measures to prevent the recurrence of incidents, and to recover from disasters.

SOURCE: Treasury Board of Canada. (2001). *Risk management policy*. Retrieved August 18, 2004, from http://www.tbs-sct.gc.ca/pubs_pol/dcgpubs/ riskmanagement/riskmanagpol1_e.asp#_Toc457619039

Risk, of course, is to some large extent a subjective assessment at both the individual and the cultural level. Some people see no risks in activities that make others quail. Societies define risk differently as well. For example, there is a case to be made that contemporary industrial societies have elevated "safety" to almost a religious level (Beck, 1992; Furedi, 2002). On almost any conceivable measure, from life expectancy to the likelihood of suffering accidents, people generally today (in developed countries, to be sure) are safer than ever before. Paradoxically, that very condition of relative safety may increase people's expectations about how safe things should be, and hence lower their tolerance to risk. Nonetheless, there are internationally recognized definitions of risk. The International Organization for Standards defines risk as a "combination of the probability of an event and its consequences." The Canadian Standards Association defines risk as "the chance of injury or loss as defined as a measure of the probability and severity of an adverse effect to health, property, the environment or other things of value." These and a myriad of other definitions highlight two key points about risk: chance or probability, and severity of consequences. This is exactly the logic behind auto insurance. Companies calibrate their insurance premiums to age, sex, type of car, driving environment, and use. These are all measure of probability. Young male drivers of sports cars in urban centres who will use their cars a lot are a greater risk (i.e., the probability of a car accident is higher) than middle-aged, rural drivers who go out only to church on Sunday in the family sedan. The other dimension is the severity of the consequence. If the consequence, usually defined in negative terms (there can be outcomes of risk that are positive: "take a chance on love") is slight, even if the probability is high, then the risk factor would be considered negligible. However, a low probability of a severe consequence (a nuclear plant explosion) can give one pause, simply because the result might be so awful. In normal language, the concept of risk is associated with probabilities that negatively valued events or outcomes will occur. We don't think it a "risk" to possibly encounter an old dear friend on the street; it is more of a chance or an opportunity. However, it makes perfect sense to view meeting up with someone you dislike as a "risk." The other common language feature of risk is that it should be a probability of not just something severe happening, but something severe that is relevant to the core mission of the risk-assessing organization. From a policy point of view, this means assessing risks that would impede program development and delivery, and risks that would challenge the organizational mission as a whole.

What does risk management entail? Clearly, it requires the assessment of risk in the first instance, and developing strategies to deal with the risk. Assessing risk is part and parcel of developing a risk profile for the organization (Treasury Board of Canada, 2001b). The first step in that process is conducting an internal and external **environmental scan**. The internal risk factors typically are organizational: personnel, resources, information technology, and so on. A standard way of assessing the external environment is in terms of the PEST schema (also known as the STEP schema): political (federal–provincial relations, turf wars with other agencies, other governments, international bodies, international and domestic social movements, and stakeholders that may take adverse positions to policy); economic (local and national markets, price fluctuations, currency fluctuations, labour force movements, competition in one's target markets); social (demographic trends, current social debates and fashions); and technological (new technologies on the horizon and how they will be integrated into operations, scientific discoveries, new uses for old technologies, adequacy of internal technologies in the face of changing external technological environment). The next step is the consideration of the types and nature of risk facing the organization:

> The environmental scan increases the organization's awareness of the key characteristics and attributes of the risks it faces. These include
>
> - *Type of risk:* technological, financial, human resources (capacity, intellectual property), health, safety;
> - *Source of risk:* external (political, economic, natural disasters); internal (reputation, security, knowledge management, information for decision making);
> - *What is at risk:* area of impact/type of exposure (people, reputation, program results, matériel, real property); and
> - *Level of ability to control the risk:* high (operational); moderate (reputation); low (natural disasters). (Treasury Board of Canada, 2001b)

As we noted earlier, risk is to some extent in the eye of the beholder. It is linked to the notion of probability, but distinct from it nonetheless. For example, it might be possible to mathematically calculate the probability of some accident at 80 percent. Some would see that figure and consider it too high. Others—less "risk averse"—would look at it and consider the 20 percent probability of it not occurring as being quite comforting. Security and stock markets work in exactly the same way, offering products with different risks attached that appeal to different segments of the market. This is to underline the point that an organization's risk profile is only the classification of the types and probabilities of risks it faces. It is not an assessment of how seriously to take those risks. This is a more difficult process, and ultimately depends on the judgment of management, based in turn on the risk aversion of key stakeholders. For private firms this is a matter of checking with stakeholders; for public organizations it is trickier since the potential stakeholder base is quite large, and in any event, the organization is supposed to be motivated by the public interest (Pal and Maxwell, 2004).

Public organizations face a special problem in developing risk profiles because of the risk aversion of most clients. Most public services are monopoly services not provided in the same degree in the private sector—education, health, and the myriad of social services are prime examples. With few or no alternatives, clients of these services demonstrate a strong negativity bias—the risk of any change or withdrawal of benefit is considered very serious. This is a standard problem that all democratic governments face when they inflict pain or losses on their citizens (Pal and Weaver, 2003). On the other hand, risk analysis can become a smokescreen for bad policy. If there is a "risk," for example, that the media will learn about a grants and contributions scheme that is not running well, and that risk is "managed"—the net effect in terms of democracy is probably negative. A risk that truth will be told, that abuses will be exposed, that malfeasance might see the light of day—these are indeed risks, but "managing" them so they do not cause problems is the antithesis of good public service. Managing risk always has to be put in the broader context of ethical government behaviour. A risk by definition is the probability of bad news—but what counts as bad has to be measured against the yardstick of ethics.

EMERGENCY MANAGEMENT

Managing emergencies might at first blush appear to be a contradiction. In times of emergency or disaster, public (and it has to be admitted, private) authorities are put to the ultimate test. The public interest always appears abstract and distant when discussed in terms of broad policy or hypotheticals. However, when a bridge crumples, when forest fires rage, when buildings collapse or terrorists strike, there is a clear and present imperative for governments to act. They need to show that in some way they were prepared, that they can deal with the emergency, and that they will manage the aftermath.

Emergency management has been defined as the "process of developing and implementing policies and programs to avoid and cope with the risks to people and property from natural and man-made hazards" (Cigler, 1988, p. 5). Obviously, there has been a response function in government as long as government has been around—to fires, medical services, disaster relief, and crime. But the field of emergency management has emerged only in the last twenty years as a distinct area of public administration. It has taken on even greater importance since September 11, 2001. The possibility of deliberate and calamitous damage to life and property has increased exponentially in the last few years. Emergency and crisis are now much more closely aligned—something that at one time might have been a mere emergency, if the result of a terrorist attack—could become a crisis that challenges the entire political and economic system. Yet the issues are similar to those discussed above— shared risk, uncertainty, response under conditions of incomplete knowledge with severe time pressures. An emergency by definition is something that happens unexpectedly, and requires immediate response. The question is how to frame that response, and how to prepare.

There have been several challenges to emergency management in the past. One is that most emergencies conventionally occur "on the ground"—that is, they require a response from local governments and communities. This places a huge burden on levels of government that are not usually well endowed with funds and personnel. The second traditional problem is that emergencies are low-probability events. In the normal course of things, people try to avoid the hazards that lead to emergencies. However, while the probability is low, the consequences can be severe. So there is a compulsion on the part of governments to prepare for possible emergencies, but not much of a public constituency pushing for that response or lobbying for it. There is also a psychological bias to underestimate broadly based risk, and a commensurate reluctance to pay the taxes required to deal with it. This has changed completely since 9/11. There is a much heightened sense of the possibilities of deliberate danger, and the pummelling that Canada and other countries have received through emergencies such as Mad Cow and SARS (see Box 8.2 and Box 8.3 on pages 347–56) has driven home the importance of preparation and the importance of having the capacity to deal with threats.

The standard framework for emergency management has four phases or elements (see Figure 8.2 on page 346). The first is **mitigation.** This includes some of the steps discussed above under the heading of Risk Assessment. A government agency has to scan its internal procedures and its external environment, assess the probabilities of disaster, and take steps to mitigate or reduce those probabilities. The reason this is part of a management framework is that risk assessment and mitigation is an ongoing process that should be woven into daily organizational practices. The second step or phase is preparedness. Whereas mitigation involves the active attempt to prevent or avoid disasters, preparedness is about being ready for the inevitable but unpredictable accidents that

Figure 8.2 The Process of Crisis and Emergency Management

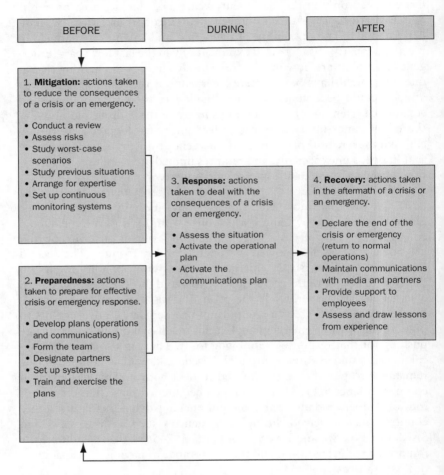

SOURCE: Canadian Centre for Management Development. (2004). *Crisis and emergency management: A guide for managers of the public service of Canada.* Table 2 at p. 9. Retrieved September, 2002, from http://www.myschool-monecole.gc.ca/Research/publications/pdfs/crisis_e.pdf

will occur. This requires planning, and indeed the establishment of some sort of emergency response plan that outlines who is in charge, what kind of coordination will take place, and the distribution of resources and responses. Part of being prepared is simulating an actual emergency and going through the steps. This can sometimes seem silly to the public

---

Box 8.2   PREPARING FOR SARS

STATE AND LOCAL HEALTH OFFICIAL EPIDEMIC SARS CHECKLIST

ARE YOU AND YOUR JURISDICTION READY FOR EPIDEMIC SEVERE ACUTE RESPIRATORY SYNDROME (SARS)?

This checklist, developed in collaboration with the Centers for Disease Control and Prevention, has been modeled on a previous Association of State and Territorial Health Officials (ASTHO) checklist for pandemic influenza preparedness (*Preparedness Planning for State Health Officials: Nature's Terrorist Attack— Pandemic Influenza* www.astho.org/ pubs/PandemicInfluenza.pdf). Preparations made to respond to other public health emergencies, including bioterror events, will generally be applicable to epidemic SARS planning.

The items on this checklist are intended for use by health officers at all levels—state, regional, district and local. The division of responsibilities between state and local levels varies among states, and often within states, according to the size of the population served by local health agencies. The items on this checklist should be interpreted in the context of the responsibilities of your public health agency and the division of responsibilities within your community, regardless of level of government. For some local public health agencies, for example, the capabilities needed for certain items may be available from a state health department but are not present locally.

Every locality should plan for the possibility of a local public health crisis such as widespread SARS-CoV transmission, in which help from other public health agencies is not available because they are facing similar crises. At the same time, there are advantages to coordinating response plans on a regional and statewide basis, partly so that isolation and quarantine procedures are applied uniformly and equitably.

SARS would be considered to be widespread in the United States if and when cases occur throughout the nation, in multiple locations, in persons without known epidemiologic links to places with community transmission of SARS-CoV or to known SARS cases. Local, district, and state public health agencies should be prepared to address all of the following items when the disease is present elsewhere in the world and to implement those

Box 8.2 (continued)

preparations when widespread disease occurs in the United States.

LEGAL AND POLICY ISSUES

❑ 1. My jurisdiction has a draft or formally adopted epidemic SARS plan.

❑ 2. Agreements have been obtained with my state's healthcare insurers, Medicaid program, and healthcare product and service providers for cooperation with public health recommendations during an epidemic.

❑ 3. I have reviewed with legal counsel my jurisdiction's laws and procedures on quarantine, isolation, closing premises and suspending public meetings and know how to implement them to help control an epidemic.

❑ 4. I am familiar with my state's medical volunteer licensure, liability, and compensation laws for in-state, out-of-state, returning retired, and non-medical volunteers.

❑ 5. I know whether my state allows hospitals and other licensed healthcare institutions to use temporary facilities for provision of medical care in the event of a public health emergency.

❑ 6. My jurisdiction's epidemic plan addresses Worker's Compensation and Unemployment Compensation issues related to health care and other workers missing work because of isolation or quarantine.

❑ 7. I have identified any deficiencies in my jurisdiction's laws and procedures on quarantine, isolation and related capacities and initiated steps to have those deficiencies corrected.

❑ 8. I know what provisions are in place, if any, for compensation of persons with economic or health injury resulting from needed SARS control measures and for limitation of liability of health care providers and agencies.

AUTHORITY

❑ 9. My state has an executive SARS epidemic planning committee that oversees the planning process, in cooperation with local health agencies.

❑ 10. My state has identified the authority responsible for declaration of a public health emergency and for officially activating our plan during a SARS epidemic.

❑ 11. My jurisdiction has identified key stakeholders responsible for development and implementation of specific components of the SARS epidemic plan, including enforcement of isolation, quarantine, and closure and decontamination of premises.

❑ 12. My jurisdiction's elected officials, appointed officials, and other agency heads know their respective responsibilities in the event of an epidemic.

❑ 13. My jurisdiction has a command system in place (e.g., the Incident Command System) to govern roles and responsibilities during a multi-agency, multi-jurisdictional event.

❑ 14. I am familiar with the controlling authority over intrastate and interstate modes of transportation, should these need to be curtailed during an epidemic (e.g., airplanes, trains, ships, highways).

❑ 15. My staff has relationships with health authorities of adjoining counties or states and with federal agencies to ensure effective communication during a public health emergency.

❑ 16. My jurisdiction has identified an overall authority in charge of coordinating different medical personnel groups during an epidemic.

❑ 17. I know personally the key individuals from the state and local authorities who will assist in maintaining public order and enforcing control measures, if needed, during an epidemic.

❑ 18. I am familiar with the procedure for enlisting the National Guard's assistance during a public health emergency.

SURGE CAPACITY

❑ 19. I know how to access current recommendations on treatment of cases and prevention of transmission in the hospital, long-term care and home care settings.

❑ 20. My jurisdiction's emergency response planning has involved health care product and service providers to determine how to best prevent and control disease spread and manage the health care of the population during an epidemic.

Box 8.2 (continued)

☐ 21. I am familiar with the required protocol for securing needed emergency healthcare services and supplies during a public health emergency.

☐ 22. My jurisdiction has identified ways to augment medical, nursing, and other health care staffing to maintain appropriate standards of care during an epidemic.

☐ 23. My jurisdiction has identified ways to augment public health laboratory, epidemiology and disease control staffing to meet emergency needs and in the event public health workers are affected by an epidemic.

☐ 24. My jurisdiction has a process to recruit and train medical volunteers for provision of care and vaccine administration during a public health emergency.

☐ 25. My jurisdiction has identified alternate facilities where overflow cases from hospitals and well persons needing quarantine away from home can be cared for and has developed processes with Emergency Medical Services to assess, communicate, and direct patients to available beds.

☐ 26. My jurisdiction has identified facilities for outpatient and inpatient care of children with SARS and their families.

☐ 27. My jurisdiction's epidemic plan addresses the mechanics of how isolation and quarantine will be carried out, such as providing support services for people who are isolated or quarantined to their homes or temporary infirmary facilities and protection for workers providing these services.

☐ 28. My jurisdiction has a plan for ensuring that appropriate personal protective equipment, including N-95 or higher level respirators, is made available for persons whose job requires exposure to people with SARS, and that needed training and fit-testing are provided.

☐ 29. My jurisdiction has a plan for dealing with mass mortality, including transportation and burial of bodies.

☐ 30. My jurisdiction has a plan for providing mental health services to mitigate the impact of a SARS epidemic.

COMMUNICATIONS AND EDUCATION

☐ 31. I have conveyed the importance of epidemic preparedness, and its overlap with bioterrorism preparedness, to my jurisdiction's chief executive and to other state and local law and policy makers.

❑ 32. I know personally the key individuals from public health agencies, the medical community, and the political community with whom I will need to communicate during an epidemic.

❑ 33. My jurisdiction has begun educating the public on epidemic SARS to instill acceptance of the epidemic response (including quarantine and isolation) and to optimize public assistance during an epidemic.

❑ 34. My jurisdiction has opened a regular channel of communication and begun educating health care providers (including first responders) and their organizations and unions on epidemic SARS (including diagnosis, treatment, and management of cases and contacts to prevent transmission).

❑ 35. My jurisdiction has opened a regular channel of communication and begun educating chief executive officers of health care organizations on epidemic SARS (including management of patients in health care settings, health care worker protection, physical facility needs, voluntary or forced furloughs of exposed workers, etc.).

❑ 36. My jurisdiction has established a multi-component communications network and plan for sharing of timely and accurate information among public health and other officials, medical providers, first responders, the media and the general public.

❑ 37. My jurisdiction has begun identifying and planning to produce and provide education and information materials for media, providers, the public, and occupational groups whose duties may expose them to SARS, in appropriate languages and in forms suitable for limited literacy populations.

❑ 38. Whoever is selected as the primary public spokesperson for my jurisdiction during an epidemic is ready to clearly and consistently answer the following types of questions:

❑ How is the SARS-associated coronavirus (SARS-CoV) transmitted?
❑ How long are people infectious after they have SARS?
❑ What is isolation? What is quarantine?
❑ What is the justification for isolation of cases and quarantine of contacts?

Box 8.2 (continued)

❑ What is the legal authority for isolation of cases and quarantine of contacts?

❑ What is the difference between a probable and a suspected SARS case?

❑ Who should be tested for the SARS-associated coronavirus?

❑ What can members of the public do to protect themselves?

❑ In the event a vaccine or antiviral treatment become available, what specific priority groups might be vaccinated or treated first?

❑ 39. My jurisdiction has identified the most effective media to get messages out to the public during an epidemic (e.g., TV, radio, print media, internet, Web sites, hotlines).

❑ 40. My jurisdiction has planned how to coordinate state, local, and federal public messages and ensure they are consistent and timely.

LABORATORY AND SURVEILLANCE

❑ 41. In the event of a SARS epidemic, I will have available daily counts of key community health indicators, such as numbers of emergency department visits, hospital admissions, deaths, available hospital beds and staff, facility closings, numbers of contacts being traced and numbers under quarantine.

❑ 42. The public health laboratory that serves my jurisdiction can test for the SARS-associated coronavirus by serology and/or PCR.

❑ 43. My state has identified those labs that can test for the SARS-associated coronavirus.

❑ 44. The public health laboratory that serves my jurisdiction has linked to clinical laboratories and provided training on the use of SARS tests, biosafety, specimen collection, packing and shipping, and rule-out testing.

❑ 45. Public health laboratories in my state have computerized record-keeping to help with data transmission, tracking, reporting of results to patients and facilities, and analysis during an epidemic.

❑ 46. My jurisdiction has determined how to assess and document the spread and impact of disease throughout the population, including special populations at risk (such as health care workers and first responders), during a SARS epidemic, including enhancements to routine surveillance.

❑ 47. My jurisdiction has computerized record-keeping for cases, suspected cases, contacts, and persons under public health isolation or quarantine orders to help with data transmission, tracking and analysis during an epidemic.

❑ 48. My jurisdiction's epidemiology staff, in cooperation with other public health agencies, has the capacity to investigate clusters of SARS cases, to determine how disease is being transmitted, to trace and monitor contacts, to implement and monitor quarantine measures, and to determine whether control measures are working.

❑ 49. My jurisdiction has plans for educating health care providers about recognition and reporting of SARS, about the current case definition, and about sources of current information on all aspects of SARS.

PREPAREDNESS IN OTHER AGENCIES

❑ 50. The emergency response system is ready to deal with epidemic SARS as called for in an all-hazards or epidemic plan.

❑ 51. My jurisdiction has carried out a community-wide epidemic SARS table-top or field exercise, to train on and evaluate its epidemic plan.

❑ 52. Community partners such as hospitals, EMS services, law enforcement agencies, health care practitioners, environmental hygiene/remediation services, news media, schools, and colleges know what part they are expected to play during an epidemic and are prepared to do so.

❑ 53. The law enforcement and court system in this jurisdiction are prepared to enforce isolation and quarantine orders and to promptly adjudicate appeals to public health orders, as provided by statute.

SOURCE: Centers for Disease Control and Prevention. (2004). *Public Health guidance for community-level preparedness and response to severe acute respiratory syndrome (SARS) Version 2 Supplement A: Command and control, Appendix A1, State and local health official epidemic SARS checklist*. Retrieved August 18, 2004, from http://www.cdc.gov/ncidod/sars/guidance/A/word/app1.doc

Box 8.3   MAD COW IN CANADA

With the threat that bovine spongiform encephalopathy—also known as BSE, or mad cow disease—has begun to appear in the U.S., once again Canadians and Canadian cattle producers are worried about the potential impact on the economy and the culture.

For years, Canada had been virtually free of mad cow disease. But in May 2003, veterinary officials in Alberta confirmed that a sick cow sent to a slaughterhouse in January of that year had been inspected, found to be substandard, and removed so that it would not end up as food for humans or other animals. The carcass was, however, sent to a processing plant for rendering into oils. Its head was kept for testing. Samples were sent to the world testing laboratories in the U.K., which confirmed the case of mad cow.

"What is important is that the system worked," said Alberta's agriculture minister, Shirley McClellan. "We have a very thorough and respected inspection system." She was insistent to remind the public that the disease is not contagious within a herd.

But McClellan's assurances didn't stop the U.S., Japan, South Korea, Australia and other countries from imposing temporary import bans of Canadian beef.

Several ranches in Alberta, B.C. and Saskatchewan were quarantined as a precaution, including the infected cow's home ranch.

In an investigation into the source of the infection, 1,400 cows were slaughtered and tested for the disease. Only the single case was ever found.

Western premiers demanded $360 million compensation from the federal government for losses to the beef industry because of the mad cow scare. Ottawa would later offer $190 million.

Over the summer of 2003, cattle ranchers held barbeques across Canada to help promote Canadian beef.

In August, the U.S. reopened its borders to some Canadian beef, but the border was still closed to live cattle. By this time, a cow that would have normally sold for $1,300 was selling for $15. Canadian beef producers asked Ottawa to approve a mass slaughter of 620,000 cattle to reduce the size of the herd and prevent further damage to the industry.

In October, CBC News reported that the border would reopen to live cattle in December 2003. But on Dec. 23, 2003, the U.S.

announced that it had discovered its first apparent case of BSE in a cow in Washington state.

Several countries banned beef from the U.S. soon after the announcement, but Canada restricted imports only on some products made from cattle and other ruminants. It still allowed the import of cattle destined for immediate slaughter, boneless beef from cattle under 30 months of age and dairy products.

DNA evidence later revealed that the cow was born in Canada, and the U.S. kept its border shut to live Canadian cattle.

THE BRITISH CONNECTION

Previously, Canada had only one case of a cow infected with BSE. The animal, reported on a farm near Red Deer, Alta., in December of 1993, was imported from Britain. Agriculture Canada opted to destroy the animal and its five herd mates.

Mexico, one of the largest importers of Canadian beef at the time, temporarily banned imports of Canadian cattle after the incident. The United States, another major consumer of Canadian beef, sent observers to Canada to see how the incident was handled.

As a result, and because of the rumours of possible human health implications circulating in Britain, the Ministry of Agriculture decided to destroy any animal imported from Britain between 1982 and 1990, the year a ban was placed on British beef imports to Canada. This slaughter also included the offspring of any of those animals.

All told, 363 animals were destroyed and their owners compensated. Some said the destruction was unnecessary, especially the farmers whose cattle were killed, but the ministry said it was better to err on the side of caution after seeing what was happening in Britain.

During the summer of 1995, the disease surfaced again. The Canadian Red Cross Society revealed two of its donors had died of Creutzfeldt-Jakob disease, CJD. Two years later, concern over blood was raised again after a man was found to be a carrier of a gene linked to a hereditary form of CJD.

In August 2002, doctors confirmed a man in Saskatchewan died from new variant CJD—the human counterpart to mad cow disease. He had spent some time in the United Kingdom and it appeared he acquired the disease while he was there, doctors said.

The man had an endoscopic examination before he died and that equipment was then used on other patients. However,

Box 8.3 (continued)

because of disinfection and cleaning procedures, the risk of cross contamination is minute. Public health officials phoned patients who had received examinations with the endoscope to inform them.

It's still not known if the disease can be transmitted through blood products.

In 1996, the Canadian government suspended imports of British beef embryos and semen. Agriculture Canada also began a review of the practice of using meat meal and bone meal as a protein source in beef cattle feed. In 1997, changes designed to keep animal parts out of animal feeds were implemented.

Canada also doesn't import meat or bone meal from nations where cows have been found to have BSE.

In spite of Canadian officials' confidence, a European Commission report released in 2000 placed Canada in the second rank of risk for mad cow disease. A top rank designates almost no risk.

The report cited the fact that, before 1992, mammalian meat and bone meal were routinely fed to cattle. It also noted that material containing nerve endings was rendered at temperatures too low to kill off the agent of mad cow disease, and was still used for feed.

For these reasons, the report concluded a small element of risk is still present for Canada's cattle. The Canadian Food Inspection Agency says it will make an appeal to the EC's scientific steering committee, asking for a better designation.

QUICK FACTS

Canada has close to 13.5 million cows and calves. About 5.7 million (or 42 per cent) are in Alberta.

Canada's total beef exports amount to $2.2 billion annually, and have risen sharply in recent years. Since 1991, beef exports have risen from 100,000 tonnes to about 500,000 tonnes. Growth in exports has been greatest to Japan, South Korea and Mexico. Alberta's share of total beef exports is 39 per cent (worth about $860 million a year).

SOURCE: CBC News Online. (2004, January 6). Mad Cow in Canada: The science and the story. Retrieved September 4, 2004, from http://www.cbc.ca/news/background/madcow

at large, but trained emergency professionals know that an effective response to disaster depends on calm threat assessment and reaction. It helps if people have gone through something similar before. The third step or phase is response—what one does when the emergency actually occurs. In part this involves following the plans made during the preparation phase, but every situation is unique. Moreover, there has to be an element of innovation and creativity in responding to a particular situation, so plans need to be supple enough that they provide guidance without tying people to the specifics. The final phase is recovery—reviewing what happened, how well the response went, and what lessons there are to be learned for the next event.

There is a temptation to think of emergency response in terms of elaborate plans and clear command and control organization. Obviously plans are important, as are drills and preparation. Some central authority and clear lines of responsibility are important as well. But the nature of disaster and emergency ultimately requires supple responses by interacting systems: local governments, communities, provinces, national authorities, and sometimes even international actors. As discussed in the theoretical section of this chapter, disaster and emergency response needs to be thought of in terms of complex systems made up of multiple actors who in the end do not have ultimate authority over anyone else. Mobilizing a complex system to respond to disaster involves an enormous amount of information processing and communication. As Comfort notes in her study of the emergency responses to eleven earthquakes around the world,

A sociotechnical approach requires a shift in the conception of response systems as reactive, command-and-control driven systems to one of inquiring systems, activated by processes of inquiry, validation, and creative self-organization. Inquiring systems function best with an appropriate investment in information infrastructure and organizational training that enables the system to assess accurately the conditions in a community that precipitate risk and to act quickly to reduce threat or minimize the consequences when destructive events occur. Combining technical with organizational systems appropriately enables communities to face complex events more effectively by monitoring changing conditions and adapting its performance accordingly, increasing the efficiency of its use of limited resources. It links human capacity to learn with the technical means to support that capacity in complex, dynamic environments. (Comfort, 1999, pp. 263–64)

Since September 11, 2001, organizing for emergency response to security threats has become a priority for both Canada and the United States. Shortly after the terrorist attacks, President Bush reorganized his administration by forming the Department of Homeland Security (DHS) to coordinate a host of functions that previously were scattered through the federal government. The DHS is massive; it employs 180 000 people throughout the country from twenty-two former government agencies such as the Immigration and Naturalization Service, the Federal Emergency Management Agency (FEMA), the Secret Service, and the Coast Guard. DHS is organized into four directorates: Border and Transportation Security, Emergency Preparedness and Response, Science and Technology, and Information Analysis and Infrastructure Protection. In its first two years, DHS listed a range of accomplishments that illustrates the scope of its activities in protecting the American public. For instance, it introduced something called the US-VISIT (United States Visitor and Immigrant Status Indicator Technology), which uses biometrics to identify travellers at major airports and seaports. Another was the unification of various border services that previously had been provided by the agriculture, immigration, and customs departments. It established the Homeland Security Operations Center, which brought together twenty-six federal and local law enforcement agencies and the intelligence community under one unified electronic warning system. The Citizen Corps initiative resulted in the formation of preparedness councils in over 900 communities. The Department of Homeland Security also promised that by the end of 2004 there would be a Unified National Database of Critical Infrastructure. These are only a few examples, but they illustrate the scope and depth of the American concerns with terror. They also demonstrate the point that emergency response in most instances happens on the ground where the emergency is first declared. The federal government can do a lot of coordination and interoperability of communications equipment, but ultimately the first line of response to any emergency is at the community level and among businesses and firms. This means that the DHS is interacting with and coordinating a vast network of governmental and nongovernmental actors to effectively deal with terrorist threats. The sad irony is that the protection of liberty and democratic government requires a highly centralized and some would say intrusive agency.

Canada has been compelled to match American efforts in emergency preparedness and security. The constant flow of trade and travel between the two countries made it imperative that Canada demonstrate to the United States that it too would take terrorist threats seriously, even though the likelihood of a terrorist attack in Canada is remote. There are two key elements to emergency preparedness in Canada—protection of critical infrastructure and emergency response, and counterterrorism. The two are related, but involve different institutional configurations. The foundations for emergency response were laid in 1980 with the creation of the Joint Emergency Preparedness Program (JEPP). This is essentially a funding program that channels federal money to provincial and local emergency preparedness projects on a cost-shared basis. It is administered by the Office of Critical Infrastructure Protection and Emergency Preparedness (OCIPEP), which was created in February 2001 to take over the activities of Emergency Preparedness Canada. Complementing JEPP, which is aimed at mitigation and preparation, is the Disaster Financial Assistance Arrangements (DFAA). DFAA provides funds to other governments in Canada to help defray the costs of response and recovery, such as emergency food, clothing and shelter, and restoration of homes, business, and infrastructure. Both these programs function under the framework of the Emergency Preparedness Act, passed in 1988. The sums involved can be staggering. In the late 1990s, for example, Canada had the misfortune to suffer three major weather-related disasters: the Saguenay River flood (1996), the Red River flood (1997) and ice storm in Eastern Canada (1998). Total costs of these three events were estimated to be over $9 billion, and the federal government alone provide $1.5 billion in disaster relief.

In December 2003 a new department was created to integrate all aspects of emergency preparedness and wider threats, Public Safety and Emergency Preparedness, headed by the deputy prime minister. It coordinates in a single portfolio activities once under the responsibility of the Solicitor General (which no longer exists as a ministry), National Defence (the Office of Critical Infrastructure Protection and Emergency Preparedness was previously under it), the National Crime Prevention Centre, and a newly created Canada Border Services Agency. As well, in May 2004, the federal government issued its first comprehensive statement on national security entitled *Securing an Open Society*. The document is revealing in several ways. First, the fact that this represents the first comprehensive policy statement on security suggests both the new priority that security issues have and the heightened threat environment in which Canada finds itself. Second, threats that at one time were parcelled out among different departments and agencies are now coordinated under one umbrella—security. This includes natural disasters and emergencies, transportation, intelligence, public health, and border security. The policy promised to put more money into security and intelligence gathering, and proposed to create a new parliamentary committee on National Security as well as a Government Operations Centre to coordinate key national players in the event of national emergencies. It also proposed the creation of a national Public Health

Agency and a Chief Public Health Officer for Canada. Finally, it pledged to create an external advisory body on National Security (Privy Council Office, 2004).

Canada's counterterrorism activities are governed by the National Counter-Terrorism policy, which was significantly updated in 2001 with the passage of the Anti-Terrorism Act in the wake of the 9/11 attacks (the act was passed December 2001). It contained amendments to the Criminal Code, the Official Secrets Act, the Canada Evidence Act, and the Proceeds of Crime (Money Laundering) Act, all intended to deal with terrorist acts as well as activities (i.e., raising money) in support of terrorism. With the act, it became a criminal offence to knowingly collect or provide funds to carry out terrorist activities, be a member of a terrorist group or facilitate its activities, or knowingly harbour or conceal a terrorist. It also increased police investigatory powers. A key element of the legislation, of course, is the definition of a terrorist group or entity. The law allows the authorities to maintain a public "list of entities" (a person, group, trust, partnership or fund, or an unincorporated association or organization) if there are reasonable grounds that that entity "has knowingly carried out, attempted to carry out, participated in or facilitated a terrorist activity; or is knowingly acting on behalf of, at the direction of or in association with an entity that has knowingly carried out, attempted to carry out, participated in or facilitated a terrorist activity." The listing is a public statement that the government believes that entity to be involved in terrorist activities, and it also freezes the entity's assets. As of June 2004, the list consisted of thirty-five entities. The first ten entities on the list are described in Box 8.4.

Emergency preparedness and counterterrorism are now part of a single continuum of policy responses, since of course the great fear now is that terrorist groups will induce emergencies as part of their campaigns. The Madrid subway bombings in March 2004, for instance, were likely an Al-Qaeda attack that resulted in 201 dead and 1500 injured. The 2003 blackout in Ontario and the northeastern United States could just as easily have been caused by a terrorist attack, and would have had the same effect of paralyzing a good part of the continent. Natural disasters still occur, of course, and there are routine ways of preparing and responding to them. The new and alarming connection between emergency preparedness and security concerns is forcing a radical rethinking across a range of policy areas that at one time would have been in separate organizational silos. The visible organizational evidence of this is the creation of agencies like Homeland Security in the United States and Public Safety and Emergency Preparedness Canada. Legislation on terrorism, charitable donations, security and intelligence gathering, customs and border control—all have changed in the last five years and been brought closer.

| Box 8.4 | LISTED ENTITIES UNDER CANADA'S ANTI-TERRORISM ACT (A SELECTION) |

1. Groupe islamique armé (Armed Islamic Group, GIA)

The GIA is a radical anti-government, anti-intellectual, anti-secularist and anti-Western Sunni Muslim group based in Algeria. The GIA is known to have targeted intellectuals, journalists and foreigners, and is known to operate outside Algeria. The group has links with terrorist organizations throughout the Middle East and Central/Southern Asia, including Al Qaida and Osama bin Laden.

2. Groupe salafiste pour la prédication et le combat (Salafist Group for Call and Combat, GSPC)

The GSPC is a radical Sunni Muslim group seeking to establish an Islamist government in Algeria. It is a breakaway faction of the GIA. The GSPC has adopted a policy that violence should be targeted on security or military targets, foreigners, intellectuals and administrative staff. The GSPC is believed to have been active outside Algeria. The group has been affiliated to Osama bin Laden and groups financed by him.

3. Al Jihad (AJ)

The AJ, founded during the 1970s, claims to offer a remedy for Egypt's social, economic and political problems by challenging the current Egyptian government. The group employs terrorism in an attempt to overthrow the current government and replace it with an Islamic state. The AJ has been actively involved in terrorism since its inception, including the assassination of then Egyptian President Anwar Sadat in 1981. AJ activity outside of Egypt has included involvement in the two 1998 US embassy bombings in Africa in which some AJ members were indicted by the US. The group has links with Osama bin Laden and the Al Qaida, and is also a signatory to the 1998 fatwa (religious decree) against the US and Israel.

4. Vanguards of Conquest (VOC)

The VOC is a radical armed wing of, but closely aligned with, the AJ that has actively been involved in terrorism including attempted assassinations against the Egyptian Interior Minister,

Box 8.4 (continued)

Prime Minister and President. The VOC has released 'assassination lists' which have included civilians.

5. Al Qaida

Al Qaida is the central component of a network of Sunni Islamic extremist groups associated with Osama bin Laden, which functions as an umbrella organization, with branches in the Middle East, Africa, Central Asia, and North America. Al Qaida is committed to overthrowing secular governments in Islamic countries and using force to eliminate all Western influences in such countries. Bin Laden, and those within his network, believe that the only way these goals can be achieved is through violence and terrorist activities up to and including martyrdom. The Bin Laden network has been directly or indirectly associated with: the 1998 bombings of two US embassies; the 2000 bombing of the USS Cole; and the 2001 World Trade Center and Pentagon attacks.

6. Al-Gama'a al-Islamiyya (AGAI)

The AGAI strives to violently overthrow the current Egyptian government and replace it with a state governed by Islamic law. It is one of the largest and most extreme Egyptian terrorist groups. The AGAI specializes in armed attacks against government and security officials, Western tourists and any others believed to be opponents of an Islamic state in Egypt. The group has been described as having links to the network of Osama bin Laden and signed his February 23, 1998 Fatwa (religious decree) against the United States and Israel saying it was the individual duty of all Muslims to kill American citizens and their allies, civilian or military, wherever possible.

7. Al-Ittihad Al-Islam (AIAI)

The AIAI is an internationally established Islamist organization that engages in terrorism in Somalia and Ethiopia. Guided by the goal of creating an Islamist theocracy based on Islamic law, the AIAI's objective is the unification of all Muslims in the region under the banner of creating a 'greater Somalia'. To achieve this goal, the AIAI is committed to using indiscriminate terror tactics, including the targeting of foreigners and political leaders of foreign states. The AIAI has ties with states that are known to support terrorism and is believed to have operational links with Al Qaida.

8. Islamic Army of Aden (IAA)

The Islamic Army of Aden is a Yemen based radical Islamic organization which advocates the overthrow of the Yemeni government and the creation of an Islamist theocracy in Yemen based on Sharia'h (Islamic law). Combating Western influences not only in Yemen but also within the Islamic world, the IAA opposes the use of Yemeni ports and bases by the United States and other Western countries, in addition to its call for the expulsion of Western forces in the gulf and the lifting of international sanctions against Iraq. Guided by these goals, the IAA has used terror tactics in order to achieve their objectives, including the targeting of foreigners and political representatives of foreign states. While the IAA is based in Yemen, its ties with terrorist groups such as Al Qaida, and states that are known to support international terrorism, make it of broad significance in the region.

9. Harakat ul-Mujahidin (HuM)

Harakat ul-Mujahidin (HuM), is a Pakistan based radical Kashmiri Islamist organization which advocates the liberation and subsequent integration of Kashmir from Indian control into Pakistan, in addition to calling for a jihad against America and India. Within this context, the HuM advocates, is devoted to, and has called for: the creation of an Islamist theocracy in Pakistan based on Sharia'h (Islamic law), as well as a jihad to 'liberate oppressed Muslims worldwide', denounces pluralist parliamentary democracy, religious tolerance and equal rights for women as corrupting influences on Islam, and views the United Nations as an institution supporting the genocide of Kashmiris. Guided by these goals and ideology, the HuM employs various methods to achieve its goals which have included, but are not limited to, the targeting, kidnapping and execution of foreigners, hijacking, as well as the targeting of Indian government officials, their representatives, and symbols of the Indian government, as well as foreigners and political representatives of other foreign states. The HuM signed the 1998 fatwa put out by Al Qaida and Osama Bin Laden and is therefore allied with, or part of, the Al Qaida coalition.

Box 8.4 (continued)

10. Asbat Al-Ansar

Asbat Al-Ansar is a Lebanon-based, Sunni extremist organization, composed primarily of Palestinians. Asbat Al-Ansar builds upon the ideology of fighting the U.S. and Israel, and seeks to establish a radical Islamic regime in Lebanon. In order to achieve its goals, Asbat Al-Ansar participated in and facilitated several terrorist attacks in Lebanon which have included targeting some Western and other embassy personnel, killing Lebanese officials, bombing public and religious places, and killing senior members from rival groups.

SOURCE: Public Safety and Emergency Preparedness Canada, *List entities.* Retrieved August 18, 2004, from http://www.psepc-sppcc.gc.ca/national_security/counter-terrorism/Entities_e.asp

There are several significant policy challenges that flow from these changes. The first and most obvious is the threat to civil liberties. This has been a mounting concern in all countries where security measures have been strengthened. Intelligence services have been given strengthened mandates and new powers; new border security measures are considerably more invasive than in the past, and there have been reported instances of racial profiling. Finding the right balance between the protection of civil liberties and public safety will be an ongoing test of public authorities. A second challenge is less philosophical than it is organizational—the challenge of coordination and implementation. As we discussed in Chapter 5, all public policy faces the problem of implementation. That challenge is more acute in the emergency and security area than in most others. The sheer size of the organizations being created—as noted above, Homeland Security employs 180 000 people—means that there will be problems in internal coordination and communication. But it is in the nature of emergencies to require widely dispersed response, which is inherently difficult to manage. In the ice storm of 1998, for example, over 4 million people in Ontario, Quebec, and New Brunswick lost power, and 600 000 had to evacuate their homes. A disaster of this magnitude cannot be responded to simply by government alone, even though Ottawa, the provinces, and local municipalities all had to work together. Nongovernmental organizations, charities, international agencies, and volunteers have to come together to respond, and all somehow have to be coordinated in a system of "shared governance" (May and Williams, 1986). And of course, the context of an emergency means that by definition time pressures are high, as are the stakes in terms of human life and property. Since most emergencies are new in some sense, relying exclusively on prepared plans can introduce inflexibilities in response. An extreme example of this comes from the initial responses by American aviation and defence authorities in the 9/11 events—they relied on protocols developed in the 1970s for airplane hijackings. For all these reasons, Comfort emphasizes the importance of adaptive systems of response that rely on self-organization: "Sustaining the process of self-organization in a continuing way requires access to communication for all the participants to support the exchange of information, stored memory for actions taken that allow reflection and redesign, and evaluation and feedback from the other participants in the group" (Comfort, 1999, p. 271). This places the emphasis on the *system* of response, including the wide availability and exchange of information among members of that response community.

CRISIS MANAGEMENT

We distinguished earlier between crisis and emergency. Emergencies are typically physical events (though not exclusively) that threaten human life and property. From a "system" perspective—the political system, the economic system, even the social system—an emergency is a threat event, but not one so severe that it will cause the system to collapse. A crisis is usually considered to fall in that category; we might think of it as an emergency that so extreme that it threatens system integrity. Also, as we noted, an emergency can evolve into a crisis is if is handled badly and people lose faith in the authorities or managers. The tainted blood scandal arose first as an emergency around the safety of Canadian blood products, but became an organizational crisis for the Red Cross, which eventually had to close its doors in Canada (see Box 8.5, page 369).

This is more than just semantics. When we are looking at crises, we are looking at specific types of events that require specific management and policy responses that are different from the responses and preparation for emergencies. And while it is difficult to find conclusive evidence on this, it seems that crisis (a threat to organizational integrity) is becoming a more important and indeed routine part of the context for developing and implementing public policy. There are several reasons this might be true. First, information about what governments are doing is much more widely available than ever before thanks to the Internet and access-to-information legislation. And information flows more rapidly and easily because of a 24/7 media environment and communications technology. For example, when SARS broke out on the

Chinese mainland in 2002, the authorities initially forbade any public discussion of the disease. Despite this, almost half the urban population in Guangzhou received news of it through unofficial means, principally text messaging over mobile phones (Huang, 2003, p. 12). Second, in a news- and media-saturated policy environment, it is easily possible for "master narratives" to be formed by the press that then feed on themselves and are very difficult to revise or rebut. Good, for example, highlights the role the media played in the 1999 HRDC scandal. Initial reports were that $1 billion in HRDC grants and contributions had gone missing, a "billion-dollar boondoggle." Once that impression was made in the public mind, it was almost impossible to shake:

> After the immediate release of the HRDC grants and contributions audit on 19 January, and for the rest of the week, the media used a simple and dramatic storyline: 'One billion dollars lost." The expression, however distorted, was dramatic and the image vivid. A seemingly dull internal administrative audit was 'recontextualized' into a newsworthy sound-bite and a catchy headline. In fact, no money was lost. After months of individually reviewing 17,000 grants and contributions files across all programs in the department, representing some $1.6 billion, HRDC officials concluded that the amount of outstanding debts owing to the government was $85,000. . . . [T]he media developed a preformed storyline that the grants were used for political purposes and, as a consequence, corruption was inevitable. (Good, 2003, p. 64)

Third, as we have noted in previous chapters, there is a pervasive mood of cynicism and distrust of government. Bad news—any type of bad news—can very easily and quickly be framed in that mental context and seen as evidence of rank incompetence, malfeasance, or corruption. A crisis can grow out of a simple error if that error gets magnified to the point where it becomes emblematic of systemic problems. The HRDC scandal—such as it was—did in the end lead to the demotion of a minister who at the time had been widely touted as a possible future prime minister, and to the splitting of the department into two.

From a policy and management perspective, the key thing about crisis is responding to it and managing it as effectively as possible. Indeed the response itself—if badly coordinated—can become the crisis once the initial triggering event is over. In the case of HRDC, the triggering event was the release of an audit of grants and contributions that appeared to suggest that the monies were badly handled. Once the media framed the story in those terms, the actual crisis was a crisis of not being able to effectively respond and get the facts of the case on the public record. A crisis gets resolved when it is handled well and overcome. Of course, the problem is that crises are typically unexpected, take place under strong time constraints and uncertainty, and usually have enough new elements that one cannot rely exclusively on prepared plans. Nonetheless, in reviewing experiences in dealing with crises and emergencies, it is possible to distill some useful lessons (Canadian Centre for Management Development, 2003a; 2003b).

Perhaps the most obvious first step is to be mentally prepared to acknowledge the existence of a possible crisis. Managers should assume that crises will occur and that they can arise from almost any possible event, however innocuous. As Good states of his own response to the HRDC stories in the press, "I believed that the matter would 'blow over.' In retrospect, I should have read the media reports in a more pessimistic manner to prepare myself, and my staff, for what lay ahead" (Good, 2003, p. 211). He goes on to say that public servants should be accustomed to expecting the unexpected and to be "overly prepared for the expected"— in this case, paying close attention to the external environment and how it might respond to information about grants and contributions. A second step involves ensuring the ability to respond quickly and accurately to the crisis and, most importantly, to the way the media handles the crisis. "Once the crisis has been confirmed, it is important to immediately establish a management team to oversee the response. The designated members of the response team and spokespersons must suspend their normal activities and devote themselves fully to the crisis. It is essential to ensure that team members are prepared to assume the responsibilities assigned to them" (Canadian Centre for Management Development, 2003a, p. 26).

A third lesson is that those who are tasked with dealing with the crisis know their respective roles and the lines of accountability and leadership. This is important for a number of reasons. In government, there are usually several departments and agencies that can plausibly take a lead role, and not coordinating them can be disastrous— conflicting messages and contradictory communications are sure to make a bad situation worse. Another dimension is that in crisis situations it is often necessary to make difficult decisions, and without clear lines of accountability those necessary decisions may be delayed or confused.

A fourth key step, possibly the most important of the list, is developing a good communications strategy. This has several elements. The right spokespersons should be designated early in the crisis, properly briefed, and properly trained to deal with media. It is often the case that the first messages that get out to the public as a crisis is developing set the frame for much of what follows, and are difficult to change or shift. Information has to be circulated within the organization responsible for dealing with the crisis, in order to facilitate learning and organizational coordination. To the extent possible, responses to the media and other external audiences should be complete and honest, and if information is missing or unavailable, it should be produced as quickly as is feasible:

> The media almost always constitute part of the external audience and represent an important means of transmitting information to the public. However, it would be a mistake to take it for granted that the public receives all its information from the media. The group of external audiences can also include interest groups and strategic partners (e.g., another level of government, NGOs, the private sector, etc). Indeed, enlightened, informed external partners can also have a major influence on public opinion—they can constitute a less obvious line of defence and can even articulate other viewpoints that can help confine the crisis. It is also important for the lead department to consult these stakeholders, keep them regularly abreast of progress and of the various types of action taken. (Canadian Centre for Management Development, 2003a, p. 27)

The fifth step, once the crisis has been resolved, is to draw lessons from the event and try to prevent a similar thing happening in the future. Mitigation and prevention strategies have their limits of course, like generals always fighting the last war. But they are essential for organizational development and for at least having a chance of dealing with the next potential crisis that comes along, as one inevitably will.

We have defined crisis as a threat event that can undermine the integrity of a system. This can mean a government, a department, or even a policy or program. It is for this reason that crises eventually have to be addressed by leaders who have key responsibilities for those organizations or programs. Crisis management is not normal, routine management, and coordinating the response to a crisis may be the single most important thing that organizational managers do. That is why crisis management, while it requires collective and coordinated response, is a severe test for those at the top of the organization. While decisive action is often required, that has to be balanced against communications, information-sharing, and teamwork.

Box 8.5   THE TAINTED BLOOD CRISIS (1998)

BACKGROUND

The Red Cross has a history in Canada almost as old as the country itself. It can be traced back to 1885, to the battlefield of Louis Riel's North West Rebellion, where a surgeon general made a Red Cross flag out of white cloth and two torn strips of red artillery cotton so he could distinguish a horse-drawn wagon being used to transport the wounded. Eleven years after the rebellion, Dr. George Sterling Ryerson, the same man who flew the makeshift flag, won approval from Britain to form a Canadian Branch of the Red Cross in Toronto. The organization grew quickly and in 1909 the federal government adopted the Canadian Red Cross Society Act. In 1927, the International Committee of the Red Cross recognized the society as an autonomous group. It went on to become the preeminent not-for-profit organization in the country.

On February 3, 1947, the Canadian Red Cross opened its first civilian blood donor clinic in Vancouver with the goal of providing free blood to anyone who needed it. Before that, patients had to pay for or replace the blood they were given in hospitals. In the late 1970s and early 1980s, Canada's blood system infected approximately 1,200 people with the HIV virus and it has been estimated that another 12,000 people were infected with hepatitis C. Many of the victims were hemophiliacs and people who had received blood during routine operations. At that time we had less knowledge than we do now about these viruses. Many of those who had been infected did not know they had received contaminated blood. Some people unknowingly passed on the viruses to their spouses and family members. As a result by the 1990s it was estimated that the number of infected people had increased substantially and exponentially. The staggering number of victims illustrated that the blood system had failed the very people it was supposed to protect. In response many people began calling for a judicial inquiry into Canada's blood system.

In 1993 Justice Horace Krever was appointed to head a Commission of Inquiry with the mandate to investigate the management and operation and contamination of the blood system in Canada. After nearly four years of a public judicial inquiry, Justice Krever issued his much-awaited final report on November 26, 1997.

Box 8.5 (continued)

Krever's report stopped short of finding the Canadian government liable for the contaminated blood or singling out individuals for blame. But he criticized federal and local authorities for their roles in distributing the tainted blood. The report also criticized the Canadian Red Cross for failing to put into place an adequate screening program for high-risk blood donors. After the report was issued the Red Cross (through Gene Durnin) apologized. "While we cannot know your suffering, we will weep with you. While we cannot feel your loss we grieve with you. We are very sorry."

Krever also recommended that the thousands of people infected with hepatitis C should be entitled to automatic compensation. He did not set an amount. The 1,200 people infected with HIV through tainted blood products had already been compensated by the federal government. Further, the Red Cross and its insurers together with the provinces contributed to a second compensation program for HIV victims—the Multi-Provincial/Territorial Assistance Program. There had been no requirement for court proceedings or legal negotiations in an overwhelming numbers of these cases.

But federal and provincial health ministers decided not to compensate hepatitis C victims at all, leaving the Red Cross with billions of dollars in claims. This led to massive complications. By the time the issue had been sorted out the Canadian Red Cross had been forced to seek bankruptcy protection under the Companies' Creditors Arrangement Act. It shook the organization to its foundation and nearly brought it tumbling down.

SOURCE: Canadian Centre for Management Development. (2003). *The federal experience: Case studies on crisis and emergency management.* Ottawa: Canadian Centre for Management Development (now known as the Canada School of Public Service). Retrieved August 18, 2004, from http://www.myschool-monecole.gc.ca/Research/publications/pdfs/crisis_e.pdf

CONCLUSION

Emergency, crisis, and pressure have attracted more attention as themes in the private sector management literature than in the public sector, until recently. Corporations face competitors, and so something like a product recall or losing a top executive can threaten the viability of a corporation. Public sector organizations, at least traditionally, enjoyed some insulation from these types of pressures, but of course political crises arise all the time. However, they do not typically pose the same kind of threat to the entire viability of a program or the existence of a public sector agency.

The ground has shifted in many ways, and public policymaking under pressure is an increasingly important feature of doing policy work. The intensification of international terrorism in recent years is one obvious example, but is not the whole story. Dealing with natural disasters such as floods and forest fires has always been part of the government's responsibility, but it may be that as a result of climate change the incidence of these events is increasing (Briceno, 2004). The combination of interdependencies in things like trade (Mad Cow) and technology (Internet) mean that emergencies and threat events can spread rapidly and paralyze whole populations, if not industries and economic processes. Pandemics and public health risks appear to be on the rise. And finally, the public mood, while perhaps more supportive of governments that are addressing emergencies or attacks, is still suspicious. Coupled with a media bias towards "gotcha journalism," this can make for a volatile environment in which to deal with emergencies. If things are badly handled, even to a modest degree, there is a new potential for expansion into full-blown crisis:

> The modern crisis is the product of several modernization processes—globalization, deregulation, information and communication technology, developments and technological advances, to name but a few. These advances promote a close-knit world that is nonetheless susceptible to infestation by a single crisis. Comparatively slight mishaps within these massive and intricate infrastructures can rapidly escalate in unforeseen ways. A prime example can be found in the European food and agriculture sector. One animal was diagnosed with foot and mouth disease in a remote English farm and, within days, the disease had affected all of Europe. Farmers, slaughterhouses, distributors, butcheries, consumers, inspection agencies, policy makers, and politicians endured enormous economic and social-psychological costs. (Boin and t'Hart, 2003, p. 546)

It is important to remember the actual, political context of crisis and policymaking under pressure. Crises and emergencies are difficult to handle at the best of times, but if they are becoming both more frequent and with wider-reaching consequences, we should not be surprised that crisis management as a real process will sometimes look different than what we might hope from a "lessons learned" approach that does not take into account the real dynamics to which decisionmakers are exposed. Boin and t'Hart's (2003) review of the literature points out six broad public expectations about crisis that are not borne out by research. To begin with, there is a public expectation that leaders should put public safety first. In fact, policy leaders always have to balance the costs and benefits of mitigation and prevention. It is simply too costly to have absolute, 100 percent safety. Rather, it is a question of how much risk can be reasonably tolerated. As well, the public is somewhat schizophrenic on risk and safety issues. On the one hand it often complains about excessive regulation that stifles individual choice (e.g., pharmaceutical regulations that prevent access to experimental drugs) but on the other it expects that drugs available on the market have been tested to be safe. As well, mitigation and prevention of nonevents do not attract political credit. There is little political incentive to invest heavily in safety.

A second public expectation is that leaders should prepare themselves for worst-case scenarios, a recommendation that we made earlier. In fact, the evidence from both private and public sector organizations seems to be that, unless one has experienced crisis in the past, or is operating in a community with similar experiences, the organizational and leadership reflex is to place a low priority on continual crisis preparation. In part this is due to a rational calculation that there may be zero benefit from investing time in preparation for an event that may never occur. As well, less rationally, organizational leaders may be reluctant to confront weaknesses in their organizations. A third expectation is that leaders should heed warnings about future crises. The reality is that many crises take time to build, and in practice all kinds of warning signals are misinterpreted or ignored, usually because the crisis by definition is a "new" event and does not fit the frame of reference of authorities. In June 2004 the National Commission on Terrorist Attacks upon the United States concluded that there had been several intelligence failures in the run-up to the 9/11 attacks. The CIA in particular missed clues that suggested the crisis was looming:

> The problems that prevent leaders from heeding warnings are manifold and fundamental. Leaders are routinely engulfed in oceans of information and advice. Moreover, they face ambiguous and contradictory signals. Warnings do not come with flashing lights; they are hidden in expert reports, advisory memos, or a colleague's casual remark. The warnings have to be distilled from a series of seemingly minor and insignificant indications. An additional problem is that information passageways to leaders often are obscured. Bad news, in particular, faces formidable obstacles on its way to the top of the organization, especially in bureaucratic organizations. These barriers are fundamentally social. Nobody wants to alarm his boss unnecessarily, and nobody wants to acquire the reputation of a troublemaker. In the absence of these signals, leaders run a big

risk of becoming the victim of "silences" in the organizational communication pattern. (Boin and t'Hart, 2003, p. 547)

A fourth expectation is that during a crisis leaders take charge and directly oversee the crisis management activities. In reality, crises are much more fluid and dynamic events than this would allow, and in practice it is systems or networks of responses from many agencies, NGOs and other actors that deal with the multiple facets of a crisis. As we noted earlier, coordination is definitely required in crisis response, but it is important to have realistic expectations of how tightly that can be managed and directed from above. A fifth public expectation is that leaders show tangible sympathy for victims of a crisis or emergency. This extends from public expressions of grief and support to financial compensation and assistance. The problem is that in the heat of the moment, leaders can make promises that they subsequently cannot keep, or raise expectations so high that they inevitably disappoint. (This was a factor in the tainted blood scandal.) The final public expectation that Boin and t'Hart identify is that leaders strive to learn the lessons of the crisis. Again, the political context in the aftermath of a crisis almost actively militates against that. A normal reaction after a crisis has been dealt with is to find its causes, and this rapidly degenerates (especially with the media) in a blame game. Leaders know that they are a target, and so instead of dispassionately "learning lessons," they focus on spin control and plausible deniability.

Chaos, risk, emergency, and crisis: these take us to the outer limits of the "normal" policy process, and yet they are themselves becoming normal aspects and challenges of doing policy work. This is the turbulence mentioned in the subtitle to this book: effective public management requires the skills and capacities to manage policy processes in conditions of great and perhaps even increasing turbulence.

KEY TERMS

crisis—a turning point or moment of danger that threatens the integrity of an entire system

emergency—an abnormal and unexpected threat event that requires immediate action

emergency management—the process of developing and implementing policies and programs to avoid and cope with the risks to people and property from natural and man-made hazards

environmental scan—an assessment of both internal and external risks, usually in terms of strengths and weaknesses, and threats and opportunities

mitigation—actions taken based on a risk assessment to lower those risks and prevent them from happening

nonlinear policy problems—problems where small changes in initial conditions can have large consequences, where uncertainty is high, and where there are discontinuities in normal events and shared responsibilities for action

risk—probability of an event with negative consequences; key dimensions are level of probability and severity of risk

risk management—a management framework that encourages the identification and assessment of risk, and its mitigation or prevention as part of a medium- to long-term strategy

tipping point—dramatic moment in an epidemic when everything can change; a sudden, unexpected change in what to that point has been a stable system

Weblinks

Department of Homeland Security (United States)
http://www.dhs.gov/dhspublic/

Public Safety and Emergency Preparedness Canada
http://www.ocipep.gc.ca/home/index_e.asp

International Association of Emergency Managers
http://www.iaem.com

Riskworld
http://www.riskworld.com/

Society for Risk Analysis
http://www.sra.org

Further Reading

Boin, A., and t'Hart, P. (2003, September–October). Public leadership in times of crisis: 'Mission Impossible'? *Public Administration Review*, 63, 544–52.

Canadian Centre for Management Development. (2003). *The federal experience: Case studies on crisis and emergency management.* Retrieved August 18, 2004, from http://www.myschool-monecole.gc .ca/Research/publications/pdfs/crisis_e.pdf

Comfort, L. K. (1999). *Shared risk: Complex systems in seismic response.* Amsterdam: Pergamon.

Comfort, L. K. (Ed.). (1988). *Managing disaster: Strategies and policy perspectives.* Durham, NC: Duke University Press.

Giuliani, R. W. (2002). *Leadership.* New York: Hyperion.

Gladwell, M. (2000). *The tipping point: How little things can make a big difference.* Boston: Little, Brown and Company.

REFERENCES

Beck, U. (1992). *The risk society: Towards a new modernity.* Newbury Park, CA: Sage.

Boin, A., and t'Hart, P. (2003, September–October). Public leadership in times of crisis: 'Mission Impossible'? *Public Administration Review, 63,* 544–52.

Briceno, S. (2004, March). Global challenges in disaster reduction. *The Australian Journal of Emergency Management, 19,* 3–5.

Canadian Centre for Management Development. (2003a). *Crisis and emergency management: A guide for managers.* Ottawa: Canadian Centre for Management Development (now known as the Canada School of Public Service). Retrieved August 18, 2004, from http://www.myschool-monecole.gc.ca/Research/publications/pdfs/crisis_e.pdf

Canadian Centre for Management Development. (2003b). *The federal experience: Case studies on crisis and emergency management.* Ottawa: Canadian Centre for Management Development (now known as the Canada School of Public Service). Retrieved August 18, 2004, from http://www.myschool-monecole.gc.ca/Research/publications/pdfs/crisis_e.pdf

Cigler, B. A. (1988). Emergency management and public administration. In M. T. Charles and J. C. K. Kim (Eds.). *Crisis management: A casebook,* (pp. 5–19). Springfield, IL: Charles C. Thomas.

Comfort, L. K. (1999). *Shared risk: Complex systems in seismic response.* Amsterdam: Pergamon.

Furedi, F. (2002). *Culture of fear: Risk-taking and the morality of low expectation.* 2nd ed. London: Continuum Internationl Publishing.

Gladwell, M. (2000). *The tipping point: How little things can make a big difference.* Boston: Little, Brown and Company.

Good, D. A. (2003). *The politics of public management: The HRDC audit of grants and contributions.* Toronto: University of Toronto Press.

Health Canada. (2004). *Fetal alcohol syndrome/Fetal alcohol effect.* Retrieved August 18, 2004, from http://www.hc-sc.gc.ca/fnihb-dgspni/fnihb/cp/fas_fae/introduction.htm

Huang, Y. (2003, Fall). The politics of China's SARS crisis. *Harvard Asia Quarterly, 7,* 9–16.

Kelling, G. L., and Coles, C. M. (1996). *Fixing broken windows.* New York: Touchstone.

May, P. J., and Williams, W. (1986). *Disaster policy implementation: Managing programs under shared governance.* New York: Plenum Press.

Morçöl, G. (2002). *A new mind for policy analysis: Towards a post-Newtonian and postpositivist epistemology and methodology.* Westport, CN: Praeger.

Pal, L. A., and Maxwell, J. (2004). *Assessing the public interest in the 21st century: A framework.* Background study for the External Advisory Committee on Smart Regulation. Retrieved August 18, 2004, from http://www.smartregulation.gc.ca/en/06/01/su-10.asp

Pal, L. A., and Weaver, R. K. (Eds.). (2003) *The government taketh away: The politics of pain in the United States and Canada.* Washington: Georgetown University Press.

Privy Council Office (Canada). (2004). *Securing an open society: Canada's national security policy.* Retrieved August 18, 2004, from http://www.pco-bcp.gc.ca/docs/Publications/NatSecurnat/natsecurnat_e.pdf

Sharkansky, I. (1986). *Policymaking under adversity.* New Brunswick, NJ: Transaction Books.

Treasury Board of Canada. (2001a). *Risk management policy.* Retrieved August 18, 2004, from http://www.tbs-sct.gc.ca/pubs_pol/dcgpubs/riskmanagement/riskmanagpol1_e.asp#_Toc457619039

Treasury Board of Canada. (2001b). *Integrated risk management framework.* Retrieved August 18, 2004, from http://www.tbs-sct.gc.ca/pubs_pol/dcgpubs/riskmanagement/rmf-cgr01-1_e.asp#Risk

U.S.–Canada Power System Outage Taskforce. (2004). *Final report on the August 14, 2003 blackout in the United States and Canada: Causes and Recommendations.* Retrieved August 18, 2004, from http://www.nrcan.gc.ca/media/docs/final/B-F-Web-Part1.pdf

Chapter 9   *Conclusions*

Readers who made it this far will probably have a mixed reaction to the arguments in this book. Some of you will be impressed at the deep changes that governments and the policy process are undergoing and generally supportive of a more quality-centred, client-focused policy-making system. Others (perhaps even the same ones who are impressed!) will be dismayed or at least uneasy with the portrait drawn in this book. Governments are becoming more businesslike, and policy is arguably more responsive to clients and stakeholders. But is businesslike government the zenith of democratic aspiration? Decentralization seems fine, but how far can it go before we lose a sense of common standards and shared community? Client satisfaction is laudable, as is responsiveness to stakeholders. But are we merely customers and interests, or is there a richer role that we play in the public sphere as citizens? All of these questions should have occurred to you as you considered the previous chapters. They raise the issue of the quality of the policy process as well as its ultimate ends. It would seem that the intensity of antigovernment sentiment witnessed in the last decade is waning and that the importance of good governance for a healthy society is being acknowledged once again. But that acknowledgment is tempered by a stronger sense of the limits of the state, both in terms of its capacities and its procedures. For various reasons that are rooted in the factors discussed in Chapter 2, we expect government not merely to be efficient but to be "good" in some ethical sense as well. This chapter briefly summarizes the main arguments and findings from previous chapters, and then addresses these deeper questions of policy and democratic governance.

POLICY ANALYSIS: RETHINKING THE TOOL KIT

Policy analysis is a relatively new discipline in the modern sense, though of course thinking about what governments do goes back as far as the invention of state structures and stable social organizations as early as the Mesopotamian period around 350 BC. As Chapter 1 pointed out, the modern roots of the policy analysis movement lie in the 1950s and particularly in the 1960s expansion of American government programs in education and social assistance. Most of what passes today for professional policy analysis and evaluation has its foundations in the application of rational models and techniques drawn from the social sciences. There was great hope in the early years that these techniques would squeeze some if not all of the politics out of decisionmaking—perhaps relegating it to higher-order value choices—and lead to improvements not only in the way that policies were made but of course in the results as well. Chapter 1 touched on some of the debates that grew up around implementation and evaluation in the 1970s and 1980s, and that ultimately contributed to the malaise in policy studies and analytical work.

The 1990s was a decade of ascendancy for new theories of public management and their application in the form of reorganizations of major agencies and programs, along with often deep expenditure cuts and steep increases in taxes. Canada was close to the middle of the OECD pack in this regard, with countries like New Zealand and Britain going much further in changing the structure and practice of government. The changes at the federal level in Canada were nonetheless profound—50 000 civil servants were either let go or retired; departments like Transport Canada were virtually eviscerated; assets such as airports and harbours were divested to local authorities; major income support programs such as unemployment insurance and major transfer programs for health and social assistance were radically altered. The changes at the provincial level were no less profound: hospitals were closed, school boards abolished, cities and regions reorganized. The Harris and Klein governments were the vanguard in tax cuts, program reductions, and re-organizations, all of which invited massive illegal strikes by public sector workers in both provinces.

The pain seems largely over now. Barring some unforeseen massive turndown in the economy, governments across the country are running modest to large surpluses and simultaneously cutting taxes and increasing expenditures, especially in health. Debt is still a worry and may come back to haunt policymakers, especially in Ottawa, but the fiscal skies seem clear. This has contributed strongly to the resurgence of interest in policy analysis. The recent era of cuts was an era principally of "management," that is, managing reductions under the veneer of making informed choices about what should go and what should stay (witness Ottawa's Program Review saga and more recently its Expenditure Review), which in reality was driven by fiscal targets and the determination to manage processes in such a way as to achieve them. Now that money is available, real policy choices are on the table once again, and decisionmakers cannot hide behind the claim that their coffers are empty. The June 2004 election was a stark reminder of this, as voters contemplated competing platforms that all promised to spend billions, though with different priorities. But as we noted in Chapter 1, this has not been the only reason for the policy revival. Around the world, there has been a growing understanding that governments—however much they might be downsized or reduced in scope and influence—have a tremendous impact on their societies. That impact is not merely instrumental in the sense of providing basic services but includes systemic effects on the economy, the environment, and social structures themselves. While good **governance** does not necessarily result in strong economies and robust societies, bad governance will yield nothing but misery.

However, the modern policy movement bears the scars and the lessons of the last decade. For one thing, there is more humility about the practice of policy analysis itself. We will return to this in a moment, but the primary point is that the limits of the rational model and social science techniques are now widely acknowledged. Outside evaluation studies, which retain a strong empiricist and technical orientation, most other types of policy work recognize the inevitably value-laden character of policy choice, design, and implementation. For another thing, the new public management (NPM) movement of the 1990s left an indelible impression on thinking about the state and the public sector. Some of this has involved the transfer of business practices to the public sector, a transfer that is not always beneficial or appropriate. But most of it has resulted in a more skeptical posture about the possibilities of state action; an affection for big spending and an automatic assumption that if there is a public problem it has to be solved through government programs have been replaced by caution and by an appreciation that problems can be addressed through a variety of means. The final major difference in the current policy revival is the sensitivity to how the world seems to be changing fundamentally and hence altering both the nature of policy problems and their responses. Those changes are summarized in Chapter 2, but subsequent chapters demonstrated their impact across the full spectrum of the policy process. The traditional categories of problem definition, design, implementation, and evaluation certainly continue to apply and continue to be applied by policy-makers themselves to make sense of what they do. But the content of those categories has shifted in important ways in order to respond to the impact of globalization, culture shifts, and management theory.

Chapter 3 showed how the nature of problem definition has shifted in recent years. Problem definition remains central to thinking about policy, but the sources and the nature of the problems governments face have changed profoundly. We noted how globalization is now at the centre of the policy research agenda being discussed and debated around the country. The question of technology and productivity is entangled in the concept of the knowledge-based economy and society (KBES), itself an artifact of globalization and the new phase of industrial or post-industrial development. These forces are generating new challenges in the areas of economic growth, human development, and social cohesion. The chapter also argued that ideas in good currency—the bedrock for the social and political process of agenda-setting—have changed as well. The key change here has been in the perceptions of the fiscal capacity of governments. While those perceptions are relaxing a bit in the face of consistent and sustained surpluses, and will possibly shift even more with a left-leaning federal government after June 2004 (though one in which both parties—the Liberals and the NDP—still claim to abhor deficits) the conceptual terrain has shifted now away from spending toward "investment."

Chapter 4 carried this analysis forward to look at instrument choice and policy design. The new context is clear: spending instruments are being used cautiously and often in the form of "boutique" programs without major expenditures commitments; regulatory practices are being redesigned as well as being held more accountable; public ownership is practically dead. Governments around the world now prefer to design policies around self-regulative instruments or set framework regulations that look to results rather than micro-management of behaviour. There is more reliance on individual responsibility. Governments are experimenting more with partnerships and alternative delivery of programs and services, especially through the Internet. At the same time, however, there are signs that there is a new interest in government as a social regulator and protector. Concerns about crime, TV violence, and pornography are driving governments to be more, not less, robust in their interventions. The impact of globalization on jobs and communities is also forcing governments, even very conservative ones, to bridle their enthusiasm for market mechanisms in favour of economic and social policies that try to insulate their populations to some degree. On other fronts, as Chapter 2 outlined, profound value shifts in Western countries have also contributed to demands that governments address broad issues like the environment.

Chapters 5, 6, and 7 expressed the same themes. Implementation of public policy is changing everywhere to be less top-down and more explicitly designed around partnerships, with a clearer division between policy design and delivery. Policy communities have accordingly become more important in the policy mix. As governments get leaner, they depend more on their partners both for policy advice and implementation. Modern policy cannot be directed by government or merely supplemented by other actors in respective policy communities. Chapter 6 provided a good illustration of how this changed context alters the way in which we think about players in the policy process. Today, the emphasis is on "governance" as opposed to government—that is, on nonhierarchical, multiple-stakeholder, diffuse systems of negotiation and compromise in which government is a player and an occasional leader but more rarely the dominant actor (Rhodes, 1997). The notion of policy communities and policy networks flows directly from this appreciation. But why are governments limited to being players in networks? They remain undeniably large institutions, but the impact of globalization and technology on government practice and power has been profound. We pointed out in Chapter 2 that this diminution of power should not be exaggerated, but it has nonetheless occurred. Western governments no longer have monopolies of knowledge or expertise, nor do they have the capacity to tackle all the really important—but huge—problems that face the country. Take the question of productivity. Even if one assumes (and not everyone does) that governments have a policy role to enhance and encourage productivity, it is clear that the key players are going to be business, labour, and the research and innovation sectors. Governments today increasingly have to work in networks to design and implement policy solutions.

Chapter 7 showed how evaluation has changed as well. It has enjoyed a renaissance of sorts as governments have emphasized results, performance, and client satisfaction. With the new focus on results and clients, however, have come new emphases in evaluative techniques, harnessing them more closely to program review and the use of innovative implementation techniques. Chapter 8 is new to this edition, but its themes were adumbrated in earlier chapters and in the second edition. Security threats—from terrorism to computer viruses to pandemics—are connected to globalization. Some of the natural disasters that loom may be connected to industrial development and climate change. Whereas risk assessment and emergency and crisis management were on the fringes of public policy and public administration studies two decades ago, they are increasingly central to the tool kit.

Normally, it is useful to be skeptical of the cult of the "new." Not everything changes radically all the time, whatever advertisers and politicians may tell us. However, in the case of policymaking and public management, it does not seem hyperbolic to talk about a substantially new context and the need for new responses. The evidence of change in society and economy is all around us, as is the evidence of change in the ways that governments behave and public servants think about the nature of governance. While some of the new thinking in policy and management may indeed be a response to fads, or driven by the interests of international agencies such as the OECD or international consultants, it is undeniable that the changes are substantial and real.

Going "beyond policy analysis" has involved trying to think about the applicability of old tools to these new circumstances and problems.

There is yet another sense in which we may go "beyond policy analysis" or the traditional orientations of the discipline. As we noted in Chapter 1, the roots of policy analysis and evaluation were in a social science tradition of rationalism and **instrumentalism**. The latter means a problem-solving orientation that thinks in terms of a solid distinction between means and ends. Policy and the programs that flow from it are technical solutions as insulated as possible from values, ethics, and concepts of higher purpose. In practice, of course, policymaking is shot through with values, even though dealing with values raises substantial practical difficulties. As Peters notes,

> Despite these practical difficulties, it is important for citizens and policymakers to think about policy in ethical terms. Perhaps too much policymaking has been conducted without attention to anything but the political and economic consequences. Of course, those economic consequences are important as criteria on which to base an evaluation of a program, but they may not be the only criteria. Both the policymaker and the citizen must be concerned also with the criteria of justice and trust in society. It may be that ultimately justice and trust make the best policies—and even the best politics. (Peters, 1999, p. 454)

The remainder of this chapter will go beyond an instrumental perspective on public policy and policy analysis and address three key issues: the nature and purpose of modern governance, the role of ethics and values in policy and public management, and benchmarks for the policymaking process.

NATURE AND PURPOSE OF MODERN GOVERNANCE

In the end, what's it all about? What is the purpose of public policy and public policy analysis? The conventional, formulaic answer of course is the improvement of the lives of the population or the maximization of the public interest. These are formulaic answers because they have no content—everything depends on the definitions of "improvement" and of "public interest." Nonetheless, it seems that modern governments are being prodded in some new directions in terms of purpose and policy, purposes that are driven to a large extent by the changed circumstances we have discussed throughout this volume. Before we address them however, we need once again to emphasize that the changes in governance we have seen in the last decade do not necessarily imply smaller and weaker governments. We argued repeatedly in the previous chapters that characterizing these changes as smaller government is simplistic, particularly in this new era of fiscal surpluses. Indeed, there are some areas where demands for government activity have increased, and there has also been a rethinking of the nature of what government does. The following list of issues or themes is obviously idiosyncratic but does touch on some contemporary concerns and debates about what governments, in the end, are all about and the major new challenges they face, both in Canada and throughout the world.

THE STATE, BUSINESS, AND CITIZENS

One interesting development that touches on the nature of government is a rethinking of the idea popular in the 1990s that governments should be more like businesses and treat citizens more like customers and clients. The backlash against this started almost at the same time as the recommendation itself, particularly in the academic community. It has gathered force over the years, however, with an increasing emphasis on the differences between governments and businesses and the importance of treating citizens as citizens and not just customers.

The NPM, and a lot of the new policy thinking described in this book, is dedicated to making government more businesslike. There is nothing wrong with this, and in some instances, such as quality services and client satisfaction, it is long overdue. However, there is a difference between making government more businesslike and treating government just like another business, particularly in a post-Enron world where business practices have been severely criticized. The best businesses recognize that they have public responsibilities, as well as governance responsibilities to their customers, competitors, and employees. But that does not make them governments. The two spheres of government and business are quite distinct, and each should function in ways that are appropriate to its sphere. Government is vital for any civilized society, not simply as an instrument to get things done but as a public space wherein we fulfill and enjoy our responsibilities and privileges as citizens.

Several observers have noted that while the emphasis on service-client relations in the NPM thinking holds promise, it is too limited a vision of the full range of responsibilities and rationales of the public sector. Gow (1995), for example, points out, "In considering citizens as clients of the administration, one must wonder about the nature of the relationship as it concerns those who fall under the disciplinary authority of the state, be they prisoners, people in regulated industries or dependents of the state" (p. 558). Doern (1994) makes a similar point: "Bureaucracy seen abstractly as an 'it' serving the customer, 'us' or 'me,' in a new form of franchised 'McState' is not all or even *most* of what democratic governance is about" (p. 92). Mintzberg (1996) argues that we actually wear four hats in relation to government: customer, client, citizen, and subject. Governments do relatively few things for us as customers, that is, as consumers of goods and services that probably could just as easily be provided through the market. A larger proportion of the services we get from government, such as health care or education, are professional services for which we are clients. But we also relate to government as subjects, in the sense of the duties and obligations that we have to obey, and that, if we do not, will incur the discipline of state authority. Our relationship as citizens is more complex still, embracing both obligations as well as rights. Respecting the integrity of government does not mean that government should do all things and be all things. What it does mean is respecting the specific nature of government as well as its importance to the exercise of our democratic citizenship. It means preserving the dignity of the public square in the knowledge that if we characterize government as just another form of business, we risk losing our own character as citizens. A world of customers and clients might be a paradise of consumption and service, but it would not be a democratic commonwealth.

As we mentioned earlier, governments will not completely retreat from the shibboleths of NPM nor should they. Being treated like a valued customer who might be able to take his or her business elsewhere is a marked improvement over being treated as a faceless and powerless citizen waiting in an endless and dreary queue for the next available official. Receiving basic services more efficiently and responsively is a good thing. Certainly, as we noted in chapters 5 and 7, governments across the country are continuing to emphasize alternative service delivery, quality services, and citizen-centred service, and we noted the more robust version under Prime Minister Blair, which sees performance (to the extent of individualizing services) as key to good governance. This will not go away, but it is being complemented by a growing sensibility to an arena wherein people engage as citizens and not just as customers. Chapter 6 explored the burgeoning interest in citizen engagement and its growing role in the policy process. Sometimes this is done to tap into reservoirs of expertise and policy-relevant information, but often it is done with an eye to shoring up a sense of legitimacy for the system as a whole and bringing people more directly into the policy process. The regular calls for parliamentary reform that would enhance the relationship between MPs and the constituents (Boyer, 1992) reflect this concern, as do various schemes to revise the electoral system. The Institute for Research on Public Policy's 2000 report *Strengthening Canadian Democracy* explicitly grounded its proposal for electoral reform on opinion surveys that showed that Canadians "continue to feel that they do not have much say over what government does and that their elected representatives are not in touch with the people; they strongly support the idea of free voting by MPs. Finding ways to help Canadians feel better connected to government should be an important aspect of any program of democratic reform" (Howe and Northrup, 2000, p. 52). The constant references to citizens and enhanced citizenship in government policy documents from all levels is another canary in the coal mine on this issue. Indeed, the emphasis on the "democratic deficit" in 2003–2004 intensified as a result of scandals and an explicit agenda by the new Martin government to enhance democratic practices. For first time, changing the electoral system may actually be seriously contemplated.

SOCIAL COHESION AND SOCIAL CAPITAL

For the last decade there has been sustained interest in the concept of "social cohesion." The Policy Research Initiative (1996) defined social cohesion as "building shared values and communities of interpretation, reducing disparities in wealth and income, and generally enabling people to have a sense that they are engaged in a common enterprise, facing shared challenges, and that they are members of the same community." In the Canadian context, some of this should be read as code for the pre-occupations of the old national unity file and making sure that Quebec in particular feels more "socially cohered" to the rest of the country. Social cohesion also has an affinity with the concept of "social union," defined as "the web of citizen rights and obligations that give effect to our shared sense of social purpose and common citizenship" (Biggs, 1996, p. v). As a concept, social cohesion is somewhat fuzzy, but it has attracted a great deal of interest in the policy research community in Canada and internationally. In practice, the concept has evolved from "cohesion" to "exclusion": "Increasingly, the problem has been formulated not only as the lack of income at a single point in time in a person's life, but rather in terms of a persistent lack of the income and other resources needed to enable people to participate in the mainstream economy and society. . . . Surrounding each of the different concepts of poverty and exclusion are related concepts whose meaning needs to be pinned down in a consistent way. Equity, equality, cohesion, inclusion, universality, targeting, and dignity are examples" (Voyer, 2003).

Part of that interest is due to the way in which it captures the angst over globalization and its economic and social impacts. This angst is not unique to Canada but has engendered debate and discussion around the world:

> In these discussions, the focus is often on "deterioration." In a general way, the concept of social cohesion assumes there are certain societal-level conditions and processes that characterise a well-functioning society and that at this time these conditions may no longer be satisfied. . . . When these economic and political, as well as social, conditions are not met or when these processes are not functioning, citizens, groups and governments begin to sense that "things are falling apart" and "it's just not working." (Jenson, 1998, p. 17)

The deterioration cuts a wide swath: it can touch communities, family, crime rates, psychological states of mind, income inequality, unemployment, youth, intergenerational conflict—in short, just about anything that would appear to be affected by the turbulence of globalization and technology and that might be considered an ingredient in the way the communities "hang together" and the way that individuals feel about their current and future circumstances. The logic of social cohesion seems plausible enough: a prosperous, stable, and happy country is possible only if people trust each either and are prepared to share. A society where some are "left out" or "left behind" is a recipe for social tension and all the costs associated with it. The Blair government launched its own version of a program to address social cohesion by establishing in 1997 the "Social Exclusion Unit" (SEU) in the Cabinet Office. In 2002 it was relocated to a new, cross-cutting office of the deputy prime minister, so that the SEU could work more closely with relevant departments. Social exclusion is defined as a "shorthand term for what can happen when people or areas suffer from a combination of linked problems such as unemployment, poor skills, low incomes, poor housing, high crime environments, bad health and family breakdown" (Cabinet Office, 2000). The notions of social exclusion and social cohesion might seem to be most popular with liberal and left governments, but they also have a cross-ideological appeal, which in part explains their popularity. Conservatives of many stripes, except the most determinedly pro-free market, have traditionally placed high value on social institutions such as the family and local community. The pressures on these institutions as a result of modernity have attracted some conservatives to concepts similar to social cohesion (Jenson, 1998, pp. 25–26). The difference is more in the means to solve the problem, where conservatives will tend to support less interventionist instruments while liberals will look to state action. It is interesting that in Canada the concept of social cohesion has been most enthusiastically embraced by policy researchers oriented to the federal government; as we saw from the PRI policy agenda, "action" on this front could conceivably involve Ottawa in a wide range of social engineering projects.

Social capital is a related concept that has taken the academic world by storm and has seeped into more general public policy discourse. The contemporary version of the concept was originally proposed in the 1960s (Jacobs, 1961) but surged in popularity with Robert Putnam's (1993) work on Italian democracy. For Putnam, social capital refers to "connections among individuals—social networks and the norms of reciprocity and trustworthiness that arise from them. . . . '[S]ocial capital' calls attention to the fact that civic virtue is most powerful when embedded in a dense network of reciprocal social relations" (Putnam, 2000, p. 19). It hinges on norms, trust, and the ongoing reciprocal relations that they engender among members of a social group. Social capital evinces itself in dense networks of participation in voluntary groups and associations, where people absorb and maintain not only the norms of civic action and engagement but also the consequent foundations for interaction in politics and the economy. The idea is that a large stock of social capital makes for both a healthy and vibrant society and also for a robust democratic practice and effective and efficient economy. Social capital would therefore appear to be a major ingredient in social cohesion and has emerged as a key target for public policy interventions. The problem is that social capital builds up slowly, even though it can erode quickly, and, moreover, it has the character of something that must be developed and absorbed autonomously rather than imposed from above through government programs. Current research suggests, however, that policies that are "family friendly," which support voluntarism, which encourage both civic equality and individual autonomy in the educational system, and that engage the voluntary sector in the delivery of social programs may be levers that can maintain and expand social capital. This, at any rate, is Hall's argument about why social capital appears not to have declined as much in Britain as in the United States. Through their policies, "governments can and do affect the levels of social capital in their nation" (Hall, 1999, p. 458).

HEALTH CARE

There is perhaps no issue more central to most Canadians than health care. It regularly tops the polls as a matter of public concern, and the extraordinary role it played in the June 2004 federal election showed that it can mobilize millions of Canadians. In the last weeks of the campaign, Liberal attack ads targeted the Conservatives over value issues such as same-sex marriage and gun control, but essentially reduced their entire campaign pitch to hospital waiting lists and allegations that the Conservatives would privatize health care. For their part, all three major opposition parties (including the Conservatives) pledged to protect and extend health care. Over the five-week campaign, health care was elevated to more than just a key social policy; it was made emblematic of Canadian values, and by implication, anyone who did not support the current configuration of services was somehow "un-Canadian." This line of argument was first developed in the Romanow Commission on health care, which argued that public health care was not merely a service, but a distinguishing characteristic of Canada:

> In their discussions with me, Canadians have been clear that they still strongly support the core values on which our health care system is premised—equity, fairness and solidarity. These values are tied to their understanding of citizenship. Canadians consider equal and timely access to medically necessary health care services on the basis of need as a right of citizenship, not a privilege of status or wealth. Building from these values, Canadians have come to view their health care system as a national program, delivered locally but structured on intergovernmental collaboration and a mutual understanding of values. They want and expect their governments to work together to ensure that the policies and programs that define medicare remain true to these values. (Commission on the Future of Health Care in Canada, 2002, p. xvi)

Health care promises to be the Canadian public policy issue for the foreseeable future for several reasons. Perhaps the most pressing is its sheer cost. It is approaching 50 percent of most provincial budgets, and has been increasing at rates of about 8 percent a year. This was the reason behind the Ontario government's decision to introduce highly unpopular health premiums—unless something was done to either generate more money for the system or contain it, there would be only one item in the provincial budget. It has also been costly for the federal government. The Health Accord signed by Prime Minister Chrétien and the provincial premiers in 2003 promised to pump almost $39 billion more into the system over five years. Despite that pledge, the Martin government promised another $10 billion over two years to fix health care "for a generation" and deal with waiting lists. These costs are driven by an aging population (the more elderly tend to draw more health resources) and increasingly effective but expensive technology. As the population ages, it can be expected that health costs will continue to increase. This is a "slow" crisis—very different from the ones discussed in Chapter 8—that builds and builds, generates constant public anxiety, and for which there does not appear to be any easy solution.

To some extent Canadians, and their leaders, have painted themselves into a corner on this policy issue by elevating its public character to almost religious significance. For example, it is no accident that a key recommendation of the Romanow Commission was a Canada Health "Covenant." Canada is virtually alone in the developed world in outlawing some version of a parallel private system of health care, usually covered by private insurance. Ironically, despite the rhetoric, substantial portions of the system are "private" in the sense that they are for-profit but reimbursed or paid for by public funds. Hospitals are the most visible, and completely public (in the sense that they are run on a nonprofit basis, and services are free to patients and covered through provincial payments) elements of the system, but even they contract out ancillary services (e.g., laundry) to private firms. Virtually all physicians in Canada are effectively small businesses, since doctors work for themselves and not the state; their services are simply reimbursed on a fee-for-service basis. Services such as laboratory testing, X-rays, and medical imaging are increasingly performed by private firms, again which are reimbursed with public funds. Most famously, abortion clinics like those owned by Henry Morgentaler, are private, as are some MRI clinics. In short, the Canadian system is actually a blend of public and private, and there is nothing in the Canada Health Act or the Constitution that forbids private provision, as long as it is covered by public funds.

Despite this reality, the overwhelming "idea in good currency" in Canada is that the system is almost entirely public, and that any element of private provision would undermine its foundations. The Romanow Commission offered forty-seven recommendations, most of which were geared to higher spending across the system: new services like home care; specific needs like rural and Aboriginal communities; and better coordination, information sharing and performance measurement. These are laudable, and if ever implemented will both expand the system and make it more transparent and accountable. But a significant range of options that would still preserve a public system while allowing more flexibility for private purposes is off the policy table.

The Romanow Commission argued that Canadians could have an enhanced health care system if they were prepared to pay for it, and also argued that they could pay for it. Maybe. But the sheer cost of increasing health care services in competition with other public policy priorities like cities, security, defence, and regional development promises to make health care a controversial issue for years to come.

SECURITY IN A THREATENING GLOBAL ENVIRONMENT

Governments have a basic responsibility to protect their societies from external threat; put more positively, they have an obligation to maintain and protect the security of their citizens. The new twist on the security agenda comes from the new types of threats that exist in the contemporary world, particularly since 9/11. Security can be now seen in two related dimensions: human security and terrorism. Since the mid-1990s Canada's foreign policy has emphasized the changing nature of **human security** in a globalized world, and indeed the concept of human security has become a centrepiece of Canada's actions abroad:

> Since the end of the Cold War, security for the majority of states has increased, while security for many of the world's people has declined. The end of the superpower confrontation has meant greater security for states touched by that rivalry. Yet during this decade we have seen new civil conflicts, large-scale atrocities, and even genocide. Globalization has brought many benefits, but it has also meant a rise in violent crime, drug trade, terrorism, disease and environmental deterioration. It clearly does not follow that when states are secure, people are secure. (Department of Foreign Affairs and International Trade, 1999)

To some degree, the concept of human security is a partisan one, congenial to a Liberal government and pushed hard by a Minister of Foreign Affairs and with a strong humanitarian bent in the mid-1990s. But other governments have been forced to face similar realizations that something important has changed in the way that we conceive security in a new global context. The EU had to deal with the eruption of ethnic conflicts in the former Yugoslavia mere hours from its borders. The same ethnic conflicts have generated massive movements of people throughout Eurasia. The AIDS epidemic in Africa is threatening to swamp all current aid and development programs in the region by Western states. Environmental disasters and species extinction threaten populations in both the countries in which they occur and countries close in location and in trade. The Canadian government's response to these threats in the late 1990s was the concept of human security and "soft power." During the election campaign in June 2004, the Liberal government continued to promote peacekeeping and peace-making as key elements of Canadian defence policy, while the Conservatives promised to put more money into conventional defence forces. The ideological differences are important—one stresses nonmilitary and peacekeeping interventions while the other emphasizes credible military commitments—but both recognize enhanced security threats around the world. The role of the state in this respect is more complex. Of course, the terrorist threat has completely eclipsed a naively pacifist or isolationist position on security; this was developed in Chapter 8 at some length in reviewing changes to emergency and public security policy.

ETHICS AND GOOD GOVERNANCE

We mentioned earlier that the dominant tradition in policy studies has been instrumentalist, a focus on means and ends. Interestingly, discussions have turned increasingly to considerations of values and ethics in the public sector as a means to support good governance. This is not entirely new of course, with codes of ethics having been promoted by various professional associations of public servants for some years. But as we have argued throughout this book, there are some new pressures that have concentrated attention on this field, pressures that began building as early as the early 1980s and blossomed in the last decade (Kernaghan, 1996). One is the decreasing trust and faith in government among Canadian citizens. Barely 60 percent of eligible voters cast a ballot in the 2004 election. A way of addressing that is to ensure that public servants—either making or implementing policy—conduct themselves to the highest standards. Another pressure has been the effects of downsizing on morale. Encouraging public servants to cleave to strong values has been a way to forestall public sector workers' cynicism and bitterness. Finally, the emphasis on entrepreneurship, innovation, and flexibility in public sector organizations has meant less detailed oversight of the work done by public servants, fewer rules and minute procedures, and a greater focus on outcomes and performance—witness the HRDC and Groupaction scandals. Unless the public sector internalizes the appropriate ethical guidelines and value systems, there is a danger that the absence of controls will lead to sloth or even corruption.

In 1995 the Clerk of the Privy Council appointed nine Deputy Ministers Task Forces to deal with issues that would arise through the Program Review exercise. One of those task forces was dedicated to public sector values and ethics, reflecting the concern about ethics expressed in the auditor general's 1995 annual report (Auditor General 1995, chap. 1) and building on a study team on the same subject that had been under way at the Canadian Centre for Management Development (CCMD) under the chairmanship of John Tait, former deputy minister of Justice. Its report, entitled *A Strong Foundation* (Canadian Centre for Management Development, 2000) highlighted some of the new pressures on the public service that were creating the need to refocus on values and ethics:

> Many public servants were shocked, and their faith in public service values was shaken, both by the *fact* of downsizing—that it was done at all—and by the way it was done. Many public servants believe that an implicit employment contract and the commitment to security of tenure were breached by personnel reductions, and by the way they were carried out. Explicit union contracts were overridden by legislation. Disrespect for public servants was read into many announcements or statements that seemed to make them scapegoats, implying they were unproductive, bureaucratic and a major reason for the problems of the debt and public distrust of government. Some downsizing processes were perceived as punitive, secretive, and capricious, in an environment where the main purpose was to cut, and there was little interest in enforcing rules or due process to protect people. Ruthlessness, some public servants believe, was permitted, or even rewarded at certain times. To them, it appears that power counted for more than values and ethics, and a focus on short-term results crowded out concern for public policy purposes and values. (Canadian Centre for Management Development, 2000, p. 32)

> Many public servants are trying to cope with issues of increasing complexity, issues moving at increasing velocity that allow them less and less time for action. They are under pressure to downsize, reorganize, and, at the same time, increase performance with reduced resources. The demands of ministers and citizens are growing, as are those of employees. There are also growing (and welcome) demands from the centre of government to participate in corporate and horizontal activities. (Canadian Centre for Management Development, 2000, p. 72)

As well, the Task Force noted in its discussions with public servants that there was unease and confusion about "new" public service values that now complemented and sometimes appeared to contradict more traditional ones such as anonymity, neutrality, loyalty, and probity. The new values, of course, stem from the NPM emphasis on clients, customers, and service, as well as on decentralization, contracting out, and partnerships. New modes of service delivery and implementation are creating new types of temptations as well as tensions—a pedestrian example is public officials who provide so much "service" to private firms that they begin to identify with them and not the sector as a whole or even the public interest. The Task Force declined to choose one set of values over another, arguing that both were necessary, though it did make a bow to the NPM in suggesting that rule-based approaches to enforcing ethics and values had to be complemented by more flexible emphases on frameworks and guidelines.

The Task Force concluded that public service values can be clustered in four families or categories: democratic values, professional values, ethical values, and people values. Democratic values are the foundation for all the rest and refer to "helping ministers, under law and the Constitution, to serve the public interest." They hinge on the concept of accountability within a parliamentary regime, on providing "fearless advice" to ministers and faithfully carrying out their decisions under the law and the Constitution. Professional values are closely related and include "excellence, professional competence, continuous improvement, merit, effectiveness, economy, frankness, objectivity and impartiality in advice, speaking truth to power, balancing complexity, and fidelity to the public trust" (Canadian Centre for Management Development, 2000, pp. 67–68). They also entail some "new" values such as innovation, creativity, client service, partnership, and networking. Ethical values include "integrity, honesty, impartiality, taking responsibility and being accountable, probity, prudence, fairness, equity, objectivity, disinterestedness, selflessness, trustworthiness, discretion, respect for law and due process, and the careful stewardship of public resources" (Canadian Centre for Management Development, 2000, p. 69). Finally, people values is a category that touches on how we relate to others and includes such things as courage, trust, integrity, reasonableness, and decency. The Tait report laid the foundation for the federal government's June 2003 Values and Ethics Code; it relied on the same categorization of values and also dealt with conflict of interest issues (Treasury Board of Canada, 2003).

In addressing ethical issues related to changes in the nature of the public sector, Canada is of course dealing with a more general problem. The OECD flagged precisely the same set of concerns:

> Public servants operate in a changing world. The nameless, faceless public servant is becoming a relic of the past. Greater transparency in government operations, through public access to official information, when coupled with an increasingly zealous media, and well organised interest groups, means that public servants today work in a virtual "fishbowl." Their actions are more visible and publicised as are their mistakes and misdemeanours. Moreover, they face pressures from increased public expectations about the quality of public services and their capacities to deliver them. This pressure is driven partly by governments' own attempts to publicly state standards to be achieved (through Citizen's Charters for example). If these standards are not met, the result is public dissatisfaction.

Public management reform itself has changed the internal environment in which public servants operate. In some countries individual government departments now enjoy substantial autonomy. This has lead to concerns that systems of "professional socialisation," that is, the inculcation of public service values across the public sector, are breaking down as departments define their own "corporate culture," standards and ways of operating. This breakdown is compounded by more recruitment from the private sector. The old style coherent public service culture or ethos may be disappearing. In any case, traditional public service values may need to be amended as countries move away from an emphasis on strict compliance with rules and procedures, towards considerations such as "efficiency and effectiveness," "value for money," "service to the citizen," and "equal opportunities." For example, is it unethical to waste taxpayers' money or give bad service? (Organisation for Economic Co-operation and Development, 2000)

Like the Canadian Task Force, the OECD recognizes the limitations of rules-based enforcement and the importance of overlapping institutional frameworks, organizational culture, and individual practice. In its work with member countries to deal with the problems of public sector ethics and corruption, the OECD uses the concept of an "ethics infrastructure," which is reproduced in detail in Box 9.1.

Box 9.1   OECD ELEMENTS OF AN ETHICS INFRASTRUCTURE

AN ETHICS INFRASTRUCTURE HAS EIGHT KEY ELEMENTS

POLITICAL COMMITMENT

Without genuine political support—clear messages from government leaders that unethical conduct will not be tolerated—initiatives to improve ethics in the public service will fall on barren ground. Recent attempts to improve public sector ethics in OECD countries have been sponsored at the highest political levels, such as the UK Committee on Standards in Public Life set up by Prime Minister Major in 1994, the Portuguese deontological charter launched by the Secretary of State for Administrative Modernisation in

1993, the integrity measures sponsored by the Dutch Minister of the Interior (1995), and the United States President's Council on Integrity and Efficiency (1991). Of course, leaders also provide important role models. They should set an example.

AN EFFECTIVE LEGAL FRAMEWORK

This is the set of laws and regulations which define standards of behaviour for public servants and enforce them through systems of investigation and prosecution. It is the 'teeth' in the overall ethics infrastructure. In reviewing its legal framework for ethics management, countries must first take stock of existing criminal codes (applying to all citizens) as well as civil service laws, conflict of interest statutes and regulations which apply to public servants. At the very least these should be clear and consistent. While the law is an inflexible tool for the day-to-day management of ethics, it provides an important safety net.

EFFICIENT ACCOUNTABILITY MECHANISMS

Accountability mechanisms set guidelines for government activities, for checking that results have been achieved, and that due process has been observed. They include internal administrative procedures, (requirements that activities or requests be recorded in writing), and comprehensive processes such as audits and evaluations of an agency's performance. They might also be external to the public service; for example, oversight mechanisms such as legislative or parliamentary committees. Whistle-blowing provisions are also important (that is, procedures for public servants to say no when asked to do something inappropriate or to expose wrongdoing committed by others). Accountability mechanisms should encourage ethical behaviour by making unethical activities hard to commit and easy to detect.

WORKABLE CODES OF CONDUCT

Codes of conduct remain important even in OECD countries that have reduced rules applying to public servants and adopted more "managerial" styles of public management. Some countries (e.g., Australia, New Zealand) now have a broad public service wide code of conduct from which individual agencies design a purpose-built code to reflect their particular objectives and mission. In other countries (Netherlands, Norway) codes are all agency-based. The ethical issues confronting an employee of a defence ministry might vary significantly from those facing social security

Box 9.1 (continued)

officials. Criticisms of codes include being too specific or too general, unworkable, unused, unknown or simply that simplistic statements of rules are not the ideal medium for answering complicated ethical dilemmas faced by public servants.

PROFESSIONAL SOCIALISATION MECHANISMS

These are the processes by which public servants learn and inculcate ethics, standards of conduct, and public service values. Training (induction and refreshers) is an essential element (including in ethics awareness), as are good role models (especially managers).

SUPPORTIVE PUBLIC SERVICE CONDITIONS

If public servants are feeling underpaid, overworked and insecure, then they are less likely to embrace initiatives to improve performance including in the ethical domain. However, too much job security can also result in complacency. And low pay is no excuse for illegal or unethical behaviour.

AN ETHICS CO-ORDINATING BODY

These take various forms—parliamentary committees, central agencies, or specially created bodies—and assume various functions; "watchdog" including investigation (such as the New South Wales Independent Commission Against Corruption), "counsellor and advisor" (such as the United Kingdom Committee on Standards in Public Life which Prime Minister Major has referred to as an ongoing "ethics workshop", or the United States Office of Government Ethics), or "general promoter" of public sector ethics (such as the New Zealand State Services Commission, the Norwegian Department of Public Administration). But the existence of a co-ordinating body should not allow departments and managers to absolve themselves of responsibility for ensuring ethical conduct within their jurisdictions. Ethics is everybody's responsibility.

AN ACTIVE CIVIC SOCIETY . . .

(including a probing media) so that citizens can act as watchdog over the actions of public officials. Access to information provisions are an important factor in this function.

SOURCE: Organisation for Economic Co-operation and Development. (2000). *What is an ethics infrastructure?* Retrieved August 19, 2004, from http://www .oecd.org/puma/ethics/infras.htm

BENCHMARKING THE POLICY PROCESS

It is difficult to develop standards for "good policy" in terms of specific programs and instruments. As we argued earlier in the book, there is usually agreement about broad objectives such as reducing poverty or crime but often wide disagreements about the problem situation and the right way to tackle those perceived problems. But there is growing agreement on one thing: effective and responsive policies (however defined) are not likely to arise from flawed policy processes. An effective policy process is no guarantee of quality outputs and outcomes, but it helps. Rethinking and reforming the policy process has emerged in recent years as a complement to more general organizational redesign and reform in the public sector. It has several distinct aspects, however. One is the sense that if governments downsize and do fewer things directly themselves, there will be greater emphasis on their capacity to develop policy objectives and monitor outcomes. As we noted in Chapter 1, the emphasis on policy capacity is also linked to a sense that the pressures on societies and governments today are increasing and are more intense. Rapid, and rational, response is increasingly important, and well-designed policy frameworks provide a filter and a foundation for concerted action. Another aspect has been the wider public sector reform project itself—in some countries like New Zealand, as we pointed out in Chapter 5, there has been a more radical separation of policy advice functions from central administration than has been characteristic of Canada. Accordingly, there is greater need for benchmarking the policy development function to ensure that it meets recognized standards.

By policy development function, we mean the process of determining and elaborating policy issues or problems, articulating solutions, and making recommendations. We do not include the process of actual decisionmaking and choice of options, which is primarily political and takes place through a host of governmental institutions, from cabinet to legislature. Nor do we include actual implementation or evaluation of selected options. Obviously these are crucial phases in making public policy but entail different sets of standards and techniques. Implementation is a management function and involves administrative skill in combining resources and personnel in the right amounts at the right time to achieve the desired policy or programmatic outcome. Evaluation, by the same token, is normally undertaken within a fairly well-defined framework with relatively clear operational standards (see Chapter 7). Policy development is the "front end" of these processes, though of course it also entails consultations and communications about policy issues from time to time. An effective policy process in the largest sense of the term will be effective at all these stages—policy development (the analysis of the problem and development of options and recommendations), implementation (putting into effect the chosen option and elaborating on its programmatic elements), and evaluation (assessing efficiency and effectiveness). But implementation and evaluation take the option as given, the choice made. Our concern here is to address the first, crucial phase of policy development and ask if there are benchmarks of standards of practice that might improve the way it is conducted.

There are three immediate problems with posing the issue this way. First, as this book has stressed repeatedly, policy development is a mix of craft and science. A good deal of what goes into problem recognition and definition is subjective and not necessarily guided by well-known techniques (indeed, the same point applies even in apparently technical arenas such as cost-benefit evaluation). By definition, something that is craft-based is difficult to improve through better technique. Second, of necessity, policy development touches on some highly politically sensitive issues. It involves "speaking truth to power," and in that sense it may seem that truth will be sacrificed to power, that politics and political orientations are the most important part of developing policy advice. It is obviously true that public servants developing policy advice for a government of one political stripe will offer different advice in some respects to a government of a completely different political stripe. However, that is not the end of the story. Many problems are simply "there" as an empirical reality—the aging of the population or globalization. From some perspectives these may not be problems, but they do encapsulate forces that no government can really ignore, however it might want to interpret those forces. As well, as we noted in Chapter 3, problem definition does rely on hard research, and this cannot be ideologically driven. And finally, while governments and politicians may have strong ideological orientations, that does not mean that they can simply dream up policy options based on these orientations. There is a still a good deal of analytical work that has to go into the mix.

The third problem is that policy development is only in part a process that takes place inside government and between officials and their political masters; it also involves citizens, interest groups, the media, and a host of other actors. It has a political/social dimension that is broader than any benchmarking procedure might suggest.

These are valid objections and issues, but the fact remains that a major responsibility for governments is to develop policy, and this function is performed in large part in central agencies and departments staffed by professional public servants. Governments have not been blind to the importance of improving the policy development function—we saw various instances throughout the previous chapters where nationally and internationally there have been calls for improved governance and, as part of that, improved policy development and implementation. The governments of Australia and New Zealand have, for example, routinely assessed and evaluated the policy development function since the early 1990s through "policy management reviews" (Uhr and Mackay, 1996). In April 2000, the Canadian federal government released a report on the law-making process that made explicit reference to improving the process of policy development and advice (Government of Canada, 2000). The report argued, for example, that policymaking could be improved by "challenging the traditional choice of instrument for effecting change; setting clear, objective outcomes and reporting on their results; putting greater emphasis on a balanced analysis; planning policy development better; and finding the most appropriate ways to engage and consult the public."

Our approach to benchmarks is guided by the conviction that policy development, despite its messiness, does have some identifiable stages or phases, principally moving through problem identification, analysis of issues, development of options, and finally recommendations based both on analysis and other input in the process. As well, we have to acknowledge the balance of craft and skill that defines policy development work. A crucial issue then is how to enhance craft, how to build in mechanisms that will improve a process that resists easy categorization. And finally, we need to acknowledge that policy work is part of a larger democratic conversation and that it should reflect strong democratic values as well as contribute to them. In these terms then, we can suggest several benchmarks that, while they will not guarantee good policy design, will certainly contribute to it:

Training of policy development staff: This should not be occasional but continuous. Policy development staff have to know what the policy process is about, the different elements of policy design and implementation and evaluation, and various techniques for both the development of policy ideas and communication. They should have a solid grounding in policy analysis and administration.

Well-organized information and research resources: Having information, being able to access it quickly, and organizing it well, is a basic requirement of good policy work.

A balance of scanning and service orientations: Good policy work not only requires immediate and effective responses to demands from political masters but also demands the scanning of the political and social environment to see what is coming up in the near to medium term. Policy work needs to be strategic.

Rigour and honesty: Policy development, as we noted above, is at the intersection of political necessity and analytical research. Policy analysts should keep that balance in mind and be wary of sacrificing professional standards and rigour for political purposes.

Transparency and consultation: Confidentiality is often unavoidable as policy problems and options are being debated and defined. To the greatest extent possible, however, policy development work should hear from all sides, consult widely both within and outside government, and put out as much information as possible for public discussion, debate, and review.

Develop a good challenge function: Further to the previous point, the policy development process should be designed in such a way as to incorporate challenge and debate—this is a key testing ground for policy ideas and proposals and an important means for working through limitations and unexpected design flaws.

Policymaking is nothing less than developing public responses, primarily through government but in cooperation with citizens and organizations, to public problems. Doing it well matters for lots of reasons, not least because the quality of the responses affects our everyday lives as well as the texture of our democracy.

KEY TERMS

governance—the process of governing or steering complex systems in cooperation with a variety of other actors

human security—a broader definition of international security that goes beyond geo-political and military considerations to consider threats to humanity and ordinary citizens such as environmental degradation, international crime, and child labour

instrumentalism—a philosophical orientation that tries to make a sharp distinction between means and ends

Weblinks

Strategy Survival Guide (UK)
http://www.strategy.gov.uk/su/survivalguide/index.htm

Values and Ethics Code for the Public Service
http://www.tbs-sct.gc.ca/pubs_pol/hrpubs/TB_851/vec-cve_e.asp

Implementation Assessment Template (Australia)
http://www.dpmc.gov.au/pdfs/ciu_assessment_guide.rtf

Guide to Preparing Implementation Plans (Australia)
http://www.dpmc.gov.au/implementation_plan/index.shtml

Further Readings

Commission on the Future of Health Care in Canada. (2002). *Building on values: The future of health care in Canada*. Retrieved August 19, 2004, from http://www.hc-sc.gc.ca/english/care/romanow/hcc0023 .html

Privy Council Office (Canada). (2004) *Ethics, responsibility, accountability: An action plan for democratic reform*. Retrieved August 19, 2004, from http://www.pco-bcp.gc.ca/ default.asp?Language=E&Page=Publications&doc=dr-rd/dr-rd_e.htm

Putnam, R. D. (1993). *Making democracy work: Civic traditions in modern Italy*. Princeton, NJ: Princeton University Press.

Putnam, R. D. (2000). *Bowling alone: The collapse and revival of American community*. New York: Simon and Schuster.

REFERENCES

Auditor General of Canada. (1995). *Annual report, 1995*. Retrieved August 19, 2004, from http://www.oag-bvg.gc.ca/domino/reports .nsf/html/95menu_e.html

Biggs, M. (1996). *Building blocks for Canada's new social union*. Ottawa: Canadian Policy Research Networks, Working Paper No. F02.

Boyer, J. P. (1992). *Direct democracy in Canada: The history and future of referendums*. Toronto: Dundurn.

Cabinet Office (Britain). (2000). Retrieved September 14, 2004, from http://www.socialexclusionunit.gov.uk

Canadian Centre for Management Development. (2000). *A strong foundation: Report of the task force on public service values and ethics*. Retrieved August 19, 2004, from http://www.myschool-monecole .gc.ca/Research/publications/html/tait_e.html

Commission on the Future of Health Care in Canada. (2002). *Building on values: The future of health care in Canada*. Retrieved August 19, 2004, from http://www.hc-sc.gc.ca/english/care/romanow/hcc0023 .html

Department of Foreign Affairs and International Trade (Canada). (1999). *Human security: Safety for people in a changing world.* Retrieved September 14, 2004, from http://www.humansecurity.gc.ca/1

Doern, G. B. (1994). *The road to better public services: Progress and constraints in five Canadian federal agencies.* Montreal: Institute for Research on Public Policy.

Government of Canada (Privy Council Office). (2000). *Report on law-making and governance: A summary of discussions held by the deputy ministers' challenge team on law-making and governance.* Retrieved August 19, 2004, from http://www.pco-bcp.gc.ca/raoicssrdc/default.asp?Language=E&Page=Publications&Sub=ReportonLaw MakingandGove

Gow, J. I. (1995, Winter). Frauds and victims: Some difficulties in applying the notion of service to the clientele in the public sector. *Canadian Public Administration, 38,* 557–77.

Hall, P. A. (1999, July). Social capital in Britain. *British Journal of Political Science, 29,* 417–61.

Howe, P., and Northrup, D. (2000). *Strengthening Canadian democracy: The views of Canadians.* Montreal: Institute for Research on Public Policy.

Jacobs, J. (1961). *The death and life of great American cities.* New York: Random House.

Jenson, J. (1998). *Mapping social cohesion: The state of Canadian research.* Ottawa: Canadian Policy Research Networks, Study No. F03. Retrieved August 19, 2004, from http://www.cprn.org/cprn. html

Kernaghan, K. (1996). *The ethics era in Canadian public administration.* Ottawa: Canadian Centre for Management Development, Research Paper no. 19. Ottawa: Supply and Services Canada.

Mintzberg, H. (1996, May–June). Managing government, governing management. *Harvard Business Review,* pp. 75–83.

Organisation for Economic Co-operation and Development. (2000). *Pressures affecting public service ethics and conduct.* Retrieved August 19, 2004, from http://www1.oecd.org/puma/ethics/pubs/pressure.htm

Peters, B. G. (1999). *American public policy.* (5th ed.). New York: Chatham House.

Policy Research Initiative. (1996). *Report on growth, human development and social cohesion.* Ottawa: Privy Council Office.

Putnam, R. D. (1993). *Making democracy work: Civic traditions in modern Italy.* Princeton, NJ: Princeton University Press.

Putnam, R. D. (2000). *Bowling alone: The collapse and revival of American community.* New York: Simon and Schuster.

Rhodes, R. A. W. (1997). *Understanding governance: Policy networks, governance, reflexivity, and accountability.* Buckingham, UK: Open University Press.

Treasury Board of Canada. (2003). *Values and ethics code for the public service.* Retrieved August 19, 2004, from http://www.tbs-sct.gc.ca/pubs_pol/hrpubs/TB_851/vec-cve_e.asp

Uhr, J., and Mackay, K. (Eds.) (1996). *Evaluating policy advice learning from Commonwealth Experience.* Canberra: Federalism Research Centre, The Australian National University, and Commonwealth Department of Finance.

Voyer, J.-P. (2003). *New approaches to poverty and exclusion: A strategic framework.* Ottawa: Policy Research Initiative. Retrieved August 19, 2004, from http://policyresearch.gc.ca/page.asp?pagenm=v6n2_ art_08

Index

Credits

p. 31: World Bank, 1997. *World development report 1997: The state in a changing world.*

p. 48: World Trade Organization, *International trade statistics 2003*, Chart II.1, p.30. Reproduced with permission.

p. 49: Adapted from the Statistics Canada publication *The performance of interprovincial and international exports by province and territory since 1992.* Catalogue no. 11-621, no. 11, March 5, 2004.

pp. 55–56: Fair World Fair, Greedy 8 Alternative Coalition, http://www.g8carnival.org. Reprinted with permission.

pp. 60–61: R. Kluver and W. Fu. (2004). *The cultural globalization index. Foreign Policy*, www.foreignpolicy.com. [On-line] Available: http://www.foreignpolicy.com/story/files/story2494.php This work is protected by copyright and the making of this copy was with the permission of Access Copyright. Any alteration of its content or further copying in any form whatsoever is strictly prohibited.

p. 74: *Reinventing government: How the entrepreneurial spirit is transforming the public sector,* D. Osborne and T. Gaebler, 1993. Perseus Books.

p. 76: From K. Kernaghan, "The post-bureaucratic organization and public service values," March 2000. © International Institute of Administrative Studies, 2000, by permission of Sage Publications Ltd.

p. 78: The President's Management Agenda: The Scorecard [On-line] Available: http://results.gov/agenda/scorecard.html

p. 80: The Prime Minister's Office of Public Services Reform, http://www.pm.gov.uk/output/page254.asp. Crown copyright material is reproduced with the permission of the Controller of HMSO and the Queen's Printer for Scotland.

pp. 82–83: *Getting Government Right,* http://www.tbs-sct.gc.ca/report/dwnld/gfce.pdf

pp. 83–84: *Results for Canadians,* March 2000. http://www.tbs-sct.gc.ca/res_can/rc_e.asp Treasury Board of Canada Secretariat, 2000. Reproduced with the permission of the Minister of Public Works and Government Services Canada, 2004.

pp. 106–7: Dunn, W. A. (2004). *Public policy analysis: An introduction,* 3rd ed. (Englewood Cliffs, NJ: Prentice Hall), Chap. 3.

pp. 108–9: Geva-May, I., and Wildavsky, A. (1997). *An operational approach to policy analysis: The craft.* (Boston: Kluwer Academic Publishers), p. 37. Reproduced with permission.

pp. 110–11: Adapted and amended from Rochefort and Cobb (1994). "Problem definition: An emerging perspective." In D. A. Rochefort and R. W. Cobb (Eds.), *The politics of problem definition: Shaping the policy agenda* (pp.1–31). Lawrence, KS: University of Kansas Press. Reproduced with permission.

pp. 120–21: *Growth, human development, and social cohesion,* Policy Research Initiative, 1996. Reproduced with permission.

pp. 122–25: Policy Research Initiative, 2004. Retrieved August 6, 2004, from http://policyresearch.gc.ca/page.asp?pagenm=root&langcd=E Reprinted with permission.

pp. 141–44: From *The tools of government* by Lester M. Salamon, copyright © 2002 by Lester M. Salamon. Used by permission of Oxford University Press, Inc.

pp. 151, 153: Office of the Auditor General and the Commissioner of the Environment and Sustainable Development, "Grants and contributions: Selected programs in Industry Canada and Department of Canadian Heritage."

pp. 166–67: *Report of Auditor-General of Canada: 2003,* Office of the Auditor General of Canada, 2003. Reproduced with the permission of the Minister of Public Works and Government Services Canada, 2004.

p. 169: World Trade Organization, *Technical regulations and standards 1996.* Available: http://gatekeeper.unicc.org/wto/comp_leg_wpf.html1#technical

p. 194: Hogwood, B. W. and Gunn, L. A. (1984). *Policy analysis for the real world.* Oxford, UK: Oxford University Press.

p. 195: Sabatier, P. A., and Mazmanian, D. A. (1981). *Effective policy implementation.* Lexington, MA: Lexington Books, a division of Rowman & Littlefield Publishing Group. p. 7. Reproduced with permission.

pp. 208–9: Guardian Unlimited. (2004). Full text of Tony Blair's Speech. Retrieved August 12, 2004, from http://society.guardian.co.uk/futureforpublicservices/comment/0,8146,1134531,00.html

p. 212: Copyright OECD (*Enhancing the effectiveness of public spending: experience in OECD countries,* 2004). Reproduced by permission of the OECD.

pp. 216–17: IPAC, *2003 Winners and finalists.* http://www.ipac.ca/awards/innovation/past_winners/2003_winners_and_finalists/index.html Reproduced with permission.

pp. 218–19: Retrieved September 4, 2004, from http://www.ashinstitute.harvard.edu/Ash/pr_20032.htm

pp. 222–23: *Citizens first 3* (2003). Ottawa: The Institute for Citizen-Centred Service and the Institute of Public Administration of Canada, p. 85. Reproduced with permission.

p. 224: "A framework for alternative service delivery." http://collection.nlc-bnc.ca/100/201/301/tbs-sct/tb_manual-ef/Pubs_pol/opepubs/TB_B4/dwnld/frdoce.doc Treasury Board of Canada Secretariat, 1996. Reproduced with the permission of the Minister of Public Works and Government Services Canada, 2004.

pp. 224–25: *Citizens first 3* (2003). Ottawa: The Institute for Citizen-Centred Service and the Institute of Public Administration of Canada, p. 86. Reproduced with permission.

p. 249: From *Group politics & public policy,* 2nd edition, by Paul A. Pross. Copyright © 1992 by Oxford University Press Canada. Reprinted by permission of the publisher.

p. 251: Lindquist, E. A. (1992, Summer). "Public managers and policy communities: Learning to meet new challenges." *Canadian Public Administration,* 35. Reproduced with permission of the Institute of Public Administration of Canada.

p. 252: Pal, L. A. (1993). *Interests of state: The politics of language, multiculturalism and feminism in Canada.* Montreal: McGill-Queen's University Press. Reproduced with permission.

p. 255: From *Policy change and learning* by Paul Sabatier. Copyright © 1993 by Westview Press. Reprinted by permission of Westview Press, a member of Perseus Books, L.L.C.

pp. 268–69: *Building on values: The future of health care in Canada,* pages 271–272 (© 2002). Reproduced with the permission of the Minister of Public Works and Government Services Canada, 2004, and courtesy of the Privy Council Office.

p. 271: *Report of the Auditor General of Canada – 2000,* Office of the Auditor General of Canada, 2000. Reproduced with the permission of the Minister of Public Works and Government Services, 2004.

p. 271: Fitzpatrick, T. (2000). *Horizontal management: Trends in governance and accountability.* Action-Research Roundtable on the Management of Horizontal Issues. Ottawa: Canadian Centre for Management Development. [On-line] Available: http://dsp-psd.pwgsc.gc.ca/Collection/SC94-112-2000E.pdf

pp. 288–89: American Evaluation Association, 2000. *Guiding principles for evaluators.* Reproduced with permission.

pp. 296–97: Howard Bloom et al., *Testing a re-employment incentive for displaced workers: The earnings supplement project.* Ottawa: Social Research and Demonstration Corporation, May 1999, pp. ES1–2, 45. Reproduced with permission.

p. 312: *Into the 90s: Government program evaluation perspectives.* Ottawa: Office of the Comptroller General.

pp. 314–15: Treasury Board of Canada Secretariat Evaluation Policy, February 1, 2001. http://www.tbs-sct.gc.ca/pubs_pol/dcgpubs/TBM_161/ep-pe_e.asp Treasury Board of Canada Secretariat, 2001. Reproduced with the permission of the Minister of Public Works and Government Services Canada, 2004.

pp. 315–16: Treasury Board of Canada (2001a). *Guide for the development of results-based management and accountability frameworks.* [On-line]. Available: http://www.tbs-sct.gc.ca/eval/pubs/RMAF-CGRR/rmafcgrr02_e.asp

pp. 316–17: *Results for Canadians,* March 2000 http://www.tbs-sct.gc.ca/res_can/rc_e.asp Treasury Board of Canada Secretariat, 2000. Reproduced with the permission of the Minister of Public Works and Government Services Canada, 2004.

p. 340: *Risk management policy, 1994* http://www.tbs-sct.gc.ca/pubs_pol/dcgpubs/RiskManagement/riskmanagpol_e.asp Treasury Board of Canada Secretariat, 1994. Reproduced with the permission of the Minister of Public Works and Government Services Canada, 2004.

pp. 340–41: *Risk management policy, 1994* http://www.tbs-sct.gc.ca/pubs_pol/dcgpubs/RiskManagement/riskmanagpol_e.asp Treasury Board of Canada Secretariat, 1994. Reproduced with the permission of the Minister of Public Works and Government Services Canada, 2004.

p. 343: *Integrated risk management framework, 2001* http://www.tbs-sct.gc.ca/pubs_pol/dcgpubs/RiskManagement/rmf-cgr01-1_e.asp#Risk Treasury Board of Canada Secretariat, 2001. Reproduced with the permission of the Minister of Public Works and Government Services Canada, 2004.

p. 346: *Crisis and emergency management: A guide for managers of the public service of Canada,* Table 2 at p. 9, Canadian Centre for Management Development, 2004. Reproduced with permission of the Canada School of Public Service, 2004.

pp. 347–53: Centers for Disease Control and Prevention. (2004). *Public health guidance for community-level preparedness and response to severe acute respiratory syndrome (SARS),* Version 2 Supplement A: Command and control, Appendix A1: State and local health official epidemic SARS checklist. [On-line] Available: http://www.cdc.gov/ncidod/sars/guidance/A/word/app1.doc

pp. 354–56: CBC News Online (2004, January 6). "Mad Cow in Canada: The science and the story." Retrieved September 4, 2004, from http://www.cbc.ca/news/background/madcow/ CBC Online Staff, CBC News. More recent update available online.

pp. 361–64: Listed entities. http://www.psepc-sppcc.gc.ca/national_security/counter-terrorism/Entities_e.asp Public Safety and Emergency Preparedness Canada 2002. Reproduced with the permission of the Minister of Public Works and Government Services Canada, 2004.

pp. 369–70: *The federal experience: Case studies on crisis and emergency management,* by Don Malpass, pp. 13–16. Ottawa: Canadian Centre for Management Development, 2003. Reproduced with permission of the Canada School of Public Service, 2004.

p. 392: Canadian Centre for Management Development. (2000). *A strong foundation: Report on the task force on public service values and ethics.* Retrieved August 19, 2004, from http://www.myschool-monecole.gc.ca/Research/publications/html/tait_e.html

pp. 393–94: Copyright OECD, *Pressures affecting public service ethics and conduct, 2000.* Reproduced by permission of the OECD.

pp. 394–96: Copyright OECD, *What is an ethics infrastructure?* (Paris: 2000). Reproduced by permission of the OECD.